Integrated Marketing Communications

Integrated Marketing Communications:

A Systems Approach

M. Joseph Sirgy

Professor of Marketing
Virginia Polytechnic Institute and State University

 Prentice Hall, Upper Saddle River, New Jersey 07458

Acquisitions Editor: Whitney Blake
Associate Editor: John Larkin
Editorial Assistant: Rachel Falk
Vice President/Editorial Director: Jim Boyd
Marketing Manager: John Chillingworth
Production Editor: Michelle Rich
Production Coordinator: Carol Samet
Permissions Coordinator: Jennifer Rella
Managing Editor: Dee Josephson
Associate Managing Editor: Linda DeLorenzo
Manufacturing Buyer: Kenneth J. Clinton
Manufacturing Supervisor: Arnold Vila
Manufacturing Manager: Vincent Scelta
Cover Design: Jayne Kelly
Composition: Pine Tree Composition

 Copyright © 1998 by Prentice-Hall, Inc.
A Simon & Schuster Company
Upper Saddle River, New Jersey 07458

Library of Congress Cataloging-in-Publication Data

Sirgy, M. Joseph
   Integrated marketing communications : a systems approach / M. Joseph Sirgy.
      p. cm.
   Includes bibliographical references and index.
   ISBN 0–13–205618–6
   1. Communication in marketing. I. Title
HF5415.123.S55 1998
658.8′02–dc21   97–19498
                                              CIP

Prentice-Hall International (UK) Limited, London
Prentice-Hall of Australia Pty. Limited, Sydney
Prentice-Hall Canada, Inc., Toronto
Prentice-Hall Hispanoamericana, S.A., Mexico
Prentice-Hall of India Private Limited, New Delhi
Prentice-Hall of Japan, Inc., Tokyo
Simon & Schuster Asia Pte. Ltd., Singapore
Editora Prentice-Hall do Brasil, Ltda., Rio de Janeiro.

Printed in the United States of America

10 9 8 7 6 5 4 3 2

I dedicate this book to my three daughters (Melissa, Danielle, and Michelle), my two brothers (Abraham and Gamil), my baby sister (Rebecca Jarrel), and the rest of my extended family. I also dedicate this book to my colleagues and friends in marketing and systems science.

Brief Contents

Contents

Preface

This book is written for advanced marketing students and marketing communications practitioners. The book is about *integrated marketing communications*. It deals with the intersection between marketing communications and strategic marketing. It connects these two important topics using a systems approach. It focuses on the *integration*, or synthesis, of marketing communications with strategic marketing. It is designed to help the advanced marketing communications student and marketing communications manager answer questions like the following: How can I *strategically* plan and manage all the varied marketing communications tasks as a system? How can I coordinate the various elements of marketing communications to ensure consistency? How can I create a learning system that will help me make periodic adjustments in the communication elements to achieve better performance? How can I plan and manage the marketing communications tools to ensure the attainment of marketing and corporate-level goals? How can I assemble the elements of the marketing communications mix and adjust them periodically in such a way to achieve marketing- and corporate-level goals?

As you can see, this book does *not* introduce the reader to marketing communications but rather builds on the reader's knowledge of marketing communications to help advanced marketing communications students better understand the planning and management process of marketing communications. The book also helps marketing communications managers perfect the tools of their trade by offering them a conceptual tool to *strategically* plan and manage marketing communications.

Specifically with respect to the *educational market*, at colleges and universities offering only one undergraduate course in marketing communications, this book can be used effectively as a supplementary text. Students should be assigned to read it after they have covered the basic marketing communications concepts. Thus, students learn how to integrate the elements of marketing communications at the end of the course. In colleges and universities offering both basic and *advanced* marketing communications courses, this book is highly suitable for the advanced course. In an advanced undergraduate course in marketing communications it can be a *stand-alone* book (or possibly one of the assigned books and/or reading materials). This book is also ideally suited for colleges and universities offering a master of science degree in marketing, advertising, or communications in either schools of business or schools of journalism/communications. Professors or instructors teaching graduate-level courses in marketing communications in these programs should seriously consider this book for classroom use. This book is well suited for an MBA course in marketing communications. Most MBA students have enough business experience and marketing communications background to allow them to fully understand and appreciate the concepts inherent in this book.

With respect to the *trade market*, this book can greatly benefit marketing communications managers, especially those with little job experience. It can help them conceptualize and plan the whole communication process by making connections among the disperse elements and the marketing and corporate levels goals and strategies. The book can help managers design a monitoring and control system in which communication can be significantly improved through trial and error. The book provides managers with a guide on how to set communications objectives that are tied to corporate- and marketing-level objectives. It can guide managers to set quantitative and concrete objectives and help them monitor communications performance using measures that closely correspond to the stated objectives. The book shows how marketing- and corporate-level decisions are an integral part of the planning and management process of marketing communications.

This book is divided into five parts. The first part introduces the reader to the concept of *integrated marketing communications* (IMC), systems concepts used to build the systems model of IMC, and an overview of the systems model of IMC presented in this book. Specifically, chapter 1 starts out with a basic definition of IMC and provides an analysis of different conceptualizations and planning approaches to IMC. Also, in this chapter we review a model of integrated marketing communications developed by Professor Schultz—the foremost authority and a pioneer in IMC. Chapter 2 discusses a particular systems model in the generic sense. The systems model involves five major components: (1) strategy and tactics, (2) objective and measures, (3) budget, (4) monitoring and control, and (5) analysis and planning. We introduce the reader to each of these systems components and describe their dynamics. Then we address the concept of *system integration*—that is, how systems can be effectively integrated by building and strengthening linkages among the systems components. Chapter 3 presents an overview of the model. Simply described, it involves three levels of analysis—corporate, marketing, and marketing communications. Each level involves a subsystem, and the components of that subsystem are strategy/tactics, objectives/measures, budget, monitoring/control, and analysis/planning.

Part II presents the core of the systems model, namely strategy and tactics. Strategy and tactics are viewed as a process hierarchy, or what some systems experts call a decision tree. Marketing communications programs (advertising, sales promotion, reseller support, direct marketing, public relations, and word-of-mouth communications) are viewed as elements of the marketing communications mix selected and guided by an overall marketing communications strategy (Informative, Affective, Habit Formation, and Self-Satisfaction). Marketing communications strategy is viewed as an element of the marketing mix (product, price, distribution, and marketing communications), which in turn is selected and guided by an overall marketing strategy (differentiation, cost leadership, and focus, as well as various positioning operationalizations of these strategies—positioning by product attribute, positioning by intangible factor, positioning by customer benefit, etc.). Fifteen positioning strategies are described in this book as directly related to marketing strategy. Similarly, marketing strategy is viewed as an element of the corporate mix (marketing, manufacturing, R&D, engineering, accounting, finance, employee relations, etc.), which in turn is selected and guided by corporate strategy (grow, maintain, harvest, innovate, and divest). These ideas are developed in chapters 4, 5, and 6.

Part III describes objectives and performance measures (chapter 7), budget (chapter 8), and monitoring and control (chapter 9). Chapter 7, on objectives and performance measures, describes how objectives are set at the corporate, marketing, and marketing communications levels. Also, specific performance measures related to corporate, marketing, and marketing communications objectives are described. Chapter 8, on resource allocation, shows how a marketing communications budget can be effectively determined through a top-down procedure. In chapter 9, we show how the marketing communications manager can monitor communications performance and make corrective adjustments in the system at various levels to align future performance with objectives.

Part IV involves analysis and planning. Here we concentrate on showing the marketing communications manager how to conduct meaningful situation analysis in order to select best strategies at the corporate, marketing, and marketing communications levels (chapter 10). Chapter 11 describes the kind of situation analysis that can assist the marketing communications manager in setting objectives at the three hierarchical levels. And similarly, chapter 12 describes situation analysis for the purpose of determining an effective marketing communications budget.

The last part of the book is devoted to highlighting the principles of systems integration. Chapter 13 discusses those principles in some detail and advises the marketing communications manager on how to best use these principles.

We hope you will enjoy reading this book and walk away with a good sense of *integration*. That is, the reader may be able to appreciate how everything fits together in the big scheme of things. We hope you will understand and appreciate how marketing communications campaigns can be *strategically* planned and managed. And we hope this book helps you appreciate the importance and the need to plan marketing communications campaigns *guided by corporate and marketing strategies*.

Happy reading!

Joe Sirgy

Acknowledgments

Writing a book is usually a major undertaking. This book took many years of development. There were so many people who contributed one way or another in the development of this book. I would like to acknowledge them all but I'm afraid that I may leave out some. So I will acknowledge only those who played a formal role in the development of this book. These people are listed alphabetically below:

Avery Abernethy, Auburn University; Reviewer
Kenneth D. Bahn, James Madison University
Whitney Blake, Prentice Hall; Acquisitions Editor
Dave Borkowsky, Prentice Hall; Acquisitions Editor
Jim Boyd, Prentice Hall; Vice President/Editorial Director
John Chillingworth; Marketing Manager
Kenneth J. Clinton, Prentice Hall; Manufacturing Buyer
Ruth Clottey, Barry University; Reviewer
John Cronin, Western CT State University; Reviewer
Linda DeLorenzo, Prentice Hall; Associate Managing Editor
Rachel Falk, Prentice Hall; Editorial Assistant
Teresa Festa, Prentice Hall; Editorial Assistant
Marianne Hutchinson, Pine Tree Composition; Composition Editor
Dee Josephson, Prentice Hall; Managing Editor
Jane Kelly, Prentice Hall; Cover Design
John Larkin, Prentice Hall; Associate Editor
Allison Larsen, Private Copy Editor; Private Consultant
Val Larsen, Northeast Missouri State University; Reviewer
Peter McClure, University of Massachusetts-Boston; Reviewer
H. Lee Meadow, Eastern Illinois University; Reviewer
Don Rahtz, College of William and Mary; Reviewer
Jennifer Rella, Prentice Hall; Permission Coordinator
Michelle Rich, Prentice Hall; Production Editor
Carol Samet, Prentice Hall; Production Coordinator
Arnold Vila, Prentice Hall, Manufacturing Supervisor

PART ONE

Introduction

The Orlando/Orange County Convention and Visitors Bureau, Inc., is charged with directing a total marketing communications program to attract visitors to the area year-round. The bureau's specific mission is "to promote the area worldwide as a premier leisure and business destination." It caters to a diverse group of stakeholders—organizational members such as Disney World, local community leaders, visitors to the area, convention planners and delegates, and the travel industry. To communicate with these various stakeholders, the bureau has used in the past all forms of marketing communications—advertising, public relations, consumer promotions, trade promotions, and direct marketing, among others.*

Now suppose you (the reader) are hired as the marketing communications director at the bureau to plan and manage the total marketing communications program. What a challenge! Where do you start, and what do you do? To do a good job planning and managing the bureau's total marketing communications program, you need to figure out strategy and tactics. First, what is the overall strategy of the bureau at the highest level—that is, corporate strategy? Is it to increase visitors in the area? Or is it to maintain the current level? What are the specific quantitative objectives? What is the current level of visitors and what level of increase is desired? What is the time frame to achieve the stated objectives? Next quarter? A year from now? How can you measure the number of visitors that come to the area? How do you monitor progress toward the stated objectives and take corrective actions when needed?

What should the marketing strategy be? Could it be a differentiation strategy? That is, should you focus on convincing tourists that the Orlando area is better than another tourist destination? If so, exactly how should the Orlando area be effectively positioned? What positioning approach should you take? Should the Orlando region be positioned by customer benefits—highlighting all the different tourist attractions that are "fun, fun, fun," are located in one small area, and don't require much traveling? Exactly what are the marketing objectives? Should you state a marketing objective in terms of brand association—that is, associate Orlando in the minds of tourists with a variety of well-known,

*For a complete discussion of the bureau's total marketing communications activities, see chapter 20 of the following book: William Wells, John Burnett, and Sandra Moriarty, *Advertising: Principles and Practice* (Upper Saddle River, N.J.: Prentice Hall, 1995).

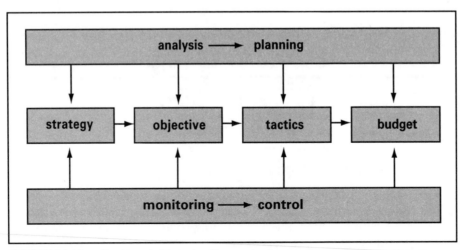

FIGURE I.1 Major Decisions in Marketing Communications

entertaining attractions? How do you measure this to keep track of how well you're doing?

How about selecting the most effective tools of marketing communications? Should you work with advertising? Why or why not? How about sales promotion? Why or why not? Direct marketing? Public relations? Trade promotions? Do you need some sort of a strategy to help you choose the right mix of marketing communication elements? What would this strategy be? What are the objectives of the total marketing communications program? Should you state the objectives in terms of awareness, knowledge, attitude, action, and repeat action in relation to the Orlando region? How do you go about doing this? Shouldn't you come up with a total marketing communications plan that has different objectives over time? How will you measure marketing communications performance and monitor performance against the stated objectives? How do you figure out an optimal marketing communications budget? Mind boggling, isn't it?

This book is designed to help the reader use conceptual tools to help come up with answers. Part I of the book is designed to introduce the reader to the concept of integrated marketing communications (IMC), systems concepts, and a model of IMC based on systems concepts. Specifically, chapter 1 introduces the reader to a basic definition of the concept of IMC and provides an analysis of its various conceptualizations. Chapter 2 describes the five major components of the systems model: (1) strategy and tactics, (2) objective and measures, (3) resource allocation, (4) monitoring and control, and (5) analysis and planning. We introduce the reader to each of these systems components and describe their dynamics. Then we address the concept of system integration—that is, how systems can be effectively integrated by building and strengthening linkages among the systems components. Chapter 3 presents an overview of the model at large. The model is simply described as involving three levels of analysis—corporate, marketing, and marketing communications. Each level involves a subsystem, and the components of that subsystem are strategy/tactics, objectives/measures, resource allocation, monitoring/control, and analysis/planning (see Figure I.1).

CHAPTER 1

Integrated Marketing Communications

Consider the following case of Acuvue disposable contact lens.[1] Marketing scholars agree that Johnson & Johnson (J&J) launched a successful integrated marketing communications (IMC) campaign. J&J started out with a direct-response advertising campaign in magazines, such as *Newsweek*. The direct-response campaign introduced the lens and discussed its benefits. Each print ad allowed readers who became interested to receive information packets by returning mail-in cards to J&J and identifying their optometrists. J&J then sent direct-mail kits to their optometrists. The optometrists, in turn, contacted their patients to set up appointments. Then optometrists notified J&J of appointments. Using this information, J&J mailed discount coupons (as a first-time trial offer) to patients who made appointments to see their optometrists. These patients turned in their coupons and placed their first orders with their optometrists. The optometrists, in turn, notified J&J about the orders. After some time, J&J mailed the eyecare patients another discount on second orders (see Figure 1.1).

Running a complicated marketing communications campaign such as the one for J&J's Acuvue lens involves multiple communications tools, directed to multiple audiences, in multiple stages, using a sophisticated coordination mechanism. That is what an IMC campaign is all about.

The purpose of this chapter is to introduce to the reader the concept of IMC. We start the chapter by first defining IMC. Second, we discuss the characteristics of an IMC campaign. Third, we describe the concept of IMC from a developmental perspective. Fourth, the conditions that paved the way for IMC are described. Then, last but not least, the reader is introduced to several planning methods or approaches to IMC.

DEFINITION OF IMC

In today's high-tech environment, there is an exponential increase in the development of new communication technologies. Marketers are compelled to use many of these technologies to reach and communicate with target consumers more effectively and in more cost-efficient ways. To do this, marketers need help. They need help to know how to plan and implement a unified marketing communications campaign. They

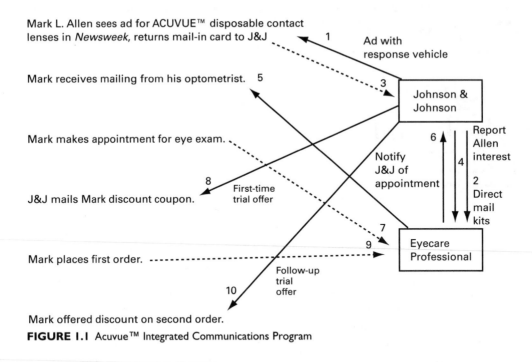

Mark L. Allen sees ad for ACUVUE™ disposable contact lenses in *Newsweek*, returns mail-in card to J&J

Mark receives mailing from his optometrist.

Mark makes appointment for eye exam.

J&J mails Mark discount coupon.

Mark places first order.

Mark offered discount on second order.

FIGURE 1.1 Acuvue™ Integrated Communications Program

need conceptual tools to guide them to pull it all together. They have to create synergies among the various marketing communications programs. For these reasons, many marketing and marketing communications scholars are increasingly recognizing the importance of integrated marketing communications. But first, what *is* "integrated marketing communication" (IMC)? It is defined as follows:

> IMC is a concept that recognizes the added value in a program that integrates a variety of strategic disciplines—for example, general advertising, direct response, sales promotion, and public relations—and combines these disciplines to provide clarity, consistency, and maximum communication impact.[2]

Professor Don Schultz, considered to be the guru of IMC, defined IMC as follows:

> The process of managing all sources of information about a product/service to which a customer or prospect is exposed which behaviorally moves the consumer toward a sale and maintains customer loyalty.[3]

IMC is the idea that a firm coordinates all its communications activities. This is very important because many firms are often content to let an advertising agency take care of the firm's advertising. It farms out its public relations (PR) work to a PR agency. The firm's marketing department handles the sales promotion program. As a result, the firm's advertising goes off in one direction, public relations in another, and the sales promotion program in still another. As a result, the overall effectiveness of the firm's marketing communications suffers significantly. IMC, as a philosophic concept, dictates that all parties involved in the firm's communications efforts coordinate to speak to target consumers with one voice, a unified message, and a consistent image.

Studies have shown that marketers value the IMC concept.[4] Four out of five marketers surveyed, when given a definition of IMC, agreed that the concept is valuable and that it would increase the effect and effectiveness of their marketing communication programs. They indicated that IMC provides greater consistency in marketing communication programs, reduces media waste, and gives a company a competitive edge.[5]

CHARACTERISTICS OF AN IMC CAMPAIGN

The Body Shop has been proclaimed as a highly successful international chain of retail stores. The company has an image of being socially and environmentally concerned. The image is consistent with the personality and values of the founder of The Body Shop, Anita Roddick. The product ingredients are all natural and are bought from developing countries; none of the testing is done on animals. The company does not use traditional advertising. The company uses a variety of marketing communications tools and has done well to integrate the disparate components in order to create impact. Although The Body Shop's marketing executive may not realize it, this company, we believe, has successfully practiced IMC. But the question here is, how can we *really* tell? What are the characteristics of The Body Shop's marketing communications campaign that makes it *integrated*?

Many of us are guilty of defining IMC in terms of effectiveness. If a marketing communications campaign were to achieve its marketing goals, we may infer that the campaign must have been integrated. Philosophers may chuckle here because what we have just described is what philosophers call "tautology," or "circular thinking." Of course, we can do better than this. An IMC campaign can be defined in terms of two distinct characteristics: campaign continuity and strategic orientation.[6] *Campaign continuity* means that all messages communicated in different media through different marketing communications tools are interrelated. Campaign continuity involves making both the physical and psychological elements of a marketing communications campaign consistent. *Physical continuity* refers to the consistent use of creative elements in all marketing communications. Physical continuity in a marketing communications campaign can be achieved by using the same slogan, taglines, and trade characters across all ads and other forms of marketing communications. For example, all Maytag ads show the same character—the lonely repairman.

In addition to physical continuity, *psychological continuity* is equally important. Psychological continuity refers to a consistent attitude toward the firm and its brand(s). It is consumers' perception of the company's "voice" and its "persona."[7] This can be achieved by using a consistent theme, image, or tone in all ads and other forms of marketing communications. The Virginia Slims marketing communications campaign has a consistent theme, that of the liberated woman who chooses to smoke because she now has a mind of her own. Marlboro cigarettes is another example of the use of a consistent image across all forms of marketing communications—the cowboy image of being tough and rugged. Many cosmetic and apparel communications are good examples of consistent tone. For example, all Calvin Klein ads and other forms of marketing communications are sexual in tone.

The second characteristic of an IMC campaign is *strategic orientation.* IMC campaigns can be effective because they are designed to achieve strategic company goals. The focus is not on developing a creative ad that simply attracts attention or gets an audience to laugh. Many marketing communication specialists get carried away by producing extraordinarily creative work that wins them communication awards. But these same communications do not help achieve the firm's strategic goals—goals such as sales, market share, and profit. What makes a marketing communications campaign integrated is its strategic focus. Messages are designed to achieve specific strategic goals; media are selected with strategic goals in mind.

A DEVELOPMENTAL VIEW OF IMC

IMC can occur in different forms at different levels of development. Seven levels of development have been identified (see Table 1.1).[8]

Awareness of the Need for Integration

In its most rudimentary form, IMC can be simply marketers' *awareness,* or recognition of the need to integrate marketing communications. Consider the following example. A media planner is involved in buying and placing ads for a political candidate who is running for the presidency. The media planner comes to recognize that media vehicles within and across media categories should be selected to reflect a consistent image of the political candidate. This is a first step toward implementing the IMC concept.

Image Integration

The second stage involves making decisions to ensure *message/media consistency.* Message/media consistency refers to consistency achieved between written and visual elements of an ad, and between ads placed in different media vehicles. That is, the picture has to reinforce and illustrate the written message. Although each ad has to be slightly varied as a function of the editorial or programming content of a media vehicle, it must be consistent with other ads placed in other media vehicles.

Derrith Lambka, the strategic planning and customer data manager for computer products at Hewlett-Packard, defined IMC in a manner consistent with image

TABLE 1.1 Developmental Stages of IMC
1. Awareness of the need for integration
2. Image integration
3. Functional integration
4. Coordinated integration
5. Consumer-based integration
6. Stakeholder-based integration
7. Relationship management integration

integration. She views IMC as "integration of messages and visual themes across the marcom mix to maximize impact of message in the marketplace. A consistent user benefit is clearly communicated in all marcom pieces."[9]

Functional Integration

The third level of development involves *functional integration.* Functional integration refers to the process in which the various marketing communication programs are formulated as a direct function of marketing goals, such as sales and market share. That is, the strengths and weaknesses of each element of the marketing communication mix are analyzed, and the mix is assembled to achieve specified marketing objectives. To reiterate, marketing goals are employed to guide the selection and implementation of the marketing communication programs.

Coordinated Integration

At a still higher level of development—*coordinated integration*—the personal selling function is directly integrated with other elements of marketing communications (advertising, public relations, sales promotion, and direct marketing). That is, measures are taken to ensure consistency between interpersonal and impersonal forms of marketing communications. What each salesperson says has to be consistent with what the ad says.

Consumer-Based Integration

At the fifth level of IMC development, marketing strategy is planned by understanding the consumers' needs and wants, targeting certain consumers, and effectively positioning the product to target consumers. This stage of IMC development is referred to as *consumer-based integration.* In other words, marketing strategy is integrated. Messages reflecting strategic positioning reach the minds of a selected consumer segment.

Stakeholder-Based Integration

The sixth level of IMC development is *stakeholder-based integration.* Here, marketers recognize that target consumers is not the only group that the firm should be communicating with. Other stakeholders that should be included in the overall IMC campaign include the firm's employees, suppliers, distributors, and stockholders as well as the community, certain government agencies, and others.

Relationship Management Integration

Finally, *relationship management integration* is considered to be the highest level of IMC development. To effectively communicate with the various stakeholders, the firm needs to develop effective strategies. These strategies are not only marketing strategies; they are manufacturing strategies, engineering strategies, finance strategies, human resource strategies, and accounting strategies, among others. That is, in order to enhance relationships with organizational stakeholders, the firm has to develop management strategies within each functional unit (manufacturing, engineering and R&D, marketing, finance, accounting, human resources, etc.) that reflect coordination among the various functional units. Once this integration is achieved, the marketer attempts to communicate to the various stakeholders in a manner reflecting total integration.[10]

We believe the IMC model described in this book reflects an integration perspective consistent with the highest three levels of IMC development—consumer-based integration, stakeholder-based integration, and relationship-management integration. We hope the reader will agree with this assessment upon completion of the book.

CONDITIONS OR TRENDS THAT PAVED THE WAY FOR IMC

At least seven conditions or trends have been identified that paved the way for IMC.[11] These are shown in Table 1.2.[12]

Trend 1—Decrease in Message Credibility

Consumers are continuously bombarded with marketing communications on all fronts. The enormity of this message bombardment has caused "clutter" in the landscape of marketing communications. This clutter is responsible for the fact that a single ad in a single medium cannot create significant impact. The result is a decreasing trend in message impact, which in turn has led to the recognition that message effectiveness is dependent on multiple messages, multiple media, and multiple forms of marketing communications tools. Therefore, marketers are beginning to feel the need for understanding the science and art of IMC. They are beginning to realize that they need to understand and implement IMC to be effective in today's cluttered marketing communications environment.

Trend 2—Decrease in Cost of Database Marketing

The advent of computer technology has created a large mailing list industry. More than ever before, marketers are now capable of gathering specific information about consumers. For example, if a marketer wants to target, let us say physical therapists, they can buy a database that provides an extensive profile of these people. Included in this profile are their media habits and various sources of information they use in making purchases related to their professional practice. Armed with this information, a marketer targeting this population can use different forms of marketing communications tools to create multiple messages. Because of the sophisticated computer technologies used in database management and the fierce competition in this industry, the

---

TABLE 1.2 Conditions or Trends That Paved the Way for IMC

Decrease in message credibility
Decrease in cost of database marketing
Increase in cost and decrease in effectiveness of mass-media communications
Increase in mergers and acquisitions of marketing communications agencies
Increase in media and audience fragmentation
Increase in parity, or "me-too" products
Shift of information technology

cost of using databases has dramatically decreased over the years. The increased viability of database marketing has made IMC increasingly attractive to many marketers.

Trend 3—Increase in Cost and Decrease in Effectiveness of Mass-Media Communications

The costs of television advertising as well as other mass-media advertising have continuously spiraled over the years. Consumers are no longer watching television as they used to. They are not reading newspapers as they used to. Radio listenership is also down. Consumers are turning to other entertainment media and leisure activities, such as playing Nintendo games and surfing the Internet. Those who still watch television are now zipping through and zapping the commercials. Many are paying to watch cable television to avoid commercials. Marketers are becoming more cost conscious than ever. They are increasingly recognizing that they can launch an aggressive and effective marketing communications campaign using marketing communication tools that are less costly than mass-media advertising. But to rely on other forms of marketing communication tools and combining these programs to achieve sales, market share, and profitability goals, marketers are beginning to realize that they need to better understand the science of integrated communications—in short, IMC.

Trend 4—Increase in Mergers and Acquisitions of Marketing Communications Agencies

In the last decade or so, we have witnessed an unprecedented level of mergers and acquisitions in the marketing communications agency business. These mergers and acquisitions may have been the result of agency executives' realizing the need to offer clients comprehensive marketing communications services. A large marketing communications agency that can assemble teams from various marketing communications departments to meet the needs of its clients is likely to be in a better competitive position than agencies that cannot offer this type of service. Those agencies that are now in a position to offer comprehensive marketing communications services are increasingly appreciative of the science and art of IMC.

Trend 5—Increase in Media and Audience Fragmentation

The fierce competition in mass media has forced the industry to become highly fragmented. Radio stations with specific programming formats are springing up all over. Television channels are specializing by content area—history, classic movies, learning, science fiction, family, news, politics, and so on. There are hundreds or thousands of specialized magazines and trade publications. Consumers are no longer watching a television station that caters to everyone. They don't have to. They tune in to those media that have programming or editorial content that matches their interest. This trend of media and audience fragmentation has been a challenge for marketers. Marketers can no longer place a 30-second television commercial in, let's say, *CBS Evening News* or *60 Minutes* and expect to get wide exposure. That used to be the case, but no more. Marketers have to identify the media habits of their target consumers and develop and place multiple messages in specialized and possibly nontraditional media. To do this effectively, they realize now more than ever that they need to fully understand IMC.

Trend 6—Increase in Parity, or "Me-Too" Products

Competition is becoming fierce. Many businesses are developing and marketing products that cannot be significantly differentiated from competitor brands. Marketing communications has become highly essential in an age of "me-too" products. The name of the game is now *share of voice*. Share of voice becomes an effective means to achieve desired returns and market share. That is, the more messages in more media, the better the chance of achieving higher returns and greater market share.

Trend 7—Shift of Information Technology

Professor Schultz has argued that changes in information technology are likely to provide consumers with the ability to communicate and even purchase through a variety of means. That is, consumers can communicate interactively with and purchase products directly from the manufacturer. Traditionally, the manufacturer announces the availability of his or her product to consumers and attempts to transmit messages to consumers in the hope of making them purchase. The trend points to the scenario in which the buyer announces his or her readiness to purchase using the latest interactive information technology. The sellers attempt to respond to the buyer's readiness. Here the buyer becomes the advertiser, and the traditional use of advertising, sales promotion, public relations, and direct marketing changes dramatically. This shift in information technology dictates a redefinition of the traditional use of the various elements of marketing communications.[13]

The increased emphasis on marketing communications has brought with it increased marketing communications clutter, decreased message credibility, database marketing, increased cost and decreased effectiveness of mass-media communications, mergers and acquisitions of marketing communications agencies, increased media and audience fragmentation, and shift of information technology. These, in turn, have made marketers very cognizant of the need and power of IMC.

APPROACHES TO PLANNING IMC

Several approaches to planning IMC have been identified and discussed.[14] These are listed in Table 1.3.

TABLE 1.3   Planning Approaches to IMC
The mandated "one look" approach
The themelines, or "matchbooks," approach
The supply-side planning approach
Ad hoc approaches
The consumer-based approach

The Mandated "One Look" Approach

Some marketers understand and implement the concept of IMC in terms of *common look*. This usually translates into having common colors, graphics, and logo treatments in all forms of marketing communications. For example, a company hires an ad agency to develop an ad campaign for one of its products but decides to develop other communication materials in-house. In this case, the company attempts to develop those in-house materials in a manner consistent with the ad campaign. In other words, the company tries to maintain a "look" of the in-house communication materials that is consistent with the colors, visuals, and logo treatments in the ads developed by the ad agency.

The major shortcoming of this approach is the fact that a common look to all forms of marketing communications is not likely to suffice. A strategic focus is needed, and that is what this book is all about. We show how IMC decisions can be made effectively using a systems model that has a strategic marketing focus.

The Themelines, or "Matchbooks," Approach

This approach is used by marketers who coordinate all forms of marketing communications around their advertising. The goal is to use nonadvertising forms of marketing communications to trigger consumers to remember the advertising message. For example, the television commercial of Coppertone suntan lotion uses a themeline of "Tan, don't burn." The same themeline is then used in skywriting over the beaches during the summer. Some research has been conducted in this area.[15] Examples of findings and their managerial usefulness are the following:

- Advertising retrieval cues, such as key visuals or distinctive slogans, can be placed on point-of-purchase displays and packaging. These cues can help consumers remember the advertising message.

- Consumers will remember a television commercial better if they also hear a radio commercial with the same audio script.

- Before running a television commercial, marketers can run radio and print ads that are directly linked to the television commercial. The print and radio ads in this case serve as a teaser and increase consumer motivation to fully process the television commercial when it is finally run.

- Television commercials can be viewed as consisting of different elements that marketers can choose to combine in different ways over time. Examples of these interchangeable elements include visual scenes, characters, symbols, verbal phrases, and slogans.

As with the "one look" approach, the themeline approach is necessary but not sufficient. Marketers need to be guided by both continuity and a strategic focus.

The Supply-Side Planning Approach

Many companies offer a system of marketing communication services that have the appearance of integration. For example, an advertising agency may have a package deal with the local cable company, several radio stations, and a local newspaper. The package deal allows a local business to advertise its offerings through a combination of cable channels, radio stations, and the local newspaper. The price of the package deal is highly attractive. The benefit that the advertising agency highlights in selling this package deal to prospective businesses is integrated communications. That is, the advertising agency will create ads with a common look and theme and will place them across varied media vehicles.

The major shortcoming of this approach is the fact that the package deal may not fit the exact needs of the business client. Many businesses may jump on the band wagon because they may think that they are getting a good bargain, but the bargain may not actually provide real value.

The Ad Hoc Approach

Many marketers attempt to integrate the disparate elements of their marketing communications programs by arranging meetings of all the parties involved. For example, a variety of people representing different interests attend a meeting and attempt to achieve consensus. The group may include the account exec from the ad agency, the public relations rep, the salesperson from the sales promotion firm, and the marketing research people. The meeting is organized and led by the marketing director. People representing the various suppliers present their ideas for marketing communications and discuss ways to establish common threads.

The major shortcoming of this approach is that the process is not likely to be efficient. No model or plan guides their integration efforts. Second, the outcome may be highly influenced by group dynamics. Certain parties with strong opinions may take over and lead the integration effort in an inappropriate and ineffective direction.

Consumer-Based Approaches

Two consumer-based approaches to IMC have been developed—one by Schultz, Tannenbaum, and Lauterborn[16] and the other by Moore and Thorson.[17] The IMC model developed by Schultz et al. is considered to be the standard model, and therefore, we will discuss this model fully and critique it to help set the stage for our IMC systems model. First, however, we will briefly describe the Moore and Thorson model.

The Moore and Thorson IMC Model

This model involves five basic steps, as shown in Table 1.4.

The first step, *identifying the market,* is the process by which the marketer identifies those consumers who are most likely to buy the company product. For example, Evian, a brand of bottled water, targets two market segments—health-conscious adults and new mothers. (New mothers are inclined to buy pure water to feed their babies.) The second step is *segmenting the market based on stage of purchase cycle.* The typical stages in the purchase cycle include awareness, acceptance, preference,

---

TABLE 1.4 The Moore and Thorson Customer-Based Approach to IMC

1. Identifying the market
2. Segmenting the market based on stage-of-purchase cycle
3. Identifying messages and communications vehicles for each target segment
4. Allocating resources
5. Evaluating program effectiveness

search, purchase, usage, and satisfaction. The stage of the purchase cycle is then identified for each market segment. For example, one can identify two market segments as having tried bottled water; therefore, most of those consumers are at the satisfaction stage. The third step is *identifying messages and communication vehicles for each target segment.* Knowing at what stage most of the consumers are allows the marketer to identify the kind of message needed. In this case, the message has to reinforce their satisfaction. The message directed to the health-conscious has to be created in such a way as to encourage them to identify with the character(s) in the ad, perhaps with a health-conscious celebrity. Similarly, the message directed to new mothers has to appeal to that audience; perhaps ads can be created that feature a new mother as a spokesperson. Furthermore, the marketer of Evian will attempt to identify those media vehicles that can reach both segments in the most cost-efficient way. For example, certain magazines can be identified for both segments. Once both message and media are identified for market segment(s), the marketer will attempt to ascertain the costs of creating and placing a certain number of messages in certain media—that is, *resource allocation.* The final step involves *evaluating program effectiveness.* For example, tracking studies can be employed to monitor brand awareness, consumer attitude, and so on.

This approach to IMC is highly consistent with the systems approach discussed in this book. However, we believe our model is more comprehensive and rigorous than the Moore and Thorson model. Our model shows in explicit ways how decisions made at the corporate level are tied to decisions made at the marketing level, which in turn are linked to decisions made at the marketing communications level. This said, the reader is now in a position to better understand and appreciate the systems model of IMC proposed in this book.

The Schultz/Tannenbaum/Lauterborn IMC Model

The most authoritative work in integrated marketing communications (IMC) is that of Schultz, Tannenbaum, and Lauterborn (1994) in their book titled *Integrated Marketing Communications: Pulling It Together and Making It Work.*[18] Schultz et al. describe IMC as a way of conceptualizing the whole process instead of focusing on parts such as advertising, public relations, sales promotion, direct marketing, and so forth. Their IMC model can be described as involving a sequence of marketing communications planning activities (see Figure 1.2).

Database Development   The first step in planning, according to the Schultz model, is developing a database. Database development involves gathering and assembling information (demographics, psychographics, purchase history, and category networks) about the product users (consumers). For example, an airline sends information to members of its frequent flier program through direct mail and solicits replies from them. The members may be asked if they want information on air travel to some exotic island in the Caribbean to spend the Christmas holidays. The reply can be in the form of a direct mail piece which the member sends in or merely a telephone call. Part of the reply card asks for additional information about the members—their likes and dislikes involving travel, the way they would like to spend their Christmas vacation, and so on. The reply information is used to create the database of potential customers who might be interested in flying to the Caribbean for a Christmas vacation

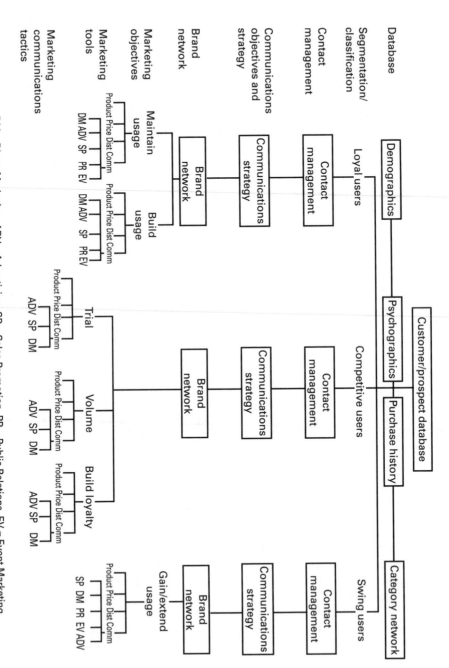

FIGURE 1.2 The Schultz et al. IMC Model

DM = Direct Marketing ADV = Advertising SP = Sales Promotion PR = Public Relations EV = Event Marketing

and to determine the kind of travel/tourist services that the airline company should provide to meet the needs of the members of its frequent flier program.

One may want to ask, "Data about what and for what purpose?" Gathering data about consumers is, of course, important. But marketing scholars have always advocated exactly the same thing. That is, we need to know our customers to be able to serve them well. The problem here is knowing exactly what we need to know about consumers. We will argue in Part IV ("Analysis and Planning"), as well as in chapter 12 ("Lessons in Integration"), that analysis has to be strongly linked with planning. That is, every piece of information we gather has to be useful. We need to figure out exactly what kind of decisions we need to make first and then try to gather *relevant* information that can help us make these decisions. In the systems model of IMC, we will show how analysis and planning are essentially and directly tied to strategy selection, objective setting, the formulation of tactics, and resource allocation at the corporate, marketing, and marketing communications levels.

Segmentation   This is a process in which consumers are divided into loyal users, competitive users, and swing users, and consumer profiles of these segments are developed. *Loyal users* are consumers who have a history of repeat use of the product brand. *Competitive users* are those who use the brand in question together with other competitive brands. *Swing users* are not loyal to any one brand or combination of brands. They are opportunistic. They buy a brand because of its price and accessibility.

Let's use the Olive Garden (a national chain of Italian restaurants) as an example. The marketing director would be interested in developing consumer profiles of those who are loyal to the Olive Garden—people who eat at the Olive Garden whenever they feel the urge to eat Italian food in a sit-down restaurant. The marketing director wants information about these loyal customers in order to serve them better and retain their business for the long term. But what kind of information would the marketing director want about the loyal customers? Information about their likes or dislikes concerning the different items on the menu, information about their likes or dislikes concerning the introduction of new dishes, and information about their media habits, for example.

What about competitive users? The marketing director of the Olive Garden may want information about these people too, the goal being to get them to increase their patronage of the Olive Garden. Again, information about their likes and dislikes concerning the menu items and about their media habits could be very helpful in appealing to this segment.

But would the marketing director of the Olive Garden be interested in the swing customers? Perhaps the marketing director could appeal to the swing customers to come during times when business is slow, perhaps for lunch and dinner in the middle of the week. These people might respond to good deals, perhaps to coupons distributed in the local newspaper. Thus, the marketing director needs to gather some information about them, at least about which local newspapers they subscribe to. If those consumers do not read newspapers, what other media vehicles could reach them in the most effective and cost-efficient way? Information about their media habits would be important.

The reader may ask: "Why segmentation on the basis of brand use and not on the multitude of other bases?" Schultz and his colleagues advance a unique method of segmentation. They suggest that consumers should be segmented into the following groups: loyal users, competitive users, and swing users. Of course this segmentation is fine. It is well known in the marketing literature. But why should we use this particular segmentation? Marketing scholars have long described many different ways of segmenting the market by using all kinds of different segmentation criteria (e.g., demographic segmentation, psychographic segmentation, segmentation based on product criteria, geographic segmentation, socio-cultural segmentation, and so on). Schultz et al.'s concept of segmentation is limited to only one very specific method of segmentation based on a product criterion, i.e., brand use. Do Schultz and his colleagues advocate that we abandon all other uses of segmentation and adopt the brand use segmentation as the best and only method? Their prescription of segmentation is too constrictive. One can imagine hundreds of scenarios in which segmentation by brand use is not likely to be effective. The systems model does not force managers to use a specific segmentation criterion. As a matter of fact, the systems model uses Porter's model, which posits that segmentation can and should only be attempted when the best marketing strategy is focus. Other marketing strategies such as differentiation and cost leadership do not require any market segmentation at all. Only in the context of the focus strategy should the manager implement segmentation. And in the context of focus, the systems model recommends the use of any of the following three positioning strategies: customer benefits (commonly known as benefit segmentation in marketing), use or applications, and user or customer. Thus, the brand use segmentation basis of Schultz is only one variation of the user or customer strategy.

Contact Management   Contact management is the process by the which the marketer determines the time, place, or situation in which to communicate to the customer or prospect. For example, the marketing director of the Olive Garden considers the situation in which most customers (potential and actual) are likely to be most disposed to processing an advertising message about the Olive Garden. Should the ad appear on the local TV news program before dinnertime? Those who may be planning to eat out may consider the Olive Garden if they were to see an ad about the Olive Garden just before they are getting ready to go out to dinner. Effective contact management in this case may be broadcasting an ad on the local television news program between 5 and 7 p.m.

The reader may ask, "Contact management—why a strategic decision?" Why talk about contact management as a strategic decision? Contact management, although it is important, is a tactical decision. In the systems model, contact management is a tactical decision made in the context of each element of the marketing communications mix. For example, when advertising is selected as an effective element of the marketing communications mix, the marketing communications manager makes media placement decisions, and only in this context should the time, place, or situation be considered. The systems model treats marketing and corporate decisions as more strategic than tactical. Contact management is strictly a tactical decision but, nevertheless, an important one.

Communications Strategy   The marketer at this point determines what main points the consumer should take away from the communications and what action the consumer should take as a result of the communication. That is, the marketer tries to identify the most effective message possible. What can be said? The goal is to create a change in the customer's or prospect's category and brand network, the kind of change that is likely to induce the desired behavior.

For example, a marketer of, let's say, Compaq Computers tries to identify the most effective message to those who bought Compaq computers several years ago. The goal is to get them to upgrade. The marketer has to find a compelling reason to do so that can be effectively communicated to those people. Could the reason be that, in view of the proliferation in the use of multimedia software, users of old Compaq computers are missing out on this wonderful new technology? Or could it be the increasing speed of computer processing? Or could it be the new communications systems? Which message is likely to be most effective? For the marketer to be able to identify effective messages, he or she needs to know something about the value systems of these prospective customers. What is important or unimportant to them in the way they use computers? This information should be part of the consumer profile that the marketer gathers about target customers.

But then one can say, "This is what positioning is all about!" According to Schultz et al., the marketer at this point determines what main points the consumer should take away from the communications and what action the consumer should take as a result of the communication. That is, the marketer tries to identify the most effective message possible. The problem is not that what Schultz et al. say is wrong or unimportant but that the term "communications strategy" is used vaguely and perhaps improperly. What is described is in essence what marketing scholars refer to as "positioning," which is communicating important things about the product in such a way as to cause target consumers to adopt the product. The systems model describes at least three marketing strategies and how these strategies are communicated through positioning. It describes well-established concepts of positioning, such as positioning by product attribute, positioning by intangible factor, positioning by product class, positioning by competitors, and so on. This positioning decision is highly strategic and governs what we call "marketing communications strategy, objectives, and tactics."

Marketing Objectives   The message has to induce some overt behavior, and this behavior is captured and measured in relation to marketing objectives. The following are some examples of marketing objectives:

- Maintain or increase product usage by brand-loyal customers
- Generate product trial, build volume, or build loyalty among competitive users
- Gain or extend product usage by swing users

Note that marketing objectives are stated in relation to selected target markets (loyal customers, competitive users, and swing users). Also, note that these marketing objectives are directly deduced from the communications strategy—that is, from the message. For example, suppose the Compaq marketer who is targeting the loyal customers (previous buyers of Compaq) settles on the following message: "You should update your Compaq because the new Compaq gives you much more power for just a few dollars more." This message should be tied to a specific marketing objective, such as increasing usage by previous Compaq customers through an increase of 20% in sales of the Compaq Presario series in the next six months.

The reader may ask: "Are these 'marketing' or 'communication' objectives?" According to Schultz et al., the message has to induce some overt behavior, and this behavior is captured and measured in relation to marketing objectives. As listed above, examples of marketing objectives include: maintain or increase product usage by brand-loyal customers; generate product trial, build volume, or build loyalty among competitive users; and gain or extend product usage by swing users. Schultz et al. are right on target in arguing that marketing objectives can be directly deduced from the strategy. Of course, we call it marketing strategy, and they call it "communications strategy." They are right on target in talking about the message as a strategic decision, which we place at the marketing level, and about how the message (i.e., positioning strategy) dictates marketing objectives. The reader will note upon reading further that their "marketing objectives" are partly accounted for in our "communications objectives." Our conception of communications objectives involves the well-accepted hierarchy of effects that starts with brand awareness, goes to brand learning, moves into brand attitude/liking, then into brand trial/purchase, and finishes off with repeat purchase. Our conception of "marketing objectives" is directly tied to the marketing strategies of differentiation, cost leadership, and focus, which in turn are further operationalized in terms of positioning. Depending on which positioning strategy is invoked, the corresponding marketing objective is also invoked. For example, if a differentiation strategy is selected, the marketer may choose to operationalize this strategy in terms of positioning by product attribute. In this context, the corresponding marketing objective may be stated in terms of increasing or maximizing brand association with an important product attribute. On the other hand, if a focus strategy is operationalized in terms of positioning by customer application, then the corresponding marketing objective can be stated as maximizing brand association with a certain customer application.

Marketing Tools   At this point, the marketer uses the elements of the marketing mix (product, price, place, and promotion) as marketing communications tools to implement the communications strategy and achieve the stated marketing objective. The message is not communicated solely through marketing communications elements such as advertising, sales promotion, public relations, and so forth. The product itself, its package, its price, and the way it is distributed can each communicate a different message. The challenge lies in ensuring message consistency across the mix of marketing elements.

For example, suppose the marketer of upscale apparel such as Polo clothing decides that the message is, "Polo clothes are for classy people." However, Polo clothes are inexpensive. Polo clothes are distributed through discount clothing stores. This example shows inconsistency between the message itself on one hand and the price and method of distribution on the other. Consumers are getting conflicting messages. The ad campaign is informing them that Polo clothes are for classy people, yet they are sold cheaply and through discount stores. Consumers would expect Polo clothes to be sold at premium prices through clothing boutiques and upscale apparel stores. Thus, the message must be consistently reflected in all elements of the marketing mix, not just the communications mix.

Schultz's idea of marketing tools is "on target." That means, according to Schultz et al., that the marketer uses the elements of the marketing mix (product, price, place, and promotion) as marketing communications tools to implement the communications strategy and achieve the stated marketing objective. If what is meant by "communications strategy" à la Schultz is what marketing scholars talk about as positioning, then our systems model appears to be highly compatible with the Schultz model since the systems model asserts that the marketing strategy is translated in terms of marketing objectives, which in turn are achieved through marketing tactics (i.e., the elements of the marketing mix—product, price, place, and promotion).

Marketing Communications Tactics At this point, the marketer chooses tactics such as advertising, direct marketing, sales promotion, public relations, and event marketing to implement the communications strategy and achieve the marketing objective. In the Polo example, the marketer attempts to choose an effective mix of communications elements to communicate the message of "class." Which communications elements are *most* effective in implementing the communications strategy of "classy clothes"? Would advertising be effective? What form of advertising? TV advertising? Radio advertising? Magazine advertising? If magazine advertising, which magazines should be selected as the most effective and cost-efficient vehicles? The *New Yorker? Forbes?*

The reader may ask, "Whatever happened to 'communications strategy and objectives'?" According to Schultz et al., the marketer then chooses tactics such as advertising, direct marketing, sales promotion, public relations, and event marketing to implement the communications strategy and achieve the marketing objective. This is fine, of course, except for the fact that they missed an entire layer of decision making. Before the marketing managers can make decisions about marketing communications tools, they have to figure out a marketing communications strategy. The systems model uses the traditional Foote-Cone-Belding (FCB) model to identify four communications strategies: informative (thinker), affective (feeler), habit formation (doer), and self-satisfaction (reactor). Choosing a strategy is an important decision because the strategy allows the marketing communications manager to figure the communications performance dimensions (marketing communications objectives). According to the FCB model, an informative (thinker) strategy leads to developing a marketing communications campaign that focuses on brand awareness and learning. The affective (feeler) strategy prompts the marketing communications manager to single out brand attitude or liking as the goal for the marketing communications campaign. The habit formation (doer) strategy motivates the manager to set the campaign objectives in terms of brand trial/purchase and brand learning. Finally, the self-satisfaction (reactor) strategy nudges the manager to set the campaign goals in terms of brand trial/purchase and brand attitude/liking. According to the systems model, all marketing communications objectives have to be spelled out in terms of the various dimensions of the hierarchy-of-effects model. The FCB Planning model allows the marketing manager to select a communications strategy and then to figure out the appropriate performance dimensions of the communications campaign.

An Overall Critique of the Schultz Model

Besides the problems with the conceptualization of the various stages or components of the Schultz et al. model, their model can be further criticized in terms of (1) not dealing with budgeting issues—an important factor in marketing communications, (2) not dealing with issues of monitoring and control, and (3) working with a model that involves a narrow and highly select use of concepts not yet established in the literature of marketing communication, marketing, and business strategy.

Not Dealing with Budgeting Issues   Developing a marketing budget that allows marketing communications managers to accomplish the stated campaign objectives is very important. Schultz et al. do not deal with budgeting at all. They briefly talk about compensation, which is entirely different from budgeting for marketing communications. Even in regard to compensation (e.g., how to compensate the ad agency based on performance), we don't know much about how this decision fits into the overall scheme of the model. Budgeting is not a decision in the model at all, and the entire topic of budgeting is conspicuously absent. This is a major shortcoming of the Schultz model.

Not Dealing with Issues of Monitoring and Control   Also conspicuously absent from the Schultz model is the issue of monitoring and control. Monitoring and control are crucial in every aspect of business. Most marketing as well as marketing communications books (e.g., Kotler's *Marketing Management* and Belch and Belch's *Marketing Communications*) do at least some justice to this very important concept. No marketing communications campaign can be effectively managed without assessing performance and taking corrective action. How can we have *integrated* marketing communications without a monitoring and control function? The Schultz model does not address the topic at all, let alone show how it can be used to enhance integration of marketing communications.

Working with a Model That Involves a Narrow and Highly Select Use of Concepts Not Yet Established in the Literature   Most important is the fact that the Schultz et al. IMC model does not clearly show students and practitioners of IMC how to put all the pieces together. The problem is that Schultz et al. do not recognize that all the pieces are equally important. Many decisions, concepts, and models that are well accepted in marketing communications, marketing, and overall business strategy are not acknowledged in the Schultz model. Students and practitioners of IMC have to put aside most of the concepts and models they have learned (and may have felt comfortable using throughout the years) and adopt the Schultz model. The systems model described in this book, on the other hand, builds on well-accepted concepts and models in marketing communications, marketing, and business strategy. The systems model uses concepts such as the FCB Planning model, which is highly popular in advertising and marketing communications, Porter's model of marketing strategies (differentiation, cost leadership, and focus), and much of the rich literature on positioning and positioning methods, as well as the Boston Consulting Group matrix and the Multifactor Portfolio model, which are very popular in business strategy. The point is that the systems model focuses on the *process* rather than the *content*. If IMC students or practitioners are highly satisfied with a particular strategic model at the corporate, marketing, or marketing communications level, they can change the content but follow the same process. The marketing communications manager has to select a marketing communications strategy that is designed to achieve marketing objectives. The marketing objectives have to reflect the selected marketing strategy. The marketing strategy has to be selected in such a way to achieve corporate objectives. Corporate objectives have to reflect the goal of corporate strategy. The *process* is the same. The *content* may differ. The process dictates that the marketing communications budget be determined by taking into account the marketing communications tactics (or tasks). The process dictates that each objective has to be quantified and measured using reliable and valid measures with established norms. The process dictates that objectives should be set to capture the essence of a superordinate strategy. The process dictates that objectives set at one hierarchical level should guide the selection of programs or tactics at the subordinate level. And so on. This systems model emphasizes the process and is versatile enough to change content whenever the state of the science reveals better strategy models (the kind of models that help us select effective marketing communication, marketing, and corporate strategies).

Summary

This chapter introduced the reader to the concept of IMC. IMC was defined as added value in a program that integrates a number of marketing communication programs, such as general advertising, direct response, sales promotion, and public relations. The goal is to provide clarity, consistency, and maximum communication impact.

An IMC campaign is recognized through two distinct characteristics: continuity and strategic focus. Campaign continuity involves making both the physical and psychological elements of a marketing communications campaign continuous. Physical continuity in a marketing communications campaign can be achieved by using the same slogan, taglines, and trade characters across all ads and other forms of marketing communications. Psychological continuity can be achieved by using a consistent theme, image, or tone in all ads and other forms of marketing communications. With respect to strategic orientation, the focus is to make marketing communication decisions to achieve the firm's strategic goals—such as sales, market share, and profit.

We showed that IMC can occur in different forms at different levels of development. Seven levels of development have been identified. These are (1) awareness of the need for integration, (2) image integration, (3) functional integration, (4) coordinated integration, (5) consumer-based integration, (6) stakeholder-based integration, and (7) relationship management integration.

At least seven trends have been identified that paved the way for IMC. These are (1) decrease in message credibility, (2) decrease in cost of database marketing, (3) increase in cost and decrease in effectiveness of mass-media communications, (4) increase in mergers and acquisitions of marketing communications agencies, (5) increase in media and audience fragmentation, (6) increase in parity, or "me-too" products, and (7) shift of information technology.

Several approaches to planning IMC have been identified and discussed. These are the mandated "one look" approach, the themelines (matchbooks) approach, the supply-side planning approach, ad hoc approaches, and the consumer-based approach. We described these approaches and provided a critique of each.

Questions for Discussion

1. Develop your own definition of IMC. Then compare and contrast your definition with the definitions provided early in the chapter.
2. Find two magazine ads for the same brand. Examine the two ads in terms of campaign continuity. Do the two ads have physical continuity—same slogans, taglines, and trade characters? How about psychological continuity? Do the two ads have a consistent theme, image, and tone? Describe those features of the ads in some detail.

3. Try to recall a recent television commercial. Think for a moment about its content and purpose. Now, can you figure out the corporate goals behind this commercial? In other words, what is the strategic focus of this commercial?

4. How do marketers try to achieve image integration in their marketing communication efforts?

5. How do marketers try to achieve functional integration in their marketing communication efforts?

6. How do marketers try to achieve coordinated integration in their marketing communication efforts?

7. How do marketers try to achieve consumer-based integration in their marketing communication efforts?

8. How do marketers try to achieve stakeholder-based integration in their marketing communication efforts?

9. Pick an industry that you are somewhat familiar with, such as banking, telecommunications, computer software, or computer hardware. Now try to think about the industry dynamics in relation to marketing communications. Do you think marketers in that industry recognize the importance of IMC? Is IMC practiced in that industry? What are the conditions or trends that have made marketers in that industry adopt or not adopt IMC? Describe those conditions.

10. Discuss the various approaches to IMC planning. What are their advantages and disadvantages?

Notes

1. John Deighton, "Features of Good Integration: Two Cases and Some Generalizations," in *Integrated Communication: Synergy of Persuasive Voices,* edited by Esther Thorson and Jeri Moore (Mahwah, N.J.: Erlbaum, 1996), pp. 243–56.

2. Bob Stone, *Successful Direct Marketing Methods,* 5th ed. (Lincolnwood, Ill.: NTC Business Books, 1994), p. 7.

3. Northwestern University's brochure, 1991.

4. C. L. Caywood, D. E. Schultz, and P. Wang, *A Survey of Consumer Goods Manufacturers* (New York: American Association of Advertising Agencies, 1991); T. Duncan and S. E. Everett, "Client Perceptions of Integrated Marketing Communications," *Journal of Advertising Research* 33, no. 3 (1993): pp 30–9.

5. Reported in Tom Duncan and Clarke Caywood, "The Concept, Process, and Evolution of Integrated Marketing Communication," in *Integrated Communication: Synergy of Persuasive Voices*, edited by Esther Thorson and Jeri Moore (Mahwah, N.J.: Erlbaum, 1996), p. 19.

6. Donald Parente, Bruce Vanden Bergh, Arnold Barban, and James Marra, *Advertising Campaign Strategy: A Guide to Marketing Communications Plans* (Fort Worth, Tex.: The Dryden Press, 1996).

7. Barbara Stern, "Integrated Communication: The Company 'Voice' and the Advertising Persona," in *Integrated Communication: Synergy of Persuasive Voices,* edited by Esther Thorson and Jeri Moore (Mahwah, N.J.: Erlbaum, 1996), pp. 87–102.

8. Tom Duncan and Clarke Caywood, "The Concept, Process, and Evolution of Integrated Marketing Communication," in *Integrated Communication: Synergy of Persuasive Voices,* edited by Esther Thorson and Jeri Moore (Mahwah, N.J.: Erlbaum, 1996), pp. 13–34.

9. Cited in Don E. Schultz, "Problems that Practitioners Have with IMC," *Marketing News* (November 4, 1996), p. 11.

10. Tom Duncan and Clarke Caywood, "The Concept, Process, and Evolution of Integrated Marketing Communication," in *Integrated Communication: Synergy of Persuasive Voices,* edited by Esther Thorson and Jeri Moore (Mahwah, N.J.: Erlbaum, 1996), pp. 13–34.

11. Tom Duncan and Clarke Caywood, "The Concept, Process, and Evolution of Integrated Marketing Communication," in *Integrated Communication: Synergy of Persuasive Voices,* edited by Esther Thorson and Jeri Moore (Mahwah, N.J.: Erlbaum, 1996), pp. 13–34.

12. Don E. Schultz, "The Inevitability of Integrated Communications," *Journal of Business Research* 37, no. 3 (1996), pp. 139–46.

13. Don E. Shultz, "The Inevitability of Integrated Communications," *Journal of Business Research* 37, no. 3 (1996), pp. 139–46.

14. Jeri Moore and Esther Thorson, "Strategic Planning for Integrated Marketing Communications Programs: An Approach to Moving From Chaotic Toward Systematic," in *Integrated Communication: Synergy of Persuasive Voices,* edited by Esther Thorson and Jeri Moore (Mahwah, N.J.: Erlbaum, 1996), pp. 135–52.

15. Kevin Lane Keller, "Brand Equity and Integrated Communication," in *Integrated Communication: Synergy of Persuasive Voices,* edited by Esther Thorson and Jeri Moore (Mahwah, N.J.: Erlbaum, 1996), pp. 103–32.

16. Don E. Schultz, Stanley I. Tannenbaum, and Robert F. Lauterborn, *Integrated Marketing Communications: Pulling It Together & Making It Work* (Lincolnwood, Ill.: NTC Business Books, 1994).

17. Jeri Moore and Esther Thorson, "Strategic Planning for Integrated Marketing Communications Programs: An Approach to Moving From Chaotic Toward Systematic," in *Integrated Communication: Synergy of Persuasive Voices,* edited by Esther Thorson and Jeri Moore (Mahwah, N.J.: Erlbaum, 1996), pp. 135–52.

18. Don E. Schultz, Stanley I. Tannenbaum, and Robert F. Lauterborn, *Integrated Marketing Communications: Pulling It Together and Making It Work* (Lincolnwood, IL: NTC Books, 1994).

Suggested Reading

Duncan, Tom, and Clarke Caywood. "The Concept, Process, and Evolution of Integrated Marketing Communication," In *Integrated Communication: Synergy of Persuasive Voices,* edited by Esther Thorson and Jeri Moore, pp. 13–34. Mahwah, N.J.: Erlbaum, 1996.

Duncan, Tom and S. E. Everett. "Client Perceptions of Integrated Marketing Communications." *Journal of Advertising Research* 33, no. 3 (1993): 30–9.

Moore, Jeri and Esther Thorson. "Strategic Planning for Integrated Marketing Communications Programs: An Approach to Moving from Chaotic toward Systematic." In *Integrated Communication: Synergy of Persuasive Voices,* edited by Esther Thorson and Jeri Moore, pp. 135–52. Mahwah, N.J.: Erlbaum, 1996.

Schultz, Don E., Stanley I. Tannenbaum, and Robert F. Lauterborn. *Integrated Marketing Communications: Pulling It Together & Making It Work.* Lincolnwood, Ill.: NTC Business Books, 1994.

Special Issue of Integrated Marketing Communications. *Journal of Business Research* 37, no. 3 (1996).

Stern, Barbara. "Integrated Communication: The Company 'Voice' and the Advertising Persona." In *Integrated Communication: Synergy of Persuasive Voices,* edited by Esther Thorson and Jeri Moore, pp. 87–102. Mahwah, N.J.: Erlbaum, 1996.

CHAPTER 2

Systems Concepts

Systems concepts and models are designed to help people—particularly decision makers and managers—make better decisions. Decisions cannot be made in a vacuum. They are made in the context of programs, projects, and campaigns. The goal is to make effective decisions that ensure the integrity of the system (i.e., the integrity of the program, project, or campaign). Let's use a person's career as an example and call it a system. The system has to be effectively planned and managed. Systems concepts can help do exactly that. You can apply concepts such as strategy and tactics, objectives, budget, monitoring and control, and analysis and planning. Think about your own career for a minute. Think about the *strategy* you have set for yourself to further develop your own career. What is it? Could it be acting professionally? Could it be following your boss's direction to the letter? Could it be exercising creativity? Could it be demonstrating leadership? Or how about getting rich? Think about your own strategy and focus on it. What have you been doing lately to carry out this strategy? For example, have you been trying to keep up with the professional trade journals so you can use the newest concepts and models at work? Perhaps this is a tactical thing you do to achieve the goal of "acting professionally." Think about two or three tactics you have used and list them.

Now focus on one or two of these career-related tactics. Can you articulate the exact *objective* pertaining to each *tactic?* For example, if you subscribe to a trade journal, your objective may be to read it completely and discuss the things you found interesting with your officemates and your immediate supervisor. Now think about the objective pertaining to your career strategy. Can you articulate it? For example, if you said that acting professionally is your strategy, then how would you know that you are progressing to becoming an ideal professional? What are those *measures,* or indicators, that will tell you whether you are making progress or not? Now shift gears and think about how you budget your *resources* (and energy) to the various tasks that help you achieve your career goal. Your resources may be money, time, and effort. Now shift gears again and focus on *monitoring* and *control.* Are you a good learner? Are you learning from trial and error? What have you learned in the past that has allowed you to enhance your career? Again, let's shift gears. Let's focus on *analysis* and *planning.* What kind of analysis do you do to help you in your career planning? For example, some people gather information about new job opportunities. Other people gather information about opportunities to help out within the firm, and so on. Of course, analysis and planning are very much related to your career strategy. You might gather information and thoroughly analyze it to help you figure out the best career strategy you should pursue. Or you might gather information that may help you allocate your time wisely. All the tactics you use to achieve your career objectives are part of a system. Your decisions will become more effective if you learn to manage the system as a whole.

The purpose of this chapter is to sensitize the reader to certain systems concepts that we use to build the IMC model. The goal is to make the reader familiar with the language of the IMC systems model as a prelude to the next chapter (chapter 3), in which many of these concepts will be used. It is very likely that many of the systems concepts addressed in this chapter will be better understood and appreciated after reading chapter 3 and will be fully appreciated by the end of the book. Some readers may find this chapter "too theoretical," but then the theory part of the model has to be flushed out, articulated, and understood before one can apply the theory to IMC. So please read this chapter with patience and try to learn the language of systems theory. You will find it not only useful in better understanding the IMC systems model but will also appreciate its practical significance.

STRATEGIES AND TACTICS

All decisions can be viewed as involving a decision tree, or a *process hierarchy*. A *decision tree* is in essence a sequential set of processes that are hierarchically organized. Thus, any organizational task can be viewed as involving a set of processes organized hierarchically. At any given level of the process hierarchy, there is a mix of process elements. Focusing on a given element of the process mix allows the system designer to identify the subordinate elements. For example, a decision tree that we will address throughout this book involves a three-level hierarchy for a company's programs—corporate, marketing, and marketing communications. Marketing communications programs, at the bottom of the decision tree, are considered to be elements of the marketing communications mix. The elements of the marketing communications mix are guided by a marketing communications strategy. But marketing communications strategy is considered an element of the next level in the hierarchy, the marketing mix. This element is guided by marketing strategy. Marketing strategy also is considered an element of the corporate mix, which in turn is guided by a corporate strategy.

More specifically, a process at a superordinate level is usually referred to as a "strategy," while the elements of that process (the subordinate processes designed to implement the superordinate process) are usually referred to as "tactics" or "strategic mix." Once we focus on a process, it becomes a strategy, and the elements employed to implement that process become tactics (elements of the strategic mix). But then a tactic becomes a strategy once we move down the hierarchy of processes and focus on that tactic. Hence, the distinction between a strategy and a tactic can be best appreciated from the vantage point of the decision maker in an overall hierarchy of processes. For example, a CEO commonly makes decisions at the top of the decision tree, decisions management scholars refer to as corporate strategy. A decision such as "Gain market share" is considered highly strategic. This decision is carried out by the various organizational departments. In other words, all corporate strategic decisions are implemented through the deployment of the various functional units of an organization (R&D, engineering, production, marketing, accounting, finance, insurance, employee relations, etc.). The tasks performed in the various functional units are tactical decisions, not strategic ones, from the vantage point of the CEO. However, a decision made by the VP for marketing is highly superordinate if it guides the performance of the entire marketing department; this decision would be strategic from the vantage point of the VP for marketing. For example, "We should position our product as a quality product" is a strategic decision that guides all marketing efforts. The various marketing tasks employed to implement this decision are considered tactics—but again, only from the vantage point of the VP for marketing. Note that the decision made by the VP for marketing is considered a tactic from the vantage point of the CEO. Similarly, the marketing communications manager may make strategic decisions at the marketing communications level; these in turn are carried out as concrete tasks, or tactics, using the various tools of marketing communications. For example, "Use coupons" would be considered a tactical decision by the marketing communications manager because this particular task would be guided by a superordinate decision such as "Develop a communications campaign that induces consumers to try the product."

In a typical decision tree, or process hierarchy, the selection of one or more subordinate process elements (elements of a strategic mix) is directly influenced by the selection of the corresponding superordinate process (strategy). Correspondingly, the selection of a specific strategy (main process at any given hierarchical level) is influenced by the implicit or explicit selection of the strategic mix (process elements). That is, the process hierarchy is designed using both top-down and bottom-up approaches. It does not matter which comes first, a given process (strategy) or its elements (strategic mix). The idea is that planning entails the selection of hierarchical processes that create means-end chains; subordinate processes (means) are selected in such a way to achieve the goals of a superordinate process (end) at any level of the process hierarchy, and vice versa (see Figure 2.1).

SETTING OBJECTIVES

The concept of *objectives* is very popular in the organizational and managerial sciences. Managers set goals and objectives and develop programs to meet these goals and objectives. First, let's distinguish between strategies/tactics and goals/objectives, and then proceed to distinguish goals from objectives. Once we get a good feel for what objectives are, then we'll discuss how objectives are set, in general.

Strategy = Goal

In the context of the process hierarchy described in the preceding section, a *strategy* can be described as a *goal* that can be attained through *tactics*. Managers always talk about implementing a program to accomplish or achieve a goal, and this goal is nothing more than the superordinate decision or action that we also call a strategy. Once a strategic decision is made and a set of tactics are conceived to carry out the strategy, progress toward achieving this strategy is considered "goal fulfillment." In other words, we translate strategy into goal only after putting into action a program designed to achieve the strategy—that is, *meet the goal*. Another way of looking at this is through the distinction of planning versus management. When managers talk about *planning,* they usually talk about strategy, strategizing, strategic planning, strategic

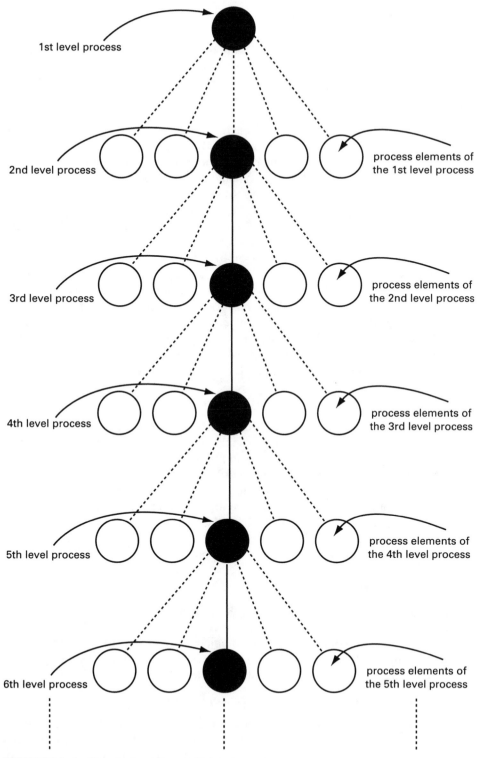

1st level process

2nd level process

process elements of
the 1st level process

3rd level process

process elements of
the 2nd level process

4th level process

process elements of
the 3rd level process

5th level process

process elements of
the 4th level process

6th level process

process elements of
the 5th level process

FIGURE 2.1 An Organizational Process Heirarchy

decision making, and the like. In this context, the focal point of the discourse is to make superordinate-level decisions, or decisions that are positioned more toward the top of the organizational hierarchy than toward the bottom. The outcome of planning is one or more strategies. People who make these superordinate-level decisions are mostly upper managers.

Once the strategic plan is put into action, then the focus becomes *management*. The emphasis is now placed on implementing the strategies through programs, or operationalizing the strategies into concrete action. Middle-level managers and supervisors tend to be concerned with operationalizing strategies. They are concerned about *achieving goals* that reflect the strategies. In other words, goals are nothing more than a middle-level management's representation of strategies to ensure that the tactics (or managerial programs) are carried out in such a way to effectively implement the strategies—that is, to achieve certain goals that reflect these strategies. For example, suppose a CEO makes a strategic decision to "Maintain position" of the firm's brand in a certain market. In other words, the focus is to fend off the competition and stop customer erosion to competitor brands. This is a corporate strategy. This strategy can be implemented through various organizational programs—marketing, R&D, engineering, manufacturing, accounting, finance, purchasing, and so forth. The marketing manager has to develop and manage product, price, place, and promotion programs in such a way to meet the "Maintain position" goal. Thus, the strategy conceived by top management becomes a goal for middle-level management.

Objective = Quantitative Formulation of a Goal

Managers usually treat objectives as quantitative operationalizations of goals. Therefore, goals are desired states that are articulated qualitatively, whereas objectives are goals' quantitative counterparts. For example, to go back to the CEO's strategy of maintaining position, which is now treated as a goal by middle-level managers, this goal can be articulated quantitatively in terms of sales and market share. More specifically, the goal of maintaining position may be quantitatively translated as "Maintain current level of market share, which is 25%." Or "Maintain current level of unit sales of 5 million units per year." These are objectives, and middle-level management is traditionally held accountable to achieve these "goals."

How Objectives Are Set

Setting objectives is an organizational task involving three key processes. These are (1) identification of an objective (or performance) dimension, (2) identification of measures to gauge outcomes related to the objective (or performance) dimension, and (3) identification of the desired level and time frame associated with the objective dimension. Let's discuss each of these tasks in some detail and provide illustrations.

Identifying an Objective (or Performance) Dimension

Here the manager tries to select an appropriate objective. The challenge here is to identify an appropriate objective that is consistent with the selected strategy and its strategic mix. Different strategies (and strategic mixes) entail different objective dimensions. For example, the objective dimension for a strategy to maintain position is sales and market share. One can quantify the goal pertaining to the maintain position strategy in terms of the sales and market share dimensions. However, a strategy such as "harvest" may entail an entirely different objective dimension, namely profit. Here the goal pertaining to the harvest strategy can be quantified in terms of maximizing profit, not sales/market share. The point here is to select the appropriate objective dimension that closely matches the selected strategy.

Identifying a Measure to Gauge Outcomes

Once one or more objective dimensions are identified (e.g., brand awareness), the manager has to identify suitable measures for each selected objective dimension. If the selected objective is "brand awareness," then what are those valid and reliable measures that are well-established in the industry that the manager can use? Not only these measures have to be identified but also the norms pertaining to the measures. For example, suppose a "brand awareness" objective is selected. The manager then should examine alternative measures of brand awareness and select a suitable measure.

Then the manager should examine the norms of that measure. Are there previous studies of comparable campaigns that used this measure with a comparable product and a comparable target market? Suppose the product is a brand of deodorant soap. The manager is planning a TV ad campaign that should last six months. Target consumers are adult women. Now suppose the manager finds several studies that deal with comparable markets, products, and ad campaigns. Now let's say that based on these studies, the average increase in brand awareness after six months of TV advertising was identified as approximately 50%. That is, previous comparable ad campaigns have generated an increase of 50% in brand awareness. Now, the manager is in a position to go to the next step and identify the desired level associated with the selected objective.

Identifying the Desired Level and the Time Frame

Knowing the norms of the measure that will be used to gauge the performance of a program (e.g., an advertising campaign), the manager is now positioned to identify the goal of that program in a very concrete and quantitative way. Should the manager set his or her objective to reflect the norm, above the norm, or below the norm? If 50% increase in brand awareness is the norm, for example, should the goal be 50%? Greater than 50%? Less than 50%? The goal now is to determine the extent of desired deviation from the norm. This can be accomplished by considering several factors such as past and anticipated performance of key competitors, anticipated changes in the market, and anticipated changes within the firm.

Note that implicit in this discussion is the notion that the time frame is also selected in a way to match comparability with previous studies. For example, if most of the previous studies conducted with comparable products and ad campaigns involve a time frame of six months (duration of the entire ad campaign), then the time frame of the planned ad campaign should also be six months.

Linking Strategy, Tactics, and Objectives

Examine Figure 2.2. The figure shows how strategies, tactics, and objectives are linked in the context of the process hierarchy. A strategy at a zero-order level of the process hierarchy (we'll call it Strategy 0) has a corresponding objective (we'll call it Objective

0). To achieve Objective 0, we have to move to the first-order level of the process hierarchy. Thus, the strategy of the first-order level in the process hierarchy (we'll call it Strategy 1) is essentially the tactic used to achieve the objective at the superordinate level. We can call this decision Strategy 1 or Tactic 0. Similarly, at the second-order level, the strategy (Strategy 2) has a corresponding objective (Objective 2). This Strategy 2 is essentially a tactic conceived to carry out the objective of the first-order level (Objective 1).

Calling a decision at any given level a "strategy" or a "tactic" is very much dependent on whether this decision is seen as the starting point of many other subordinate decisions or a decision that is subordinate to others. Thus, a decision that initiates the system (considered as a starting point) is a strategy, whereas a tactic is a decision that is subordinate in nature, as shown in Figure 2.2.

Let's use an example to illustrate the links among strategy, objective, and tactic. Let's conceive of a process hierarchy involving three process levels—corporate (zero-order level), marketing, (first-order level), and marketing communications (second-order level). At the zero-order level (i.e., corporate level), most organizations make decisions to "grow," "maintain position," "innovate," "harvest," "divest," and so on. We can view any of these decisions as a zero-order strategy. A grow strategy may be translated into a goal and quantified in terms of an objective such as "5% increase in sales." This objective is then the zero-order objective. This objective becomes the goal that guides the decision maker to formulate tactics to achieve the stated objective. Now move to the marketing level (first-order level). Let's say the decision maker decides that a differentiation strategy is best to achieve the 5% sales increase. This is Strategy 1 or Tactic 0. This strategy can be translated into a concrete goal: "Associate the brand with key product benefit X so that 60% of consumers come to recognize the brand in terms of that benefit." This is Objective 1. This objective creates the impetus for the decision maker to identify a suitable marketing communications tactic that can achieve this goal. Now we're at the marketing communications level (second-order level). Perhaps an informative (thinker) communications tactic would do the job. This

FIGURE 2.2 Linking Strategy, Tactics, and Objectives

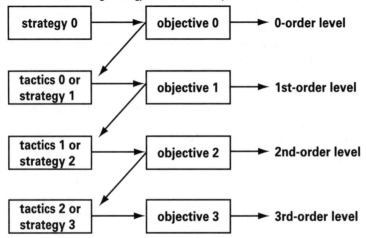

is Tactic 1 or Strategy 2. This decision can be translated in terms of specific goals, such as "We need to increase brand awareness and learning such that at least 80% of consumers become aware of the brand and its key benefit."

BUDGETING

Allocating resources to the elements of the strategic mix is, in essence, a budgeting decision. The manager must decide what resources are needed to implement the selected strategy and its respective strategic mix. For example, given the decision to advertise the product on TV, the manager determines the amount of money needed to launch a TV advertising campaign to achieve a certain level of brand awareness.

This example shows the power of a particular budgeting method called the "build-up approach" commonly used in advertising (sometimes this budgeting method is also referred to as the "objective-task method"). In the build-up method, a decision maker can effectively allocate resources by starting at the top of the decision hierarchy so that strategy → objectives → tactics → strategy → objectives → tactics →, . . . , and so on all the way down the process hierarchy. At the bottom of the hierarchy, the decision maker tabulates the costs of all those tasks at that level needed to achieve the stated objective at the superordinate level. The sum of these costs is viewed as the required budget to effectively achieve the stated objectives (all those objectives stated at the different levels of the process hierarchy).

MONITORING AND CONTROL

The control function involves the use of a *feedback mechanism.* A feedback mechanism generates a warning signal when a specific measured outcome is detected to be significantly below (or above) the stated objective. For example, a marketing communications objective may be phrased as follows: "The marketing communications objective is a 50% increase in brand awareness as measured by a brand recognition method after six months from the launch of the ad campaign." After six months, the marketing communications manager assesses the outcome using the designated method and finds out that brand awareness inched up only 10%. That is, a negative deviation of 40% from the desired level of the objective dimension was detected. Significant negative deviations "raise red flags" and motivate the manager to make adjustments. These adjustments may involve one or more of the following: (1) change strategy and tactics, (3) change objective, and/or (2) change budget.

Change Strategy and Tactics

Through negative feedback, a manager realizes that perhaps the selected strategy was not the best strategy. Or perhaps the way the strategy was implemented was faulty. Perhaps certain elements of the strategic mix (or tactical programs) were misconceived. Thus, based on feedback, the manager may develop a new strategy or a new configuration of the strategic mix for future action. This is viewed as corrective action.

Change Objective

In many instances, managers set their objectives too high, perhaps unrealistically high. If performance is assessed to be significantly below the objective, then perhaps the objective was too high to begin with and needs to be lowered in future planning and implementation. Conversely, some managers may underestimate their strengths and set their objectives too low. Feedback may indicate performance above and beyond the stated objective. In that case, those managers may realize that the objective was set too conservatively and may raise the objective in future action.

Change Budget

Corrective action can also come in the form of reallocating resources. Through negative feedback, a manager may realize that perhaps the amount of money budgeted to implement a strategy is not adequate; more money is needed. Or the converse is also possible—too much money has been allocated to implement a certain program, creating misallocations to other programs, which together may have contributed to failure in meeting the stated objective.

ANALYSIS AND PLANNING

Analysis and planning, in systems language, is referred to as *feedforward*. Feedforward is the kind of analysis that anticipates the future situation. In many instances, managers rely on studies that have successfully predicted certain phenomena to anticipate how things are likely to unfold. These studies reflect a feedforward function, looking into the future, anticipating events by relying on our understanding of what happened in the past. Managers usually conduct what has been referred to as *situation analysis* to help them anticipate how things are likely to unfold and therefore make decisions based on anticipated events and attempt to control them. Situation analysis, for example, as commonly used by marketing strategists involves market analysis, environmental analysis, competitive analysis, customer analysis, and self-analysis. Thus, when selecting a positioning strategy, a marketer needs to make that decision based on customer analysis— that is, how consumers perceive the ideal product and the various brands in terms of product attributes. This kind of analysis is used to help the marketer make a positioning decision. This analysis allows the marketer to understand how consumers perceive his/her brand in relation to competitor brands. Therefore, the marketer anticipates how consumers are likely to react to the brand if it is given certain attributes in the near future. In particular, analysis and planning assist the manager in (1) selecting effective strategies and tactics, (2) setting objectives, and (3) budgeting.

Analysis and Planning in Relation to Strategies and Tactics

Situation analysis (or feedforward) allows the manager to understand and anticipate the effects of certain actions (strategies and tactics). Specifically, the manager needs to plan a process hierarchy that is most effective and to determine which elements of a strategic mix (which tactics) are likely to be most effective in achieving the goals of a superordinate strategy. For example, a CEO studies the situation pertaining to a certain product offered by her firm in a certain market. She needs to make a strategic decision: whether to attempt to grow further in that market, to maintain position, to harvest, to improve the product through innovation, or to divest. Which strategic option is likely to be most effective in enhancing the stock value of the firm? The CEO has to rely on situation analysis to make this decision. The application of models such as the Boston Consulting Group Matrix and other portfolio models may help the CEO gather appropriate information to help her select the most effective strategy. Depending on which portfolio model is used in the situation analysis, the CEO may gather information about market growth, market share, and other characteristics pertaining both to the industry as a whole and to her particular business position. The models assist the decision maker in selecting the best strategy.

An example closer to the heart of marketing communications may be the following: Suppose the marketing communications manager is working with a habit formation (doer) strategy. That is, the manager is charged with the task of inducing consumers to try the product and experience its benefits directly. What is the best element of the marketing communications mix that can carry out this strategy? Could it be sales promotion? Advertising? Public relations? Direct marketing? Reseller support? Word-of-mouth communications? What does the marketing communications manager know about the effectiveness of each of the communications mix elements? Under what conditions are certain elements of the communications mix likely to be most effective? To answer these questions, the manager has to apply certain marketing communications models that are designed for the specific purpose of answering these questions. The manager applies the model, gathers the necessary information to operationalize the model, and voilà!—the answer.

Analysis and Planning in Relation to Setting Objectives

Situation analysis is also very important in helping managers set objectives. To set reasonable objectives, managers have to translate goals (which are reflections of strategies) into quantitative desired states. To do this effectively, the manager has to establish a conception of a desired state based on information concerning

- the *firm's strengths and weaknesses*—what the firm can realistically achieve in the future, given its strengths and weaknesses;
- the *competition*—how key competitors have acted in the past and how they are likely to act given certain market conditions;
- *market changes*—whether these changes present opportunities or threats and how the firm can react to them; and
- *changes within the firm*—whether these changes present opportunities or threats, and how the firm should react to them.

Analysis and Planning in Relation to Budgeting

Situation analysis also can be invaluable in allocating resources. Through the analysis, managers commonly gather information about

- the *firm's past expenditures*—how much the firm has traditionally spent on what program and how effective the various programs have been, given certain levels of expenditures;

- key *competitors*—how much the competition has spent on what program in the past and how much the competition is likely to spend in the future;
- the *industry* at large—how much most firms in the industry have spent on what programs and the effectiveness of different levels of expenditures;
- *changes in the market* that are likely to increase or decrease the cost of certain programs and tools; and
- *changes within the firm* that are likely to increase or decrease the cost of certain programs or tools.

SYSTEM INTEGRATION

Having gotten a feel for the different system components, the reader is now in a position to appreciate the concept of *system integration*. System integration is achieved by ensuring strong links among the system components, specifically the following: (1) link connecting strategy, objective, and tactics, (2) link between strategy/objective/tactics and budget, (3) link between monitoring and control, (4) link between monitoring/control and strategy/tactics, (5) link between monitoring/control and objectives, (6) link between monitoring/control and budget, (7) link between analysis and planning, (8) link between analysis/planning and strategy/tactics, (9) link between analysis/planning and objectives, and (10) link between analysis/planning and budget. (See Figure 2.3.)

Link Connecting Strategy, Objective, and Tactics

Systems tend to break down and become ineffective when there is no clear logic connecting a given strategy to the way this strategy becomes a goal-guiding tactic and to the tactics formulated to achieve the objective. For a system to be effectively integrated, a strategy has to be translated into a quantifiable objective, and tactics have to be developed to achieve the stated objective. Each tactic in turn becomes a strategy, which in

FIGURE 2.3 System Integration

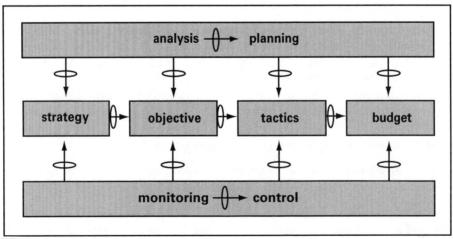

turn is transformed into a goal to guide subordinate-level tactics, and so on. This is a necessary but not sufficient principle of system integration. For example, suppose a marketing communications manager is charged with getting consumers to adopt the product on a trial basis. The manager has a history of using TV advertising and nothing but TV advertising. Consequently, he uses TV advertising to accomplish this goal. The goal of getting consumers to adopt the product on a trial basis is a goal that reflects the habit formation (doer) communications strategy. The objective of this goal is to increase consumers' product trial by a certain percentage within a given time frame. The tactics used to carry out this strategy include sales promotion and direct marketing; TV advertising may not be very effective in implementing the doer strategy. In this situation there is no link that connects strategy, objective, and tactics. No logic ties them together.

Objectives are concrete and quantitative translations of strategies. The system is jeopardized when a manager sets objectives that have little or nothing to do with the selected strategy. The supporting programs cannot be developed and effectively managed without higher-order objectives. For example, a marketing communications manager is working with a habit formation (doer) strategy, but sets an objective related to brand awareness and learning. He states that the objective is to maximize awareness and learning from the current level of 50% to a desired level of 80%. Now what does the awareness/learning objective have to do with the habit formation (doer) strategy?! This strategy can be translated only in terms of product trial or purchase, *not* awareness and learning. This is another example of lack of system integration.

Link between Strategy/Objective/Tactics and Budget

The system is said to lack integration when resources are allocated in a manner that is completely oblivious to the resource requirements of the selected tactics (those programs selected to achieve specific objectives). In many instances top management allocates resources using methods that do not take into account the resource requirements to accomplish the goals of certain strategies. Such misallocation of funds can place the system in jeopardy. For example, a marketing communications manager is working with a habit formation (doer) strategy, the goal of trying to get target consumers to adopt the firm's product on a trial basis. The corresponding objective is to increase product trial by 30% in the next six months. She knows that such an objective will require at least two mass mailing campaigns to target consumers and will cost approximately $100,000. However, top management has traditionally allocated a marketing communications budget based on 2% of the previous year's sales. Last year's sales were $4 million, and 2% of $4 million allocates $80,000. The marketing communications manager needs at least $100,000 to accomplish the goals of the communications strategy and its stated objective. There is a problem here! The resources allocated do not mesh with the required strategies and the cost of the program required to achieve the goal of the strategy.

Link between Monitoring and Control

Lack of system integration occurs when performance monitoring is not followed by control. In other words, the manager may monitor system performance but exert no control. The manager fails to observe deviations from desired states and to respond by taking corrective action. Corrective action may have been completely dissociated from monitoring. For example, suppose the marketing communications manager observes that the direct mail campaign designed to increase product trial by 30% in the next sixth months is failing. He does nothing! There is no corrective action! There is no learning from mistakes! Failure is terminal! Effective systems learn from trial and error. Effective systems take corrective action to improve future performance. If the link between monitoring and control is weak, then the system doesn't learn. The system deteriorates and eventually dies.

Link between Monitoring/Control and Strategy-Objective-Tactics Links

We've already discussed how monitoring and control is exerted to change strategy-objective-tactics links. This is part of the monitoring and control function. If the system fails to meet certain performance objectives, corrective action can be instituted by changing the strategy, its objective, and the corresponding tactics (supporting programs). The system is said to lack integration if the monitoring and control function, given negative feedback, fails to reassess the strategy-objective-tactics link.

Link between Monitoring/Control and Objectives

When a program fails, the manager must reassess the level of the objective. The manager asks whether the objective was set unrealistically high and whether it should be adjusted to reflect the system's true capabilities. The system lacks integration if the manager fails to reassess the objectives in light of poor performance outcomes.

Link between Monitoring/Control and Budget

As previously stated, the monitoring and control function serves to motivate the manager to reassess the appropriateness of the resources allocated. If the program fails, the manager asks whether failure may be attributed to lack of resources or to misallocation of resources. If corrections are needed, the manager should change resource allocations. Failure to reassess the method and outcome of resource allocation is a signal of system breakdown or lack of system integration.

Link between Analysis and Planning

Many managers engage in research; they set up elaborate intelligence apparatus; they hire consultants and gather enormous amounts of data. And they feel good about all of this. Unfortunately, in the real world of management, much of this information is typically not used in planning. Most business strategy books and guides show managers how to conduct a *thorough* situation analysis. They assert that managers should gather information about competitors and the market. They promote studies of consumer behavior in order to establish demographic and psychographic profiles of consumers. They urge managers to segment the market into groups and profile the various groups. They show how past sales can be analyzed and how regression equations can be developed to predict sales. Do all these tasks result in sophisticated information gathering? Yes! The failure lies in the way much of this information is—or is not—used. Most books provide very little guidance on using the information to plan strategies. A breakdown between analysis and planning is a strong sign of lack of system integration.

Link between Analysis/Planning and Strategy-Objective-Tactics Links

Previously we talked about how managers can use analysis and planning to help them plot strategy, articulate objectives from strategy, and formulate tactics guided by objectives. Proper analysis and planning are imperative. Strategy selection that is not guided by a thorough analysis of the situation can lead to a disaster. If the wrong strategy is selected, the wrong objectives are articulated, and the wrong tactics are deduced. The literature of marketing strategy and management as well as marketing communications is rich with models that allow managers to determine what strategies are effective under what conditions. Failure to use these analytic models may lead the manager to make misguided decisions, leading to system disintegration.

Link between Analysis/Planning and Objectives

Objective setting that is not guided by situation analysis may lead managers to set unrealistic and unreasonable objectives. Again, this is symptomatic of lack of system integration.

Link between Analysis/Planning and Budget

Similarly, lack of system integration occurs when resources are allocated ineffectively with very little guidance from a thorough and suitable analysis of the situation.

Summary

In this chapter the reader was exposed to rudimentary systems concepts, such as strategy and tactics, objective setting, budget, monitoring and control, and analysis and planning. Strategy and tactics are described as decisions in a decision tree, or a process hierarchy. Objectives are described as quantitative statements of a desired state represented as a strategy. Objectives serve as goals for lower-level decisions—that is, tactics. Objectives are set guided by three processes: (1) identification of an objective dimension, (2) identification of measures to gauge outcomes related to the objective dimension, and (3) identification of the desired level and time frame associated with the objective dimension. Budgeting is described as an allocation process guided by a build-up method; that is, the manager allocates resources by starting at the top of the decision hierarchy such that strategy → objectives → tactics → . . . all the way down the process hierarchy. At the bottom of the hierarchy, the manager tabulates the costs of all those tasks at the level needed to achieve the stated objectives. Monitoring and control are described as a feedback mechanism in which a warning signal is generated when a specific measured outcome is detected to be significantly below (or above) the stated objective. Significant deviations motivate the manager to make adjustments. These adjustments may involve (1) change of strategy, (2) change of objective, and/or (3) change of budget. Analysis and planning are described as a feedforward mechanism in which information is gathered and analyzed to predict future performance. Based on these predictions, the manager is in a better position to plan strategy and tactics, set objectives, and budget resources. System integration is described in terms of breakdown of links connecting (1) strategy, objective, and tactics, (2) strategy/objective/tactics and budget, (3) monitoring and control, (4) monitoring/control and strategy/tactics, (5) monitoring/control and objectives, (6) monitoring/control and budget, (7) analysis and planning, (8) analysis/planning and strategy/objective/tactics, (9) analysis/planning and objectives, and (10) analysis/planning and budget.

Questions for Discussion

Let's see if we can apply some of these systems concepts to your own personal experiences. Focus on a particular project, whatever the project is, that you have been very much involved with in the last few months, and answer the following questions.

1. Develop a process hierarchy in relation to the project. Figure out what are the major goals of the project; then figure out the major tasks or programs used to achieve the goal. Within each program, try to figure out the various subtasks. Lay this out in a tree form. That is, construct a decision tree.
2. Now focus on one major program or task. Try to figure out the goal of that program. Now try to quantify that goal and make it as concrete as you can. This will be the objective of the program.
3. Again focusing on that program, try to figure out the kind and amount of resources allocated to that program. Were these resources allocated effectively? Why or why not?
4. Again focus on the same program. How would you go about monitoring the performance of that program? What performance measures would you use? What would you do if the performance outcomes point to failure? That is, how would you go about controlling the program in an attempt to improve future performance?
5. Now let's focus on analysis and planning. What analysis would you need to conduct to help you make better decisions in terms of selecting the most appropriate subtasks, setting objectives, and allocating resources?
6. How can you enhance program integration? Is the program effective overall? Comment.

Suggested Reading

Baumier, J. (1971), "Defined Criteria of Performance in Organizational Control." *Administrative Science Quarterly* (September 1971): p. 340.

Cavaleri, Steven, and Krzysztof Obloj. *Management Systems: A Global Perspective.* Belmont, Calif.: Wadsworth, 1993.

Churchman, C. W. *The Systems Approach.* New York: Dell, 1968.

Flamholtz, E. "Organizational Control Systems as a Managerial Tool." *California Management Review* 22, no. 2 (1979): pp. 50–59.

Katz, D. and R. Kahn. *The Social Psychology of Organizations.* New York: John Wiley, 1966.

Lerner, A. Y. *Fundamentals of Cybernetics.* London: Chapman and Hall, 1972.

Miller, James G. *Living Systems.* New York: McGraw-Hill, 1978.

Morell, R. W. *Management: Ends and Means.* San Francisco: Chandler, 1969.

Powers, W. T. *Behavior: The Control of Perception.* Chicago: Aldine, 1973.

Powers, W. T. "Control Theory: A Model of Organisms." *Systems Dynamics Review*, 6, no. 1 (1990): pp. 1–20.

Rahmation, S. "The Hierarchy of Objectives: Toward an Integrating Construct in Systems Science." *Systems Research*, 2, no. 3 (1985): pp. 237–245.

Richardson, G. *Feedback Thought in Social Science and Systems Theory.* Philadelphia: University of Pennsylvania Press, 1991.

Robb, F. F. "Cybernetics in Management Thinking." *Systems Research,* 1 no. 1 (1985): pp. 5–23.

Simon, Herbert A. *Administrative Behavior.* New York: The Free Press, 1965.

Sirgy, M. Joseph "Toward a Theory of Social Organization: A Systems Approach." *Behavioral Science*, 34, no. 4 (1989): pp. 272–85.

Sirgy, M. Joseph "Toward a Theory of Social Relations: The Regression Analog." *Behavioral Science*, 35, no. 4 (1990): pp. 195–206.

Sirgy, M. Joseph "Self-Cybernetics: Toward an Integrated Model of Self-Concept Processes." *Systems Research*, 7, no. 1 (1990): pp. 19–32.

CHAPTER 3

A Systems Model for Integrated Marketing Communications

Marketers of a variety of products, from shaving cream and razors to magazines and credit cards, are all going after the college market. Kellogg's, for example, has distributed free samples of Pop-Tarts to incoming students at the beginning of the school year. Calvin Klein has sponsored movie previews, making sure there are samples of cK scent for everyone. Marketers pay much to advertise in college newspapers. They advertise their ware on television series such as *Melrose Place.* They pitch their products in cyberspace. Magazines such as Link, U, and MarketSource target the college market, and many advertisers place their ads in them hoping to appeal to college students.

Marketers have developed programs tied to on-campus movies that appeal to students. They would place several ads timed to run before movies were shown. Corporate sponsors of these ads would then promote the movies in campus newspapers and hand out literature and samples at the campus theater. However, many marketers got burned in the college student market because of lack of integration of their marketing efforts. There were all kinds of other problems. For example, different promotional materials carried different slogans and often contradictory messages. Some messages appeared to emphasize certain product benefits; other messages emphasized other benefits. Some promotional materials included trademarks and logo; others didn't. No attempt had been made to set concrete objectives and measure performance. Tactical problems were rampant. For example, free samples distributed in the dorms were snapped-up by visiting high school students. Posters promoting specific events were not put up. Ads were run in the campus paper after the target event had already taken place. Samples distributed at bookstores were not effective because store employees were too busy to enforce the company's policy requiring students taking samples to sign a log sheet and show a school ID. Promotional materials that were supposed to go into mailboxes were not distributed. The people delivering them would drop a big pile of the materials next to the mailboxes, come back a couple of days later, and throw away whatever was not picked up.[1]

Problems such as these, which are very common in promoting all kinds of products in all kinds of markets, are directly related to lack of marketing integration. The elements of any marketing communications program have to be managed in such a way as to achieve corporate and marketing objectives. The management process requires that the elements selected can achieve the marketing objectives (which in turn should be instrumental in achieving corporate objectives). Each element of the marketing communications mix has to be driven by specific and explicit objectives that have to be monitored over time to ensure continuous progress. The objectives pertaining to each element of the marketing communications mix have to be consistent with the strategies and tactics associated with that element.

Implementing these strategies and tactics requires resources, and these resources have to be effectively budgeted. A process of control has to be in place to identify problem areas and implement immediate corrective action. These are all issues of integration, the subject of this book. This chapter introduces the student to a systems model of integrated marketing communications. The systems model shows how the entire process of marketing communications can be planned to ensure integration. All marketing communications processes are structured hierarchically: at the top, processes related to the corporate level; next, the marketing department level; then, the marketing communications level; and finally, each element of the marketing communications mix. In addition, specific objectives and subordinate processes can be identified as a direct function of a given process at any hierarchical level. The model shows that systems integration can be effectively achieved by analyzing and planning, allocating adequate resources for the implementation of the process elements within a given hierarchical level, monitoring performance against the stated objectives, and exerting continuous control.

A SYSTEMS MODEL

The systems model forms the theoretical framework that organizes the topics in this book and shows how these topics are wholly integrated. The model posits that all organizational processes are structured hierarchically. Each specific objective and subordinate process is identified as a direct function of a given process at any hierarchical level. Thus, marketing communications planning can be described in terms of a process hierarchy involving at least three levels: corporate, marketing, marketing communications, and within each element of the marketing communications mix (advertising, public relations, direct marketing, sales promotions, reseller support, and word-of-mouth communications). Within each level of this process hierarchy, the marketing communications manager selects a strategy from a pool of optional strategies. The selected strategy at a given hierarchical level guides the manager to articulate quantitative objectives consistent with that strategy. Similarly, the marketing communications manager selects a strategic mix (subordinate processes) that is designed to meet the goal objectives of the selected strategy. Integration can be achieved by building and reinforcing links among the system's components within each level of the process hierarchy (see Figure 3.1).

STRATEGY → OBJECTIVE → TACTICS

A systems model is developed here for the specific purpose of integrating the various elements of the marketing communications mix. Organizational process is viewed as a hierarchy of processes. At any given level of the process hierarchy, there is a mix of

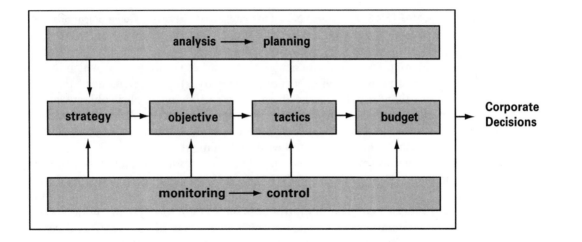

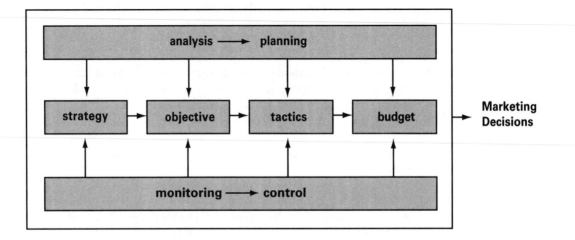

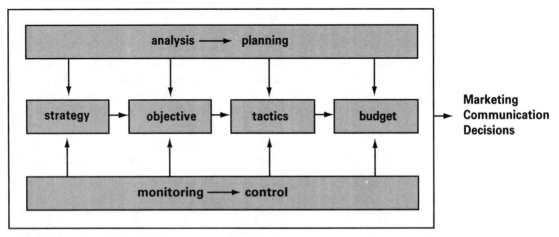

FIGURE 3.1 The Marketing Communications System at Large

process elements. Focusing on a given element of the process mix allows the identification of the subordinate elements.

More specifically, a process at a superordinate level is usually referred to as a "strategy." Subordinate processes used to implement the superordinate process are referred to as "tactics" or "strategic mix." Once we focus on a process, it becomes a strategy, and the elements employed to implement that process are tactics (elements of the strategic mix). But then a tactic becomes a strategy by moving down the hierarchy and focusing on that tactic. Therefore, the distinction between a strategy and a tactic can best be appreciated from the vantage point of the decision maker in an overall hierarchy of processes. Furthermore, to implement a strategy, the strategy becomes a goal, which is achieved through objectives. Thus, objectives are nothing more than quantitative goals that reflect a strategy. Objectives guide the formulation and the implementation of tactics.

Also, in this systems model, the selection of one or more elements elements of a strategic mix is directly influenced by the selection of the corresponding strategy. Correspondingly, the selection of a specific strategy is influenced by the selection of the strategic mix. That is, the process hierarchy is designed using both top-down and bottom-up approaches. It does not matter which comes first, a given strategy or strategic mix. Planning entails the selection of hierarchical processes that create means-end chains; subordinate processes (means) are selected in such a way to achieve the goals of a superordinate process (end) at any level of the process hierarchy, and vice versa.

Applying the process hierarchy to marketing communications, the marketing communications manager must, first and foremost, identify all superordinate processes of marketing communications. There are two types of superordinate processes in marketing communications. These are processes related to the corporate level and, next in line, processes related to the marketing level (again, see Figure 3.1). Thus, at the corporate level, a given corporate strategy is implemented through a corporate mix (process elements at that level). The elements of the corporate mix may be viewed as organizational functions related to research and development (R&D), engineering, manufacturing, finance, accounting, personnel, and marketing. More specifically, managers typically choose from among these traditional corporate strategies: grow, maintain position, harvest, innovate, and divest. These corporate-level strategies are popular and commonly used. The corporate mix here is viewed as involving the traditional functional units of an organization: R&D, engineering, manufacturing, marketing, accounting, finance, employee relations, insurance, and legal. Thus, a corporate strategy tends to configure the corporate mix in such a way that certain elements of the corporate mix are emphasized. For example, a growth strategy dictates that emphasis be placed on marketing because marketing most effectively communicates the product's benefits to new consumers in new markets.[2] In contrast, an innovation strategy places more emphasis on the working dynamics of R&D and engineering. A divestment strategy places the emphasis on the finance element of the corporate mix, and so on.

The implementation of any corporate strategy necessitates the articulation of specific objectives. These objectives guide the formulation of the selected corporate strategy. For example, a growth strategy is usually articulated in terms of increases in sales and market share, which are stated as corporate objectives. A maintain-position strategy is typically articulated in terms of maintenance of sales and market share. A harvest strategy, on the other hand, is typically expressed as maximization of profit.

An innovation strategy aims for a certain level of sales. And finally, a divestment strategy typically calls for increases in cash flow.

The model acknowledges three typical marketing strategies. These are differentiation, cost leadership, and focus. Each of these strategies is described in terms of several positioning methods. For example, differentiation can be accomplished through positioning by product attribute, intangible factor, relative price, brand-distributor tie-in, distributor location, distributor serviceability, celebrity or spokesperson, lifestyle or personality, product class, competitors, and country of origin. The cost-leadership strategy usually involves positioning by low price. The focus strategy usually involves targeting specific segments identified by using segmentation techniques. The focus strategy involves at least three positioning techniques: positioning by customer benefit (benefit segmentation), positioning by user or customer, and positioning by use or application.

Any of these marketing strategies (related to a specific strategic business unit or SBU) is in turn implemented through the marketing mix (product, price, distribution, and marketing communications). Also, just as each corporate strategy entails a different configuration of the corporate mix, each marketing strategy entails a different configuration of the marketing mix. For example, positioning by product attribute is a marketing strategy that is effectively carried out through a host of product and marketing communications decisions, while positioning by relative price places more emphasis on the price element of the marketing mix than on other elements.

To carry out any marketing strategy through implementation of the marketing mix, the marketing communications manager has to identify the objectives that reflect the marketing strategy. For example, if a differentiation strategy is selected and operationalized in terms of positioning by product attribute, then the objective is to establish a brand association with an important product attribute. Thus, marketing objectives are a direct function of the marketing strategy and its operationalization in terms of positioning.

With respect to marketing communications strategies and tactics, the model posits that the marketing communications manager usually has at least four strategic options. As previously described, these are traditionally expressed as informative (thinker), affective (feeler), habit formation (doer), and self-satisfaction (reactor). These strategies are well known in advertising but can be easily applied to all forms of marketing communications. The informative (thinker) strategy is typically applied to marketing products that are highly involving[3] and are of the thinking[4] type. For thinking high-involving type products, messages about the product are usually processed semantically, cognitively, or "rationally" (left-brain processed). Thus, marketing communications programs for this strategy focus on brand awareness and learning; that is, its objective is to reach as many consumers as possible to create brand awareness and brand associations or knowledge. The affective (feeler) strategy commonly applies to high-involvement products of the "feeling" type. This strategy is typically expressed in terms of desired increases in brand attitude, liking, or preference. The habit formation (doer) strategy applies to low-involvement products that are of the "thinking" type. The objectives are usually stated in terms of brand trial/purchase and brand learning. Finally, the self-satisfaction (reactor) strategy typically applies to low-involvement products that are of the "feeling" type. The objectives are articulated in terms of brand trial/purchase and attitude.

The implementation of any marketing communications strategy is done through the marketing communications mix—advertising, sales promotion, reseller support, direct marketing, public relations, and word-of-mouth communications. Also, just as corporate and marketing strategies dictate the configurations of the corporate and marketing mix respectively, marketing communications strategy guides the marketing manager to work with certain elements of the communications mix and not others. For example, the informative (thinker) strategy can be effectively implemented through print advertising, certain forms of public relations (such as the press release), certain forms of reseller support programs (such as trade shows), and word-of-mouth communications (such as the use of referrals). A self-satisfaction (reactor) strategy can be effectively implemented through outdoor advertising, sales promotion (such as the use of premiums and contests and sweepstakes), and direct marketing (such as selling parties and teleshopping).

BUDGETING

Allocating resources to the elements of the strategic mix is, in essence, a budgeting decision. The manager must decide what resources are needed to implement the selected strategy and its respective strategic mix. For example, given the decision to advertise the product through TV, the marketing communications manager determines the amount of money needed to launch a TV advertising campaign to achieve the goal of the marketing communications strategy—for example, a certain level of brand awareness. This method is referred to as the "build-up approach" commonly used in advertising (sometimes also referred to as the "objective-task method"). The build-up method can be used effectively to find out the costs of the marketing communications programs needed to achieve the marketing communications objectives. Then, the manager sums up the total costs related to the implementation of these subordinate tasks to derive the required budget. Of course, this method of allocating marketing communications resources is predicated upon the assumption that each task or tactic is effectively designed to meet higher-order objectives.

SETTING OBJECTIVES

Setting objectives is an organizational task involving three key processes: (1) identification of one or more objective dimensions, (2) identification of the measures used to gauge outcomes related to each objective, and (3) identification of the desired level and time frame associated with each objective dimension. Since this is an introduction to the model, we will discuss how marketing communications managers go about identifying objective dimensions that reflect the selected strategies. The other remaining processes will be discussed in some detail in chapter 6 in the section on objectives and measures.

The marketing communications manager tries to select appropriate objectives related to each strategy at the three hierarchical levels (corporate, marketing, and marketing communications). The selection of the objective dimensions have to reflect the essence of the selected strategies. You will recall that these are *corporate* strategies:

grow, maintain position, harvest, innovate, and divest. The growth strategy usually entails the use of sales and market share objectives. That is, the marketing communications manager may translate the corporate vision of growth in a certain market into a marked increase in sales and market share in the specified market. Similarly, the corporate vision of maintaining position may translate into maintenance of current levels of sales and market share. In contrast, a harvest strategy may entail different objective dimensions altogether. The appropriate objective dimension for a harvest strategy is to increase or maximize profit but not necessarily through increases in sales and market share. Usually, a harvest strategy signals the manager to be cost efficient and to generate profit through cost reductions. The objective dimension for an innovation strategy is only sales. Newly launched products may not have competitors; therefore, market share is not an appropriate objective. Profit is also not an objective, since new products are expected to be in the red for some time. Finally, the divestment strategy entails a cash flow objective. Most firms divest SBUs that are continuously losing sales, market share, and profit. The goal in divestment is to increase cash flow.

At the *marketing level*, objectives are selected in direct correspondence with the selected positioning strategy. All objectives at this level relate to brand equity (i.e., brand associations). For example, positioning by product attribute entails creating or reinforcing a brand association with an important product attribute (usually an attribute that consumers consider when making decisions). As another example, positioning by customer benefit entails creating or reinforcing a brand association with an important customer benefit (usually a benefit that is an important criterion in consumer purchase decision).

At the *marketing communications level*, objectives are selected as a direct function of marketing communications strategies—informative (thinker), affective (feeler), habit formation (doer), and self-satisfaction (reactor). Based on these strategies, marketing communications objectives are typically articulated in terms of brand awareness, learning, attitude (or liking), trial (or purchase), and repeat purchase over an extended time frame. The informative (thinker) strategy entails a LEARN → FEEL → DO sequence. That is, brand awareness and learning objectives are considered the most important in the initial phase of the campaign. Brand attitude is considered the most important objective in the second phase of the campaign, while brand trial/purchase is considered the most important in the last phase of the campaign. The affective (feeler) strategy entails a FEEL → LEARN → DO sequence. That is, the initial phase of the marketing communications campaign should emphasize establishing brand liking. The second phase should emphasize positive brand associations, while the last phase of the campaign should emphasize brand trial and purchase. The habit formation (doer) strategy reflects a DO → LEARN → FEEL sequence. That is, the initial phase of the campaign should attempt to induce target consumers to buy the product on a trial basis. The second phase of the campaign tries to educate consumers about the product benefits (brand associations), while the third phase of the campaign concentrates on establishing good feelings about the product (brand liking). Finally, the self-satisfaction (reactor) strategy entails a DO → FEEL → LEARN sequence. That is, the initial phase of the campaign should emphasize brand trial and purchase. The second phase of the campaign focuses on establishing good feelings toward the brand, while the third phase concentrates on learning about the brand.

For example, a communications campaign of a national pizza restaurant called Roni has pizza places on college campuses throughout the United States. The marketing communications manager targets freshman students by directing messages to the freshman students at the beginning of every school year, changing the nature of the message in the middle part of the school year, and changing it again during the last part of the school year. The idea is to guide freshman students through a sequence of actions and reactions, such as LEARN → FEEL → DO, FEEL → LEARN → DO, DO → LEARN → FEEL, or DO → FEEL → LEARN. Doing so will ensure that these students will be able to learn about the product benefits, establish good feelings for it, and try it at least once. A freshman student who has learned about the pizza, established good feelings about the pizza, and tried it at least once is likely to buy it repeatedly during the next three years in college. The next questions are, "What marketing communications strategy is most appropriate for Roni's Pizza? and how does the marketing communications manager set objectives varying in time?" Table 3.1 shows examples of marketing communications objectives that reflect the four different strategies.

Note in the table how the desired level of each communication objective changes as a direct function of the marketing communications strategy. If the man-

TABLE 3.1	Marketing Communications Objectives as a Direct Function of Marketing Communications Strategy		
Strategy	*Brand Learning (LEARN)*	*Brand Liking (FEEL)*	*Brand Purchase (DO)*
Informative (thinker) strategy (LEARN→FEEL→DO)			
First three months	80%	20%	10%
Second three months	90%	50%	20%
Third three months	95%	60%	50%
Affective (feeler) strategy (FEEL→LEARN→DO)			
First three months	20%	80%	10%
Second three months	50%	90%	20%
Third three months	60%	95%	50%
Habit formation (doer) strategy (DO→LEARN→FEEL)			
First three months	20%	10%	80%
Second three months	50%	20%	90%
Third three months	60%	50%	95%
Self-satisfaction (reactor) strategy (DO→FEEL→LEARN)			
First three months	10%	20%	80%
Second three months	20%	50%	90%
Third three months	50%	60%	95%

Note: The first three, second three, and third three months add up to a nine-month marketing communications campaign. The percentages in the table refer to quantitative goals. For example, if the marketing communications manager has decided to use an informative (thinker) strategy, then the first three months of the campaign should strive to establish awareness and learning in the minds of 80% of the target market, establish positive feelings toward the brand in 20% of the target market, and persuade 10% of the target market to purchase the brand on a trial basis.

ager chooses an informative (thinker) strategy, this leads the manager to use educational messages to initiate the campaign. Thus, during the first three months of the academic year, Roni's marketing communications manager may expect 80% of the freshman students to learn about the benefits of Roni's Pizza, 20% to form a positive attitude toward Roni's Pizza, and 10% to try it. Note that the 80% brand learning objective reflects the importance placed on that goal compared to brand liking and brand purchase. In the next three months, about 10% *more* of the freshman students are expected to be educated about Roni's Pizza (to a total of 90%). But note that the emphasis is now placed on the second component of the hierarchy of effects—the FEEL component. Here the goal is established at 50%. The underlying assumption is that consumers are now ready to establish an attitude toward Roni's Pizza, after being educated about its benefits during the first three months of the academic year. Thus, the nature of the message changes in tone, from cognitive to affective. This shift underscores the notion that brand attitude develops after brand learning (LEARN → FEEL). The third three months of the campaign focuses on brand purchase. Here the goal is established at 50%; that is, 50% of the freshman students should have tried Roni's Pizza at least once. Again, this reflects the notion that consumers are likely to purchase the product after feeling good about it (FEEL → DO). Now note how objectives pertaining to brand learning, liking, and purchase dramatically change with other marketing communications strategies—the affective (feeler) strategy, the habit formation (doer) strategy, and the self-satisfaction (reactor) strategy. Therefore, the point to remember is: *Select the appropriate objectives that closely match the selected strategy and its strategic mix.*

MONITORING AND CONTROL

The control function involves the use of a feedback mechanism. A feedback mechanism generates a warning signal when a specific measured outcome is significantly below the stated objective. Negative feedback can occur at the corporate level, marketing level, and/or marketing communications level. Negative deviations observed at any hierarchical level necessitate corrective action. Corrective action may take the form of changing the strategy and/or tactics, changing the budget, and/or changing the stated objectives.

For example, a communications objective may be a 70% increase in brand awareness as measured by a brand recognition method six months from the launch of the campaign. After six months, the marketing communications manager assesses the outcome using the designated method and finds out that brand awareness inched up only 30%. That is, a negative deviation of 40% from the goal was detected. Significant negative deviations "raise red flags" and motivate the manager to make adjustments. These adjustments may involve one or more of the following: (1) change the strategy and corresponding tactics, (2) change the budget, and/or (3) change the objective.

Change the Budget

For example, through negative feedback, the marketing communications manager may realize that the amount of money budgeted to implement the strategic mix of the informative (thinker) strategy is not adequate; more money is needed.

Change the Strategy and Corresponding Tactics

For example, through negative feedback, the marketing communications manager realizes that perhaps the informative (thinker) strategy is not the best strategy; perhaps an affective (feeler) strategy would be more effective. Thus, based on feedback, the marketing communications manager develops a new communications campaign that is consistent with an affective (feeler) strategy.

Change the Objective

For example, expecting a 50% increase in brand awareness may not be realistic, perhaps because the marketing communications manager has failed to take into account certain conditions that are detrimental to the communications campaign. Thus, the marketing communications manager may lower the desired level to 40% in planning the next campaign.

Failure to meet objectives at either the marketing or the corporate level also requires the marketing communications manager to take similar corrective action—that is, change marketing or corporate strategy and/or tactics, change resource allocation at either the marketing or corporate level, and/or change the stated objectives to align them with actual performance.

ANALYSIS AND PLANNING

The marketing communications manager gathers much information, analyzes this information, and makes decisions at the corporate, marketing, and marketing communications level. These decisions involve strategy selection, setting objectives, and allocating resources. Analysis and planning facilitates decision making by providing the marketing manager with relevant information.

Analysis and Planning in Strategy Selection

Remember that the marketing communications manager may be directly or indirectly involved with selecting (or changing) strategies at the corporate, marketing, and marketing communications levels. Also, remember that all strategies and tactics are formulated in relation to a specific strategic business unit (SBU). At the corporate level, optional strategies are to grow, maintain position, harvest, innovate, and divest. At the marketing level, optional strategies include differentiation, cost leadership, and focus. At the marketing communications level, optional strategies are informative (thinker), affective (feeler), habit formation (doer), and self-satisfaction (reactor). How does the marketing communications manager select the best strategy at each level? By doing *situation analysis*.

At the corporate level, situation analysis is conducted through the use of a strategy selection model such as the Boston Consulting Group (BCG) Matrix and the Multifactor Portfolio Matrix. These models direct the manager to gather specific information such as market share and market growth to assess the strengths and weaknesses of the SBU in question. For example, knowing that the SBU has a low market share but is in a high-growth market may lead the manager to select a growth strategy. This selection of corporate strategy is a direct logical deduction of the BCG Matrix.

At the marketing level, the selection of a positioning strategy is facilitated by situation analysis. Here the manager gathers information about a host of factors—customer demographics and psychographics, consumers' perception of the brand in relation to competitor brands, consumers' perception of the ideal product, and consumers' decision-making criteria, among others. There are many positioning models such as perceptual maps, means-end chain, conjoint analysis, multiattribute attitude models, and so on. All these models are designed to help marketing communications managers select an optimal positioning for the brand in question.

At the marketing communications level, the manager has to select one or more strategies from the following optional strategies: informative (thinker), affective (feeler), habit formation (doer), and self-satisfaction (reactor). In doing so, the manager gathers information about many factors that can facilitate strategy selection. Two factors commonly used in situation analysis are product involvement and product type (thinking versus feeling). For instance, if consumers are likely to be highly involved with a thinking-type product, they may be highly motivated to seek information and learn about the product and alternative brands. Thus, an informative (thinker) strategy may be best.

Analysis and Planning in Setting Objectives

The marketing communications manager has to be involved directly or indirectly in the setting of corporate, marketing, and marketing communications objectives. Situation analysis is used to assist in this endeavor. At the corporate level, the objectives are usually stated in terms of sales, market share, profit, and cash flow. Each strategy has its own objective dimensions. Specifically, the goal of the growth strategy is usually articulated in terms of sales and market share: maintain position in terms of sales and market share, harvest to increase profits, innovate to stimulate sales, and divest to raise cash flow. The desired level of the selected objective dimension is determined by information obtained through situation analysis. The manager relies heavily on information regarding the firm's strengths and weaknesses and the competition to set a desired level of the selected objective. For example, the manager decides to increase sales by 50% within the next year because the product is undergoing a radical improvement (innovation strategy) and the competition is not expected to develop a comparable improvement.

At the marketing level, the manager may rely heavily on information regarding the norm of the brand association measure. Different methods used to measure brand association may have different norms. In addition to the norms of the measure, the manager may conduct a consumer survey to measure the level of brand association that has been achieved so far and to determine what can be achieved in light of the strengths and weaknesses of the firm's communications campaign and the competition. The final objective may be stated as, "Increase brand association with . . . by . . . % in the next . . . months."

At the marketing communications level, the manager also may rely heavily on the norm of the measure pertaining to the selected objective dimension (brand awareness, brand association, brand preference, brand trial or purchase, and repeat purchase). Again through a consumer survey, the manager may find out what the current level is in relation to the selected objective dimension (e.g., current level of brand awareness is 30%). Knowing something about the competition, the firm's skills and capabilities, and anticipated changes in the marketplace and within the firm, the manager may be in a position to set the desired level of the selected objective (e.g., "Increase brand awareness by . . . % in the next . . . months.").

Analysis and Planning in Budgeting

The marketing communications manager is likely to be directly or indirectly involved in determining the marketing communications budget. In setting the budget using the build-up method (objective-and-task method), the manager gathers much information about the cost of the various marketing communications tasks. As a matter of fact, every marketing communications manager has to have an information database about the costs of using every possible marketing communications tool, especially ones that are more frequently used than others, and the manager must update this information periodically. This is imperative if the manager uses the build-up method to determine the budget needed to accomplish various objectives.

We recommend the use of the build-up method in determining a preliminary marketing communications budget. The final marketing communications budget is adjusted as a direct function of analysis and planning. That is, the manager takes into account factors such as the firm's past expenditures on marketing communication, past and anticipated expenditures by key competitors, average marketing communications expenditures by the industry at large, current and forecasted changes in the marketplace, and anticipated changes within the firm. Information about these factors should help the marketing communications manager adjust the budget. Thus, a final budget is developed.

MARKETING COMMUNICATIONS INTEGRATION

Integrated marketing communications can be achieved by ensuring strong links among the various decision processes made at the corporate, marketing, and marketing communications levels. Lack of integration may occur at any one or combination of the following system links.

- Link connecting strategy, objective, and tactics
- Link between strategy/objective/tactics and budget
- Link between monitoring and control
- Link between monitoring/control and strategy/objective/tactics
- Link between monitoring/control and objectives
- Link between monitoring/control and budget
- Link between analysis and planning
- Link between analysis/planning and strategy/objective/tactics
- Link between analysis/planning and objectives
- Link between analysis/planning and budget

Let's examine one of these system links and see how the problem of integration can be understood in terms of one of these links. Let's focus on the first link connecting strategy, objective, and tactics. Suppose the corporate strategy is determined to be "Maintain position." This may be due to the realization that competition is becoming fierce, and the best the firm can do is to defend the current market position. However, the corporate objective is stated as "Increase market share by 5% in the next quarter." Now this corporate objective is certainly not consistent with the corporate strategy of "Maintain position"; that is, there is no link between corporate strategy and corporate objective. To exacerbate the situation, suppose the CEO has instructed all departments to implement a drastic cost cutting measure of 10%. Cost cutting, however, is a corporate tactic that is supposed to be guided by a "harvest" strategy, *not* a "Maintain position" strategy. This is because a "harvest" strategy is most effective when the product is in the declining stages of its life cycle and the firm cannot make further improvements to the product to offset the competition. In this situation, cost cutting becomes important to maximize profitability before the product is "pronounced dead." Again, lack of consistency between strategy and tactics means *system breakdown,* or specifically, a breakdown of an important link in the system.

Summary

In this chapter, the reader has been introduced to a systems model of marketing communications. An effective system, by definition, is an integrated system. System integration can be achieved through ensuring that (1) the processes are integrated hierarchically, (2) the objectives of each process are consistent with the selected process elements, (3) resources are allocated in a manner consistent with the selected processes and their corresponding objectives, (4) performance is monitored against the objectives, and (5) control is continuously exerted throughout the process hierarchy. We described in a cursory fashion how the model works and how strategies and tactics are formulated at the corporate, marketing, and marketing communications levels. We discussed how objectives are set in direct relation to corporate, marketing, and marketing communications strategies. We talked about determining how to allocate resources to achieve an effective marketing communications budget and hinted at the use of an effective method—the build-up method. We briefly addressed monitoring and control and explained how this is done at the three different levels. Finally, we touched on the kind of analysis and planning that marketing communications managers perform to select strategies, set objectives, and allocate resources at the three different levels.

Questions for Discussion

Assume you are a marketer for a large print shop in a metropolitan area, and you realize that you need to launch an aggressive marketing communications campaign. You have recently bought new digital printing equipment. Digital printing is different from offset printing in that it can print directly from a computer disk and print copies only as needed. Offset printing has the advantage of economies of scale; that is, the more copies one prints, the less cost per unit. In contrast, digital printing has the advantage of economies of scope; that is, for less cost, the consumer can print a few copies, make changes, and print more copies based on the altered version. Offset printing costs too much to print only a few copies, and it has little or no flexibility to customize orders.

1. What do you think is an effective marketing communications strategy for this print shop? Would you choose to work with an informative (thinker) strategy? Affective (feeler) strategy? Habit formation (doer) strategy? Or self-satisfaction (reactor) strategy? Why?
2. What do you think is an effective marketing strategy for this print shop? Select a marketing strategy and justify your selection.
3. What do you think is an effective corporate strategy for this print shop? Would you select a growth strategy? Maintain position strategy? Harvest strategy? Innovation strategy? Or divestment strategy? Why?
4. Tie the selected marketing communications strategy with the superordinate strategies at the marketing and corporate levels. Do the strategies fit together? If they do not fit, revise the strategies and make them fit.
5. Now set corporate, marketing, and marketing communications objectives that are directly deduced from the strategies.
6. What kind of monitoring would you recommend for the print shop? What kind of corrective action would you recommend to exert control and improve marketing communications performance?
7. Now think about analysis and planning. What information do you think you need in order to develop an effective strategy at the corporate level? At the marketing level? At the marketing communications level?
8. What information do you think you need in order to set effective objectives at the corporate level? At the marketing level? At the marketing communications level?
9. How would you go about determining a marketing communications budget for the print shop? What information do you think you need in order to determine an optimal budget?

Notes

1. Cyndee Miller, "College Campaigns Get Low Scores," *Marketing News* (May 8, 1995), pp. 1–2.
2. It should be noted that our systems model starts out with a focus on a specific strategic business unit (SBU). Each firm can easily identify its strategic business units by developing a two-dimensional matrix in which all its products can be specified along one dimension and all markets specified along the other dimension. The starting point of the systems model is a specific SBU or a product/market unit. All decisions are then constrained to that SBU (corporate, marketing, and marketing communications decisions).
3. A highly involving product is the kind of product that prompts consumers to deliberate its costs and benefits, e.g., car, television set, and camcorder. In contrast, a low involving product prompts consumers to purchase based on impulse, e.g., candy, soft drink, and gum.
4. A thinking type product is one that is considered for its utility, e.g., microwave oven. However, a feeling product prompts consumers to consider purchasing for emotional end states, e.g., perfume.

Suggested Reading

Advertising Age. "Ad Age Conference to Explore Effects of Integrated Marketing." *Advertising Age* (18 October 1993), p. 2.

Aaker, David A., Rajeev Batra, and John G. Myers. *Advertising Management*, 4th ed., Upper Saddle River, N.J.: Prentice Hall, 1992.

Belch, George E., and Michael A. Belch. *Advertising and Promotion: An Integrated Marketing Communications Perspective,* Burr Ridge, Ill.: Irwin, 1993.

Kotler, Philip. *Marketing Management: Analysis, Planning, Implementation, and Control*, 8th ed., Upper Saddle River, N.J.: Prentice Hall, 1994.

Park, C. W., and Gerald Zaltman. *Marketing Management*. Hinsdale, Ill.: Dryden Press, 1987.

Robin, Donald P., and Clyde E. Harris, Jr. "An Integrated Approach for Applying Marketing Strategy." *Business Ideas and Facts*, (winter 1973), pp. 35–40.

Schultz, Don E., Stanley I. Tannenbaum, and Robert F. Lauterborn. *Integrated Marketing Communications: Pulling It Together and Making It Work*. Lincolnwood (Chicago), Ill.: NTC Business Books, 1994.

Schultz, Don E., and Dennis G. Martin. *Strategic Advertising Campaigns*. Chicago, Ill.: Crain Books, 1979.

Thorson, Esther, and Jeri Moore, eds. *Integrated Communication: Synergy of Persuasive Voices*. Mahwah, N.J.: Erlbaum, 1996.

Wang, P., and L. Petrison. *"Integrated Marketing Communications and Its Potential Effects on Media Planning." Journal of Media Planning* (Fall 1991), pp. 11–17.

PART TWO

Strategies and Tactics

Consider the following IMC case of the Indiana Middle Grades Reading program.* In December 1989, Dr. Jack Humphrey, the director of reading services for the Evansville-Vanderburgh School Corporation in Evansville, Indiana, hired a marketing communications agency (the Keller-Crescent Company) to develop a marketing communications campaign. The goal of the campaign was to reinforce the importance of reading to children. Two market segments were targeted: Indiana youth in grades six through nine who attended school in the fifty-three targeted school corporations; and teachers, parents, and all other residents who lived in the area of the targeted school corporations. A project team was assembled from account service, creative, research, public relations, and the production departments of the agency. Originally, the focus was to develop public service announcements for television and radio. Then the focus shifted from one of a traditional advertising campaign to a comprehensive communications program. The theme for the campaign reflected the ideas that reading opens doors to the imagination and that a child's imagination is much more powerful than any video game. This led to the use of the metaphor of the "theater of the mind." Therefore all communications had a closing line: "Enter the Theater of the Mind. Read, Because Only Reading Makes It Real." The logo used on all forms of communications was, "Only Reading Makes It Real." The television commercial used interesting visual effects. The children were shown in color against a black-and-white background. The background scene varied as a function of the story the child was reading, creating the impression that imagination is "the theater of the mind." The print ads and the outdoor posters were also designed in the same manner. The radio commercial used the audio portion of the television commercial, creating the feeling that the books had come to life. Collateral materials such as press releases and press kits featured the same logo and tag line. All materials were on display at the news conference, and special logo boards were prominently featured on speaker podiums.

* Diana L. Haytko, "Integrated Marketing Communication in a Public Service Context: The Indiana Middle Grades Reading Program," in *Integrated Communication: Synergy of Persuasive Voices*, edited by Esther Thorson and Jeri Moore (Mahwah, N.J.: Erlbaum, 1996), pp. 233–42.

The campaign started with public relations activities in the form of direct mail and personal selling (phone conversations with media representatives, state officials, and programming directors). The mail campaign was directed to the principals of the 144 schools in the 53 targeted school corporations. The letters requested the school principals to get involved by asking teachers to select students to be involved as characters in the ad campaign. The student casting event was heavily publicized through the use of the wire services and extensive distribution of press releases and press kits to 27 television stations, 200 radio stations, and 500 newspapers. Fifteen students were selected at the casting sessions from the 400 who auditioned. The names of the finalists were then publicized around the state. The production of the ad campaign was also well publicized. A few months later the public service announcements on television were aired and ran for two years. The public service announcements were publicized in the major television, radio, and newspaper media throughout the state.

This IMC campaign illustrates the importance of strategies and tactics in an IMC campaign. What was the corporate strategy? It was to increase children's reading activities. What was the marketing strategy? It was to position reading as an effective means to opening doors to children's imagination. What were the communication strategies and tactics? It was an affective strategy designed to instill positive feelings in the act of reading. What communication tools were used? Advertising and public relations were used in implementing the marketing communications strategy. The three chapters in this part of the book will help the reader develop specific skills in identifying strategies and tactics at the corporate, marketing, and marketing communications levels. The reader will be able to come up with answers to questions regarding strategy and tactics using well-established analytical models.

Specifically, Part II presents the core of the systems model, namely strategy and tactics. Strategy and tactics are viewed as a process hierarchy, or what some systems people call a decision tree. Marketing communications programs (adver-

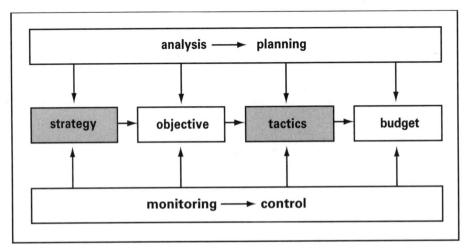

FIGURE II.1 Strategy and Tactics

tising, sales promotion, reseller support, direct marketing, public relations, and word-of-mouth communications) are elements of the marketing communications mix and are selected and guided by an overall marketing communications strategy—informative, affective, habit formation, and self-satisfaction. Marketing communications strategy is viewed as an element of the marketing mix (product, price, distribution, and marketing communications), which in turn is selected and guided by an overall marketing strategy—differentiation, cost leadership, and focus (operationalized through fifteen alternative positions, such as positioning by product attribute, positioning by intangible factor, positioning by customer benefit, etc.). Similarly, marketing strategy is viewed as an element of the corporate mix (marketing, manufacturing, R&D, engineering, accounting, finance, employee relations, etc.), which in turn is selected and guided by corporate strategy (grow, maintain, harvest, innovate, and divest). These concepts are developed in chapters 4, 5, and 6 (see Figure II.1).

CHAPTER 4

Corporate Strategies and Tactics

W hile I was first writing this chapter, I became aware of the following "news" events. IBM Corp. was attempting a hostile takeover of Lotus Development Corp. And it was using all means, including the Internet, to publicize the event. IBM went all out on a public relations media blitz to convince the public that the acquisition was in Lotus's best interests. IBM wanted to buy it for $3.3 billion. IBM had set a home page on the World Wide Web of the Internet to explain its move, and more than 23,000 people gained access to the IBM Web page announcing the hostile bid.[1] In other news, Hewlett-Packard Co. was stepping up a marketing campaign to grab more of the corporate PC market. Compaq Computer Corp. was introducing many new products and was growing quickly. CompUSA had cut costs and had begun a marketing push into the home computer market.[2]

These events represent corporate decisions—decisions to grow, to diversify, to divest, to maintain position, to retrench, and so on. These are decisions made at the highest superordinate level of an organization. Any marketing program, and particularly a marketing communications program, involves decisions and actions taken in an attempt to carry out strategies at the corporate level. Therefore, one cannot do justice to marketing strategy, and marketing communications strategy in particular, without first understanding corporate decisions. This chapter is designed to help the reader understand how corporate decisions are made and how these decisions provide the foundation for marketing action (see Figure 4.1). Specifically, the reader will learn the answers to these questions:

- What is a strategic business unit or product/market?
- What is corporate strategy, and how it is made?
- How is the corporate mix assembled as a direct function of corporate strategy? (See Figure 4.1.)

STRATEGIES AND TACTICS AT THE CORPORATE LEVEL

To understand corporate strategy and tactics, we first have to understand the concepts of *strategic business units* and *product/market* because most corporate strategies and tactics are directly related to product/markets. We'll see how they are related in the discussion about corporate strategy and tactics in this chapter.

59

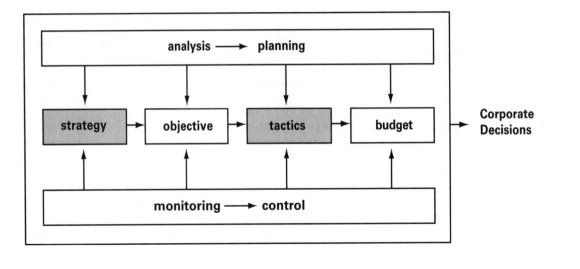

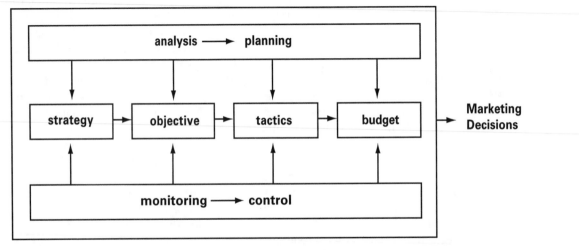

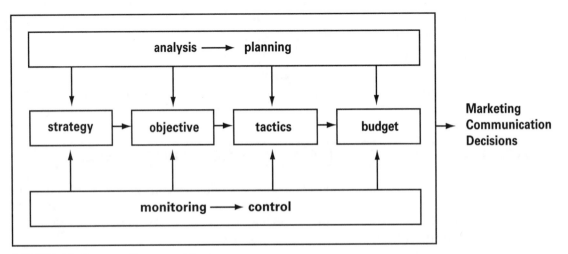

FIGURE 4.1 Corporate Strategy and Tactics

First, what is a *strategic business unit (SBU)?* Most business firms actually operate *several* businesses. For example, a firm such as General Electric is involved in many businesses—forty-nine SBUs, to be exact. An SBU has three characteristics: (1) It is a single business that can be planned separately from other businesses of the firm; (2) The business has its own set of competitors; and (3) the business has a manager who is responsible for its planning and management.[3]

Keep in mind that all corporate decisions discussed from this point on are constrained to a specific SBU. That is, corporate decisions are *not* made in a vacuum. They are made in relation to specific products in specific markets.

At the corporate level, the basic process is essentially a selection of a corporate strategy. Examples of popular corporate-level strategies are to gain market share, hold market share, harvest, divest, and innovate. The organization attempts to implement a given strategy at the corporate level through a strategic mix—that is, process elements that are carried out together to achieve the goals of the overall strategy at the superordinate level. The strategic mix at the corporate level may involve organizational processes related to R&D, engineering, manufacturing, finance, accounting, personnel, and/or marketing. Each of the corporate mix elements may be construed as a "tactic" designed to accomplish the corporate strategy. The traditional breakdown of the organization in terms of functional units is a common way to conceptualize the strategic mix at the corporate level. Each element of the strategic mix is carried out to achieve the *goal* of the overall strategy, which means that for each corporate strategy there is a corresponding goal. Table 4.1 shows an example of a typology of corporate strategies. Please bear in mind that this typology is only an example, not a definitive model of corporate strategies. The idea here is that the marketer should employ an established strategic model to identify optional strategies. This observation applies to all the strategic typologies discussed throughout this paper. The table shows a traditional typology of corporate strategies popular in both marketing and business strategy.[4]

THE GROWTH STRATEGY AND CORRESPONDING TACTICS

In implementing the *growth* strategy, the *marketing, R&D,* and *engineering* functions are likely to be viewed as important elements of the strategic mix. This is because growth usually entails expanding the scope of operations through establishing new distribution outlets, encroaching on new geographic markets, and introducing new product variations to the market. Establishing new distribution outlets and encroaching on new geographic markets are goals that can be achieved through marketing. Introducing new product variations is a goal that can be met through R&D and engineering with the guidance of marketing.

Implicit in this discussion are the corporate objectives corresponding to the growth strategy. The following are examples of corporate objectives directly related to the growth strategy:

- Establish ___ level of sales by ___ date.
- Increase sales by ___ amount by ___ date.
- Establish ___ level of market share by ___ date.
- Increase market share by ___ amount by ___ date.

TABLE 4.1 Corporate Strategy, Tactics, and Objectives

Corporate Strategy	Corporate Tactics (Strategic Mix)	Corporate Objective
Grow	**MARKETING** **R&D** **ENGINEERING** Manufacturing Personnel Finance Accounting	Maximize sales and market share
Maintain position	**MARKETING** R&D **ENGINEERING** Manufacturing **PERSONNEL** Finance Accounting	Minimize negative % change in sales and market share
Harvest	Marketing R&D Engineering **MANUFACTURING** **PERSONNEL** Finance **ACCOUNTING**	Maximize profit
Innovate	**MARKETING** **R&D** Engineering Manufacturing Personnel Finance Accounting	Establish or increase sales and gain market leadership (through high market share)
Divest	Marketing R&D Engineering Manufacturing Personnel **FINANCE** Accounting	Maximize cash flow

Note: Strategic mix elements in boldface reflect major focus or emphasis.

When a firm is aspiring to expand and grow in its operations, the implicit corporate strategy is growth. Implementing this strategy entails treating the marketing, R&D, and engineering functions within the firm as more important than the other functional units. Therefore, more resources should be allocated to marketing, R&D, and engineering in order to help accomplish the growth goals. Furthermore, the growth goal should be closely monitored, and the performances of marketing, R&D, and engineering programs should be evaluated in relation to the growth goal. Control is likely to be exerted if the marketing, R&D, and engineering departments fail to deliver. In many instances, growth tactics (operationalized through marketing, R&D, and engineering) can take on the following goals:

- Increase the number of new distribution outlets by ___amount by ___ date.
- Penetrate geographic markets ___ by ___ date.
- Introduce to the market product variations ___ by ___ date.

Let's use an example of a medium-size advertising agency to illustrate these points. This hypothetical advertising agency is focusing on a specific product/market that is advertising on the Internet by creating home pages on the World Wide Web. The target market is business firms. The agency's plan is to grow in interactive advertising. What would be the agency's corporate objectives? An example of an objective congruent with the growth strategy is to establish about eight satellite offices in key metropolitan areas within a 400-mile radius in the next two years. These satellite offices will each comprise the following: one account executive who will sell interactive advertising to local businesses; two creative people who will be responsible for creating client-tailored interactive ads; and an office manager who will act as receptionist and bookkeeper and who will coordinate the activities of the account executive and the creative staff.

Note that this strategic move requires the deployment of marketing, R&D, and engineering, in the generic sense. The marketing personnel at the agency would oversee the recruitment of the key account execs and train them. The R&D personnel would work hard at perfecting the science of interactive advertising. The engineering personnel, who in this case may involve the creative director at the agency, would help set up the necessary technologies at the satellite offices.

THE MAINTAIN-POSITION STRATEGY AND CORRESPONDING TACTICS

With respect to the *maintain-position* strategy, the *marketing, engineering*, and *personnel* functions are likely to be viewed as important process elements of the strategic mix. The corporate objective corresponding to the maintain-position strategy may be stated as "Minimize negative percentage change of sales and market share." Achieving this stability goal entails treating the marketing, engineering, and personnel functions within the firm as more important than the other functional units. This is because marketing has to increase its efforts to offset threats from encroaching competitors. Engineering has to ensure that product quality is held to standards. The firm cannot afford any significant "goof-ups." A few poorly produced products can cause a great deal of damage to the company. Personnel has to do a better job of keeping employees motivated and satisfied with their jobs while keeping employee compensation and fringe benefits stable. Also, personnel has to recruit qualified people in case replacements are needed.

Let's use the advertising agency example to illustrate this strategy. Suppose this agency is becoming keenly aware that competitor agencies are serving the local business market with traditional mass media advertising. This agency has been the market leader for many years and wants to maintain its leadership position. The goal is articulated by the president of the agency: "The goal for next year is to maintain the twenty largest accounts, which produce 80% of the billings." How can this be accomplished? The president realizes that marketing has to play a bigger role in meeting this objective. Marketing has to ensure that these twenty accounts are satisfied customers who are not likely to be tempted by the encroaching competition. Thus, marketing has to work harder than ever to meet this challenge. They may need a larger budget.

Also, the personnel department has to work hard to prevent employee turnover. Employees who quit are likely to be hired by competitors. These employees are likely to take with them certain accounts, some of which may be key accounts. Therefore, personnel needs to ensure that the core people at the agency—creative people and account execs—are happy with their jobs. Also, personnel needs to ensure that the creative people and account execs feel committed to the agency. This is a tough challenge. Therefore, personnel may need additional resources to meet this important goal.

Furthermore, this maintenance goal needs all the help it can get from the engineering people. At the agency, the engineering person is essentially the creative director. This person has to work harder and do a better job in monitoring quality control. Since the agency can't afford to lose key accounts, it becomes imperative to make sure that product quality must always be maintained.

THE HARVEST STRATEGY AND CORRESPONDING TACTICS

With respect to the *harvest* strategy, the *manufacturing*, *personnel*, and *accounting* functions are likely to be most important. The corporate objective corresponding to the harvest strategy is, "Maximize profit." That is, a firm implementing a harvest strategy needs to be cost efficient in its operations. Carrying out this strategy entails treating the manufacturing, personnel, and accounting functions within the firm as more important than the other functional units. This is because minimizing costs to increase profit is a goal that can be accomplished through cost-efficiency programs. These programs should be directed at manufacturing and personnel and overseen by accounting.

Let's use the medium-sized ad agency example to illustrate this situation. Let's focus on a specific product/market, newspaper advertising. The president realizes that this product/market is declining for the advertising agency business because many businesses now have their own graphics and design capabilities through desktop publishing software. Businesses can design their own newspaper ads without outside help. Even if they can't, a newspaper's advertising department can design an ad for a client since all newspapers have adopted computer technology. As a result, media organizations now must provide their clients the additional service of ad design for little or no added cost. So what can the agency do? *Harvest* this product/market. What does this mean? Rather than pour any money into marketing the newspaper advertising part of the business, the president should cut down on any promotion effort related to this part of the business. Therefore, marketing decreases in importance. The personnel department has to cut back the creative staff who specialize in newspaper advertising, perhaps by layoffs or eliminating vacated positions. Accounting has to pay close attention to cost control, especially in relation to personnel and tasks related to newspaper advertising. The goal is to reduce the cost of goods related to producing newspaper advertising. This step, in turn, would maximize gross profits and reduce overhead costs (and thus maximize net profits).

THE INNOVATION STRATEGY AND CORRESPONDING TACTICS

With respect to the *innovation* strategy, the *marketing* and *R&D* functions are likely to be important process elements because both marketing and R&D are the primary means for carrying out the innovation strategy. The corporate objective corresponding to the innovation strategy is, "Establish X level of sales and gain market leadership through high market share." That is, given that the firm is aspiring to be the first to market a given product, the firm's strategy can be implicitly recognized as an innovation strategy. Carrying out this strategy entails treating the marketing and R&D functions as more important than the other functional units. More specifically, the innovation strategy can be operationalized in terms of introducing a new product (see Table 4.1).

Let's apply the innovation strategy to the ad agency business. The product/market is a form of radio communications that allows an advertiser to broadcast his or her message on a radio frequency that has a reach of 250 feet. This advertising medium is well suited to businesses that have parking lots and drive-through windows. For example, customers of some fast-food restaurants must wait in line to be served at the drive-through window. The restaurant could post a big sign reading, "To know what today's specials are, tune your radio dial to AM 73.5." The customer tunes his radio to the designated frequency and gets the list of specials over the radio before he or she reaches the drive-through window. Advertising agencies can use this new advertising medium to better serve both present and prospective clients, such as local businesses with drive-through windows.

Let's say the president of the ad agency decides to introduce this advertising medium to certain clients. To do this, the R&D people must fully develop and test this technology and develop a rate card showing prices with discounts proportional to the number of purchases. The account execs have to be involved too. They would help tailor the technology and the rate card to meet the demands of the agency's clients or prospective clients. The president might target a specific date to offer this new advertising medium to local clients and prospects. She would monitor the progress of its development and pave the way for its introduction. The president must also closely monitor the performance of the people assigned to this project and take corrective action if the product development deviates from course toward the goal. Sufficient resources must be allocated to carry out this task. We'll address the question of resource allocation and control in some detail in part III of this book.

THE DIVESTMENT STRATEGY AND CORRESPONDING TACTICS

Finally, for the *divestment* strategy, the *finance* function is likely to be the most important process element of the strategic mix. This is because the finance people are likely to be directly involved in implementing the divestment decision. The corporate objective corresponding to the divestment strategy may be, "Maximize cash flow."

When a corporation is trying to minimize financial losses and bring in some badly needed cash, a divestment strategy is employed. Implementing this strategy entails treating the finance function within the firm as more important than the other functional units in minimizing the firm's losses (again, see Table 4.1).

Going back to the ad agency example, suppose the ad agency is structured as follows. The president oversees the operations of five separate groups or departments: (1) production of TV and radio advertising, print advertising, interactive advertising, and bulletin board and transit advertising; (2) collateral services; (3) media planning and placement; (4) marketing and advertising research; and (5) account executives. (See Figure 4.2.)

The president realizes that the bulletin board/transit advertising department has not been profitable for a while. It is very difficult to keep costs down, especially below the costs of other outdoor advertising companies competing in the same geographic area and targeting the same business clients. The president decides to divest this organizational unit. Perhaps one way to achieve this is to offer to sell the entire department to the people who are presently employed in that department. The goal here is to obtain a return that is at or above market value and thus bring in some badly

FIGURE 4.2 Organizational Structure of the Ad Agency

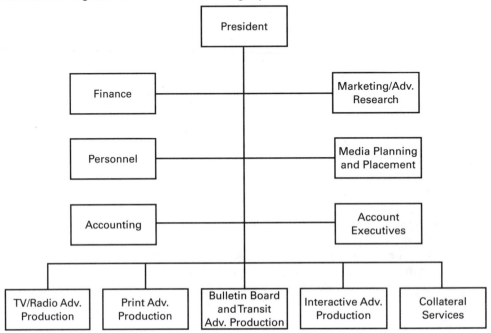

needed extra cash. This task is likely to be effectively handled by the finance people. The president gives this charge to the finance staff and monitors their progress toward divesting this unit at or above market value. Certain resources that the finance staff need to accomplish this task are provided.

Summary

This chapter introduced the reader to conceptual tools related to corporate strategy and tactics. The purpose is not to teach the reader how to become an expert in making corporate decisions but only to provide some degree of familiarity with the topic. Marketing communications managers do not usually make corporate decisions directly but are likely to influence these decisions. Also, they need to make sure that marketing communications decisions are consistent with marketing and corporate decisions.

The chapter began by showing how marketing communications managers define a strategic business unit and a product/market. Knowing the exact product/market units (strategic business units) of an organization is extremely important because most corporate decisions are made in relation to each definable product/market.

The various corporate strategies were discussed, including the corporate decisions to grow, maintain position, harvest, innovate, and divest. Each strategic alternative has a corresponding objective. For example, the growth strategy may aim at an increase in sales and market share. Each strategic alternative is carried out through a unique configuration of the strategic mix. The elements of the corporate strategic mix include manufacturing, engineering, marketing, R&D, personnel, accounting, and finance. A strategic alternative is implemented through the deployment of certain elements of the strategic mix. For instance, the elements of the corporate mix which are likely to be deployed for growth may be marketing, R&D, and engineering. The deployment of specific elements of the strategic mix entails the allocation of resources to those elements. Similarly, the performance of those deployed elements is monitored, and deviations from the objectives are noted, triggering corrective action.

Questions for Discussion

1. What is a strategic business unit? Product/market? How do marketers identify product/markets? Illustrate with examples.
2. What is corporate strategy? Describe at least three alternative corporate strategies. Illustrate with examples.
3. Identify corporate objectives associated with each alternative corporate strategy. Illustrate with examples.
4. Identify the corporate strategic mix needed to implement each alternative corporate strategy. Illustrate with examples.
5. Suppose you are an owner of a local restaurant that makes approximately $2 million a year. The restaurant is located in a university town and specializes in deli sandwiches. It also has a game room (pool, billiards, darts, etc.) and a staging area used at night for live band and comedy shows. Define the various strategic business units of this restaurant.

6. Still assuming that you are the owner of that restaurant, think about how you could expand the restaurant to make more money. In other words, your corporate strategy is to grow. How would you implement this growth strategy? Decide which specific tactics may be viable in expanding the operations. Which of the following functional units become more central to the growth strategy: marketing, R&D, engineering, manufacturing, personnel, finance, or accounting?

7. Still assuming that you are the owner of that restaurant, you become aware that another deli-type restaurant (with night club setting) is now directly competing with your business. Your strategy is now to maintain market share. How would you go about implementing this strategy? What are those corporate strategic elements that you would be likely to deploy? Be specific.

8. Still assuming that you are the owner of that restaurant, you realize that you can no longer compete with two or three other deli-type restaurants in town. You are now thinking of harvesting the deli operation and channeling your energy into the night club operation. How would you go about doing this? Which functional units of the restaurant will become more central and which less central? Explain.

9. Still assuming that you are the owner of that restaurant, you realize that the only way to effectively compete with the two or three new deli-type restaurants is to be innovative. You have to come up with something new, a new gimmick that will attract patrons to your restaurant. What could this be? Think of a new gimmick and describe how you would go about implementing it.

Notes

1. Associated Press, "The Internet is Newest Corporate Battleground," *Roanoke Times and World News* (June 9, 1995), pp. A15, A17.

2. Gary McWilliams, "At Compaq, a Desktop Crystal Ball," *Business Week* (March 20, 1995), pp. 96–8; Larry Armstrong, Ira Sager, Kathy Rebello, and Peter Burrows, "Home Computers: Sales Explode As New Uses Turn PCs into All-Purpose Information Appliances," *Business Week* (November 28, 1994), pp. 88–96; Peter Burrows, "It's All Starting to Compute Now," *Business Week* (March 13, 1995), p. 94.

3. Philip Kotler, *Marketing Management,* 8th ed. (Upper Saddle River, N.J.: Prentice Hall, 1994), p. 69.

4. Robert D. Buzzell and Frederick D. Wiersema, "Successful Share-Building Strategies," *Harvard Business Review* (January-February 1981), 135–44; Donald C. Hambrick and Ian C. MacMillan, "The Product Portfolio and Man's Best Friend," *California Management Review* (fall 1982), 84–95; R. G. Hammermesh, M. J. Anderson, and J. E. Harris, "Strategies for Low Market Share Business," *Harvard Business Review* (May-June 1978), 95–102; Philip Kotler, "Harvesting for Weak Products," *Business Horizons* (July 1978), 15–22; Steven A. Shnaars, "When Entering Growth Markets, Are Pioneers Better Than Poachers?" *Business Horizons* (March-April 1986), 27–36.

Suggested Reading

Day, George. "Diagnosing the Product Portfolio." *Journal of Marketing* (April 1977): pp. 29–38.

Ferrell, O. C., George H. Lucas Jr., and David Luck. *Strategic Marketing Management.* Cincinnati, Ohio: South-Western Publishing Co., 1994.

Hambrick, Donald C., and Ian C. MacMillan. "The Product Portfolio and Man's Best Friend." *California Management Review* (Fall) pp. 84–95.

Haspeslagh, Philippe. "Portfolio Planning: Uses and Limits." *Harvard Business Review* (January-February 1982): pp. 60, 73.

Schnaars, Steven P. *Marketing Strategy: A Customer-Driven Approach.* New York: The Free Press, 1991.

Wind, Yoram, and Vijay Mahajan. "Designing Product and Business Portfolios," *Harvard Business Review* (January-February 1980): pp. 155–65.

Wind, Yoram, Vijay Mahajan, and Donald J. Swire. "An Empirical Comparison of Standardized Portfolio Models." *Journal of Marketing* (Spring 1983): pp. 89–99.

CHAPTER 5

Marketing Strategies and Tactics

Refer to the storyboard of "The Heaven" commercial for the California Milk Processor Board (see Figure 5.1). The commercial shows a person who has been run over by a truck and now is in heaven. In heaven, he eats his favorite chocolate chip cookie. But wait a minute! Something is missing! Milk. This commercial is designed to reinforce the association that eating cookies goes with drinking milk. The marketer is *positioning* milk (the advertised product) with a specific *use* or *application* (eating cookies). This chapter will introduce the reader to a marketing strategy called *positioning by use or application*.

Now examine the storyboard of the Norwegian Cruise Line (see Figure 5.2). The commercial shows a woman experiencing sensual pleasure and adventure. The ad uses an analogy to articles in the Constitution that guarantee certain rights to U.S. citizens. The point is that people are entitled to get away from work and experience sensual pleasure, relaxation, and a little adventure. The marketing strategy behind this commercial is called *positioning by customer benefit*. The marketer of the Norwegian Cruise Line is attempting to associate customer benefits such as sensual pleasure, relaxation, and adventure with the cruise line. In this chapter, we will discuss this strategy and many other similar marketing strategies that guide marketing communications.

Thus, this chapter will introduce the reader to a variety of marketing strategies that are operationalized through *positioning*—highlighting, emphasizing, and communicating particular aspects of a brand to target consumers. Also, we'll discuss how each of the positioning strategies can be operationalized through marketing research and how appropriate models can be used to guide this research (see Figure 5.3).

The marketing communications manager attempts to identify an overall strategy that will guide the marketing mix. This is a strategic decision at the marketing level. We'll call this the *marketing strategy*. There are many models of marketing strategy in the marketing literature. The most popular is Porter's model of competitive strategy.[1] The model identifies three major marketing strategies: (1) differentiation, (2) cost leadership, and (3) focus. We'll describe these three strategies in some detail.

CALIFORNIA MILK PROCESSOR BOARD

TITLE: "HEAVEN" :30 COMM'L NO.: ZGRE 4348

MAN: Tom, can I make a suggestion? You're fired!!! (HE LAUGHS, KNOCKS OVER OLD LADY AND STEPS INTO TO CROSS WALK) (SFX: TRUCK HORN) (MAN SCREAMS)

(SOFT MUSIC UP) WOMAN: Welcome... to eternity... (MUSIC UP) (MAN TAKES BITE OF HUGE COOKIE)

MAN: Heaven! (HE LAUGHS) (OPENS REFRIGERATOR, SEES MILK CARTONS) MAN: Yes! Huh...? (SHAKING EMPTY CARTON)

Hmmm... (ALL CARTONS ARE EMPTY) Milk! ...Wait a minute... Where am I? ANNCR VO: Got milk? (SFX: FIRE CRACKLING)

FIGURE 5.1 Positioning by Use or Application

California Milk Processor Board: "Heaven" (Goodby, Silverstein & Partners; Propaganda Films; :60) Our grocery products category winner also was selected as Best of Show among TV entries.

FIGURE 5.2 Positioning by Customer Benefit

Norwegian Cruise Line: "Constitution" (Goodby, Silverstein & Partners; Ritts/Hayden; :60). Smouldering passion in black and white.

Silky-voiced, shapely young woman recites various elements of a "new constitution for the world" (among them: "Article 1, Section 3, we shall form a more perfect union" and "Article 4, Section 7, work shall be abolished"), while she and male companion frolic, embrace underwater and go boating in tropical settings. Spot closes with a shot of one of the Norwegian Cruise Line ships. Category winner also was named best in cinematography.

THE DIFFERENTIATION STRATEGY AND CORRESPONDING TACTICS

The differentiation strategy asserts that marketing performance can be enhanced if the product is unique in the industry along some dimension widely valued by consumers. Uniqueness may be based on product (e.g., product design, service, options), price (e.g., price connoting status and prestige), distribution (e.g., excellent customer service available at each distributor), and marketing communications (e.g., the prod-

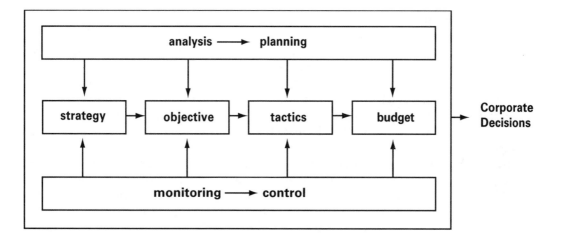

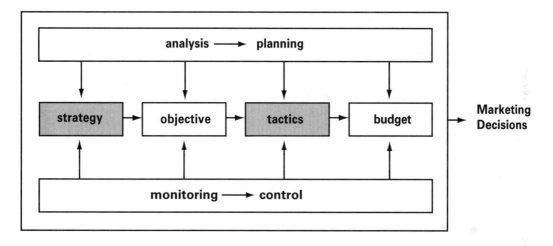

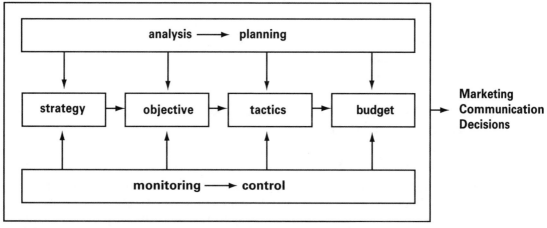

FIGURE 5.3 Marketing Strategy and Tactics

uct is associated with a celebrity spokesperson). Focusing on a unique and valued marketing mix dimension is referred to as *positioning*.

Specifically, positioning is a unique configuration of the marketing mix (product, price, distribution, marketing communications).[2] In other words, the manner in which a marketing manager emphasizes or de-emphasizes certain elements of the marketing mix is, in essence, positioning. If, for example, the marketing manager thinks that the success of the marketing program depends on competing with price, then the marketing strategy is price-based. Positioning scholars have developed an extensive repertoire of positioning techniques. Among the significant ones are these: product attribute, intangible factor, customer benefits, relative price, low price, use/application, user/customer, celebrity/person, lifestyle/personality, product class, competitors, and country/geographic area of origin.[3] Each positioning technique reflects a specific emphasis on selected elements of the marketing mix (product, price, distribution, marketing communication). Therefore, we'll group the various positioning techniques according to the element of the marketing mix most emphasized. The grouping is as follows:

Positioning strategies emphasizing the *product:*

- Positioning by product class
- Positioning by product attribute
- Positioning by intangible factor
- Positioning by competitors
- Positioning by country of origin

Positioning strategies emphasizing price:

- Positioning by relative price

Positioning strategies emphasizing distribution:

- Positioning by brand-distributor tie-ins
- Positioning by distributor location
- Positioning by distributor service

Positioning strategies emphasizing marketing communication:

- Positioning by celebrity or spokesperson
- Positioning by lifestyle or personality

In the following sections, we'll discuss these positioning strategies and how they are implemented (see Table 5.1).

Positioning by Product Class

Some brands can be positioned at the product-class level—that is, by using product-class associations. To understand the concept of product class, the reader has to understand the distinction between product category, product form, and brand. A product category is the highest level of abstraction of a given product. For example, we can talk about automobiles as a *product category.* Within the product category there are various *product forms:* for instance, cars can be differentiated as sports cars, compact economy cars, pickups, jeeps, station wagons, vans, minivans, and so on. All these are

TABLE 5.1 Positioning Strategies Related to Differentiation

Positioning Strategy	Marketing Mix Elements	Marketing Objectives
Positioning by product attribute	**Product** Price Distribution Mktg. comm.	Establish, increase, or maintain brand association with product attribute X
Positioning by intangible factor	**Product** Price Distribution Mktg. comm.	Establish, increase, or maintain brand association with intangible factor X
Positioning by product class	**Product** Price Distribution Mktg. comm.	Establish, increase, or maintain brand association with product class
Positioning by competitors	**Product** Price Distribution Mktg. comm.	Establish, increase, maintain brand and/or association with leading competitor X
Positioning by country of origin	**Product** Price Distribution Mktg. comm.	Establish, increase, or maintain brand association with country or geographic area
Positioning by relative price	Product **Price** Distribution Mktg. comm.	Establish, increase, or maintain brand association with quality through price
Positioning by product-distributor tie-In	Product Price **Distribution** Mktg. comm.	Establish, increase, or maintain brand association with distributor X
Positioning by distributor location	Product Price **Distribution** Mktg. comm.	Establish, increase, or maintain brand association with distributor location X
Positioning by distributor service ability	Product Price **Distribution** Mktg. comm.	Establish, increase, or maintain brand association with distributor X's service ability
Positioning by celebrity or person	Product Price Distribution **Mktg. Comm.**	Establish, increase, or maintain brand association with celebrity or person X
Positioning by lifestyle/personality	Product Price Distribution **Mktg. Comm.**	Establish, increase, or maintain brand association with lifestyle/personality

Note: Terms in boldface reflect focus or emphasis.

forms of the automobile. Within a product form, there are *product brands*. Thus, in relation to vans, we may have a Ford van, a Chrysler van, and so on. Product-class associations means connecting the brand to a particular benefit related to either the product form or the category itself.

For example, 7-Up soft drink positioned itself as the logical alternative to the "colas" but with better taste. Because of the ad campaign, 7-Up became known as the "uncola." Caress hand soap positioned itself apart from other brands of soap by associating its brand with bath oil (a product that is different from soap).[4] Examine the ad in Figure 5.4. The ad is about Nivea gels. The product is positioned at the product-class level. It is positioned as a moisturizing gel for shower and bath.

The major marketing mix element used to implement the positioning-by-product class strategy is the *product* element (see Table 5.1). Specifically, resources have to be allocated to do the following:

1. Conduct product research to identify the extent to which most of the target consumers are satisfied or dissatisfied with their current product. If the majority of the target consumers are dissatisfied with their current product, the next step is to determine why and in what situations. If the majority of the target consumers are satisfied with their current product, the marketer should determine new product opportunities. For example, if consumer research indicates that women who use moisturizers are dissatisfied with the current moisturizer products that can be used when taking a bath or shower, the marketing communications manager would position Nivea Shower and Bath as a moisturizer for use when taking a bath or shower.

2. Communicate selected situations reflecting dissatisfaction with the current product or satisfaction with the new product. The Nivea ad (in Figure 5.4) shows an example of consumer satisfaction with the new product.

Positioning by Product Attribute

The most popular of all brand positioning strategies is the *product attribute* strategy. Here, the marketer attempts to link certain important product features to the brand in question. These product features are concrete and specific: for example, Crest toothpaste is associated with fluoride; Hewlett-Packard Laser Jet printers are associated with excellent resolution on computer printouts; Viva paper towels emphasize the paper's absorbency.[5]

Examine the ad shown in Figure 5.5. The ad shows a software application, MapLinx, that maps customer, sales, or other business data. The focal point of the ad is the visual display of the data in a map-like form. The ad emphasizes this product attribute in the most visual way possible.

Remember our definition of positioning—a selected configuration of the marketing mix. In this section, we'll describe the marketing mix configuration that is used to operationalize the positioning-by-product-attribute strategy. The element of the marketing mix that has to be mobilized to implement the positioning-by-product-attribute strategy is the *product* element (see Table 5.1). That is, resources have to be allocated (or reallocated) so that the marketing communications manager can do the following:

1. Conduct product research to ascertain the most effective *product attribute*(s) (see Appendix 5.1 for a model and method that marketers use to select important product attrib-

FIGURE 5.4 Ad Illustration for Positioning by Product Class

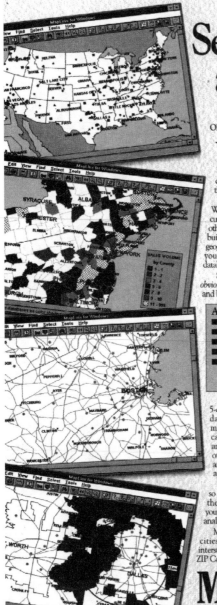

See your business in a whole new way!

MapLinx™ for Windows *maps* your customer, sales or other business data – for profitable decision-making.

You've got all the data you need to plan and act with deadly accuracy. But without a visual *picture* of this data, you're making decisions in the dark.

That's why you *need* MapLinx for Windows. MapLinx instantly maps your customer or prospect lists, sales figures or other business data on detailed U.S. maps built right into the product. You get a geographical picture of your business that your contact manager, spreadsheet or database simply can't deliver.

Suddenly, the right decisions are *obvious*. You'll spot new opportunities – and beat the competition to them.

A must for users of:
- ACT!®
- Access®
- Excel®
- dBASE®
- Other contact managers, spreadsheets and databases.

MapLinx pinpoints locations using 5-digit ZIP Codes. Use it to map your database records on pushpin-style maps. Or use the color coding capabilities to visually display and analyze sales levels, market activity or other data. Print your maps, or copy and paste them into other Windows applications for dazzling presentations.

The built-in maps are customizable, so you can illustrate your data exactly the way you want. And you can save your maps with associated data for future analysis or record-keeping.

MapLinx incorporates over 27,000 cities, all U.S. and state highways and interstates, and every county, area code and ZIP Code in the country.

MapLinx™
for Windows

Some of the ways people are using MapLinx:

Sales. Increase your sales by analyzing where the profits are coming from, and which areas need attention. Create balanced territories. Plan efficient calls on prospects and customers in a given area (for example, ask MapLinx to display all within a 20-mile radius of Chicago). Stay one step ahead of your competition!

Marketing. Plan geographically and demographically-targeted direct mail campaigns that maximize your resources. Plan and analyze the success of regional promotions and campaigns for constant improvement. Create strategic growth plans, and turn bold new ideas into bottom-line results!

Service. Boost your customer service and success by being able to instantly refer customers to their nearest dealer, agent, etc., or offer other geographically-based information.

MapLinx will turn your database into the ultimate competitive weapon. Take advantage of our limited-time special offer and call today!

LIMITED-TIME OFFER

Call now and get MapLinx for the special price of only $79.95 (reg. $149.95). You save $70! Or visit your nearest CompUSA, Computer City, Egghead or other fine software retailer.*

90-DAY MONEY BACK GUARANTEE
Call free now by dialing *278 on the Airfone® Service from GTE.

GTE Airfone

Or call anytime
1-800-370-8966

FIGURE 5.5 An Ad Illustration for Positioning by Product Attribute

utes). In the example of MapLinx, perhaps research may show that the visual clarity of the map is the most important feature of a sales-tracking software.

2. Work with the firm's product engineers to redesign the product to make the selected product attribute central to the product. Or perhaps the marketer can display that attribute on the product itself and/or the package. For MapLinx, the marketer should work closely with the software development engineers to guide them into developing the map-like visual features that are likely to be most appealing to sales managers (target consumers).

3. Communicate to the target consumers the fact that the brand has the desired product attribute. The marketing communications manager for MapLinx has to launch a marketing communications campaign in which the visual clarity of the maps is demonstrated. All elements of the marketing communications mix work together to highlight the visual clarity feature of the software.

Positioning by Intangible Factor

An intangible factor is a general attribute that serves to capture a host of important attributes.[6] In contrast to product attributes, which are concrete and objective, intangible factors are abstract and subjective. For example, product quality, technological leadership, and value are all intangibles. Ford has an on-going ad campaign focusing on "quality." Not much is said about particular car models. The marketing communications manager here is trying to associate Ford automobiles with high quality across all car makes and models.

Consider the following study that demonstrated the power of an intangible attribute. Subjects were shown two camera brands; they were told that one was more technically sophisticated and the other was easier to use. However, detailed information provided to the subjects clearly showed that the easier-to-use brand had the superior technology. After a couple of days, the subjects did not remember much of the detailed information; they merely recalled how the brands were presented—easy-to-use versus technically sophisticated. Although the easy-to-use brand could have been recognized as technically superior, subjects identified the brand that was presented to them as "more technically sophisticated" as the brand with higher technology. This study shows that consumers rely on intangible attributes, not detailed specifications about the brand, to store brand information in memory.[7]

The SIEMENS ad shown in Figure 5.6 illustrates positioning by an intangible factor, namely technological innovation.

The element of the marketing mix that is used to operationalize the positioning-by-intangible-factor strategy is the product element (see Table 5.1). Resources have to be allocated toward the following tasks:

1. Conduct product research to identify the product's strengths and *associated intangible factors*. In the case of Siemens, the marketer should conduct a product analysis. For example, a thorough product analysis may reveal several strengths; perhaps one of them is found to be technological innovation, the intangible factor that can be used as a focus of a marketing communications campaign.

2. Communicate to the target consumers the fact that the brand has the intangible factor, since the results of product research show that the intangible factor may play a salient role in the purchase decision. That is, the Siemens' marketing communications manager would conduct a study to ascertain the importance of the intangible factor of technological innovation as a criterion in buying corporate stock. Given that technological innova-

SIEMENS

1895. That was then.

Working in a small laboratory, Wilhelm Roentgen made the world's first x-ray images. Working with him, Siemens patented and manufactured its first x-ray tubes in 896.

1996. This is now.

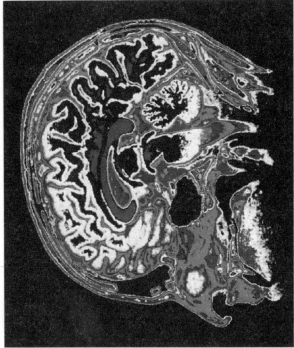

This modern magnetic resonance image lets doctors see into the human body more clearly than ever before. It is a product of years of Siemens investment in research and development. Happily, you don't have to be a scientist to appreciate the results. Doctors, hospitals and clinics throughout America are giving their patients better care because of Siemens advances in many forms of diagnostic imaging, including ultrasound, magnetic resonance, nuclear imaging and computed tomography. And that's the kind of results we can all feel good about. **Siemens. Precision Thinking.**

FIGURE 5.6 An Ad Illustration for Positioning by Intangible Factor

tion is found to be an important decision criterion for stockholders, the marketing communications manager can use this intangible factor as a basis for a marketing communications campaign.

Positioning by Competitor

Some brands are positioned in direct association with leading competitor brands. This is usually done when the leading competitor has a well-established image in the minds of the target consumers. Here, a brand follower tries to capitalize on this well-established image by anchoring its brand next to the well-established brand in the minds of the target consumers. Claiming better performance than the leading brand may result in consumers making positive inferences about the brand. The widely cited example of Avis, "We're number two; we try harder," is the epitome of this positioning strategy. The message is that although Hertz is the leading company in car rentals, Avis is positioned next to Hertz as a major car-rental option.[8] Examine the ad in Figure 5.7. The ad is about Aleve, the nonprescription pain reliever. Aleve is positioned directly against Tylenol, Advil, and Bayer.

The element of the marketing mix used to operationalize the positioning-by-competitors strategy is again the product element (see Table 5.1). Specifically, resources have to be allocated to do the following:

1. Conduct product research to ascertain consumers' perception of the product's strengths and weaknesses in relation to selected competitors, preferably the leading competitors. For example, the marketer of Aleve would conduct consumer research using a sample of consumers who have used Aleve, Tylenol, Advil, and Bayer. These consumers would be asked to compare Aleve against the competitors along a set of criteria. The findings may show that Aleve is perceived as longer-lasting and gentler to the stomach than the three leading competitors, and that longer-lasting and gentler to the stomach are criteria that consumers weigh heavily in their decision to buy a pain reliever. [See Appendix 5.2 for a model and method to conduct this type of research.]

2. Work with product engineers to correct noted product weaknesses and enhance strengths. If Aleve is found weak in relation to Tylenol, Advil, and Bayer along an important attribute, then the marketer should provide this data to the pharmaceutical engineers and R&D personnel to correct the problem.

3. Set prices that are likely to be perceived by target consumers as more appealing than those of competitors. Set a price for Aleve that is likely to be acceptable in light of the prices of Tylenol, Advil, and Bayer.

4. Distribute the product using the same channels as the leading brands. For example, Aleve should be distributed to drugstores and supermarkets where Tylenol, Advil, and Bayer are also found.

5. Communicate to target consumers information concerning strengths and/or information showing how weaknesses are being addressed to satisfy customers. The ad pertaining to Aleve shows the product's strength in relation to competitor brands.

Positioning by Country of Origin

Certain countries are known for producing certain high-quality products. For example, Japan is associated with high-quality automobiles and electronic gadgets; France is associated with high-quality perfumes and fashion; Italy is associated with high-

Before You Take Advil or Tylenol Again, Get a Second Opinion

It's been about a year since a pain reliever called Aleve® was made available to consumers without a prescription, and its benefits are being discovered by more and more people each day.

In fact, clinical studies show that Aleve has key advantages over other brands. At the end of the day, a two-pill dose of Aleve provides stronger pain relief than a dose of Advil®.* It provides longer-lasting relief than Extra Strength Tylenol® and is gentler on the stomach lining than aspirin. So if you haven't been satisfied with your current pain reliever, you may want to try Aleve.

Aleve is the only non-prescription pain relief product that offers Americans in pain a completely different active ingredient — naproxen sodium†. It was developed from Naprosyn® (naproxen) and Anaprox® (naproxen sodium), two of the world's most widely used prescription pain relievers. That's probably why so many doctors have already recommended Aleve for their patients.

Here are some additional things you may want to think about when considering this new choice:

THE DOSING ADVANTAGE

Most pain relievers are labeled to be taken up to four or six times a day, which may not be convenient if you want to work all day or sleep through the night. However, in looking at the recommended dosing chart (above right), you will notice a basic difference with Aleve. Aleve is labeled to be dosed every 8 to 12 hours instead of every 6 to 8 hours like Extra Strength Tylenol, or 4 to 6 hours like Advil.

*Based on a single, 2-pill dose pain relief comparison at 11 and 12 hours.
†Do not take this product if you had either hives or a severe allergic reaction after taking any pain reliever.

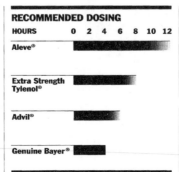

RECOMMENDED DOSING

HOURS	0	2	4	6	8	10	12
Aleve®							
Extra Strength Tylenol®							
Advil®							
Genuine Bayer®							

THE VALUE DIFFERENCE

How often you have to take a pain reliever also affects your wallet.

These days, it's important to get the most for your money. The table below shows that the price on the bottle is not the best guide to value. The cost for the number of pills you have to take for the maximum daily dose varies greatly. The cost for Aleve shows it may be an excellent choice for value-conscious consumers.

THE SAFETY STORY

Finally, even though you can buy them almost everywhere, remember OTC pain relievers are serious medicine. It's important to read the product's label and directions carefully.

COST PER 24 HOURS OF PAIN RELIEF
(Based on Maximum Daily Dose)

BRAND		COST
Aleve (3 pills)		$0.31
Advil (6 pills)		$0.63
Extra Strength Tylenol (8 pills)		$0.78
Genuine Bayer (12 pills)		$0.94

Based on IRI drug outlet pricing data on 50 count bottles (1/1/95–4/2/95).

You may have recently heard of reports in leading medical journals, such as the Journal of the American Medical Association, linking acetaminophen (the active ingredient in Tylenol) to possible liver damage. These patients took more than the maximum daily dose of acetaminophen, and many of these patients were either fasting and/or consuming alcohol. If you consume three or more alcohol-containing drinks per day, you should ask your doctor for advice for when and how you should take any OTC pain reliever. In fact, it was recently announced that all OTC pain relievers should have an alcohol warning.

Look for a list of the approved uses for the product, how often and for how long you can take it, and especially for any warnings or side effects of which you should be aware. For example, if you suffer from stomach pain, you should check with your doctor or pharmacist before taking aspirin, ibuprofen or naproxen sodium. Remember, when used properly, OTC pain relievers can provide safe and effective relief from most common aches and pains.

THE BOTTOM LINE

For the first time in more than 10 years, there's a pain relief choice that's really different — Aleve. And having a new choice means that you are better able to find pain relief that's right for you.

If you are in doubt about what to take, ask your doctor or pharmacist. Chances are, he or she may recommend Aleve. Even though it's been around for only one year, many doctors have already recommended it.

© P&G 1995

FIGURE 5.7 An Ad Illustration for Positioning by Competitor.

quality shoes and leather goods; Germany is associated with high-quality beer and automobiles; and Russia is associated with high-quality vodka.

Many "country-of-origin" studies have documented the effectiveness of brand positioning by certain countries.[9] However, it should be noted that consumers' reactions to imports can vary considerably. In general, people tend to rate products from industrialized countries more favorably than those from developing countries. Recent evidence suggests that country-of-origin information serves to stimulate consumers' interest in the product. Consumers, thus, do more thinking about products in which country-of-origin information is presented and evaluate them more carefully than when such information is not presented.[10]

Examine the ad in Figure 5.8 about Walkers cookies. This brand of cookies is positioned by using a country, or geographic region. The region in the Walkers cookies ad is Scotland, specifically the Scottish Highlands. People in the Scottish Highlands have been known for decades for making the finest shortbread cookies. The association with Scotland and the Scottish Highlands is made in every ad using a variety of creative cues, such as the picture of the package that is typically "Scottish."

The marketing mix element used to operationalize the positioning-by-country/geographic-area strategy is again *product* (see Table 5.1). Specifically, resources have to be allocated to do the following:

1. Conduct product research to ascertain consumers' perception of product *quality* as a direct function of manufacturing the product in selected countries, and identify countries that are perceived to generally produce a quality product. Select a set of countries for possible manufacture based on this analysis, and pass the recommendation to corporate executives for future action. In the case of Walkers cookies, market research could be done to ascertain the extent to which Walkers cookies would be perceived as being of high quality if consumers know that the recipe is a long-cherished Scottish tradition.

2. If the product is then manufactured in countries to which target consumers attribute product quality, then the marketer should communicate to target consumers the fact that the product is manufactured in the designated country. The example of Walkers cookies shown in Figure 5.8 illustrates how a message that is grounded in a country-of-origin position can be created in print advertising.

Positioning by Relative Price

A brand can be positioned in terms of relative price—that is, its price compared to the price of other product brands. Many products have brands that are perceived along a price/quality hierarchy, with certain brands of lower price/quality, others with midrange price/quality, and still others of higher price/quality. Consider how hotels/motels are perceived in the minds of many consumers. The budget hotels/motels (low price/quality) may include hotels/motels such as Motel 6, Econolodge, McSleep, Days Inn, Hampton, and Comfort Inn. Midrange hotels/motels may include Courtyard, Ramada, and Holiday Inn. Luxury ones may include the Marriott, Renaissance, Clarion, Hyatt Regency, Westin Hotels, and Embassy Suites.[11]

Marketing communications managers choose to position their product at the higher end of the price dimension to connote high quality. An ad about the Aurora luxury automobile serves to illustrate the positioning-by-relative-price strategy. The

FIGURE 5.8 An Ad Illustration for Positioning by Country/Geographic Area

ad refers to a "bull market" and "luxury." By doing so, the marketing manager is establishing the fact that this car is highly priced and is of high quality (see Figure 5.9).

The major marketing element that is employed to carry out the relative-price positioning is *price* (see Table 5.1). Specifically, resources have to be allocated to do the following:

1. Conduct research to ascertain if *price* is associated with quality. Consider the following example of the Aurora. Are business executives more likely to perceive Aurora as being a high-quality sedan if it were to be labeled as a luxury car and priced at a level comparable to other luxury sedans? If so, follow step 2.

2. Set a price level that would be associated with the desirable level of quality. See Appendix 5.3 for an illustration of how a specific price can be determined consistently with the positioning-by-relative-price strategy.

3. Communicate to the target consumers the price level and corresponding quality. The ad for Aurora is a good example of how a message can be guided by the positioning-by-relative-price strategy.

Positioning by Brand-Distributor Tie-In

This positioning strategy asserts that marketing success is likely to be assured by creating a brand association with a credible and reputable distributor. For example, Sears has a good reputation in kitchen and laundry appliances. A new manufacturer of washing machines may strike a deal with Sears to carry its product line. Based on this deal, the new washing machine can be effectively positioned by associating it with Sears. The reverse situation is also commonplace. That is, distributors attempt to create tie-ins with credible and reputable manufacturers. For example, an ad that ties Fortune Magazine ("manufacturer") to Compuserve ("distributor") is a reverse situation, one in which the "distributor" uses a credible and reputable "manufacturer" to position itself effectively.

The way to implement this positioning strategy is as follows (see Table 5.1):

1. Conduct research to identify all possible *distributors*, if you are a manufacturer. Manufacturers should contact these distributors and ascertain the possibility of doing business with them and select a set of distributors that have better offers. If you are a distributor, do the reverse—conduct research to identify all possible *manufacturers* whose products you may want to distribute. And so on.

2. Now focus on this set of optional distributors or manufacturers. Administer a consumer survey to measure the image favorableness of each distributor or manufacturer. If these distributors are retail outlets, consult the retailing literature about store image and how measures of store image can help you select the distributor with the most favorable image in the minds of potential consumers. If these are manufacturers, tap into the measurement literature concerning corporate image. Of course, before attempting to conduct your own study, see if past studies have been conducted regarding these particular distributors or manufacturers. Most large distributors and manufacturers conduct their own image surveys, and they can provide you with this information without you having to gather it yourself (see Appendix 5.4).

3. Based on the image research, select a distributor or manufacturer with the most favorable image and create the tie-in with that distributor or manufacturer.

It can go 100,000 miles before its first tune-up. It has a 32-valve, DOHC V8 that broke 47 different speed-endurance records during development. Ninety percent of its peak torque is available between 1,700 and 5,600 RPM. And with 250 horsepower, it might be just the boost that the market is looking for. The new Aurora luxury-performance sedan by Oldsmobile. See what happens when you Demand Better. 1-800-718-7778.

FIGURE 5.9 An Ad Illustration for Positioning by Relative Price

4. Develop a communications message to target consumers emphasizing and highlighting the brand-distributor tie-in.

Positioning by Distributor Location

This positioning strategy posits that "location, location, location" is a very important decision criterion in purchase. Therefore, showing consumers how to access the product in the most convenient way is likely to improve marketing performance. For example, the marketing success of most fast-food restaurants and motels depends on their location. Similarly, location is significant for hospitals and health clinics. Where they erect their establishments is likely to make a big difference in terms of corporate goals such as sales, market share, profit, and cash flow. Examine the IBM ad in Figure 5.10. The ad communicates a basic message—*location*. It shows consumers how to access IBM through the internet. Of course, once they access IBM through the World Wide Web, consumers expect to find clear and relevant information. Nevertheless, the focus here is on convenient access.

To implement this positioning strategy, we recommend the following tasks (see Table 5.1):

1. First, find out how your product (product class or related products) is usually distributed. Is it traditionally distributed through a direct channel, and if so, what form of direct channel (e.g., teleshopping, electronic shopping)? Is it traditionally distributed through indirect channels, and if so, through what kind of retailers? Where are these retailers housed—in a shopping mall, a shopping plaza, a configuration of stores next to the entrance/exit of a major highway, for example?

2. Conduct research to ascertain the shopping habits of the target market in relation to the product in question. Do most consumers use a direct or an indirect channel? If a direct channel, then what form of direct channel is most convenient for them? If they go out shopping, do they usually go to the nearest shopping plaza, nearest shopping mall, or where? If the product is new and no comparable products are on the market, then consumers can be asked to evaluate the convenience of different methods of access to the product.

3. Based on this research, select a distributor based on location and convenience to the target consumers.

4. Inform target consumers how to access the product and stress the convenience of the distribution access.

Positioning by Distributor's Service Ability

This positioning strategy focuses on providing customer service at the distributor level. The strength of a manufacturing firm may lie in providing excellent customer service through its dealership network. Many department stores tend to position themselves as providing excellent customer service. The Acura automobile positions itself on customer service and satisfaction. The focus is to serve the customer the best way possible at the retail level. Most product manufacturers that realize the importance of a distributor's ability to serve customers have their own channels of distribution. Take the example of Brooks Brothers (upscale, conservative men's wear). Products are distributed solely through Brooks Brothers' own retailers. Salespeople serve as fashion advisors rather than sales personnel. They build first-name relationships

Refresh

http://www.ibm.com

IBM
Solutions for a small planet™

FIGURE 5.10 Positioning by Distributor Locations

with lifelong customers. This is ideal customer service.[12] Another example is First Union Bank. This bank is $5.89 billion strong and is the sixth largest U.S. banking company. It positions itself on service.[13]

Examine the ad in Figure 5.11. This is a clever ad that focuses on customer service but in a nontraditional way. Federal Express realizes that customer service is extremely important, so they're providing their customers with software that allows customers to order and track their shipping packages on-line. This is good customer service.

How can this positioning strategy be effectively implemented? The following tasks are recommended:

1. Conduct a consumer survey of the target market to determine the relative importance of *distributor's service ability* as a purchase and/or repeat purchase criterion.

2. Given that the distributor's service ability is found to be a very important criterion, study different ideal customer service programs housed at the retail level. Then select the program that best matches the requirements and conditions of your distributors.

3. Collaborate with the managers of the distribution outlets to set up the selected customer service program.

4. Communicate to target consumers the message that customers are entitled to the best service possible and that the distributors can best serve their needs.

Positioning by Celebrity/Person

A brand can be associated with a celebrity. Usually certain celebrities are perceived by the public as having certain personalities. The marketer can benefit from the celebrity's personality and the cognitive and emotional responses the celebrity may elicit from the public. Marketing communications managers want some positive responses to "spill over" to the brand.

For example, when Nike developed the "pump" basketball shoes called Air Jordans (basketball shoes having pressurized-gas pockets in the soles as a cushioning feature), they used Michael Jordan (basketball celebrity). This brand was a smashing success, and its success was directly attributable to the association with Michael Jordan.[14] Perhaps people felt that if they wore the shoes they could jump as high as Jordan. Perhaps the brand association was with Jordan's happy and friendly personality.

Examine the ad in Figure 5.12. The ad shows the senior chairman of the board of Wendy's, Dave, as the spokesperson for Wendy's fast-food restaurants. The idea is to position Wendy's by emphasizing Wendy's association with Dave. He appears in all TV commercials and most forms of marketing communications.

The major marketing mix element that is used to implement the positioning-by-celebrity/person strategy is essentially marketing communications (see Table 5.1). Specifically, resources have to be allocated to do the following:

1. Conduct marketing communications research to identify *celebrities* or *spokespersons* who have images matching the product and the self-concept of target consumers. Determine which media categories and vehicles are associated with the selected celebrity or spokesperson image. Consider the Wendy's situation and the ad shown in Figure 5.12. It is possible that the image of Wendy's senior chairman of the board is a humorous fatherly figure who cares about good and tasty traditional food (hamburgers made the old-fashioned way). People who prefer Wendy's may be old-fashioned, "meat-and-potato" kind of people. Wendy's has the image of an "old-fashioned hamburger joint." The im-

Now the hardest thing about shipping is mastering the complexities of the double click.

Introducing FedEx Ship™ the revolutionary new desktop shipping software from FedEx. Now with FedEx Ship, you can handle virtually any aspect of shipping a package with just a few clicks of your mouse.

Using your modem, the software connects your computer directly to FedEx. It creates shipping labels and prints them on your own laser printer. Maintains a data base of your customers. Schedules pickups, tracks and confirms delivery of your packages. All faster and easier than ever before. Without so much as picking up the phone. FedEx Ship. Once you get the double click down, it's a whole new way of shipping packages. For a free copy of FedEx Ship software for Windows™ or Macintosh®, just call 1-800-GO-FEDEX® or download at http://www.fedex.com.

FedEx
Federal Express
Our Most Important Package Is Yours.®

JUST POINT, CLICK AND SHIP.

©1995 Federal Express Corporation. Windows is a trademark of Microsoft Corp. Macintosh is a registered trademark of Apple Computer, Inc. *TDD: 1-800-238-4461.

FIGURE 5.11 Positioning by Distributor's Service Ability

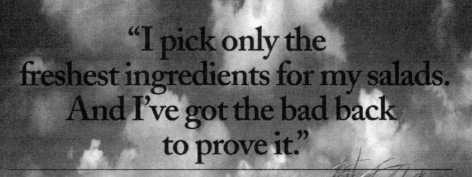

FIGURE 5.12 An Ad Illustration for Positioning by Celebrity/Person

ages of Wendy's, the spokesperson, and Wendy's customers all match, making this positioning strategy very effective (see Appendix 5.5).

2. Develop messages with selected celebrities or spokespersons and place these messages in media categories and vehicles that are associated with each celebrity's or spokesperson's image. The Wendy's ad placed in a traditional women's magazine, such as *Ladies' Home Journal,* is a good example of how marketing communications can be guided effectively by this positioning strategy.

Positioning by Lifestyle/Personality

Over time, brands develop their own "personalities." Consider the Betty Crocker personality. Research has shown that most women perceive Betty Crocker brands as honest, dependable, friendly, concerned about consumers, an expert in baked goods, time-tested, and traditional. Also, research has shown that Coke has a strong all-American, all-around image—family and flag, rural America. Pepsi's personality on the other hand, is exciting, innovative, fast-growing, and somewhat brash and pushy.[15]

In the ads you've seen for Cover Girl make-up, the personality symbol is that of a magazine cover girl, and it is used consistently in all forms of marketing communications. The image of Cover Girl make-up is that of a young, wholesome, and very attractive model. These ads reflect a positioning strategy based on lifestyle or personality.

The major marketing mix element used to implement the positioning-by-lifestyle/personality strategy is marketing communications (see Table 5.1). Specifically, resources have to be allocated to do the following:

1. Conduct marketing communications research to identify lifestyles or personalities that have desired images that can be injected into the product to establish its unique identity. Select the most effective lifestyle or personality. Determine which media categories and vehicles are associated with the selected lifestyle or personality. How do marketing communications managers select lifestyle or personality symbols for their products? For example, how was the Cover Girl personality established? Such product personalities usually occur by focusing on an icon or symbol having certain cultural connotations that can be "injected" into the product. The Cover Girl symbol is seen as the epitome of youth, good looks, and a "flirty" personality. This lifestyle personality of Cover Girl makeup is selected as a direct function of what may appeal to the target consumers—young women who cherish good looks—because it idealizes models as glamorous women who are admired by society.

2. Develop messages with the selected lifestyle or personality and place these messages in media categories and vehicles that are associated with the same lifestyle or personality symbols.

THE COST LEADERSHIP STRATEGY AND CORRESPONDING TACTICS

In contrast to positioning by relative price, many marketers position by *low price.* Entire marketing communications campaigns are designed around price reductions and promotional deals. Consumers react to price reductions and promotional deals as a direct function of motivations.[16] The first motivation is related to stockpiling. Some customers who are committed to the brand may decide to take advantage of the price discount and stockpile. The second motivation is to receive an incentive for switching brands. Finally, experimentation may be a motive. Consumers who have not yet consumed the product category may decide to try the product by buying the brand with the reduced price as a way to reduce their risk in the product. If they don't like the product, they won't feel too bad, since they haven't invested much money in buying it. For example, one ad for the HealthMax Treadmill is a good example of a positioning-by-low-price strategy. The ad shows that HealthMax is significantly lower in price than NordicTrack.

The major element of the marketing mix that is deployed to carry out the positioning-by-low-price strategy is *price*. Specifically, resources have to be allocated to do the following:

1. Conduct pricing research to ascertain the price level that would set the firm's brand apart from competitor brands and be perceived as a bargain by most of target consumers. Using the HealthMax Treadmill example, the question becomes: At what level below the price of the NordicTrack will the perception of a bargain be created? A $50 differential? A $100 differential? A $200 differential? A $300 differential? A $400 differential? A $500 differential? Research may show that the perception of a bargain can be established somewhere between a $300 and $400 differential (see Appendix 5.6).

2. Set a price level that would be associated with the desirable level of value to be perceived as a bargain. For example, the HealthMax Treadmill is less than half the price of the NordicTrack.

3. Communicate to the target consumers the price level and corresponding value. An ad for the HealthMax Treadmill targets women who exercise regularly at home and may be thinking of buying a treadmill. They can save hundreds of dollars by buying the HealthMax Treadmill instead of the NordicTrack.

FOCUS-RELATED STRATEGIES AND CORRESPONDING TACTICS

Michael Porter, a Harvard Business School professor and a management guru, has long argued that ruthless specialist firms are likely to be successful in today's market conditions. Specialist firms are those firms that tailor all their activities to serve narrow market segments in ways that cannot be easily imitated by competitors. For example, Jiffy Lube specializes in oil and filter changes, and, therefore, serves a narrow segment. Similarly, Southwest Airlines provides frequent flights at low cost between pairs of cities—again, a very narrow market—compared to most airlines that have a world-wide hub-and-spoke network that can take air travelers from somewhere to anywhere. According to Professor Porter, a focus strategy entails tailoring every facet of the business to serve a narrow market segment. By doing so, focused-driven firms gain a competitive advantage over competitor firms who try to be all things to all people.[17]

Most scholars view marketing strategy as involving two key decisions, market selection and positioning. We have addressed many positioning strategies in the context of the differentiation strategy. *Market selection* involves identifying all the possible markets for the firm's product(s) and then making a deliberate decision to go after certain markets while ignoring others. In doing so, the manager attempts to segment the market using certain segmentation criteria and then analyzes the viability of each segment. Market selection is thus a decision based on prioritizing the identified markets and targeting the most viable ones. What is a *market?* Here are some definitions of "market" by marketing scholars:

- "An aggregate demand by potential buyers of a product or service."[18]
- "People with needs to satisfy, the money to spend, and the willingness to spend it."[19]
- "By market here is meant the interrelated class of brands or products whose relations of substitution and competition are powerful enough so that the sales of each are strongly influenced by the sales of the other."[20]

Segments are customer groups, or a "homogeneous" set of buyers—an identifiable group of customers with the same generic need. The example illustrated in Figure 5.12 shows a thermometer manufacturer with the capability to cater to three market segments: (1) health care facilities, (2) restaurants, and (3) households.

Needs are the functions or purposes a product serves for customers. For example, thermometers can serve three customer functions: (1) measuring body temperature, (2) measuring cooking temperature, and (3) measuring atmospheric temperature.

FIGURE 5.12 Product/Market Is Based on Typology of Segments X Needs X Technologies

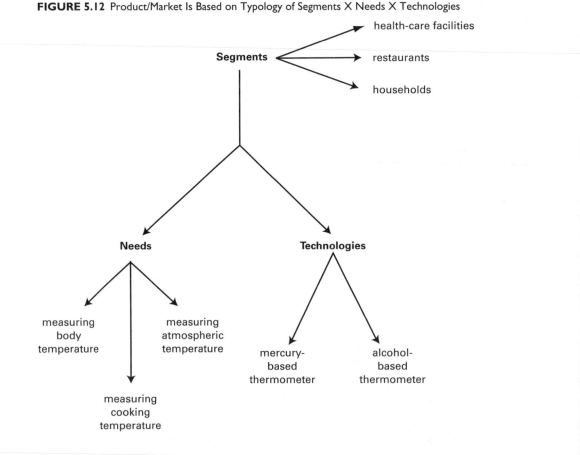

*Technologie*s refer to those particular products that can be defined and distinguished from other products through technological features. For example, there are two types of thermometers, technologically speaking—one that is mercury-based and another that is alcohol based.

By articulating different segments by different needs and by different technologies, we can construct a product-market matrix as shown in Figure 5.13. The product-market matrix specifies each business unit that is the basis of all subsequent corporate, marketing, and marketing communications decisions. The product-market matrix shows the possibility of 10 different business units. Focusing on the household segment, we can identify six product-markets: (1) households using mercury-based thermometers to measure body temperature as a symptom of illness, (2) households using alcohol-based thermometers to measure body temperature as a symptom of illness, (3) households using mercury-based thermometers to measure cooking temperature in preparing oven-cooked meals, (4) households using alcohol-based thermometers to measure cooking temperature in preparing oven-cooked meals, (5) households using mercury-based thermometers to measure atmospheric temperature to figure out how warmly to dress, and (6) households using alcohol-based thermometers to measure atmospheric temperature to figure out how warmly to dress.

Restaurants use thermometers mostly for one purpose, to measure cooking temperature. The thermometers can be mercury-based or alcohol-based. Health-care facilities use mercury- or alcohol-based thermometers to measure body temperature as a diagnostic medical tool.

It may be that mercury-based thermometers are more appropriate than alcohol-based ones for certain markets. If so, certain cells within that matrix would make up the possible business units.

How do marketers identify various possible market segments and needs? It is beyond the scope of this book to delve into the huge amount of literature concerning

FIGURE 5.13 The Resulting Product/Markets

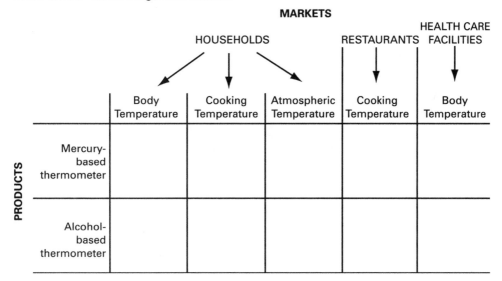

segmentation, but it may suffice to point out that segmentation criteria are highly varied. Representative segmentation criteria traditionally used by consumer and industrial marketers are shown in Table 5.2.

Once a market segment is selected, the marketer can communicate to this segment *directly,* using those marketing communications tools that can precisely target consumers in the market segment, or *indirectly,* through messages that are designed to speak to them, or both. The direct method involves selecting the best marketing communications tools that have the best reach. For example, a direct mailing to restaurant managers obtained from a mailing list house is likely to serve the targeting goal. However, suppose that no such lists exist and the target segment cannot be effectively reached through specific communication media. What then? In this situation, marketers typically devise communication messages that can appeal to the target consumers. For example, airing a television commercial about Ensure (a nutritional drink offered as a meal substitute) on the *CBS Evening News* is likely to reach a huge audience. Part of the audience includes elderly consumers, who constitute the target market for Ensure. The ad is designed so that elderly consumers can realize that the commercial is "speaking" to them.

We can talk about these message strategies also in terms of positioning, as we've done in discussing differentiation. The focus here is on the customer, *not* on the product, price, distribution, or marketing communication. There are at least three positioning strategies here:

- Positioning by customer benefit or problem
- Positioning by user or customer image
- Positioning by use or application

TABLE 5.2 Segmentation Criteria Commonly Used by Consumer and Industrial Marketers

Segmentation criteria used by consumer marketers:
- demographic factors (gender, income, education, . . .)
- sociocultural factors (social class, family life cycle, social integration, opinion leadership, . . .)
- geographic factors (local, regional, international, . . .)
- psychographic factors (activities, interests, opinions, personality, self-concept, lifestyle, . . .)
- motivational factors (benefits, needs, wants, . . .)
- consumption factors (product usage, brand loyalty, . . .)

Segmentation criteria used by industrial marketers:
- end use (Standard Industrial Classification code)
- customer size (no. of employees, annual sales, . . .)
- geographic factors (local, regional, international, . . .)
- motivational factors (benefits, needs, wants, . . .)
- consumption factors (product usage, brand loyalty, . . .)
- channel type (type of wholesaler, type of retailer, . . .)
- personal selling method (deals, allowances, co-op adv. . . .)

Positioning by Customer Benefit or Problem

Consumer researchers distinguish between *attributes* and *benefits*. An ad campaign can focus on one or more attributes or it can focus on one or more customer benefits. *Customer benefits,* like intangible factors, are product features that can be characterized as abstract and subjective. However, in contrast to intangible factors, these product features can be easily described in terms of how the product is used by the customer and what its value is to the customer.

Consider the example of an advertising campaign for a brand of shampoo that contains natural protein. The marketer can translate the natural protein into customer benefits, such as "It is safe to use every day," and "It is exciting and sexy." A computer with a touch-screen entry feature (attribute) can be advertised as "easy to use" (customer benefit).[21] An ad for pickles can be positioned by a customer benefit, namely its extra crunchiness.

Similarly, an advertising campaign can appeal to customers with certain *problems*. For example, a financial institution wants to target business entrepreneurs who may have wonderful business ideas but cannot get any bank to lend them money to operationalize their ideas and start a business. Most banks shy away from risky investments, especially investments by entrepreneurs without collateral. Thus, the financial institution may place an ad in the local newspaper in the business section with a headline that reads, "If You Can't Get Your Bank to Finance a Business Venture, Then You Should Check Us Out."

How can this positioning strategy be carried out in the most effective way possible? Resources are allocated to perform the following tasks:

1. Conduct customer research to ascertain *customer benefits* or *problems* commonly perceived in relation to the product and product purchase. See Appendix 5.7 for a model and method commonly used to select important customer benefits. For example, the marketing communications manager of Claussen pickles would conduct a study to ascertain important customer benefits that pickle eaters seek in a good brand of pickles. The research may show "crunchier pickles" is an important benefit sought by a sizable part of the pickle-eating market.

2. Work with the product, price, and/or distribution personnel and functions to enhance product attributes that are directly related to the customer benefit (or problem). That is, the marketing communications manager at Claussen should work with the engineers and manufacturing people to ensure the production of a "crunchier pickle." He or she has to price Claussen pickles in a way to ensure the connotation of quality—crunchier than other brands of pickles. Perhaps a premium price may be consistent with this customer benefit. The manager has to ensure that the pickles are distributed in a manner to preserve the "crunchier" texture. Timing is essential in distribution to ensure freshness and of course "crunchiness."

3. Communicate to the target customers the most important customer benefits related to the product (or the way the product solves an important customer problem). In the case of Claussen pickles, the marketing communications campaign has to focus on "crunchier pickles." The message should be placed in media vehicles that can reach most pickle eaters.

Positioning by Use or Application

Brands can be positioned by *use or application* too. Here the focus is on how and when the consumer uses the consumer uses the product. One study discovered nine use contexts for coffee.[22] These are: (1) to start the day, (2) between meals alone, (3) between meals with others, (4) with lunch, (5) with supper, (6) at dinner with guests, (7) in the evening, (8) to keep awake in the evening, and (9) on weekends. A marketer may decide to associate a brand of coffee with one of the most popular uses. Campbell's soup has been positioned as a lunchtime product; Gatorade is positioned for athletes, particularly in the summer months. An ad for Coppertone sunblock and tanning lotion may show a woman relaxing on the beach. Coppertone has been positioned for people who like to lie in the sun at the beach for a long time.

This positioning strategy can be implemented as follows:

1. Conduct customer research to identify how and when the target consumers *use* (or can use) the product and determine which uses or applications are most appealing or significant to the customers. For a Coppertone campaign, research may discover that many situations are equally appealing, including lying in the sun on the beach or by the swimming pool or enjoying outdoor activities such as tennis, running, bicycling, sailing, canoeing, and fishing. Suppose that, based on this customer research, the marketing communications manager selects the following applications: at the beach, at the swimming pool, and playing tennis.

2. Work closely with the product engineers to redesign the product to make it highly conducive to one or more set of applications that are highly appealing or significant to target customers. Suppose the marketer of a sunblock lotion selects the beach situation. He or she would need to work closely with the product engineers to ensure that the sunblock and tanning lotion can be used in the best way possible at the beach. For example, users of sunblock lotion at the beach may get sandy. How does the lotion feel with sand on the body? If there is a feeling of discomfort, can the lotion be redesigned to solve this problem? Does swimming or perspiring affect the sunblock's protection? If so, then can the sunblock be redesigned to make it waterproof? Similar questions have to be raised and addressed in relation to such recreational situations.

3. Communicate to the target customers select uses or possible applications that they are likely to find most appealing. A sunblock ad may show the use of the product at the beach. Also, suppose that other ads show its use at the swimming pool and on the tennis court. Therefore, the entire marketing communications campaign would involve showing the use of the sunblock and tanning lotion in three different situations—relaxing at the beach, lying by the swimming pool, and playing tennis.

Positioning by User or Customer

Another effective brand association strategy is the *user/customer association*. Here the marketer associates the brand with a particular kind of person, the kind of person who typically uses the product. For example, Nike shoes traditionally associates its shoes with the serious athlete. Cover Girl cosmetics is associated with wholesome, healthy, young, and very attractive women. Canada Dry has positioned itself for adults, leaving Coke and Pepsi for the younger market.[23]

This strategy can be implemented as follows:

1. Conduct customer research to identify user images associated with the product and determine which *user images* are most congruent with customers' self-concept (actual self, ideal self, social self, and/or ideal social self). Select a user image that is most congruent with target customers' self-concept. Determine which product accessories, price level, channels of distribution or retail outlets, and media categories and vehicles are associated with the selected user image.

    Let's use women's athletic shoes as an example. The marketing communications manager determines how a typical woman who likes to work out sees herself, how she would like to see herself, how she thinks she is seen by others, and how she would like to be seen by others. It may be that this woman sees herself as the kind of person who loves to work out; she loves to feel pumped up and aching after a good workout. She sees herself that way (her actual self-image); she thinks other people see her that way (her social self-image); she likes herself that way (her ideal self-image), and she likes knowing that others see her in the same light (her ideal social self-image). The customer research may show several things: that special aerobic shoes with special aerobic outfits appeal most to this target segment; that this segment is willing to pay a moderate-to-premium price for a good pair of athletic shoes and sport outfits; that this segment shops for athletic shoes and outfits in sporting goods stores and specialty outlet stores; that this segment reads magazines such as the *New Woman, Redbook*, and *McCall*; that it doesn't watch much television but listens to soft rock and country music on the radio (see Appendix 5.8).

2. Work closely with the product engineers to modify the product with accessories that are symbolic of the selected user image. For example, the manager would guide the shoe designers and apparel designers to select those designs that are most appealing to the target segment, based on customers' self-concept.

3. Set a price consistent with the user image. For example, the manager would price the athletic shoes and apparel at moderate and premium prices because these price levels may be most appealing to the target customers.

4. Distribute the product through channels and outlets that are associated with the selected user image. The manager may place the aerobic shoes and apparel in sporting goods stores and the brand's outlet stores because these stores are used most often by the target customers.

5. Develop messages with sources (spokespersons, models, characters, celebrities, etc.) that reinforce the selected user image and place these messages in media categories and vehicles that are associated with the user image too. The manager would develop ads and place them in media vehicles such as *New Woman* magazine.

Summary

Marketing strategy involves selecting among three major strategies—differentiation, cost leadership, and focus. The differentiation strategy may consist of several positioning approaches: positioning by product class, by product attribute, by intangible factor, by competitors, by country of origin, by relative price, by brand-distributor tie-in, by distributor location, by distributor's service ability, by celebrity or person, or by lifestyle or personality. Cost leadership is positioning by low price. The focus strategy is positioning by customer benefits or problem, by user or customer image, or by use or application. Each of these marketing strategies has a unique marketing mix. Once managers know precisely what is required to implement the strategy, they can effectively allot resources to implement that strategy. Also, the marketing mix helps the marketer spell out one or more objectives consistent with the strategy. Once objectives are articulated, the marketing communications manager monitors the performance of the marketing programs in relation to the stated objectives. If the objectives are not met, the manager changes the system to create future outcomes that are more aligned with the objectives.

Questions for Discussion

1. Describe a communications campaign you know about in which the objective is to associate the brand with an important product attribute. What is the central theme of the campaign? How are the product attributes identified through marketing research?

2. Suppose you are the marketing communications manager of a regional hospital. The hospital has just built a fitness club as part of a preventive program to promote physical health through exercise and nutrition programs. The hospital board of directors is now expecting you to effectively promote the fitness club. Now you need to plot a strategy. Design a campaign strategy by identifying at least two positioning strategies that may be highly effective for the fitness center.

3. Suppose you are part of the marketing communications team working on the AT&T account. It seems obvious to you and the rest of the team that the primary campaign objective of AT&T is to convince current and previous customers of AT&T that AT&T is not more expensive than the competition and that it offers better service. What is this positioning strategy called? Give a general description of this strategy. Describe the optimal conditions under which to use this positioning approach. What is the appropriate marketing mix for this strategy? Give an example of an objective that is highly consistent with the strategy.

4. Suppose you are part of the marketing communications team working on the MCI account. What is MCI's current positioning strategy? Do you think it is effective? Why or why not?

5. Suppose you are the marketing communications manager of Nike athletic shoes. You realize that the campaign objective is to create certain kinds of associations that are powerful in inducing a long-term positive image for Nike shoes. What would these brand associations be? How would you do a study to discover these brand associations?

6. Suppose you are the marketing communications manager of the Macintosh line of personal computers. Your objective is to reinforce the positive image among Macintosh users. You realize that the typical Macintosh user perceives the Macintosh in very complex ways. Apply the means-end model to map out how the Macintosh is perceived by its long-time users. Design a campaign strategy based on the findings.

7. Suppose you are the marketing communications manager of a pharmaceutical company that has just produced a new pharmaceutical substance to fight gum disease, which is most common among the elderly. The substance is much more effective than the ingredients currently used by most of the major toothpaste manufacturers. The company decides to package the substance as toothpaste and penetrate the toothpaste market. You realize that you need to do some research to investigate how the various toothpaste brands are perceived and evaluated by the elderly. Your first task is to identify the toothpaste brands currently on the market. Second, use the ideal-point model and develop hypotheses about the elderly's perception and evaluation of the current brands. Third, based on the hypothetical findings, make recommendations about the optimal attribute configuration of the new brand and how you would advertise it to appeal to a significant segment of elderly consumers in North America and Europe.

8. Suppose you are working for a large advertising/marketing communications agency, and you are assigned to work with the team handling the Wendy's account (fast food). Your team is given specific instructions that the ad campaign objective should aim to achieve a higher level of sales and market share from older consumers. That is, it is very important to get a mature person who is thinking of eating fast food out to consider Wendy's as a viable and very likely alternative. Determine a positioning strategy for Wendy's and design a marketing communications campaign for the company. Justify your decisions.

9. You are the communications manager of a large pharmaceutical company that recently has developed a new antiperspirant that is highly effective for athletically-inclined women. The brand name of the new product is Sweat Free. You realize that your communications campaign objective is to instill a positive attitude of Sweat Free among women who exercise a lot. Develop a positioning strategy that can help you figure out the message of the entire campaign. Make sure to justify your decisions.

Notes

1. Michael E. Porter, *Competitive Strategy* (New York: The Free Press, 1980).

2. Al Ries and Jack Trout, *Positioning: The Battle for Your Mind* (New York: Warner Books, 1982); David Aaker and J. Gary Shansby, "Positioning Your Product," *Business Horizons,* May-June 1982, pp. 56–62.

3. David A. Aaker, *Managing Brand Equity: Capitalizing on the Value of a Brand Name* (New York: The Free Press, 1991), ch. 5.

4. Ibid, p. 127.

5. Ibid, pp. 114–15.

6. Ibid, p. 116.

7. Joseph W. Alba and J. Wesley Hutchinson, "Dimensions of Consumer Expertise," *Journal of Consumer Research*, 13, (March 1987), pp. 411–54.

8. David A. Aaker, *Managing Brand Equity: Capitalizing on the Value of a Brand Name* (New York: The Free Press, 1991), p. 127.

8. David A. Aaker, *Managing Brand Equity: Capitalizing on the Value of a Brand Name* (New York: The Free Press, 1991), pp. 127; C. Min Ha and Vern Terpstra, "Country-of-Origin Effects for Uni-National and Bi-national Products," *Journal of International Business Studies* (Summer 1988), p. 242; N. G. Papadopoulos, L. A. Heslop, F. Garby, and G. Avlonitis, "Does Country-of-Origin Matter?" Working Paper, Marketing Science Institute.

10. Richard Ettenson, Janet Wagner, and Gary Gaeth, "Evaluating the Effect of Country of Origin and the 'Made in the U.S.A.' Campaign: A Conjoint Approach," *Journal of Retailing* 64 (Spring 1988), pp. 85–100; C. Min Ha and Vern Terpstra, "Country-of-Origin Effects for Uni-National and Bi-National Products," *Journal of International Business* (Summer 1988), pp. 235–55; Michelle A. Morganosky and Michelle M. Lazarde, "Foreign-Made Apparel: Influences on Consumers' Perceptions of Brand and Store Quality," *International Journal of Advertising* (Fall 1987), pp. 339–48; Gary M. Ericksen, Johnny K. Johansson, and Paul Chao, "Image Variables in Multi-Attribute Product Evaluations: Country-of-Origin Effects," *Journal of Consumer Research*, (September 1984), pp. 694–9; Sung-Tai Hong and Robert S. Wyer, Jr., "Effects of Country-of-Origin and Product-Attribute Information on Product Evaluation: An Information Processing Perspective," *Journal of Consumer Research* (September 1989), pp. 175–87; Marjorie Wall, John Liefeld, and Loiuse A. Heslop, "Impact of Country-of-Origin Cues on Consumer Judgments in Multi-Cue Situations: A Covariance Analysis," *Journal of the Academy of Marketing Science* 19, no. 2 (1991), pp. 105–13.

11. David A. Aaker, *Managing Brand Equity: Capitalizing on the Value of a Brand Name* (New York: The Free Press, 1991), pp. 120–2; Stuart Agres, *Emotion in Advertising: An Agency's View* (New York: The Marschalk Company, 1986).

12. G. Bruce Boyer, "The Man (and the Woman) in the Brooks Brothers Shirt," *Town and Country* (May 1981), 58–66.

13. Mag Poff, "First Union's Goal: Service," *Roanoke Times* (January 12, 1996), p. A7.

14. David A. Aaker, *Managing Brand Equity: Capitalizing on the Value of a Brand Name* (New York: The Free Press, 1991), p. 125; Tom Murray, "The Wind at Nike's Back," *Adweek's Marketing Week* (March 27, 1986), pp. 28–31.

15. David A. Aaker, *Managing Brand Equity: Capitalizing on the Value of a Brand Name* (New York: The Free Press, 1991), p. 126; Roger Enrico, *The Other Guy Blinked* (New York: Bantam Books, 1986).

16. M. M. Moriarity, "Retail Promotional Effects on Intra- and Interbrand Sales Performance," *Journal of Retailing* (Fall 1985), pp. 27–47; B. E. Kahn and D. C. Schmittlein, "The Relationship between Purchase Made on Promotion and Shopping Trip Behavior," *Journal of Retailing* (Fall 1992), pp. 294–315; K. Helsen and D.C. Schmittlein, "How Does a Product Market's Typical Price-Promotion Pattern Affect the Timing of Households' Purchases?" *Journal of Retailing* (Fall 1992), pp. 316–38.

17. Jill Dutt, "Hedging Your Bets in 1997: Diversify to Survive Markets' Ups and Downs," *The Washington Post* (December 29, 1996), pp. H1, H4.

18. W. J. Stanton, M. S. Sommers, and J. B. Barnes, *Fundamentals of Marketing,* 2nd Canadian ed. (Ryerson, Toronto: McGraw-Hill, 1977).

19. Philip Kotler, *Marketing Management: Analysis, Planning, and Control,* 2nd ed. (Upper Saddle River: Prentice Hall, 1976), p. 7.

20. Frank Bass, C. W. King, and E. A. Pessemier, *Applications of the Sciences in Marketing Management* (New York: John Wiley, 1968), p. 252.

21. David A. Aaker, *Managing Brand Equity: Capitalizing on the Value of a Brand Name* (New York: The Free Press, 1991), p. 120; Stuart Agres, *Emotion in Advertising: An Agency's View* (New York: The Marschalk Company, 1986).

22. Glen L. Urban, Philip L. Johnson, and Hohn R. Hauser, "Testing Competitive Market Structures," *Marketing Science* 3 (Spring 1984), pp. 83–112.

23. David A. Aaker, *Managing Brand Equity: Capitalizing on the Value of a Brand Name* (New York: The Free Press, 1991), pp. 123–4.

Suggested Reading

Aaker, David A. *Managing Brand Equity: Capitalizing on the Value of a Brand Name.* New York: The Free Press, 1991.

Atkin, C., and M. Block. "Effectiveness of Celebrity Endorsers." *Journal of Advertising Research,* 23, no. 1 (1983): pp. 57–61.

Burnkrant, Robert E., and Thomas A. Page Jr. "The Structure and Antecedents of the Normative and Attitudinal Components of Fishbein's Theory of Reasoned Action." *Journal of Experimental Social Psychology,* 24 (January 1988): pp. 66–87.

Claiborne, C. B., and M. Joseph Sirgy. "Self-Congruity as a Model of Attitude Formation and Change: Conceptual Review and Guide for Future Research." In *Development in Marketing Science,* vol. 13, edited by B. J. Dunlap, pp. 1–7. Cullowhee, N.C.: Academy of Marketing Science, 1990.

Enrico, Roger. *The Other Guy Blinked.* New York: Bantam Books, 1986.

Fishbein, Martin, and Icek Ajzen. *Belief, Attitude, Intention, and Behavior: An Introduction to Theory and Research.* Reading, MA: Addisson-Wesley, 1975.

Friedman, H. H., and L. Friedman. "Endorser Effectiveness by Product Type." *Journal of Advertising Research,* 19, no. 5 (1979): pp. 63–71.

Ginter, James L. "An Experimental Investigation of Attitude Change and Choice of a New Brand." *Journal of Marketing Research,* 11(February 1974): pp. 30–40.

Guttman, Jonathan. "A Means-End Chain Model Based on Consumer Categorization Processes." *Journal of Marketing* (Spring 1982): pp. 60–72.

Ha, C. Min, and Vern Terpstra. "Country-of-Origin Effects for Uni-National and Bi-National Products." *Journal of International Business Studies* (Summer 1988): p. 242.

Johar, J. S., and M. Joseph Sirgy. "Value-Expressive versus Utilitarian Advertising Appeals: When and Why to Use Which Appeal." *Journal of Advertising,* 20 (September 1991): pp. 23–33.

Kamens, Joseph M., Abdul C. Azhari, et al. "What a Spokesman Does for a Sponsor." *Journal of Advertising Research,* 15, no. 2 (1975): pp. 17–24.

Kamins, Michael A. "An Investigation into the 'Match-Up' Hypothesis in Celebrity Advertising: When Beauty May Be Only Skin Deep." *Journal of Advertising,* 19, no. 1 (1990): pp. 4–13.

Lehmann, Donald R. "Television Show Preference: Application of a Choice Model." *Journal of Marketing Research,* 8 (February 1972): pp. 47–55.

Papadopoulos, N. G., L. A. Heslop, F. Graby, and G. Avlonitis. "Country-of-Origin Matter?" Working Paper, Marketing Science Institute, 1989.

Percy, Larry, and John R. Rossiter. "A Model of Brand Awareness and Brand Attitude Advertising Strategies." *Psychology and Marketing,* 9 (July/Aug. 1992): pp. 263–74.

Ries, Al, and Jack Trout. *Positioning: The Battle for Your Mind.* New York: Warner Books, 1982.

Sirgy, M. Joseph. "Self-Concept in Consumer Behavior: A Critical Review." *Journal of Consumer Research,* 9 (December 1982): pp. 287–300.

Appendix

APPENDIX 5.1: SELECTING IMPORTANT PRODUCT ATTRIBUTES

Marketing communications managers use a variety of models to help them identify those product attributes that may be effective in brand positioning. A popular model, which has been well accepted in marketing, is the *means-end chain model.*[1] This model involves a hierarchical knowledge structure that can be decomposed into attributes, consequences, and values (see Figure A5.1.1).

The model shows that a given brand may have associations that can be categorized in terms of six different levels. The attributes include both concrete and abstract attributes. The consequences can be functional or psychosocial. The values include instrumental and terminal values. A *concrete attribute* involves the cognitive representation of a physical characteristic of the brand. For example, the price of a certain brand of car may be construed as a concrete attribute. An *abstract attribute* involves the abstract representation of one or more concrete attributes. An abstract attribute is more subjective and less perceptual, such as the high quality of the car. A *functional consequence* refers to the extent to which the brand does what it is supposed to do. Does it function as intended? For example, does the car function so as to provide tangible benefits such as performance, safety, and reliability to the consumer? A *psychosocial consequence* refers to the psychological or social costs or benefits associated with the consumption of the brand. For example, does the car make the consumer feel young, feel proud, feel foolish? An *instrumental value* is defined in terms of a preferred mode of conduct. For example, does the car help project a positive image to significant others and help the user gain approval? Other instrumental values may project the image of the consumer as hardworking, independent, imaginative, courageous, forgiving, cheerful, polite, responsible, and so on. A *terminal value* is the preferred end state. For example, does the car enhance one's self-esteem? Self-esteem is an end goal, a terminal value. Other terminal values may include pleasure, comfort, sense of accomplishment, beauty, inner harmony, self-respect, friendship, and happiness.

Figure A5.1.2 shows an example of a mineral water product that is decomposed into a means-end chain "map." Note that the attributes such as the "in-between color," "nonalcoholic," and "not too sweet, less sugar" are all concrete attributes. The meaning nodes of "light taste" and "dry clean taste" may be abstract attributes. Nodes such as "soft drink substitute," "doesn't inhibit ability to concentrate," "strong taste preference," "not bad for me," and "doesn't mask taste of food" are all functional consequences. Cognitions such as "make others feel at ease," "belonging," "sophistication shows good taste," and "personal enjoyment" are all psychosocial consequences. Those related to "social acceptability," "social recognition," "in control," "individualism," "independence," "health," and "achievement" are all instrumental values. Finally the terminal values are "security" and "self-esteem."

FIGURE A5.1.1 The Means-End Chain Model

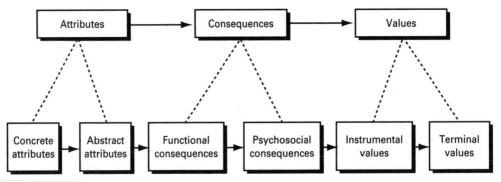

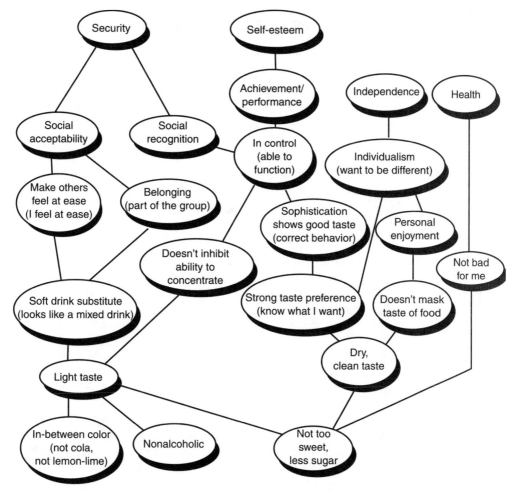

FIGURE A5.1.2 An Example of a Means-End Chain Related to Mineral Water

This model allows the manager to select product attributes that are likely to create or reinforce positive means-end chains. Product attributes that are part of a positive means-end chain are those that lead to positive instrumental and/or terminal values (e.g., good health, self-esteem, social recognition). Once these are identified, the marketer can formulate an entire campaign around the product attributes that are psychologically connected with positive values. For example, looking back at the mineral water example, the marketer knows that "in-between color," "nonalcoholic," and "not too sweet, less sugar" are all attributes associated with the brand, and all have means-end chains connecting to positive personal values. A communications campaign designed to reinforce any one or combination of these attributes may be quite effective.

APPENDIX 5.2: SELECTING MESSAGE CLAIMS THAT ARE COMPETITOR ORIENTED

How do marketing communications managers identify concepts or message claims that are competitor oriented? Many models have been developed for this purpose. Among the popular models is the *ideal point model*.[2] The ideal point model allows the perception of a certain attribute to be compared directly to its ideal point. Suppose we have a brand in question that is pitted against consumers' ideal conception of what the brand should be. The manager of the brand in question would like to assess his/her brand's major strengths and weaknesses as perceived by a certain consumer group and in relation to the ideal conception of what the brand should be, as well as in relation to other brands. The model can be presented as follows:

$$A_o = \sum_{i=1}^{m} W_i \ |I_i - X_i|$$

where $\quad A_o$ = attitude toward Brand (o)

I_i = the "ideal" performance of Brand (o) on attribute dimension (i)

X_i = the belief about the brand's actual performance on attribute dimension (i)

W_i = importance of attribute dimension (i)

Here is an example of a new brand of athletic shoes called Asahi pitted against the leading brand, Reebok. Let us say that the advertiser is considering directing an ad campaign toward mature adults. These are some hypothetical figures for illustrative purposes.

The measure for the importance (I_i) construct can be as follows: "How important is the following criteria in an ideal athletic shoe? How important is price in relation to the other criteria listed below?" The scale used varies from 1 to 10, with 1 being "least important" and 10 being "most important." Each attribute dimension is then represented on a bipolar scale varying from 1 to 10, and the respondents are in-

Attribute Dimension (I)	Importance (W_i)	Ideal Point (I_i)	Reebok (X_i)	Asahi (X_i)
Lo price (1)–hi price (10)	10	5	8	6
Shock absorbency: lo (1)–hi (10)	4	7	6	6
Durability: lo (1)–hi (10)	7	10	7	6
Color/Style: trad.(1)–fash.(10)	6	3	7	3
Comfort: lo (1)–hi (10)	8	10	8	9
Arch support: lo (1)–hi (10)	4	5	9	5
Fastener: velcro (1)–lace (10)	3	8	3	8
Material: canvas (1)–leather (10)	3	2	10	2
Specialty performance: all-purpose (1)–specialty (10)	5	1	10	1
Country of manufacture: made in USA (1)–others (10)	2	1	3	9

structed to locate their ideal point on the bipolar scale and then to indicate their perception of the brands being evaluated on the same scale.

The ideal point (I_i) and the belief (X_i) constructs can be measured as follows:

> Rate your ideal brand along each criterion listed below; then rate how each brand performs along the same criterion. Compare the brands with each other and with the ideal brand while you rate each of them. How do you rate your ideal brand of athletic shoes on price? Locate the ideal point on the scale and mark it with "I." Then, rate Reebok and Asahi with respect to price." Locate where you think Reebok is on the same scale and mark it as "R." Finally, rate Asahi performance on price in the same manner as you did Reebok. Locate where you think Asahi is with respect to price and mark it with an "A." Here is an example:

Low Price _____I_____A_____R_____ High Price
   (around $10)   (around $90)

In this example, the respondent rated his or her ideal brand of athletic shoes as priced toward the low end of the price dimension. Reebok is perceived to be closer to the high price end of the dimension, whereas Asahi is close to the middle of the dimension.

Two strategies can be directly deduced from this model: (1) a strategy addressing the brand's weakness, and (2) a strategy addressing the brand's strengths.

Strategy Addressing the Brand's Weakness

Note that in the example above Asahi was rated more positively than Reebok. The mathematical formulation involves a difference score. Therefore, the lower the score, the more positive the attitude. This analysis allows marketers to assess the strengths and weaknesses of their brand in relation to competitor brands. In the case of Asahi, the advertising strategist knows from inspecting the belief figures (the Bi's) that Asahi is perceived to be weak on two attributes: country of manufacture and durability. The mature adults in the United States seem to place more value on products manufactured in the United States than overseas. This is indicated by a difference score of 8 for Asahi compared to that of 2 for Reebok. In other words, Reebok does much better than Asahi in relation to the ideal point with respect to the country-of-manufacture attribute. Consumers know that Reebok manufactures its shoes in the United States,* while Asahi manufactures its shoes in Asia. However, the importance of this attribute in the overall scheme of things (i.e., the relative contribution of this attribute to the overall attitude toward Asahi) seems negligible. Consequently, the marketer may simply decide not to do anything tangible about this weakness.

With respect to durability, the target consumers perceive Asahi to have a level of durability which is somewhat discrepant from their ideal point (a difference score of 4). Reebok does slightly better in this area (a difference score of 3). Examining the importance weight of the durability attribute, we find that the target consumers believe that this is a relatively important attribute in their overall attitude toward any brand of athletic shoes. Therefore, to remedy the perceptual weaknesses in the Asahi brand, the

---

* Material above is hypothetical and is for illustrative purposes only.

manager is likely to recommend that the R&D people do a better job with respect to durability and come up with a new and improved Asahi model that is highly durable. A claim to high durability can be the basis of a new communications campaign.

Strategy Addressing the Brand's Strength

In the example pertaining to Reebok and Asahi, the reader should note that the Asahi brand also has strengths captured in eight criteria (i.e., Asahi does well on some attributes in relation to the ideal brand of athletic shoes and somewhat better than Reebok too). These strengths involve price, shock absorbency, color/style, comfort, arch support, fastener, material, and specialty performance. However, after examining the importance weight of these criteria, we note that some are more important than others. The criteria that are believed to be highly important in the formation of brand attitude are price and comfort (10 and 8, respectively). Therefore, a communications campaign can be developed to emphasize the brand's strength in relation to the competition—that is, to emphasize that Asahi shoes are very comfortable and low in price.

APPENDIX 5.3: SELECTING THE MOST EFFECTIVE RELATIVE PRICE

Marketing communications managers can use the concept of the *price-quality relationship* to guide them in choosing the most effective relative price. The concept of the price-quality relationship asserts that consumers infer quality as a direct function of price. The higher the price is, the higher the perceived quality. Many consumers believe in such aphorisms as "You get what you pay for."[3]

A typical method used to ascertain the level of perceived quality as a direct function of price is a consumer survey in which a sample of consumers (representative of the target market) is shown a picture of the target product, its price, and a description of the product. Other brands with their respective prices are also shown. Subjects are asked to make inferences about the quality of each brand. Examine the example diagrammed below. The example shows that consumers of hotels and motels make judgments of quality directly based on price. Therefore, a marketer of a certain hotel or motel such as Comfort Inn who would like to position the hotel/motel as having high-quality service may elect to increase its price toward Marriott's prices, and then, through a marketing communications campaign, refer to the new Comfort Inn as a high-quality service organization.

$0/night			$150/night		$300/night
		Comfort Inn			
	Econo Lodge	Holiday Inn	Marriott	Hyatt Omni	
Poor Quality			Moderate Quality		Excellent Quality

APPENDIX 5.4: MEASURING STORE IMAGE

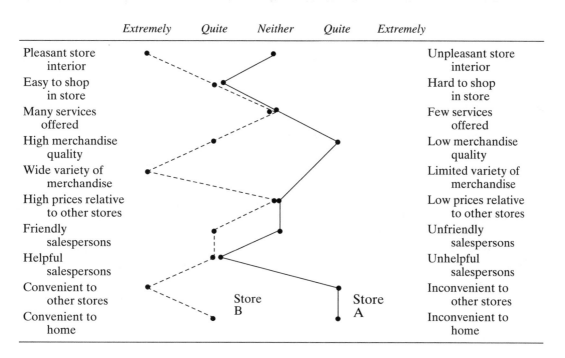

	Extremely	Quite	Neither	Quite	Extremely	
Pleasant store interior						Unpleasant store interior
Easy to shop in store						Hard to shop in store
Many services offered						Few services offered
High merchandise quality						Low merchandise quality
Wide variety of merchandise						Limited variety of merchandise
High prices relative to other stores						Low prices relative to other stores
Friendly salespersons						Unfriendly salespersons
Helpful salespersons						Unhelpful salespersons
Convenient to other stores		Store B		Store A		Inconvenient to other stores
Convenient to home						Inconvenient to home

APPENDIX 5.5: SELECTING AN EFFECTIVE CELEBRITY ENDORSER

Marketing communications managers must try to match the product image, the characteristics of the target market, and the personality or celebrity.[4] That is, consider the example of Candice Bergen as the spokesperson for Sprint. Most consumers associate her with her role on *Murphy Brown* (the popular television show about an independent and defiant TV journalist). The image of Sprint is the independent and defiant long-distance telephone company that is battling it out against AT&T, the monster Goliath, with Sprint being little David. Thus, there is a match between Sprint and Candice Bergen. The question remains: Is there a match between the target market and both Sprint and its spokesperson? It may be argued that this image of the defiant, independent, little guy appeals to a sizable segment of the target market, who see themselves similarly.[5]

APPENDIX 5.6: SELECTING THE MOST EFFECTIVE LOW PRICE

The manager selecting this strategy knows that he or she should price a product at a lower level than the major competitors. But how much lower is the important question. In the literature of the psychology of pricing, marketing researchers have long used a model referred to as the *differential price threshold,* based on the concept of the "just noticeable difference" or (j.n.d.).[6]

The model asserts that the perception of low price is always relative to some referent. This referent may be the original price of the product or the price of a leading competitor's product. Hence, the new price must be advertised in relation to another price. For example, one can position a PC as a bargain by communicating a significant price reduction, say from $2,200 to $1,600. The question is whether consumers are likely to perceive that the reduction from $2,200 to $1,600 is a significant bargain. Would they be willing to buy the PC at that price level? Research is conducted to ascertain consumers' willingness to buy the product at various discount levels. One method divides a representative sample of target consumers into several groups. Each group is asked to indicate their willingness to buy the product given a certain level of price reduction. The results of a hypothetical example are shown as follows:

Price Reductions	Willingness to Buy
from $2,200 to $2,100	30%
from $2,200 to $2,000	32%
from $2,200 to $1,900	35%
from $2,200 to $1,800	36%
from $2,200 to $1,700	57%
from $2,200 to $1,600	62%
from $2,200 to $1,500	65%

As illustrated in the table, given that the product market in question is at least somewhat elastic, willingness to buy normally increases as price reductions increase. However, what marketers look for is the threshold at which there is a significant jump in the willingness to buy. Note that reductions from $2,100 to $1,800 generate small increases in the willingness to buy. However, at $1,700 the willingness to buy increases by a large margin, then stabilizes again with additional price reductions. The manager should select the price level that increases the willingness to buy by a significant margin, and the price here is $1,700. This is the price that exceeds the differential price threshold. Price reductions below that level are said to fall below the differential price threshold. A significant number of the target population perceive buying the PC at $1,700 reduced from $2,220 as a bargain and would be willing to buy at that level.

APPENDIX 5.7: SELECTING IMPORTANT CUSTOMER BENEFITS

How can marketing communications managers identify important customer benefits? Many models have been developed for this purpose. A very popular model that is well accepted in marketing is the *Fishbein model*.[7] This model posits that a brand attitude is a function of the multiplicative product of belief strengths and evaluation weights pertaining to all the attributes that the brand is perceived as possessing. Mathematically formulated,

$$A = \sum_{i=1}^{m} B_i E_i$$

where A = attitude toward the brand
B_i = belief that brand possesses attribute i
E_i = desirability of attribute i

Here is an example concerning a radio station which is planning a marketing communications campaign.

Attribute, i = 1, 2, 3, & 4	B_i	E_i	$B_i \times E_i$
Plays lots of music	+3	+3	+9
Plays lots of commercials	+3	−3	−9
Gives news updates	+1	+1	+1
Has interesting DJs	+2	+3	+6

sum +7

Here is an illustration of how a belief strength about one of the attributes (plays lots of music) can be measured:

Radio station (Brand X) plays lots of music:
 true +3 +2 +1 0 −1 −2 −3 false
The evaluation weight can be measured as follows:
Lots of music is:

very appealing +3 +2 +1 0 −1 −2 −3 not appealing at all
  to me   to me

Let's examine this hypothetical example further. The first thing that the manager should do is to examine the outcome of the belief strengths (Bi's). The figures above show that the target consumers strongly believe (+3) that the radio station in question plays lots of music; they strongly believe (+3) that the radio station plays lots of commercials; moderately believe (+1) that the radio station gives news updates; and moderately-to-strongly believe (+2) that the radio station has interesting DJs. Examining the pattern of the evaluation weights (Ei's), we find that the attribute pertaining to "plays lots of music" seems to be highly desirable (+3) to the target market. "Plays lots of commercials" is found to be highly undesirable (−3). The attribute "gives news updates" is moderately desirable (+1), while the attribute "has interesting DJs" is highly desirable (+3).

At this point the manager should focus on the multiplicative product of the B_i's and E_i's and try to understand the station's strengths versus weaknesses. There are two attributes that require the strategist's attention. These are the attributes of "plays lots of music" and "plays lots of commercials." Scores for the former are very positive (an area of strength), while those for the latter are very negative (area of weakness). The manager may decide to capitalize on areas of strength, correct areas of weakness, or do both. In this case, the manager may decide to recommend to upper management that the radio station should decrease its commercials (possibly through playing the commercials in major blocks of time rather than having the commercials dispersed intermittently throughout the program). Also, the manager may recommend to either replace the current DJs with more "interesting" ones or instruct the current DJs to do certain things to come across as more "interesting" to target listeners. With these recommendations approved, the manager can launch a communications campaign playing up the virtues of the radio station: that it plays lots of music, that it has decreased commercial interruptions of music programming, and that now the station's DJs are more "interesting."

APPENDIX 5.8: SELECTING IMPORTANT USER/CUSTOMER IMAGES

How can marketing communications managers identify product user images that are effective in positioning their brand in the minds of a target market? Over the years, marketers have adopted a popular model called the *self-image congruence model*. This model is based on the cognitive matching between value-expressive attributes of a given brand and the consumer self-concept.[8] There are four types of matching between the brand-user image and the consumer self-concept. These are: actual self-congruity, ideal self-congruity, social self-congruity, and ideal social self-congruity (see Figure A5.8.1.)

Actual self-congruity involves the match between the brand-user image and the actual self-image of the consumer. The brand-user image involves stereotypical beliefs about the typical user of a certain product brand. For example, many believe that owners or drivers of jeep-type automobiles, such as the Jeep, are "outdoorsy types"; drivers of vans, such as the Dodge Astro, are "family-types"; drivers of sports cars, such as the Corvette, are "young, rich, and outgoing-types"; drivers of a car such as the Honda Civic are "single, young, and economy-minded." The actual self-image, on the other hand, is the belief about one's self in direct relation to the brand-user image. In other words, when a consumer is exposed to a car such as the Corvette, he or she conjures up the image of the typical person who would drive such a car—"young, rich, and outgoing." This is the brand-user image. Then the consumer asks himself or herself, "Am I the young, rich, and outgoing type?" The answer may be, "Yes, indeed, I am the young, rich, and outgoing type." This response reflects the actual self-image of the consumer. Or, the actual self-image, perhaps, may be: "No, I am far from being young, rich, and outgoing." Therefore, consumer self-concept researchers refer to a

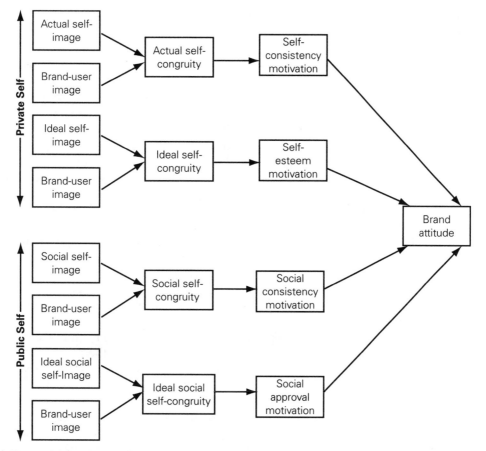

Figure A5.8.1 The Self-Image Congruence Model

high actual self-congruity as a match between the brand-user image and the actual self-image of target consumers. Conversely, a low actual self-congruity is a mismatch between the brand-user image and the actual self-image.

Consumer self-concept researchers explain that a state of high actual self-congruity contributes to a positive attitude toward the brand, while low actual self-congruity contributes to a negative brand attitude. This is because consumers are motivated to purchase products and brands that reinforce their conceptions of themselves and personal identities. Psychologists refer to this motivational state as *self-consistency*. In other words, people are motivated to hold favorable attitudes about objects, persons, and events that are consistent with their actual self-image. By doing so, people preserve and enhance the integrity of their belief system regarding themselves. Without a coherent and integrated belief system about the self, the individual cannot function effectively.

Ideal self-congruity refers to the match or mismatch between the brand-user image and the consumer's ideal self-image. In other words, the consumer compares the brand-user image with the image he or she would like to have (aspirational goal). For example, a consumer examining a Corvette thinks, "The person who typically would drive a car like this is young, rich, and outgoing, and I would like to feel young, rich and outgoing." Here we have a match between the brand-user image and the consumer's ideal self-image (high ideal self-congruity). In this case, the consumer is likely to form a favorable attitude toward the brand. Ideal-self-congruity is motivated by the need for *self-esteem*. In other words, people are motivated to hold positive attitudes toward objects, persons, and events when these objects, persons, and events are likely to be perceived as self-enhancing—that is, they serve to move the person's actual self-image one step closer to his or her ideal self-image.

Social self-congruity involves a comparison between the brand-user image and the consumer's social self-image. The social self-image is the image that one believes others have of oneself. For example, a man may evaluate a certain kind of charity organization, such as the American Heart Association. He realizes that his friends know that he contributed generously to the American Heart Association after his heart attack several years ago. In other words, this person has a social self-image of "I am known to contribute to the American Heart Association." This is his social self-image. He may also think that people with his reputation contribute to the American Heart Association. Here we have a case of high social self-congruity—a good match between the brand-user image and the social self-image. High social self-congruity is likely to significantly contribute to a positive attitude about the object under evaluation. This occurs because people are motivated by what social psychologists refer to as the *social consistency* motive, the drive to form a positive disposition toward objects, persons, and events that are likely to confirm one's view of oneself in the eyes of significant others.

Finally, *ideal social self-congruity* involves a match or mismatch between the brand-user image and the consumer's ideal social self-image. The ideal social self-image is defined as the image one would like to attain for *social approval* reasons. For example, a woman might belong to an environmental organization such as the Sierra Club. Within the Sierra Club, she is surrounded by significant others whose approval and disapproval matter a great deal. Therefore, if a brand has an environmental type of image, the consumer is likely to hold a favorable attitude toward it because her reference group is likely to express approval of this behavior.

Two major strategies can be employed to position a product through user or customer image: the passive strategy and the active strategy.

The Passive Strategy

This strategy calls for focusing on the brand-user population. The manager conducts research to ascertain the brand-user image and the actual users' self-concept (actual, ideal, social, and ideal social self-image). If the research uncovers that the brand users have distinct perceptions of the brand-user image and this image is consistent with one or more of the brand users' self-images (actual, ideal, social, and/or ideal social self-image), then a marketing communications campaign can be planned to reinforce this congruity and to appeal to new consumers who have comparable self-images.

For example, suppose we are dealing with a certain automobile, and we find out from market research that those who have already bought it are the college-student types (young, liberal, and thrifty). The research shows that the owners perceive that the typical person who drives this brand of car is a college student who is young, liberal, and thrifty. They also acknowledge that they see themselves the same way. They regard this image as ideal; others see them that way, and they like others to see them that way. A marketing communications campaign should be launched in which the image of the brand user is young, liberal, and thrifty; thus, it will appeal to potential car buyers who have actual, ideal, social, and ideal social self-images that are young, liberal, and thrifty.

The Active Strategy

The passive approach to identifying the user or customer images assumes that the brand is not a new brand and that it has some following. However, what happens with new brands that are trying to penetrate an existing market? Certainly the manager does not have the luxury of doing research to uncover the image attributes that have created self-congruity in the brand-user population. Here, the marketer should consider the active approach to identifying a user/customer image. The active approach entails developing alternative scenarios of brand-user images. For example, the manager who is trying to penetrate the watch market with a new brand of watches needs to conduct research to ascertain self-image congruence for the competitor brands. This kind of research is likely to uncover strategic gaps. Perhaps competitor Brand A appeals to those who have a self-image of themselves of being young and thrifty; Brand B appeals to those who have a self-image of themselves as being professional; and Brand C appeals to those with a self-image of affluence. If the manager of a new brand knows what kind of self-image watch owners in general have, and what competitor brand is appealing to whom with what self-image, the manager then can identify gaps, niches, or areas in which to compete head-on with certain brands.

Notes

1. Jonathan Guttman, "A Means-End Chain Model Based on Consumer Categorization Processes," *Journal of Marketing* (Spring 1982), pp. 60–72; Jonathan Guttman and Thomas J. Reynolds, "An Investigation of the Levels of Cognitive Abstraction Utilized by Consumers in Product Differentiation," in *Attitude Research Under the Sun*, edited by J. Eighemy (Chicago: American Marketing Association, 1979), pp. 125–50; Jerry C. Olson and Thomas J. Reynolds, "Understanding Consumers' Cognitive Structures: Implications for Marketing Strategy," in *Advertising and Consumer Psychology*, edited by L. Percy and A. G. Woodside (Lexington, Mass.: Lexington Books, 1983), pp. 77–90.

2. James L. Ginter. "An Experimental Investigation of Attitude Change and Choice of a New Brand," *Journal of Marketing Research* 11 (February 1974), pp. 30–40; Donald R. Lehmann, "Television Show Preference: Application of a Choice Model," *Journal of Marketing Research* 8 (February 1971), pp. 47–55.

3. Douglas J. McConnel, "Effect of Pricing on the Perception of Quality," *Journal of Applied Psychology* (August 1968), pp. 331–4.

4. J. Forkan, "Product Matchup Key to Effective Star Presentations," *Advertising Age* (October 6, 1980), p. 42; Michael A. Kamins, "An Investigation into the 'Match-up Hypothesis' in Celebrity Advertising," *Journal of Advertising* 19, no. 1 (1990), pp. 4–13.

5. Grant McCracken, "Who Is the Celebrity Endorser? Cultural Foundations of the Endorsement Process," *Journal of Consumer Research* 16, no. 3 (December 1988), pp. 310–21.

6. Bruce Buchanan, Moshe Givon, and Arieh Goldman, "Measurement of Discrimination Ability in Taste Tests: An Empirical Investigation," *Journal of Marketing Research* 24, (May 1987), pp. 154–63.

7. Martin Fishbein, "An Investigation of the Relationship Between Beliefs About an Object and the Attitude Toward That Object," *Human Relations* 16 (1963), pp. 233–40.

8. M. Joseph Sirgy, "Self-Concept in Consumer Behavior: A Critical Review," *Journal of Consumer Research* 9 (December 1982), pp. 287–300; M. Joseph Sirgy, "Self-Image/Product-Image Congruity and Consumer Decision Making," *International Journal of Management* 2 (December 1985), pp. 49–63; C. B. Claiborne and M. Joseph Sirgy, "Self-Congruity as a Model of Attitude Formation and Change: Conceptual Review and Guide for Future Research," in *Developments in Marketing Science* 13, edited by B. J. Dunlap (Cullowhee, N.C.: Academy of Marketing Science, 1990), pp. 1–7.

CHAPTER 6

Marketing Communications Strategies and Tactics

Consider the following scenario: The Discovery Channel—a TV channel associated with learning—has been cultivated to the point that it now ranks No. 2 among cable media brands in terms of consumer recognition. This has come about as a direct result of a large marketing communications budget, $20 million annually. Chris Moseley, senior VP for marketing and communications of the Discovery Channel, devised an effective marketing communications strategy that involved a mix of communications elements from using moving LED signs on telephone kiosks and using the new multimedia, theatrical, and even retail venues to making buys on competing cable channels.[1] The Discovery Channel is an example of how diverse elements of marketing communications can be integrated effectively to meet marketing objectives such as brand association.

In contrast, IBM had a problem a few years back. It was advertising in 24 magazines, and each ad presented a different image of the IBM Corp. To correct this problem, Abby Kohnstamm, IBM's VP for corporate marketing, fired some 80 ad agencies around the globe and gave its account to Ogilvy & Mather Worldwide. Ms. Kohnstamm also unified the look of the company's packaging and brochures. She pulled together the scattered booths of IBM divisions at trade shows to present a consistent image of IBM. The goal has yet to be reached, however, to create a unified image of IBM. To meet this challenge, the various elements of marketing communications must be integrated, and the disparate communications must be viewed as components of a system.[2]

These two scenarios exemplify the challenges of making marketing communications decisions and integrating these decisions into the big picture. This chapter sensitizes the reader to this awesome challenge. Specifically, this chapter introduces the reader to marketing communications decisions. Having gotten a good feel for corporate and marketing strategy and tactics, the reader is now ready to appreciate how marketing communications decisions can be effectively made in light of corporate and marketing decisions. Like corporate and marketing decisions, marketing communications decisions involve selecting a marketing communications strategy, determining the optimal marketing communications mix to implement the strategy, setting concrete and quantifiable marketing communications objectives that reflect the overall thrust of the strategy and tactics, allocating resources for the marketing communications mix, and engaging in monitoring and control to ensure the strategy's effectiveness over time. In this chapter, we'll concentrate only on marketing communications strategy and tactics. The topics of objectives, budget, analysis and planning, and monitoring and control are relegated to the third and fourth third part of the book and will be discussed in some detail there (see Figure 6.1).

STRATEGIES AND TACTICS RELATED TO MARKETING COMMUNICATIONS

In one of his recent *Marketing News* columns, Professor Schultz gave advice to marketing communications practitioners as to how to allocate expenditures across the various elements of the marketing communication mix (e.g., advertising, PR, sales promotion, and direct marketing). He advised practitioners to have the customers determine the value of these different communication elements. That is, practitioners should ask customers and prospects how they would like to receive information or materials.[3] He used Lexus as an example of this selection strategy. When a person purchases a Lexus, a short questionnaire asks how he or she would like to receive information. Through direct mail? Through a phone call from the dealership? Should a phone call be directed to the home or to the office? And if so, what are the most convenient times? And so on. The idea here is to let the customer or prospect tell you and to use this customer/prospect input to select the appropriate mix of marketing communication tools. Although this selection method is highly intuitive and plausible, it ignores corporate, marketing, and marketing communications strategies and objectives. Our position is that the elements of the marketing communications mix should be assembled as a direct function of marketing communications strategy (informative, affective, habit formation, and self-satisfaction), which in turn is guided by marketing strategy (differentiation, cost leadership, and focus), which in turn is guided by corporate strategy (grow, maintain position, harvest, innovate, and divest). In this section, we will show how specific elements of the marketing communications mix go hand-in-hand with certain marketing communications strategies, which in turn are selected to meet marketing and corporate goals.

The various communications strategies, their tactics, and objectives are all shown in Table 6.1. The table shows four marketing communications strategies, namely, informative ("thinker"), affective ("feeler"), habit formation ("doer"), and self-satisfaction ("reactor"). These strategies are borrowed (and adapted) from a popular and well-established model in advertising called the Foote-Cone-Belding (FCB) planning model.[4] This model was first envisioned in the context of advertising, but I believe it is applicable to marketing communications at large.

THE INFORMATIVE (THINKER) STRATEGY TACTICS

An *informative (thinker) strategy* seeks to expose target consumers to the messages and to educate them about a product's important costs and/or benefits. For example, a firm selling lofts (a high bed that stands on four poles, so that a desk, for example, may be placed under the bed) to college students at the beginning of the fall semester

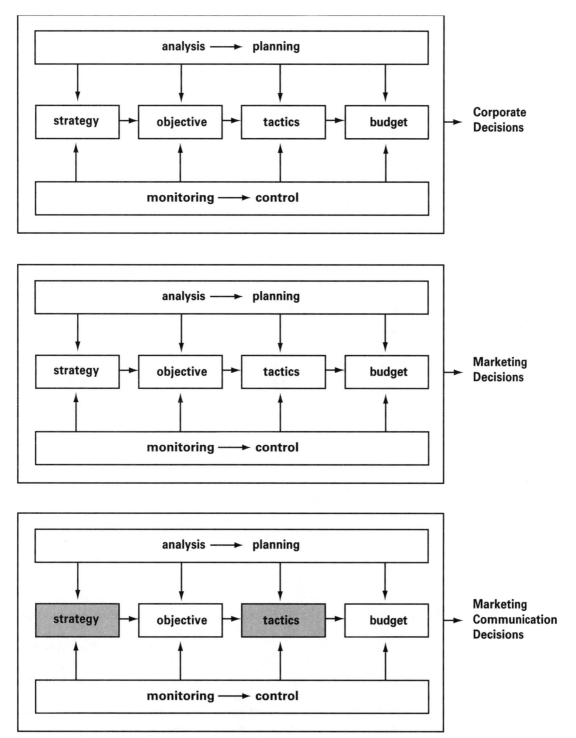

FIGURE 6.1 Marketing Communications Strategy and Tactics

TABLE 6.1 Marketing Communications Strategies, Tactics, and Objectives

Strategy	Tactics (strategic mix)	Objectives
Informative (thinker)	Advertising (mostly print) Reseller support (training & trade shows) Public relations (press release & publicity) WOM Communications (stimulating WOM through advertising & sampling, referral system)	Generate maximum brand awareness and learning
Affective (feeler)	Advertising (mostly broadcast) Reseller support (cooperative advertising) Public relations (press conference, corporate advertising, & event sponsorship) WOM Communications (simulating WOM through advertising)	Generate maximum brand awareness and positive attitude (liking)
Habit Formation (doer)	Advertising (mostly print & interactive) Direct marketing (direct mail, newsletter, direct response advertising) Sales promotion (coupons, sampling, refunds & rebates, bonus packs, & price-off deals) Reseller support (trade allowances) Public relations (publicity)	Induce trial purchase and learning from product use (first-time users) and reinforce learning (repeat users)
Self-Satisfaction (reactor)	Advertising (outdoor & specialty) Direct marketing (catalogs, direct response advertising, telemarketing, & direct selling) Sales promotion (premiums & contests sweepstakes) Reseller support (contests & incentives, in-store advertising, POP displays, & personal selling) Public relations (corporate advertising, event sponsorship, & placement of product in movies & TV)	Induce trial purchase and brand liking from product use (first-time users) and reinforce positive attitude (repeat users)

might launch a marketing communications campaign with the objectives of making students aware of the availability of these lofts and educating them about the benefits of buying a loft instead of a regular bed.

Once the marketing communications manager selects a marketing communications strategy, the elements of the communications mix have to be assembled. Table 6.1 shows elements of the marketing communications mix that can be effectively employed to meet the requirements of the informative (thinker) strategy, namely advertising, reseller support, public relations, and word-of-mouth (WOM) communications. These communications tools help achieve the maximum brand awareness and learning possible. The other elements of the marketing communications mix (direct marketing and sales promotion) are not likely to be as effective.

Now the question is how to implement the informative (thinker) strategy through each of the recommended elements of the communications mix, starting with advertising.

Advertising

Advertising is a marketing communications tool that focuses on the mass media. That is, messages are placed in impersonal types of media such as television, radio, newspapers, and magazines, among others. Advertising is an excellent communications tool to generate the highest possible brand awareness. To accomplish this, the marketing communications manager should select the appropriate mix of media categories (intermedia selection) and the appropriate mix of media vehicles (intramedia selection), then compute the net reach of the media schedule and adjust the media components to achieve the maximum reach.

Intermedia Selection

Examine Table 6.2. This table shows advertising to involve the use of a variety of media. The major media include television, radio, newspapers, magazines, outdoor, and transit, among others. Within each medium are different forms of media. For example, within television, there are various types of media such as network, spot, local, and syndicated TV programs.

TABLE 6.2 List of Advertising Media Categories

TV advertising
  Network TV
  Spot TV
  Local TV
  Cable TV
Radio advertising
  Network radio
  Spot radio
  Local radio
    Regular :30/:60 ads
    Live/On-site advertising
Newspaper advertising
  National and daily newspapers
    Display advertising
    Classified advertising
    Reading notice
    Inserts
    Supplements
  Weekly newspapers
  Special audience newspapers
Magazine advertising
  International and national magazines
    Consumer magazines
      Regular print ad (b&w/4c, different sizes)
      Back cover (inside of front/back cover)
      Fold-out
      Talking ads (5-second play)
      Anaglyphic images (3-dimensional materials that are viewed w/colored glasses)
      Lenticular images (color images printed on finely corrugated plastic
        that seem to move when tilted)
      Singing ads
      Heat/Pressure-sensitive ink (images that change color on contact)   *(continued)*

TABLE 6.2 List of Advertising Media Categories

Business magazines
   Regular print ad (b&w/4c, different sizes)
   Back cover (inside of front/back cover)
   Fold-out
   Talking ads (5-second play)
  Farm magazines
   Regular print ad (b&w/4c, different sizes)
   Back cover (inside of front/back cover)
   Fold-out
  Academic and trade journals
   Regular print ad (b&w/4c, different sizes)
   Back cover (inside of front/back cover)
   Fold-out
 Regional magazines
  Regular print ad (b&w/4c, different sizes)
  Back cover (inside of front/back cover)
  Fold-out
Out-of-home advertising
  Outdoor advertising
   National and local outdoor advertising
    Poster panels
    Painted bulletins
    Spectaculars
  Transit advertising
   Mobile advertising
    Inside cards
    Outside posters
    Taxi exteriors
   Immobile advertising (station/terminal posters)
  Aerial advertising
  Mobile billboards
  Miscellaneous outdoor media (e.g., parking meters, automatic teller machines, trash cans, ski
    lift poles, restroom walls, public phones)
Specialty advertising
Directory advertising
  Yellow pages advertising
  Specialized directories
Interactive advertising
In-store advertising
In-flight advertising
Movie theater advertising
Videotape advertising

Factors that influence intermedia selection are divided into two groups: "eliminating criteria" and "discriminating criteria." The manager has to consider the eliminating criteria first to eliminate media categories that do not meet the company's requirements and then make discriminating judgments among the remaining media categories (see Table 6.3).

Eliminating criteria include attribute sensory modality, production flexibility, absolute cost, geographic selectivity, and legal requirements. *Attribute sensory modality*

TABLE 6.3 Criteria for Selecting among Advertising Media Categories as a Way to Implement the Aware Strategy

Eliminating Criteria	Discriminating Criteria
Attribute sensory modality	Media habits
Production flexibility	Media selectivity
Absolute cost	Seasonal usage in media
Geographic selectivity	Ethical considerations
Legal requirements	

refers to the sensory component associated with information processing of a particular medium. Certain messages have to be communicated in a medium with a certain sensory modality. The sensory modalities of TV, for example, are greater than those of radio, newspapers, or magazines because TV relies on the visual (dynamic) and auditory sensory modalities. Radio strictly relies on the auditory sensory modality, while newspapers and magazines rely on the visual (static) modality. Even newspapers and magazines differ in sensory modality in that newspapers rely mostly on black and white photography (or dull colors), while magazines use glossy colors. For example, if one is trying to advertise a graphics software program, one needs to select an advertising medium that allows the display of color graphics in the most vivid way possible. The sensory modalities of television, magazines, and outdoor advertising may fit the message requirements of this product. Newspapers and radio advertising may be easily ruled out.

Another possible eliminating criterion is *production flexibility*. In many cases managers do not have the luxury of time. They may be forced to select certain media simply as a function of production flexibility. Radio advertising is the most flexible, timewise, followed by newspaper advertising. Outdoor, magazine, and TV placements are usually the least flexible. Magazines have "closing dates"—dates by which the ad must arrive at the publisher to make a particular issue—sometimes eight weeks ahead of the "cover date," or the time when the issue actually goes on sale.

With respect to *absolute cost*, in many cases managers do not have the luxury of a large media budget, and, therefore, they are forced to select certain media simply as a function of absolute cost. For example, placing an ad on network TV usually requires a large media budget. Newspaper and radio can be selected with a meager budget. Table 6.4 shows some figures to give the reader a sense of typical unit costs in national advertising.

The manager considers not only the absolute cost of media but also the production costs within the different media categories. Production costs do not include the cost of running an ad. Costs incurred in producing an ad may include hiring actors and directors for TV ads, paying copy editors for magazine and newspaper ads, and so on. For example, a 30-second commercial on prime time network TV costs about $100,000 to produce, while a one-page four-color ad in *Readers Digest* takes at $104,600. Alternatively, an advertiser can produce ads for cable TV, radio, or local newspaper at a very small fraction of those costs. An ad on cable, for example, may cost only $250 to produce.[5]

What about *geographic selectivity* as an eliminating criterion? In many cases managers are constrained to promote the assigned product within a specific geo-

TABLE 6.4 Typical Unit Costs in National Advertising

TV (network)	=	$90,000/:30 spot
TV (spot)	=	$50,000/:30 spot
TV (cable)	=	$2,000/:30 spot
Radio (network)	=	$3,000/:60 spot
Radio (spot)	=	$8,000/:60 spot
Newspapers (national)	=	$48,000/1-page ad
Newspaper (local)	=	N/A
Newspapers (supplement)	=	$200,000/1-page insert
Magazines (consumer)	=	$75,000/1-page ad
Magazines (business)	=	$10,000+/1-page ad
Magazines (farm)	=	$5,000+/1-page ad

graphic territory. Hence, they are forced to select certain media categories that target the chosen area. In this situation, placing an ad on network TV is inconceivable not only because it usually requires a large media budget but also because it provides more coverage than is needed. For example, suppose a marketing communications manager is trying to promote a new brand of ice cream that is presently being distributed within a 300-mile radius from the manufacturer's location. This marketing communications manager is necessarily constrained to use specific media categories such as spot TV, cable TV, spot radio, local newspapers, regional editions of consumer magazines, regional magazines, and outdoor media.

What about *legal requirements?* In some cases, marketing communications managers are automatically constrained by legal rulings or laws prohibiting the use of certain media. For example, tobacco companies are prohibited by law from advertising on TV, period.

Once the eliminating criteria have been evaluated, the discriminating criteria must be examined. One of the most important factors in selecting media categories to implement the informative (thinker) strategy is media habits. The term *media habits* refers to the extent to which a certain audience is exposed to a particular media category. Some people tend to watch TV more than others. Some listen to the radio more than others. Some subscribe to magazines, while others don't. Usually, secondary data sources such as Simmons provide data about consumers' media habits.

Another important discriminating factor is *media selectivity*. Media selectivity refers to the extent to which a particular media category targets a specific or unique audience that can be clearly identified demographically and/or psychographically. If the marketing communications manager is dealing with a general audience (e.g., all adults), then nonselective media such as network TV, newspapers, newspaper supplements, and outdoor advertising are appropriate. However, if the marketing communications manager is trying to reach a highly select target market that can be clearly identified demographically or psychographically, then magazines and cable TV are likely to be better choices since specific media vehicles within magazines or cable TV can match the demographic or psychographic profile of the target market.

Still another important discriminating factor in intermedia selection is *seasonal usage in media*. Different media categories are used more or less frequently at certain times of the year. For example, most people watch network TV during fall and early spring. TV network viewing declines in late spring and the summer months. The opposite is true for radio. Radio listenership peaks in the summer months. Advertisers (such as retailers) who direct their ad campaigns to general audiences usually consider the seasonal usage of specific media. To maximize their reach, they advertise heavily on network TV during the fall and winter seasons and switch to radio and magazines in the summer months.

Finally, the advertiser may consider any *ethical* ramifications of using a specific media. Some products or ads may irritate or offend the general public. Examples include feminine hygiene products, medicinal products such as hemorrhoid medicines, contraceptives such as condoms, liquor and cigarette ads, and ads with strong sexual overtones. Marketing communications managers of products that are likely to offend certain people are advised not to use general media, such as network TV or outdoor advertising. They should use those media that are targeted to certain populations, thereby reducing the extent of spillover to the general population.

The previous discussion covered the implementation of the informative (thinker) strategy through advertising only in relation to brand awareness and learning—specifically, how advertising media categories and vehicles can be selected to maximize awareness. In relation to *intermedia* selection, a set of eliminating and discriminating criteria was introduced. These same criteria apply also to brand learning and knowledge. The informative (thinker) strategy guides the marketing communications manager in selecting a media category that lends itself to an informational message. Audience learning is maximized if the informational message is placed in a print medium. When target consumers are likely to demand more information, then it is imperative to place the ad in a print medium rather than a broadcast medium. The print media allow marketing communications managers to design ads with much information.

Intramedia Selection

Once the broader advertising media categories are selected (network TV, spot TV, local TV, cable TV, network radio, and so on), the marketing communications manager now has to select specific media vehicles within the broader range of media categories. For example, if network TV is selected, then the next question is, Which network TV programs should be selected to maximize reach? Since there is a large pool of media vehicles within a media category, the marketing communications manager must choose a manageable set of media vehicles. How can this be done? By using a set of eliminating criteria, such as media ratings and cost per thousand.

With respect to *media ratings*, media vehicles are usually rated by rating services such as Neilson and Arbitron. Typical ratings are stated as a percentage of the target market. For example, *60 Minutes* on CBS may have a rating of 20. This means that 20% of those who watch TV between 7 and 8 p.m. or Sunday evenings watch this program. Secondary data pertaining to media ratings can be easily obtained through Standard Rate and Data Service (SRDS).

In addition to media ratings, marketing communications managers compute a *cost-per-thousand* (CPM) of a variety of possible vehicles and select vehicles that are found to have low CPMs. Thus, a CPM figure of a certain vehicle denotes its cost in reaching a thousand people. The precise CPM index is computed as follows:

$$\text{CPM (media vehicle } Z) = \frac{\text{Cost of one ad insertion} \times 1,000}{\text{Population} \times \text{\% exposed to media}}$$
$$\text{vehicle } Z \text{ of target consumers}$$

For example, what is the CPM of the following three magazines? The cost of a four-color ad is $108,800 in *Readers Digest* (RD), $89,300 for *TV Guide* (TVG), and $69,245 for *Good Housekeeping* (GH). Suppose that we are interested in the adult women population in the United States that totals approximately 100,000,000. The ratings of these three magazines are 26.6, 25.4, and 20.8. (among adult women). Therefore:

$$\text{CPM (RD)} = (\$108,800 \times 1,000) / (100,000,000 \times 0.266) = \$4.09$$
$$\text{CPM (TVG)} = (\$89,300 \times 1,000) / (100,000,000 \times 0.254) = \$3.52$$
$$\text{CPM (GH)} = (\$69,245 \times 1,000) / (100,000,000 \times 0.208) = \$3.33$$

As we see from the CPM figures of the three potential media vehicles, *Good Housekeeping* magazine is the most cost-efficient. The second most cost-efficient vehicle is *TV Guide*, and the third is *Readers Digest*.

Remember that *brand awareness/learning* is the marketing communications goal. In making an *intramedia* selection, the marketing communications manager should consider two additional factors, namely the *image of the media vehicle* and its *attention level*. To effect maximum learning, the selected media vehicles have to be perceived as credible. Lack of media credibility affects message credibility, which in turn affects message acceptance. For example, consider placing a political message in a tabloid magazine such as the *National Enquirer*. The *National Enquirer* is perceived as a magazine that exploits sensationalism and would not hesitate to print stories and accounts based on fiction rather than fact. Placing a political message in such a media vehicle is likely to render the message incredible. Furthermore, for learning to take place, the audience has to attend to the vehicle and its programming (or editorial) content. Some media vehicles may have high rating points but low attention levels. Compare *CBS Evening News* to the *Late Show*. Most people tend to be attentive while watching the news, but they are getting ready to go to bed while watching the *Late Show*. One program draws a high level of attention; the other doesn't. As a result, learning is likely to be enhanced for ads in media vehicles that command high levels of attention. Market research services such as Simmons provide data concerning attention levels of national television programs.

Computing the Net Reach of the Media Mix and Making Adjustments

Now the question becomes, How do we compute the combined reach of the selected media vehicles? See Table 6.5.

The table shows a hypothetical example of three media vehicles and their combined reach. Three media vehicles are proposed (X, Y, and Z). Vehicle X is estimated to reach 8,000, while vehicles Y and Z reach 5,000 and 3,000, respectively. Therefore, the combined vehicles can reach a *gross audience* of 16,000 (8,000 + 5,000 + 3,000) and

TABLE 6.5   How to Compute Net Reach of a Number of Media Vehicles

Media Vehicle	Audience Figure	Paired Audience	Net Ratio	Cumulative Net Ratio	Net Added
X	8,000				8,000
Y	5,000	1,000 (Y + X)	.8	.8	4,000
Z	3,000	500 (Z + X)	.83		
		700 (Z + Y)	.77		
				.64	1,900
	16,000				13,900

Total market = 20,000
Gross audience = 16,000
Gross reach = 16,000/20,000 = .8 or 80%
Net audience = 13,900
Net reach = 13,900/20,000 = .7 or 70%

the *gross reach* is 80% (16,000 consumers reached by the combined vehicles out of 20,000 consumers in the target market).

We refer to the 16,000 reach as gross audience because this estimate does not take into account the duplication between/among the different vehicles. For example, the table shows that 1,000 consumers are likely to be exposed to both X and Y vehicles. This is called a *paired audience*. So the goal here is to start by figuring out the reach from a certain vehicle (Vehicle X). Then we account for the duplication between the reach of that vehicle (Vehicle X) and another program (Vehicle Y). Then we add the extent of unduplicated reach of the other vehicle (Vehicle Y) to the reach of the base program (Vehicle X). We do this by first estimating the paired audience and then by obtaining a *net ratio*, which is the audience figure of the other vehicle (Vehicle Y), minus the paired audience, divided by the audience figure. The example in the table shows that Vehicle X reaches 8,000 target consumers. Vehicle Y reaches 80% of 5,000 consumers who cannot be reached through Vehicle X. Therefore, the net added audience of Vehicle Y is 4,000 consumers.

Now let's count the added reach of Vehicle Z after taking into account the paired audience (or duplication) between Vehicle Z and the two preceding vehicles (X and Y). In this case, we have to partial out the duplication between Z and Y and Z and X. That means we need to estimate the net ratio of both $Z + X$ and $Z + Y$, and then get the cumulative net ratio of these two by multiplying them. Once the cumulative net ratio is obtained, then the net added reach of Z (after partialling out the duplication between Z and X and between Z and Y) becomes the cumulative net ratio times the audience figure pertaining to Z alone. This figure is 1,900. Therefore, the net audience reached by the combined media vehicles is 13,900 (8,000 + 4,000 + 1,900). Dividing this figure by the estimate of the total market (20,000) produces the net reach, which is 70% (13,900/20,000). That is, the combined effects of these three vehicles reach 70% of the target consumers. Assume that vehicles X, Y, and Z are three different magazines. By accounting for the individual effects of these programs, we may be misled into believing that the total reach of these three vehicles is 16,000, or 80% of the total market. However, after partialling out the duplication among the three vehicles, the marketing communications manager can accurately calculate that the ad reaches 13,900 (or 70%) of the target market, not 16,000 (or 80%) as originally postulated. The goal of this exercise is to put together a set of media vehicles that is likely to maximize net reach—that is, reach the most people in the target market. The questions then become, "Is 70% reach good enough?" "Can the marketing communications manager do any better through an alternative set of vehicles? "If so, which vehicles might these be?"

The reader may wonder where these estimates come from. The audience figures pertaining to each vehicle are derived by analyzing the individual vehicles. The paired audience figures are estimated through primary or secondary research. A marketing communications manager does primary research on his or her own for the specific purpose of deriving these estimates. Secondary research is conducted by research firms and sold to whoever needs the data. Examples of secondary data include the data from Nielsen, Simmons, MarketFacts, and Arbitron, among others. Thus, to compute the net reach of a set of media vehicles, the marketing communications manager needs to have estimates of the audience reached by each individual vehicle and the duplication between each pair of vehicles. The rest of the figures shown in Table 6.5 are arithmetic derivations.

Creative Aspects in Advertising

To achieve maximum brand awareness, certain creative decisions have to be made. The most important decision is to select the kind of advertising that draws audience attention. For example, in network television, the marketing communications manager should be very creative in developing an ad that can capture attention, that can stand out from the clutter of other advertising. This may be done through an emotional appeal or possibly an out-of-the-ordinary concept or event. Radio advertising must likewise draw attention. Radio has a unique tool—live/on-site advertising. This method of advertising is very powerful in drawing attention and creating brand awareness. In newspaper advertising, the use of provocative display ads can do the trick. Classified advertising, reading notices, inserts, and supplements are less likely to be as effective. In magazine advertising, the use of back cover ads, fold-outs, talking ads, anaglyphic images (images of ornaments sculptured or embossed in low relief, as a cameo), lenticular images (images that are biconvex), singing ads, and heat- or pressure-sensitive ink are all methods that can capture readers' attention. Similarly, in outdoor advertising, the use of spectaculars (large-scale displays) can be very effective in creating brand awareness. Transit advertising has to be very creative to draw attention. Aerial advertising and mobile billboards are likely to draw attention by the mere fact that they are out of the ordinary. Similarly, any new form of advertising placed in a new, unfamiliar media is likely to draw attention and create brand awareness. Therefore, marketing communications managers seeking to create maximal brand awareness should be very creative in their advertising efforts because the greater the creativity, the higher the brand awareness.

When the goal is brand learning, creativity plays a different role. Here the ad has to be designed to be informative, rational, and utilitarian. The novelty and emotional aspects of the ad should draw attention, but much of the copy should be informative. An ad that is too emotional should not be used, because it may distract the audience from the true goal—fully processing the content of the message.

Reseller Support

Reseller support is a marketing communications tool that is directed to "resellers" or distributors. It is also known as "trade promotion." Table 6.6 shows a listing of the various elements or tools involved in reseller support. These tools are used only by business-to-business marketing communications managers or manufacturer-to-retailer promotions and include contests and incentives, trade allowances, in-store displays and point-of-purchase materials, training programs, trade shows, and cooperative advertising. Not all these reseller support tools effectively implement the informative (thinker) strategy. Some work better than others. The ones that can be used to implement the informative (thinker) strategy include sales training programs and trade shows.

Training is a form of manufacturer-sponsored educational program. For example, in the medical equipment industry, manufacturers usually offer to both train physicians and health care personnel (the buyers) how to best use the equipment and also educate them about the product's benefits.

Trade shows are also very effective in educating potential customers about the product benefits. Trade show sellers get a chance to interact with potential buyers and educate them about the product's benefits and its various applications.

Public Relations

Public relations is a marketing communications tool that is used to promote the goodwill of the firm as a whole. Many marketing communications scholars recognize the effectiveness of public relations as an information tool, as a tool to educate consumers about the product benefits. However, its use is mostly limited to newsworthy events such as the introduction of a new product, the new use or application of existing products, or product improvements. Many tools of public relations are shown in Table 6.7.

TABLE 6.6   Reseller Support Tools and Techniques

Contests and incentives
Trade allowances
   Buying allowances (free goods)
   Promotional allowances
   Slotting allowances
In-store displays and point-of-purchase materials
Training programs
Trade shows
Cooperative advertising
   Horizontal cooperative advertising
   Ingredient-sponsored cooperative advertising
   Vertical cooperative advertising
Personal selling

TABLE 6.7 List of Public Relations Tools and Techniques

The press release
Press conferences
Exclusives
Interviews
Publicity
Corporate advertising
Event sponsorship
Product placements in movies and TV

Public relations tools include press releases, press conferences, exclusives, interviews, publicity, corporate advertising, event sponsorship, and product placements in movies and TV. The tools that serve the informative (thinker) strategy and objectives the best are the press release and publicity. The *press release* is information about the company and/or its products sent to the news media for dissemination. Of course, for the news media to disseminate information about a product or its company, the information has to be newsworthy. *Publicity*, on the other hand, is information about the company and/or one or more of its products that originates from sources beyond the control of the company. The information may be either positive or negative. The marketing function comes in when the company attempts to react to publicity. For example, J.D. Power Associates is a reputable marketing research firm that conducts customer satisfaction surveys in the automobile industry. If J.D. Power Associates rates Lexus as having the highest customer satisfaction, the Lexus marketing communications manager could turn around and use this information in an advertising campaign. The Lexus ad would boast about its high customer satisfaction ratings.

Word-of-Mouth (WOM) Communications

Just as publicity does not originate with the company itself, WOM communications involve information about the company and/or one or more of its products that originates from *customers*. The information can be either positive or negative. Customers talk to other potential customers about their experience with the company's product(s), and they recommend for or against purchase. These recommendations are powerful because they do indeed influence potential customers' purchase decisions. So what can marketing communications managers do about WOM communications? Can they influence WOM communications to the company's advantage? The answer is, *possibly*. There are at least three ways in which WOM communications can be induced and influenced. One way is by stimulating WOM communications through advertising, and another is through sampling. The third method is by creating a referral network. All of these tools can be effective in achieving maximum learning.

Stimulating *WOM communications through advertising* can be accomplished by creating a message that encourages the audience to talk about the advertised product. For example, consumers are offered a reward if they refer a friend or relative to try the product. Each referral would entitle them to a price discount or some premium or bonus.

In contrast, *WOM communications through sampling* relies on opinion leadership. Some product users are more likely to be opinion leaders than others. Opinion leaders are those who have a certain expertise about a product category and, therefore, are more likely to give advice to others about the product and the various brands of that product. For example, business professors receive many samples of business magazines and software. Business professors are considered opinion leaders because their advice and opinions are sought by students and professionals in the business community. If professors form a favorable opinion of the product, they are likely to communicate to others favorable information about the product.

The final way to stimulate WOM communications, by creating a *referral system,* is a major effort, but nevertheless, it can be a very worthwhile effort in some industries. A referral system can be established by a certain company to provide customers and potential customers with information about the myriad of products and services available to the consumer. For example, most HMOs in the United States have their own referral system. A patient within the geographic boundaries of the HMO can call its physician referral office to get information and advice about which physician within the HMO network has the proper background and expertise to treat a specific health problem. Also, the physician referral office provides callers with information about the many educational seminars related to specific medical conditions that are offered by the HMO. Referral systems can also be created at the industry level. For example, the automobile industry can set up a referral system in which each automobile company provides information about all their cars, prices, and options. Potential buyers then can contact the referral system to obtain information about the options of specific car forms (e.g., sports cars within a certain price range) and which models may be available through which dealers within a specific geographic radius.

THE AFFECTIVE (FEELER) STRATEGY AND TACTICS

The *affective (feeler) strategy* involves the application of marketing communications tools to generate maximum awareness and create the most positive attitude toward the brand. Examples of statements of objectives reflecting this strategy include: "We need to get the target consumers to become fully aware of our brand and develop a preference for it." "We want the marketing communications campaign to increase brand preference by 20% in the next six months." "We want 70% of the target consumers to feel good about our product by the end of next month." "Our goal is to strengthen positive attitudes toward the product by increasing positive brand attitude from the current 50% to 70% by the end of this year."

According to Table 6.1, the affective (feeler) strategy can be most effectively implemented through advertising, reseller support, public relations, and WOM communications, the same communications tools used to implement the informative (thinker) strategy, but with some variations. We'll address these in the context of the affective (feeler) strategy.

Advertising

In relation to *intermedia* selection, we discussed a set of eliminating and discriminating criteria applied to the informative (thinker) strategy. Now we will focus on a certain criterion that should be closely examined in implementing the affective strategy through advertising. This criterion is *message valence.* We previously recommended that the marketing communications manager should use the print media mainly because print allows the audience to process more easily the technical and detailed information describing the product and brand benefits. That is, audience learning is maximized if the informational message is placed in a *print* medium. However, given an affective (feeler) strategy, the marketing communications manager should use the *broadcast* medium because the broadcast medium is more effective in inducing emotion and creating affect.

In making an *intramedia* selection, the same criteria employed in the informative (thinker) strategy also apply in the implementation of the affective (feeler) strategy. In relation to the *creative aspects of the ad*, marketing communications managers are advised to use emotional rather than rational appeals. Examples of emotional appeals include the use of humor, sex, fear, love, romance, and nostalgia, among others. These emotional appeals can be effective in building positive affect toward the product.

Reseller Support

Table 6.6 lists the various elements or tools involved in reseller support. In discussing the implementation of the informative (thinker) strategy, we recommended the use of sales training programs and trade shows. In implementing the affective (feeler) strategy we recommend the use of the same tools with the addition of cooperative advertising.

Cooperative advertising allows the cost of advertising to be shared by the marketing communications manager and the reseller. There are three forms of cooperative advertising programs: horizontal, ingredient-sponsored, and vertical. In *horizontal cooperative advertising,* the manufacturer shares the advertising cost of a number of resellers. The ad shows the product and highlights the various retailers where it is sold. *Ingredient-sponsored cooperative advertising* is a form of advertising in which the manufacturer of a product's ingredient collaborates with other manufacturers or resellers to promote the ingredient jointly. For example, Nutrasweet may collaborate with Breyer's Ice Cream to advertise the use of Nutrasweet in Breyer's ice creams. Finally, *vertical cooperative advertising* is the most common form of cooperative advertising. Here, the ad shows several products for sale. The manufacturers of all the advertised products share the advertising costs with the retailer. Have you seen a supermarket ad in the newspaper advertising a variety of products? Some of these ads are based on cooperative advertising programs with the products' manufacturers. Of course, the idea of cooperative advertising is to associate one's product with a reseller for which the target consumers have positive feelings. By doing so, the positive affect transfers or spills over to the manufacturer's product, thereby achieving the goals of the affective (feeler) strategy.

Public Relations

In the section pertaining to the informative (thinker) strategy, we discussed the use of the press release and publicity. Of course, these same public relations tools should also be used to implement the affective (feeler) strategy. However, uniquely suited to the affective (feeler) strategy are other public relations tools, such as the press conference, interviews, exclusives, corporate advertising, and event sponsorship (see Table 6.7).

With respect to the *press conference*, the topic, of course, has to be of major interest to the news media. For example, holding a press conference about the Super Bowl is likely to draw the attention of news organizations. Here, the marketing communications manager contacts the various local offices of the news media and alerts them about the date, time, and place of the press conference and the topic to be addressed. The news media send in their news reporters to cover the event and elicit more responses from the spokesperson by asking pointed questions. The press conference is an effective tool in accomplishing the goals of the affective (feeler) strategy because usually the topic and the public attention devoted to the product or issue is emotionally charged to begin with. Thus, the audience is likely to experience certain emotions while viewing (or listening to or reading about) the press conference. These emotions, although uncontrolled by marketing communications managers, can be positively charged, resulting in the building or strengthening of a positive attitude toward the product or the company. The same can be said in relation to *interviews* and *exclusives*.

Corporate advertising and *event sponsorship* are public relations programs designed to build and strengthen a positive attitude toward the firm at large and all its products. Corporate advertising is image-based advertising in which the company is shown in a positive light. It is formally defined as "the provision of assistance either financially or in-kind to an activity by a commercial organization for the purpose of achieving commercial objectives."[6] Have you seen the Dow Corning ads on television in which college graduates are excited about finishing college and starting a career at Dow Corning? The idea here is to build positive feelings about the company. Event sponsorships, on the other hand, are programs in which a marketing communications manager shares the cost of an event that is attended by customers or potential customers, or perhaps an event that is picked up by a communications medium such as television. For example, a community baseball game may be sponsored by a local bank. The bank's name and logo appear on the baseball program as the sponsor of the event. People attending the baseball game are likely to develop positive feelings about the bank, knowing that it sponsored the event.

Word-of-Mouth (WOM) Communications

We discussed how three key WOM communications tools can be used to implement the informative (thinker) strategy. These tools are stimulating WOM communications through advertising, stimulating WOM communications through sampling, and creating a referral system. We believe that these tools are not likely to be effective in the affective (feeler) strategy—that is, to build positive affect for a product. Another form of WOM communications that is likely to be effective in carrying out the affective (feeler) strategy is *simulating WOM,* mostly through advertising.

Simulating WOM communications is commonly used in television advertising; a typical ad shows two consumers talking about the product, and one consumer is recommending to the other a particular brand based on certain benefits. The consumer recommending the brand describes the benefits of the brand over competitor brands. Usually the actor who recommends the brand to others is selected to reflect the profile of an opinion leader for that product category. For example, suppose a company is trying to market a business magazine to college students majoring in business. Market research indicates that a significant segment of business students watch CNN, and they do look up to business professors as opinion leaders in relation to selecting business magazines. So a television commercial is made showing a young, vibrant, and intelligent business professor interacting with several of his students. The actors playing the students are shown to revere the professor and hold him in high esteem. One student notices that the business professor has *Business Magazine X* in his briefcase. The briefcase is sitting on the professor's table in the classroom, and this interaction occurs immediately after a business class. A couple of students ask the professor about the business magazine. The professor discusses the virtues of the magazine and makes an explicit recommendation to the students about how the magazine is likely to help them with their business classes and also help them establish their business careers. This is a good example of using WOM communications through simulation in television advertising.

Recently I received a letter with no return address on it. The envelope had my name typed on it and a postage stamp, as though a person (not a company) had mailed this letter. Inside the envelope was a newspaper article that looked as though it had been cut out of a management magazine. The article addressed the use of trend analysis in making better management decisions. The two-page article (back-to-back) had a yellow Post-it sticker that said "Joseph, try this. It's really good!" It was signed "J." It looked like a hand-written note from someone I know. The end of the article had information about how to subscribe to this magazine. After reading the article and closely examining the Post-it note, I realized that this was merely a clever way to make me believe a friend had referred this product. The letter was actually a direct mail ad. Here we have an example in which the marketer of this magazine used advertising (more specifically direct mail) to create the illusion of WOM communications. Please note that this marketing communications method that simulates WOM is highly *unethical,* perhaps even illegal, and is not recommended.

THE HABIT FORMATION (DOER) STRATEGY AND TACTICS

For the *habit formation strategy,* marketing communications tasks aim to maximize product trial, purchase, and learning from experience for first-time users. With respect to repeat users, the goal is to enhance repeat purchase and reinforce brand learning. Examples of statements of objectives reflecting this strategy include: "We need to get 35% of the target market to express a purchase intention for our advertised product by the year's end." "We want to induce trial and direct experience of our product so that at least 30% of the target market will have experienced the product within six month's time." "We need to get our old customers to do more business with us."

As you saw in Table 6.1, the habit formation (doer) strategy can be implemented mostly through direct marketing, sales promotion, and reseller support. We'll address these in some detail.

Advertising

Advertising does an effective job of reminding consumers to buy. Therefore, when consumers need to purchase a given product, they are more likely to consider brands that are in their "evoked set" (top-of-the-mind awareness) than brands that are not.

Advertising does an effective job in maintaining a brand name in the consumers' evoked set. Thus, the same tactical aspects of advertising discussed in the context of the informative (thinker) strategy also apply here. However, it should be noted that this "reminder" advertising may be somewhat different in that shorter ads or commercials can be used. Recently, *interactive advertising* has been used to encourage customers to repeat purchase. This advertising constantly updates descriptions and explanations of a product line and any other information to help customers maintain their commitment to the firm. These updates are posted on a home page through a computer on-line web site.

Direct Marketing

Direct marketing will be addressed as a marketing communications tool used in the context of direct forms of distribution. Table 6.8 shows the various tools and techniques of direct marketing: direct mail, catalogs, telemarketing (telephone-in and telephone-out), direct response advertising (broadcast and print), new electronic media (teleshopping and videotext), and direct selling (repetitive person-to-person selling, nonrepetitive person-to-person selling, and party plans.

To reiterate, direct marketing tools and techniques are limited to businesses that promote their products through direct channels. In other words, the company products cannot be distributed to resellers (wholesalers and retailers) who in turn sell the products to the ultimate consumers. Direct marketing involves promotion to the ultimate consumers *directly*. Firms that market their product through intermediaries and resellers should use the tools and techniques of sales promotion and reseller support. We'll discuss these too, but for now let's turn our attention to the tools and techniques of direct marketing that are considered most effective in implementing the habit formation (doer) strategy. These are direct mail and direct response advertising.

Direct mail is the most prevalent form of promotion by direct marketing communications managers. Consumers refer to it as "junk mail"—the unsolicited mail

---

TABLE 6.8 List of Direct Marketing Tools and Techniques

Direct mail
Catalogs
Telemarketing
  Telephone-in
  Telephone-out
Direct response advertising
  Broadcast direct response advertising
    The 1-minute commercial
    Infomercials
  Print media
New electronic media
  Teleshopping (home shopping channels)
  Videotext (electronic shopping)
Direct selling
  One-to-one selling
  Group selling

consumers find in their mailboxes. Direct marketing communications managers who use direct mail start out by developing their own databases of actual and potential customers, using a variety of sources. Those who don't have their own database of target consumers purchase mailing lists from mailing list houses. Direct marketing communications managers use the Standard Rate and Data Service (SRDS) to identify the various mailing list companies and compare prices. Direct marketing communications managers can order a mailing list that can target highly select groups of consumers. These are usually defined in terms of where they live (through their ZIP codes), demographics (e.g., incomes, occupations, ages, and genders), and to a certain extent lifestyles (e.g., bikers, skiers, and fitness enthusiasts). Most mailing list houses identify consumers' lifestyles through past purchases of related products. For example, golfers are identified through recent purchases of golf-related materials in golf specialty shops and sporting-goods stores. This information is bought from retailers and used to develop the mailing lists of likely golfers. In many instances, mailing list houses buy information about consumers from various sources and merge them into a comprehensive database. Direct mail can encourage consumers to respond immediately by offering them special incentives to act immediately. Offers such as special discounts are also common.[7]

In terms of enhancing repeat purchase, the use of a *newsletter* is also very effective. The newsletter would contain news and information about the marketing communications manager's product line, updates, any favorable publicity cited from other sources, and possibly endorsements and testimonials from certain customers. The newsletter may also contain information about employees who have won certain awards for quality work, updates about industry trends, and so forth.

Direct response advertising is also an effective direct marketing tool designed to achieve the goals of a habit formation (doer) strategy. Part of the message in direct response advertising is information about how to order the product directly from the manufacturer (or distributor). Direct response advertising is usually done through either the broadcast or print media. In the broadcast medium, direct response advertising sometimes takes the form of *infomercials* (long commercials). In these commercials, a sales response is elicited immediately. Many products, such as Soloflex and Nordic Track fitness equipment, are promoted through one- or two-minute commercials. Infomercials, on the other hand, can range from 3 minutes to an hour. The 30- and 60-minute infomercials are designed to look like regular TV shows. The purpose is to induce an immediate purchase response by having the audience dial an 800 or 900 number to place an order on the spot. An example is the Richard Simmons *Deal-A-Meal* show that promotes diet programs.

Sales Promotion

Sales promotion is a marketing communications tool specifically designed to provide consumers with some incentive inducing an immediate response, possibly in the form of purchase. Table 6.9 shows a list of sales promotion tools and techniques: coupons (printed and electronic), sampling, refunds and rebates, bonus packs, and price-off deals.

Coupons are the most widely used sales promotion tool. A coupon is a printed document that allows the holder to get a price discount for the purchase of a product. We all are familiar with pizza coupons. Most pizza places use coupons to entice pizza

TABLE 6.9 List of Sales Promotion Tools and Techniques

Coupons
   Printed coupons
   Electronic coupons
Sampling
Premiums
   Free premiums (e.g., an inexpensive gift in a cereal box)
   Self-liquidating premiums (related products offered at cost only to customers)
Contests and sweepstakes
Refunds and rebates
Bonus packs
Price-off deals

eaters to purchase their pizza. Coupons are printed in display ads in newspapers or magazines that are mailed directly to target consumers. They are also mailed through promotion firms specializing in that type of service; one example is Val Pak. In many tourist locations, coupons are placed in tourist guides and brochures. Sometimes they are placed on the product package itself. The coupon that encourages an immediate purchase response is called an *instant* coupon. Usually it is pasted on top of the package. The consumer sees it and may be motivated to use it to purchase the product on the spot. A common form of coupon designed to encourage a product trial is called the *cross-ruff* coupon. This is placed inside or outside the package of a related product, usually a product sold by the same company. For example, Kellogg's may come up with a new brand of cereal. To encourage product trial, Kellogg's may place a coupon in Kellogg's Corn Flakes. The cross-ruff coupon may encourage those who purchase and use Kellogg's Corn Flakes to try the new Kellogg brand.

A special form of coupon that is used to elicit repeat response is called a *bounceback coupon*. This is a coupon that is placed inside or outside the product package. The coupon is redeemable for the next purchase of the same brand. Have you ever ordered a pizza and found a bounce-back coupon taped on the pizza box? The idea is to encourage you to make a repeat purchase of the same brand. *Electronic coupons* are also designed to encourage repeat purchase. At the supermarket, when you pay the bill at the cash register, you get a receipt. The back of the receipt may have coupons that can be redeemed for certain products. Product selection is determined by what you have purchased. If you have purchased Philadelphia Cream Cheese, you may get a coupon for that brand to encourage you to buy the same brand of cream cheese on your next visit to the supermarket.

In designing a coupon, the marketing communications manager typically shows a picture of the product, a very brief message (reflecting the positioning of the product) usually in the form of a slogan, the firm's logo, address, and phone number, and the terms of the coupon. Usually at the bottom of the coupon, coupon constraints are spelled out—for example, "This coupon may not be combined with any other offer." The expiration date is usually spelled out too. Coupons are an effective means to motivate consumers to purchase.[8]

Sampling is another sales promotion tool commonly used to induce product trial and purchase. For example, Procter & Gamble has always used sampling to get homemakers to try a new brand of detergent. They mail a sample to adult females in house-holds across the United States. Sampling is also very common with food items. The consumer tries a sample; she likes it; she ends up buying it.

Rebates are another sales promotion technique. A rebate is usually used to en-tice a potential consumer to purchase the manufacturer's brand. Once the purchase is made, the consumer provides proof of purchase and gets a partial refund. Many car manufacturers use rebates to entice consumers to buy during certain periods. Like-wise, *refund* offers are often used to encourage repeat purchase. Marketing communi-cations managers require consumers to send in proof of purchase as a condition to re-ceiving the refund. Many firms offer consumers special discounts and premiums with more purchase in order to encourage their customers to remain loyal. For example, many airlines use the frequent flier program to reward fliers who stick with one air-line. The nature of the reward varies from free tickets for future flights to special dis-counts on car rentals and hotels/resorts.

Bonus packs provide an extra amount of the product at regular price. Consumers may feel motivated to switch from one brand to another brand if the other brand offers a bonus pack. Thus, marketing communications managers use this sales promotion tool to induce consumers to purchase their brand or switch from competitor brands.

Price-off deals differ from coupons in that the price reduction is marked on the product package itself. Many retailers use this sales promotion tool to get rid of extra inventory. For example, car dealers mark the sticker price down by a certain margin at the end of the year to get rid of the remaining cars sitting on the lot, thus making room for the new cars for the beginning of the year. Marketing communications man-agers seeking repeat purchase may mail notices to past customers reminding them to take advantage of *price-off deals*. This form of sales promotion may be combined with other promotional materials sent to the customers through direct mail.

Reseller Support

Reseller support tools are used only by business-to-business marketing communica-tions managers or manufacturer-to-retailer promotions and include contests and incen-tives, trade allowances, in-store displays and point-of-purchase materials, training pro-grams, trade shows, and cooperative advertising (refer to Table 6.6). Some of these were addressed in the context of the informative (thinker) strategy, namely training programs and trade shows. The same programs are effective in achieving affective goals when cooperative advertising is added to the list. In relation to the habit formation (doer) strategy, *trade allowances* are the most effective communications tool.

Trade allowances are the most commonly used for trade promotion. They usu-ally involve some form of a discount or deal to encourage the reseller to carry, pro-mote, and display the product. There are three types of trade allowances—*buying al-lowances*, *promotional allowances*, and *slotting allowances*. A buying allowance is a price discount offered to resellers. The resellers can take advantage of this allowance only during the fixed period in which the allowance is offered. Another form of a buy-ing allowance is a deal in which resellers get more free products if they buy immedi-ately. A promotional allowance, on the other hand, is a price reduction if the reseller agrees to promote the product, perhaps by advertising or displaying the product more prominently than the competing brands. Slotting allowances are somewhat related to promotional allowances. Slotting allowances involve the payment of a certain fee for shelf space. Slotting allowances are therefore viewed as a reward for resellers to agree to carry and devote shelf space to a manufacturers' products. The higher the slotting fee, the greater the shelf space.

Public Relations

Public relations is an important tool to maintain a positive image of the firm in the minds of customers to enhance repeat patronage. The most common use of public relations tools to achieve goals of the habit formation (doer) strategy is *publicity*. Publicity is important because it is most credible. Any favorable publicity about the product and/or the company has to be fully exploited. We previously talked about how this information can be presented as news items in a newsletter to customers. Favorable publicity can also be used in all forms of advertising to strengthen the positive image of the product and the company.

THE SELF-SATISFACTION (REACTOR) MARKETING COMMUNICATIONS STRATEGY

Finally, the *self-satisfaction (reactor) strategy* can be viewed as the application of marketing communications tasks designed to maximize trial and repeat purchases while also increasing positive feelings about the firm's brand. Examples of statements reflecting objectives derived from this strategy include: "We want to increase trial purchase by 40% by the end of next year." "We need to get at least 80% of those who tried our brand to express liking for it." "We need to increase the number of purchases per individual consumer. Approximately 80% of our target consumers are purchasing our product once a month, and 20% twice a month. We want to get 50% to purchase the product twice a month by the end of next year." "We need to reinforce commitment to the brand so that by the end of next year at least 60% of our customers will express their loyalty to our brand." Table 6.1 indicates that all the elements of the marketing communications mix, except for WOM communications, can be effectively used to achieve the goals of the self-satisfaction (reactor) strategy.

Advertising

Advertising does an effective job of reminding consumers of certain brands. Thus, the same tactical aspects of advertising discussed in the context of the affective (feeler) strategy also apply here. However, it should be noted that this "reminder" advertising may be somewhat different in that shorter ads or commercials can be used. Furthermore, other forms of advertising can be used besides broadcast. Here, *outdoor advertising* can be effective in reminding consumers to repeat purchase. Also, *specialty advertising* does an effective job of reminding current customers of previous transactions, thus enhancing customer loyalty. Specialty advertising involves giving consumers inexpensive items such as calendars, pens, pen sets, and paper holders on which are inscribed the name of the marketing communications manager's firm, its logo and slogan, and its address and phone number.

Direct Marketing

Direct marketing tools are direct mail, catalogs, telemarketing (telephone-in and telephone-out), direct response advertising (broadcast and print), new electronic media (teleshopping and videotext), and direct selling (repetitive person-to-person selling, nonrepetitive person-to-person selling, and party plans). Of these, the most effective tools that can be used to carry out the self-satisfaction (reactor) strategy are catalogs, direct response advertising, telemarketing, and direct personal selling.

Catalogs are a traditional method of direct marketing. Many companies like Sears, Nordstrom, and J. C. Penney sell directly through catalogs. These catalogs are usually distributed on-site or can be mailed directly to consumers when consumers request them. Other catalogs (the ones that are not too expensive to produce) are classified as part of a direct mail campaign. Catalogs help consumers make decisions on the spot and therefore are viewed as effective in achieving product trial and purchase as well as repeat purchase.

Direct response advertising is also an effective direct marketing tool designed to achieve the goals of the self-satisfaction (reactor) strategy. For example, the broadcast medium can be used to appeal to consumers in a very emotional way, which is befitting of the self-satisfaction (reactor) strategy. Direct response advertising sometimes takes the form of *infomercials* (long commercials). An example is the Richard Simmons *Deal-A-Meal* show that promotes diet programs. Dieting is a highly emotional area in which a TV infomercial can be effective in inducing consumers to act and act repeatedly.

Telemarketing is another direct marketing promotional tool. It requires the use of telephones. Two forms of telemarketing are used: telephone-in and telephone-out. *Telephone-in* refers to situations where consumers dial an 800 number to place their orders. Usually, the 800 number is advertised or promoted through other sources such as direct response advertising. A new form of telephone-in is increasing in popularity and is called *tele-media* or *audiotext*. This tool involves the use of an 800, 900, or 976 number to promote a certain product. Most tele-media systems are interactive in that the consumer dials in and interacts with a computer. For example, a new audiotext system is being developed to allow health care providers to call a computer that can help diagnose the medical condition of patients. The system interacts with the caller and guides the caller to respond to questions by pressing numbers on the dial. The outcome is a medical diagnosis. This system is less typical than those designed to promote a specific product. A more common example is an audiotext used by a restaurant to promote its menu. Callers dial in to find out what is on the menu on certain days. Most systems are automated. *Telephone-out*, on the other hand, involves the use of the telephone by a salesperson to call on current and potential customers in order to persuade them to make an immediate purchase.

Direct marketing communications managers are now increasingly using new forms of *electronic media* to promote their products and elicit an immediate purchase response. For example, *teleshopping* is now widespread. The use of certain television channels that are exclusively devoted to selling products directly is now commonplace. Most of us know about the Home Shopping Network and QVC. Consumers watch these cable channels, and if they like whatever product is being advertised, they pick up the telephone and place an order on the spot through an 800 number. Similarly, electronic shopping is now becoming a fad. It is called *videotext*. Consumers can shop electronically through their personal computers. Most on-line services such as America Online, Compuserve, and Prodigy offer consumers a link to many manufacturers and resellers, allowing consumers to place an order directly.

Finally we have *direct personal selling* as another tool of direct marketing. In direct selling, a salesperson presents and demonstrates the product to consumers and elicits an immediate sales response. There are two forms of direct selling: one-to-one selling and group selling. In *one-to-one selling,* a salesperson interacts with an individual consumer. The salesperson explains and demonstrates the product to that consumer. Most industrial marketing communications managers use this form of direct marketing. They send their sales reps to visit potential customers at the job site. In many cases, one-to-one selling is difficult and costly. In these situations, group selling is attempted. *Group selling* involves assembling potential consumers in a group and presenting and demonstrating the product to them in one location. For example, many investment brokers send out invitations to prospective clients and invite them to attend a seminar on investment and to discuss the various services that the firm offers. Another form of group selling is the "party plan." For example, Mary Kay Cosmetics typically uses this sales technique.

Sales Promotion

Two types of sales promotion tools are especially well suited to the self-satisfaction (reactor) strategy: premiums and contests (or sweepstakes). There are two forms of *premiums*—free and self-liquidating ones. *Free premiums* are inexpensive gifts placed in the product package. For example, in many children's cereal boxes, marketing communications managers place inexpensive toys. These are free premiums. Have you ever seen a child exerting pressure on his or her mother to buy a certain brand of cereal that contains a toy? The child is eager to get the gift. *Self-liquidating premiums*, on the other hand, are "gifts" that require the consumer to pay some or all of the premium plus the costs of handling and mailing. For example, local fast-food restaurants may sell beverages in containers with logos of local sports teams. These are sold to the fast-food patron at cost only.

Premiums are also commonly used to encourage repeat purchase. Premiums are a method of rewarding customers for purchasing a certain brand. This reward strengthens positive feelings toward the firm and its products, enhancing the likelihood of future purchases. Similar to premiums are *bonus packs*. They operate the same way. Because they receive more of the product at the regular price, customers feel rewarded for doing business with a specific firm, and the bonus pack is seen as the reward.

Contests and *sweepstakes* are other popular forms of sales promotion. A *contest* is a game in which consumers compete for prizes or money on the basis of a specific skill. Many radio stations use contests by challenging listeners to answer trivia questions. The first caller who gives the right answer wins the prize. If there is more than one winner, then a lottery may be used to pick the winner. A *sweepstakes*, on the other hand, is a game based on chance. McDonald's has run the Monopoly game. With every purchase of certain products, the customer receives a sticker that allows him or her to purchase a piece of land on the Monopoly board. Once the customer collects an entire set of a particular color of property, he or she wins a prize. Contests and sweepstakes also reinforce customers' involvement with the marketing firm. This enhanced involvement increases repeat patronage.

Reseller Support

Contests and *incentives* are programs manufacturers use to stimulate sales. These contests are often directed to the managers and purchasing managers of the reseller firms. For example, an incentive for resellers may be in the form of free merchandise or a bonus for having met a sales quota. Although the goal of contests and incentive programs is to encourage purchase of the manufacturer's product, it should be noted that learning is also enhanced. These contests and incentives motivate the resellers to learn more about the manufacturer's product and are therefore effective in implementing the learning communications strategy.

In-store advertising and *point-of-purchase displays* are also special types of incentives that encourage resellers to buy and stock manufacturers' products. A manufacturer that can set up point-of-purchase displays and promote its products within the store is very attractive to the reseller. This is because in-store advertising and point-of-purchase displays help move the manufacturer's products, thus allowing the store to do more selling. The more selling, the more profit for the reseller.

Personal selling is also commonly used in the context of reseller support. In this context, there are three types of personal selling jobs—creative selling, order taking, and missionary sales reps.[9] *Creative selling* involves the following personal selling tasks: prospecting, assessing needs, recommending a means of satisfying needs, demonstrating the capabilities of the firm, and closing the sale. Here, the salesperson is the "point person" who establishes the initial contact and has the major responsibility for completing the transaction. *Order taking* is very different from creative selling. The order taker services an account. This situation is commonly referred to as a "straight rebuy." That is, the order does not change much. For example, a food manufacturer's salesperson may call on a wholesale food company and present them with a list of food products to sell. The *missionary sales rep* type of personal selling involves a combination of creative selling and order taking. The position calls for introducing new products and programs to both current and potential customers.

Public Relations

Public relations help enhance repeat patronage by maintaining a positive image of the firm in the minds of customers. The most common public relations tools to achieve goals of the self-satisfaction (reactor) strategy are corporate advertising, event sponsorship, and product placements in TV programs and movies. They serve to maintain and enhance the company's image in the minds of customers and other publics.[10] *Corporate advertising* is usually affectively based. Have you seen corporate advertising lately on television? The Dow Chemical commercials? The Dupont commercials? The GE commercials? These are all affectively based, and none of them provide much information about their respective companies. They are simply designed to reinforce positive feelings about the company.

The same can be said for *event sponsorship*. Many companies sponsor specific sports events. For example, DuPont has had a long tradition sponsoring Tour

DuPont—an internationally known bicycle race. Many companies—McDonald's is one of them—sponsor the Olympics. These sponsorships do not communicate a specific message about the company and its product line. The communications is affectively rather than cognitively based. Positive affect is transferred in the minds of consumers from the sporting event to the sponsoring company.[11]

A much more subtle way of inducing positive feelings about a product is to work out a deal with a popular movie in which the product appears and is used by favored characters. Since the audience has positive feelings about the movie character, positive affect transfer is a likely result. The positive feelings the audience may have for the movie character transfer to the product. This technique is referred to as *product placements in movies and TV*. For example, a BMW automobile was used in the latest James Bond movie. In many of the comedy shows on television, a variety of brand-name products appear in the background. In many shows, the products are shown to be used in explicit ways by the actors and actresses on the show.

Summary

This chapter introduced to the reader ideas to help conceptualize the marketing communications subsystem. Four different communications strategies were identified: (1) informative (thinker), (2) affective (feeler), (3) habit formation (doer), and (4) self-satisfaction (reactor). For each strategy, the reader was shown a method of implementing the strategy—that is, assembling the appropriate elements of the marketing communications mix. In relation to the informative (thinker) strategy, we recommended the use of certain forms of advertising (mostly print advertising), certain forms of reseller support programs (mostly training programs and trade shows), certain forms of public relations programs (press releases and publicity), and word-of-mouth (WOM) communications (stimulating WOM through advertising, sampling, and creating a referral system).

In relation to the affective (feeler) strategy, we recommended the use of certain forms of advertising (mostly broadcast advertising), certain forms of reseller support programs (mostly cooperative advertising), certain forms of public relations programs (press conferences, corporate advertising, and event sponsorship), and WOM communications (stimulating WOM through advertising and sampling).

In relation to the habit formation (doer) strategy, we recommended the use of advertising (mostly in the form of print and interactive advertising), direct marketing (mostly through direct mail, newsletter, and direct response advertising), sales promotion programs (coupons, sampling, refunds and rebates, bonus packs, and price-off deals), reseller support programs (mostly in the form of trade allowances), and public relations (mostly in the form of publicity).

Finally, in relation to the self-satisfaction (reactor) strategy, we recommended the use of certain forms of advertising (such as outdoor and specialty advertising), certain forms of direct marketing (catalogs, direct response advertising, telemarketing, and direct selling), sales promotion (the use of premiums and contests and sweepstakes), reseller support programs (contests and incentives, in-store advertising, point-of-purchase displays, and personal selling), and certain forms of public relations (corporate advertising, event sponsorship, and placement of the product in movies and TV).

Questions for Discussion

1. Describe a model that offers a set of marketing communications strategies. Describe these strategies.

2. Describe the objectives associated with each of the marketing communications strategies.

3. Suppose you're a marketing communications manager of a new chain of restaurants that specializes in Middle Eastern food. You're beginning to plan the marketing communications campaign. What is your first priority? That is, what is the most important goal during the first year of the campaign? What is the appropriate strategy here? What elements of the marketing communications mix will you choose to implement the selected strategy? Explain.

4. Now you are six months into the campaign for this Middle Eastern national restaurant. What should be the campaign goal? Should you now change your strategy? What elements of the marketing communications mix would you use? Explain.

5. Now it is one full year since the launch of the campaign. Again, should your goal and strategy change? If you now choose a new strategy, how will you go about implementing it?

6. This is now the end of the second year. Upper management is exerting pressure on you to show a high level of sales. Will you change your marketing communications strategy? From what to what? What are your goals now? How will you go about implementing the new strategy?

7. You have built a patron base now after a couple of years. A majority of people in the United States have tried your restaurant at least several times. Your goal is to make sure that these patrons come back and come back often. Articulate your marketing communications goals. What is your strategy? What marketing communications tactics would you use to carry out the strategy?

Notes

1. Joe Mandese and Chris Moseley, "Discovery Channel," *Advertising Age* (June 26, 1995), p. S-4.

2. Bradley Johnson and Abby Kohnstamm, "IBM," *Advertising Age*, (June 26, 1995), p. S-4.

3. Don E. Schultz, "Customers Determine Value of Your Marketing Tactics," *Marketing News* (October 7, 1996), p. 7.

4. Richard Vaughn, "How Advertising Works: A Planning Model," *Journal of Advertising Research* 20 (October 1980), pp. 27–33; Richard Vaughn, "How Advertisng Works: A Planning Model Revisited," *Journal of Advertising Research* 26 (February-March 1986), pp. 57–66.

5. Kent M. Lancaster and Helen E. Katz, *Strategic Media Planning* (Lincolnwood, Ill.: NTC Business Books, 1989).

6. John Meenaghan, "Commercial Sponsorship," *European Journal of Marketing* 7, no. 7 (1983) p. 9. Also see John Meenaghan, "Sponsorship—Legitimizing the Medium," *European Journal of Marketing*, 25 no. 11 (1991) pp. 5–10.

7. Martin S. Bressler, "Mainstream Companies Find Direct Mail Profitable," *Marketing News* (July 29, 1996), p. 7.

8. It should be noted that Procter & Gamble, the maker of hundreds of staples including Tide, Pampers, and Folgers Coffee, is undergoing an experiment to eliminate coupons. P&G has realized that the long-run use of coupons has a negative effect on brand equity. Instead of coupons, P&G will lower price. "Procter & Gamble to Try Clipping Coupons—Out," an article from the *Knight-Ridder/Tribune* that appeared in the *Roanoke Times*, January 12, 1996, p. A9.

9. Thayer C. Taylor, "A Letup in the Rise of Sales Call Costs," *Sales & Marketing Management* (February 25, 1980), p. 24.

10. David Schumann, Jan M. Hathcote, and Susan West, "Corporate Advertising in America: A Review of Published Studies on Use, Measurement, and Effectiveness," *Journal of Advertising* 20, no. 3 (1991) pp. 35–56.

11. Howard Thomas, "Sponsorship—An Advertiser's Guide*," International Journal of Advertising* 4 (1985), pp. 319–26. William L. Shanklin and John R. Kuzma, "Buying That Sporting Image," *Marketing Management* (Spring 1992), pp. 59–67. Christian Ryssel and Eric Stamminger, "Sponsoring World-Class Tennis Players," *European Research* (May 1988), pp. 110–16.

SUGGESTED READING

Barban, Arnold M., Donald W. Jugenheimer, and Peter B. Turk. *Advertising Media Sourcebook,* 3rd ed. Lincolnwood, Ill.: Crain Books / NTC Business Books, 1989.

Blattberg, Robert C., and Scott A. Nelson. *Sales Promotion: Concepts, Methods, and Strategies.* Upper Saddle River, N.J.: Prentice Hall, 1990.

Block, Tamara Brezen, and William A. Robinson, eds. *Sales Promotion Handbook*, 8th ed. Chicago, Ill.: Dartnell Press, 1994.

Bogart, Leo. *Strategy in Advertising*, 2nd ed. Lincolnwood, Ill.: Crain Books / NTC Business Books, 1984.

Houston, Michael A. "Consumer Evaluations and Product Information Choices." *Journal of Current Issues and Research in Advertising* (1979) pp. 135–44.

Kaatz, Ron. *Advertising and Marketing Checklists,* 2nd ed. Lincolnwood, Ill.: Crain Books/ NTC Business Books, 1995.

Lancaster, Kent M., and Helen E. Katz. *Strategic Media Planning.* Lincolnwood, Ill.: Crain Books / NTC Books, 1992.

Lodish, Leonard M. *The Advertising & Promotion Challenge: Vaguely Right or Precisely Wrong.* New York: Oxford University Press, 1986.

McGann, Anthony F., and J. Thomas Russell. *Advertising Media: A Managerial Approach,* 2nd ed. Homewood, Ill.: Irwin, 1988.

Nelson, Carol. *The New Road to Successful Advertising*: *How to Integrate Image and Response.* Chicago, Ill.: Bonus Books, 1991.

Parente, Donald, Bruce Vanden Bergh, Arnold Barban, and James Marra. *Advertising Campaign Strategy: A Guide to Marketing Communication Plans.* Fort Worth, Tex: The Dryden Press, 1996.

Schultz, Don, and Beth Barnes. *Strategic Advertising Campaigns,* 4th ed. Lincolnwood, Ill.: Crain Books / NTC Business Books, 1993.

Stone, Bob. *Successful Direct Marketing Methods*, 5th ed. Lincolnwood, Ill.: NTC Business Books, 1994.

Vaughn, Richard. "How Advertising Works: A Planning Model." *Journal of Advertising Research*, 20 (October 1980), pp. 27–33.

Vaughn, Richard. "How Advertising Works: A Planning Model Revisited." *Journal of Advertising Research*, 26 (February-March 1986), pp. 57–66.

Wall, Robert W. *Media Math: Basic Techniques of Media Evaluation.* Lincolnwood, Ill.: Crain Books / NTC Business Books, 1987.

Yale, David R. *The Publicity Handbook.* Lincolnwood, Ill.: NTC Business Books, 1995.

PART THREE

Objectives, Resources, and Control

Effective marketing communications usually entail an effective system of control. The firm has to articulate its goals clearly and quantitatively. It has to determine the exact amount of resources that are needed to accomplish the stated goals. It has to identify the tests or measures needed to assess performance and use these tests or measures to collect data. It has to ascertain deviations between desired and actual levels and take corrective action. An example of a firm with an effective marketing communications budgeting and control system is Hewlett-Packard (HP), which produces technical products for business. HP tests the effectiveness of every aspect of its marketing program, such as product features, price changes, advertising programs, and channels of distribution. This research has contributed to HP's profitability by allowing it to improve product offerings, set optimal prices, and enhance the quality of its marketing communications.*

Part III describes objectives and measures (chapter 7), budget (chapter 8), and monitoring and control (chapter 9). Chapter 7 on objectives and measures describes how objectives are set at the corporate, marketing, and marketing communications levels. Also, specific measures of the corporate, marketing, and marketing communications objectives are described. Chapter 8 on resource allocation shows how a marketing communication budget can be effectively determined through a top-down procedure. Chapter 9 shows how the marketing communications manager can monitor communication performance and make corrective adjustments in the system at various levels to align future performance with objectives (see Figure III.1).

*William R. BonDurant, "Research: The 'HP Way'," *Marketing Research* (June 1992), pp. 28–33.

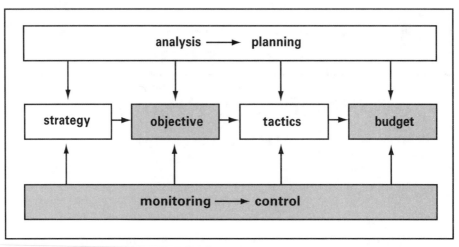

FIGURE III.1 Objectives, Resources, and Control

CHAPTER 7

Objectives and Performance Measures

The Eveready company conducted a marketing communications campaign in 1989 for Energizer batteries. Part of the campaign involved a television commercial that featured a pink bunny toy that kept on "going . . . and going . . . and going." Research has shown that among consumers who named the popular commercial as their favorite of the year, 40% mistakenly attributed it to Duracell, Energizer's main competitor. That is, only 60% correctly identified it. An analysis of one week of prime time television advertising (*Advertising Age*, October 14–20, 1991) showed that out of 57 commercials that ran in an average hour, 24, or 42%, faced at least one competitor running an ad during that same period.[1] These data highlight the importance of research to measure marketing communication performance against explicitly stated objectives. Marketers cannot simply assume that their corporate, marketing, or marketing communications objectives are being met. They have to measure performance explicitly using reliable and valid measures of performance dimensions. This chapter is about research and measurement. We need to be very clear and specific about the objectives that we set for a given marketing communications campaign and monitor its progress and performance.

This chapter introduces the reader to marketing communications objectives, their conceptualizations, and the particular methods and measures used to tap them. All marketing communications decisions are designed to meet particular objectives. These are designated as brand awareness, association, preference, trial, and repeat purchase, and decision outcomes are evaluated against these goals (see Figure 7.1). But before we discuss how corporate and marketing objectives are formulated, let's first discuss the advantages of specifying objectives that are quantifiable and measurable.

ADVANTAGES OF STATING AND QUANTIFYING OBJECTIVES

One study examined ad agency and marketing communications managers' uses of various research methods to evaluate communications effectiveness against objectives.[2] The study found the percentage of organizations that evaluate TV ad campaigns is very high. Specifically, 87.5% responded that marketing/advertising research is used to test the effectiveness of TV campaigns (with 94.9% of ad agencies and 83.6% of advertisers concurring).

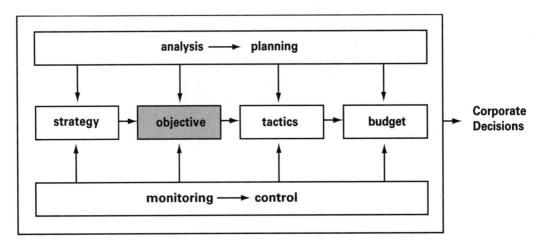

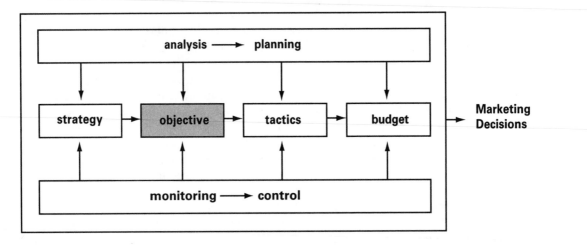

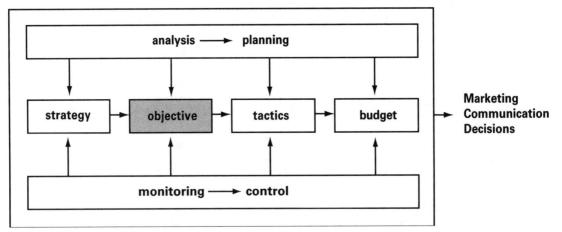

FIGURE 7.1 Corporate, Marketing, and Marketing Communication Objectives

No marketing communications campaign can be effectively planned and executed without specific objectives. Lack of marketing communications objectives has the following disadvantages:

Effectiveness of Marketing Communications Cannot be Assessed: Without marketing communications objectives, a company cannot determine the effectiveness of a marketing communications campaign. This is because it would not know which measurement instruments to use for assessing campaign effectiveness. Effectiveness measures are numerous and varied. To find out which measures to use to assess effectiveness, we first need to know what we are supposed to be measuring. What we are supposed to be measuring is very much dependent on the exact objectives the marketing communications campaign was designed to accomplish. For example, suppose a pharmaceutical company is advertising a brand of analgesic. The ad campaign addresses the benefits of the company's analgesic relative to the leading brand of analgesics. How can we assess the effectiveness of the ad campaign? Should we look at brand sales? How about measuring consumers' purchases? Purchase intention? How about preference for the analgesic brand in relation to the leading brand? Satisfaction with the brand? Extent of repeat purchase? How about brand awareness? The list could go on and on. The idea here is that every marketing communications campaign is designed to accomplish some specific objectives. It may be that the pharmaceutical company developed the ad campaign to increase consumers' preference for their brand over the leading brand by a certain margin. Suppose that the preference for the company's brand of analgesic was currently 10% before the ad campaign. The company wanted to increase the preference to 20% by launching the ad campaign. At the end of the campaign period, the company would assess the effectiveness of the ad campaign by measuring the consumers' preference for the analgesic brand. Suppose the preference effectiveness measure indicates 15%. This means that the ad campaign was moderately effective in that it increased preference from 10% to 15%. However, the objective was 20%. In other words, they fell short by 5%.

Marketing Communications Tactics Cannot be Formulated: Without marketing communications objectives, the marketing communications manager is not likely to know what marketing communications tactics or programs to use. There are varied elements of the marketing communications mix to choose from in developing a communications campaign. Specifically, the manager is very much concerned with the question, "What configuration of the marketing communications mix would best accomplish the marketing communications objectives?" Should the marketing communications manager develop a campaign through advertising? How about a mix of advertising and personal selling? How about a mix of direct marketing and sales promotion? We need to know marketing communications objectives first and foremost before we can select the right tools to accomplish the stated objectives. As an analogy, think of a tool box. There are many tools in a tool box. Each tool is designed to accomplish something, something concrete and specific. Similarly, the elements of the marketing communications mix are like tools. Without marketing communications objectives, we would not be able to effectively choose the appropriate mix. The selection of a marketing communications mix is partly guided by marketing communications objectives.

Market Communications Budget Cannot be Determined: Without marketing communications tactics, the marketing communications manager cannot figure out an optimal budget to develop a marketing communications campaign. "How much should we spend on a communications campaign?" is a very common question. The marketing communications manager doesn't want to overspend or underspend. To figure out exactly how much to spend, first and foremost the manager needs to define what he or she is trying to accomplish. Then, it is much easier to figure out the tools needed to accomplish the objectives and the cost of using these tools.

SETTING OBJECTIVES

Setting objectives is an organizational task involving three key processes: (1) identification of one or more objective dimensions, (2) identification of the measures used to gauge outcomes related to each objective; and (3) identification of the desired level and time frame associated with each objective dimension. Let's discuss each of these tasks in some detail and provide illustrations.

Identification of One or More Objective Dimensions

Here, the marketing communications manager tries to select appropriate goals or objectives. For example, in the last chapter (chapter 6), we addressed at least four strategies, each having its own distinctive objective: *brand awareness, learning, attitude, trial purchase,* and *repeat purchase.* The awareness objective is the goal to achieve a certain level of brand awareness in the minds of a target market. For example, a pizza restaurant in a college town launches a marketing communications campaign directed to college students. The owner states his objective as follows: "I want 95% of college freshmen students to become aware of my pizza place in the next three months."

A *brand learning* objective is the goal to achieve a certain level of comprehension of the products' benefits of the product. "We need to get target consumers to understand what our product is all about." The owner of the pizza place may say, "I want at least 60% of the college freshman students to know that my pizza tastes better because of the special tomato sauce I use. I want them to know this in the next three months." Both brand awareness and learning objectives are consistent with the informative (thinker) strategy (refer back to Table 6.1). As you may recall, the informative strategy applies to products that are highly involving and of the thinking type. For example, the purchase of a kitchen appliance such as a refrigerator or a microwave oven dictates that consumers are likely to adopt such a product if they become aware of its existence and are educated about its benefits and costs. Therefore, the goal is to make target consumers aware of the advertised brand and educated about its benefits and costs, i.e., brand learning.

A *brand attitude* objective is the goal to achieve a certain level of positive attitude toward the product. Statements reflecting this objective are: "We need to get the target consumers to develop a preference for our product." "We want the communications campaign to increase brand preference by 20% in the next six months." The pizza place owner may say, "I want at least 40% of all college students to prefer my pizza place over the other pizza places we have in town." Both brand awareness and attitude objectives are consistent with the affective (feeler) strategy (refer back to Table 6.1). The affective strategy applies to products that are highly involving but are of the feeling rather than thinking type. For example, the purchase of a sports car fits the profile in question. Consumers are likely to purchase a sports car if they not only become aware of it but also establish positive feelings for it. Thus, the goal is to make target consumers aware of the advertised brand and feel good about the brand at a gut level, i.e., brand attitude or liking.

A *brand trial* objective is the goal to induce a certain level of the target market to purchase (or at least to plan to purchase) the product. Statements reflecting this objective might be: "We need to get 35% of the target market to express a purchase intention of our product by the years end," or (as the owner of the pizza place might say) "I want at least 40% of the college freshmen students to try my pizza at least once in the next three months."

Finally, the *repeat purchase* objective is the goal to achieve a certain level of purchases in a given period of time as a direct function of the campaign. "We need to increase the number of purchases per individual consumer. Approximately 80% of our target consumers are purchasing our product once a month, and 20% twice a month. We want to get 50% to purchase the product twice a month by the end of next year." The pizza place owner might say, "I want 80% of my college student patrons to express a great deal of satisfaction with my pizza and to indicate that they will eat pizza in my place again in the next few weeks." Brand trial and repeat purchase objectives are consistent with both the habit formation (doer) and self-satisfaction (reactor) strategies. The habit formation (doer) strategy applies to products that are low in involvement and of the thinking type. For example, the purchase of toothpaste is a low involvement product and most consumers purchase a specific brand of toothpaste because of a utilitarian feature such as tartar control, fluoride, taste, and so on. These utilitarian features reflect thinking rather than feeling. Therefore, the goal of a marketing communications campaign is to induce trial purchase and learning from product use for first-time users and reinforce learning for repeat users (refer back to Table 6.1).

The self-satisfaction (reactor) strategy applies to products that are low in involvement and of the feeling type. For example, the purchase of perfume qualifies as being a low involvement/feeling-type product. Most consumers adopt a brand of perfume after a trial purchase and given that they feel good about it. Therefore, the goal of a marketing communications campaign is to induce trial purchase and generate positive feelings for first-time users and reinforce these positive feelings over and over for repeat users (refer back to Table 6.1).

The challenge is to identify the appropriate objectives that are consistent with the selected strategy and its strategic mix. This again was the subject of the preceding chapter. Having read the chapter 6 (or, more broadly speaking, Part II of the book), you now know what objective dimensions go with what strategies and what elements of the strategic mix go with what strategy and what objective. The point is to: select the appropriate objectives that closely match the selected strategy and its strategic mix.

Identify the Measures Used to Gauge Outcomes

Once one or more objective dimensions are specified, the marketing communications manager has to identify the valid and reliable measures that are well established in the industry for each selected objective. In addition, the norms pertaining to that measure must be identified. For example, suppose we select a brand awareness objective. We must examine alternative measures of awareness and select a suitable method and measure.

Next, we examine the norms of that measure. Are there previous studies using this measure with our product, a comparable product, a comparable target market, and a comparable marketing communications campaign? Suppose our product is a brand of deodorant soap. We're planning an awareness strategy to be implemented through a TV ad campaign that should last six months. Our target consumers are adult women. Now suppose we find several studies that deal with a comparable market, product, and ad campaign. Now let's say that, based on these studies, the average increase in brand awareness after sixth months of TV advertising seems to hover around 50%. Now, we are in a position to go to the next step and identify the desired level associated with the selected objective.

Identify the Desired Level and the Time Frame

Knowing the norms of the measure that will be used to gauge the performance of our advertising campaign, we are now positioned to identify the goal of the communications campaign in a very concrete and quantitative way. Should the marketing communications manager set his or her goal to reflect the norm, above the norm, or below the norm? If a 50% increase in brand awareness is the norm, should the goal be 50%? Greater than 50%? Or less than 50%?

Setting one's objective above the norm is possible when the marketing communications manager knows that his or her communications campaign is likely to be more effective than the campaigns of comparable products. Conversely, if the marketing communications manager believes that his or her campaign is not likely to be as effective, then perhaps setting objectives below the norm is better. In the absence of strong feelings one way or the other, the marketing communications manager should set objectives at a level reflecting the norm.

Note that the time frame must also match comparability with previous studies to be guided by the norms of these previous studies. For example, if most of the previous studies conducted with comparable products and communications campaigns involve a time frame of six months (duration of the entire ad campaign), then the time frame of the planned campaign should also be six months.

In the analysis and planning chapter (chapter 11), we will describe how situation analysis is conducted to assist the marketing communications manager in determining the exact level of the desired state. The manager considers factors such as the firm's past and forecasted performance, the competition's past and anticipated performance, anticipated changes in the industry and marketplace, and anticipated changes in the firm itself.

EXAMPLES OF OBJECTIVES

Here are three examples of possible objectives for MapLinx (the software program that keeps track of sales data using geographic plots, as shown in Figure 5.4). Objectives are stated in terms of next quarter (the next three months), the second quarter (the three months after next quarter), and the third quarter (the three months after the second quarter).

Corporate Objectives

- **Objectives for Next Quarter:** MapLinx will be introduced at the beginning of next quarter. Therefore the goal is to establish sales of MapLinx by capturing 2% of the global market. This translates into 100,000 units sold by the end of next quarter.

- **Objectives for the Second Quarter:** Capture another 5% of the global market. This translates into 250,000 additional unit sales by the end of the second quarter. The total units sold at the end of the second quarter should be 350,000.

- **Objectives for the Third Quarter:** Capture another 10% of the global market. This translates into 500,000 additional unit sales by the end of the third quarter. The total units sold at the end of the third quarter should be 850,000.

Marketing Objectives

- **Objectives for Next Quarter:** Establish an *association* between MapLinx (brand) and the visual clarity of the maps (product attribute) so that at least 7% of sales managers in the global market (or 350,000 sales managers out of the entire population of 5 million) will come to describe MapLinx by referring to its visual clarity. This should be accomplished by the end of next quarter.

- **Objectives for Second Quarter:** Increase the *association* between MapLinx (brand) and the visual clarity of the maps (product attribute) so that at least 15% of sales managers in the global market (or 750,000 sales managers out of the entire population of 5 million) will come to describe MapLinx by referring to its visual clarity. This should be accomplished by the end of the second quarter.

- **Objectives for Third Quarter:** Increase the *association* between MapLinx (brand) and the visual clarity of the maps (product attribute) so that at least 30% of sales managers in the global market (or 1.5 million sales managers out of the entire population of 5 million) will come to describe MapLinx by referring to its visual clarity. This should be accomplished by the end of the third quarter.

Marketing Communications Objectives

- **Objectives for Next Quarter:** Establish *brand awareness* of MapLinx so that at least 10% of sales managers in the global market (or 500,000 sales managers out of the entire population of 5 million) will recognize MapLinx as a sales management software. This should be accomplished by the end of next quarter. Establish *brand association* between MapLinx (brand) and the visual clarity of the maps (product attribute) so that at least 7% of sales managers in the global market (or 350,000 sales managers out of the entire population of 5 million) will come to describe MapLinx by referring to its visual clarity. This should be accomplished by the end of the next quarter. Establish *brand preference* for MapLinx so that at least 5% of sales managers in the global market (or 250,000 sales managers out of the entire population of 5 million) will come to express liking and preference for MapLinx by the end of next quarter. Establish *brand trial* for MapLinx so that at least 3% of sales managers in the global market (or 150,000 sales managers out of the entire population of 5 million) will come to order it on a trial basis by the end of next quarter.

- **Objectives for the Second Quarter:** Increase *brand awareness* of MapLinx so that at least 20% of sales managers in the global market (or 1 million sales managers out of the entire population of 5 million) will recognize MapLinx as a sales management software. This should be accomplished by the end of the second quarter. Increase the *brand association* between MapLinx (brand) and the visual clarity of the maps (product attribute) so that at least 15% of sales managers in the global market (or 750,000 sales managers out of the entire population of 5 million) will come to describe MapLinx by referring to its visual clarity. This should be accomplished by the end of the second quarter. Increase *brand preference* for MapLinx so that at least 10% of sales managers in the global market (or 500,000 sales managers out of the entire population of 5 million) will come to express liking and preference for MapLinx by the end of the second quarter. Increase *brand trial* for MapLinx so that at least 7% of sales managers in the global market (or 350,000 sales managers out of the entire population of 5 million) will come to order it on a trial basis by the end of the second quarter.

- **Objectives for the Third Quarter:** Increase *brand awareness* of MapLinx so that at least 40% of sales managers in the global market (or 2 million sales managers out of the entire population of 5 million) will recognize MapLinx as a sales management software. This should be accomplished by the end of the third quarter. Increase the *brand association* between MapLinx (brand) and the visual clarity of the maps (product attribute) so that at least 40% of sales managers in the global market (or 2 million sales managers out of the entire population of 5 million) will come to describe MapLinx by referring to its visual clarity. This should be accomplished by the end of the third quarter. Increase *brand preference* for MapLinx so that at least 20% of sales managers in the global market (or 1 million sales managers out of the entire population of 5 million) will come to express liking and preference for MapLinx by the end of the third quarter. Increase *brand trial* for MapLinx so that at least 13% of sales managers in the global market (or 650,000 sales managers out of the entire population of 5 million) will come to order it on a trial basis by the end of the third quarter.

The corporate, marketing, and marketing communications objectives are summarized in Table 7.1.

TABLE 7.1 Examples of Corporate, Marketing, and Marketing Communications Objectives

	Next Quarter Objectives	Second Quarter Objectives	Third Quarter Objectives
Corporate Objective:			
Sales	2%	5%	10%
Marketing Objectives:			
Brand association	7%	15%	30%
Marketing Communications Objectives:			
Brand awareness	10%	20%	40%
Brand preference	5%	10%	20%
Brand trial	3%	7%	13%

Note: The size of the target consumer population is 5 million. For example, the 2% sales objective for the next quarter means that the goal is to capture 2% of the market in sales by the end of next quarter, which amounts to 100,000 units (2% × 5 million). The 7% brand association for next quarter means that the goal is to establish a mental association between the brand and an important feature so that at least 7% of the market will come to describe the brand in terms of that feature, and this has to be accomplished by the end of next quarter. The 10% brand awareness objective for next quarter means that the goal is to make 10% of the target consumers aware of the brand by the end of next quarter. The 5% brand preference for next quarter means that the goal is to make 5% of the target consumers prefer the brand in question over competitor brands, and this should be accomplished by the end of next quarter. The 3% brand trial for next quarter means that the goal is to make 3% of the market order the product on a trial basis by the end of next quarter.

MEASURES OF CORPORATE OBJECTIVES

Corporate objectives are usually classified as either long term or short term. Long-term marketing objectives involve measurable standards such as brand sales and market share. Short-term objectives usually involve measures of profit and cash flow. Usually, short-term marketing effectiveness is judged at the corporate level in terms of profits. In this section we will show the reader how marketing communications managers conceptualize and measure profit, cash flow, brand sales, market share, and conduct market tests (see Table 7.2).

Profit and Cash Flow

The most common measures of short-term marketing effectiveness are profit and cash flow. *Profit* is usually defined as the difference between the company's sales revenue and the cost of producing and selling the good.[3] Mathematically formulated:[4]

$$Z = R - C$$

where

Z = product's profit

R = product's revenue

C = product's costs

in which

$$R = P' \times Q$$

where

P' = product's net price

Q = quantity sold

where

$$P' = P - k$$

in which

P = product's list price

k = unit allowance representing freight, commissions, and/or discounts

where

$$C = cQ + F + M$$

in which

c = unit variable nonmarketing costs (e.g., labor costs, delivery costs)

F = fixed costs (e.g., salaries, rent, electricity)

M = marketing costs (e.g., advertising, sales promotion)

therefore

$$Z = [(P - k)Q] - (cQ - F - M)$$

Cash flow, on the other hand, is nothing more than a figure that indicates how much cash the firm has in-hand. Usually a profit/loss statement is generated after the completion of a project or periodically, such as every quarter, every year, and so on. A

TABLE 7.2 Measures of Corporate Objectives and Performance

Profit (Gross Profit or Net Profit in relation to a specific brand)
Cash flow (Net Income in relation to a specific brand)
Sales (Sales in $ or units belonging to a specific brand)
Market share (Percent of sales belonging to a specific brand)

cash flow statement can be generated any time to indicate how much cash is available, whether the firm has enough cash to pay its bills this month, next month, and so on.

Brand Sales and Market Share

A common way to measure marketing effectiveness is to plot sales figures over time and to overlap the plot with marketing communications expenditures and the different types of marketing communications that have been used over the same period. The graphs may clearly show that changes in sales are being influenced by changes in marketing communications type and expenditure levels. For example, the graph may show that sales peaked at a time when marketing communications expenditures were highest. The inference then might well be that high expenditures are likely to drive up sales.

The market share measure is a variation of the brand sales measure in that it accounts for the relation of the company's brand sales in relation to competitor brands within the same period (e.g., last quarter). We will focus on two popular forms of measuring brand sales and market share. These are the proportion of sales method and the market test method.

Proportion of Sales Method

Market share is usually formulated as follows:

$$M1 = S1 / (S2 + S3 + S4 + \ldots Sn)$$

where

$M1$ = market share belonging to Brand 1
$S1$ = sales belonging to Brand 1
$S2$ = sales belonging to Brand 2
$S3$ = sales belonging to Brand 3
$S4$ = sales belonging to Brand 4
Sn = sales belonging to Brand n

Market Test Method

The focus of a market test is to select a representative geographic area and conduct a periodic survey to measure the level of sales over time. Changes in sales are interpreted to be a function of the marketing communications campaign over time.

In particular, market tests are employed to test the viability of a new brand before its introduction at the national or international level. High levels of brand sales (and/or market share) in the test market is taken as an indication of the effectiveness of the marketing communications campaign.

Another use of the market test method is to test the effectiveness of different marketing communications campaigns. For example, suppose that three different marketing communications campaigns are selected. The campaigns are implemented in different test markets, and brand sales (and/or market share) are monitored in each of the test markets. The test market that records the highest levels of sales (and/or market share) signifies a successful marketing communications campaign.

MEASURES OF MARKETING OBJECTIVES

Let us review what we talked about in the Marketing Strategy and Tactics chapter (chapter 5). We described several marketing strategies and the objectives of each of these strategies. The strategies and objectives all sought to positively influence brand equity—*brand associations, brand knowledge,* or *brand image.* Brand image is an outcome of learning something about the brand, its performance features, and other features such as reliability, durability, quality, price, stereotypic image of the user, and so on. A major goal of any marketing program is to mold the right image of the brand in the minds of the target consumers. This means that the marketing communications manager has to educate the consumer about certain attributes of the brand.

Consumer researchers usually show brand knowledge as a connection between a node representing the brand and other nodes representing attributes (see Figure 7.2). For example, "Crest toothpaste whitens teeth" is a brand belief. This belief links the brand, Crest, with an attribute—"whitens teeth." Each belief can be characterized in terms of strength and valence. The strength of a belief reflects the strength of the linkage between the brand node and the attribute node. Looking at Figure 7.2, we can see that the belief strength of "Crest toothpaste has nice color" is the strongest belief; the second strongest is "Crest toothpaste whitens teeth"; the weakest belief is "Crest toothpaste fights plaque."

The valence property of a belief reflects the desirability of that belief in relation to other beliefs. For Crest toothpaste, note that in the mind of that particular consumer, the consumer regards the attributes of "whitens teeth," "freshens breath," "tastes good," and "cavity prevention" to be highly desirable (four positive signs). The desirability of "tartar control" is moderate, while "fights plaque," "has nice color," and "is reasonably priced" are somewhat desirable.

The marketing communications manager's task is to identify strengths and weaknesses within the brand belief/knowledge structure. An attribute that is considered highly desirable but may not be strongly linked with the brand in the minds of the target consumers signals a weakness, or a strategic gap. The marketing communications manager, thus, can set a marketing objective to strengthen a weak belief (e.g., Crest toothpaste fights plaque) by formulating a communications campaign aimed at strengthening this belief in the minds of the target consumers. Of course, the communications claims about the attribute have to be substantiated. Strategic opportunities also are identified based on strengths. In other words, instead of formulating a campaign to address a weak belief and attempt to strengthen it, the focus can be on strong beliefs. By focusing on established beliefs, the marketing communications manager thus can capitalize on positive characteristics and further reinforce these. One approach is corrective action; the other is reinforcement.

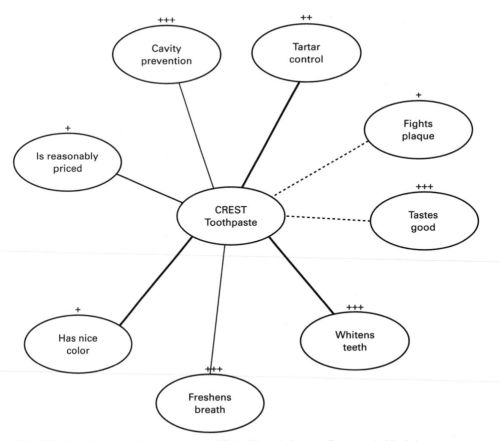

FIGURE 7.2 A Schematic Representation of Belief/Knowledge in a Consumer's Mind about Crest Toothpaste

Marketing communications researchers use measures of brand knowledge not only to ensure that the target consumers have formed the "right" beliefs about the brand in question, but also to understand which beliefs are most related to brand purchase. For example, suppose you are a marketing communications manager of a new brand of toothpaste. Your brand has been advertised to emphasize the following benefits: tartar control, plaque prevention, tooth decay prevention, teeth whitening, fresh breath, good taste, and pump dispenser.

Suppose research reveals that brand purchase among teenagers, the target market, is directly related to the following benefits: whitens teeth, freshens breath, and tastes good. That is, brand purchase may be determined by consumers' beliefs about these benefits; hence, these particular benefits should be treated as more important than others. Future marketing communications efforts thus can be adjusted to emphasize the benefits that are directly related to purchase behavior (and to deemphasize those not directly related to behavior).

The following sections will discuss and review common measures of marketing objectives (see Table 7.3).

TABLE 7.3 Measures of Marketing Objectives and Performance

Recognition measures of brand knowledge
Aided recall measures of brand knowledge
The image measure of brand knowledge
The cognitive structure index
The belief strength measure
Projective methods of brand associations
Associative strength measures of brand awareness

Recognition Measures of Brand Knowledge

Recognition measures of brand knowledge deal with the recognition of specific aspects (mostly product benefits) formed about the brand in question. For example, Johnson Controls company is an industrial company that introduced a total building automation system permitting all automatic building systems to be monitored, coordinated, and operated by a single computer. The company was advertised in the *Wall Street Journal* for six months. The company may then wonder what kind of impression potential customers have formed about the company after the six-month ad campaign in the *Wall Street Journal.* Johnson Controls' goal was to instill certain beliefs about the company, namely that the company can install the building automation system and that the building automation system can monitor, coordinate, and operate all automated aspects of the building. Measuring brand knowledge in this case is a matter of asking respondents whether they recognize that the company offers these benefits.

Responses are usually coded as "yes" or "no," and a percentage of those who said "yes" is determined by each belief statement (e.g., the total building system can monitor all automatic building systems; the total building system can coordinate all automatic building systems; the total building system can operate all automatic building systems; Johnson Controls can install the total building system, etc.). Of course, like all tests and measures testing the effectiveness of the marketing program, the before-the-campaign scores are compared with the after-the-campaign scores. This measure of brand knowledge is highly suitable to assess the effects of marketing communications campaigns guided by any of the 15 positioning strategies described in chapter 5.

Aided Recall Measures of Brand Knowledge

Aided recall measures usually involve asking a sample of consumers from the target market in an open-ended manner to list everything they know about the brand in question.[5] The open-ended responses are then analyzed, and brand beliefs statements are identified and tabulated. This is done before and after the launch of the communications program. The percentage of subjects identifying a certain brand attribute before the communications campaign is then compared to the percentage of subjects identifying the same attribute after the campaign. Like the recognition measure, this measure too can be used to assess the effects of all 15 positioning strategies.

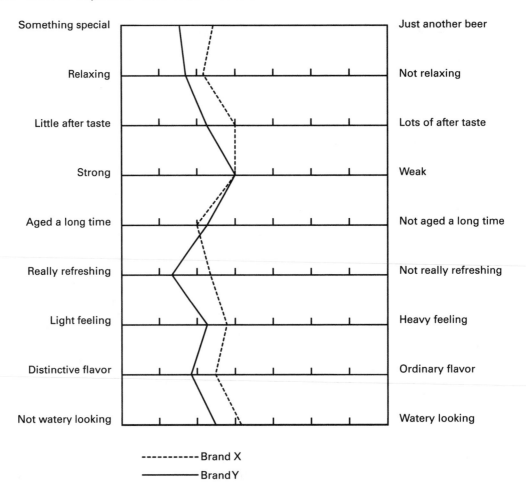

FIGURE 7.3 A Semantic Differential Comparison of Branded Beers

The Image Measure of Brand Knowledge

A very popular instrument that has been commonly used to measure beliefs or knowledge of a particular brand is a modified version of the semantic differential scale. Figure 7.3 shows an example of a profile of beliefs/knowledge pertaining to three brands of beer.

This measure involves a certain configuration of beliefs represented on bipolar scales, thus: something special/just another beer; relaxing/not relaxing; little after-taste/lots of aftertaste; strong/weak, aged a long time/not aged a long time, and so on. The respondent evaluates a certain brand of beer in relation to other brands of beer by marking a response somewhere between the polar extremes of each of the bipolar scales. The responses for each attribute dimension are averaged across all respondents. The result is a belief/knowledge profile of the brand in question contrasted with belief/knowledge profiles of the competing brands.

As in all tests and measures of marketing program effectiveness, premeasures and postmeasures are administered, and the effectiveness of the communications campaign is judged in terms of the degree of change in the brand image profile. This measure is particularly suitable to assess the effectiveness of the following positioning strategies: *positioning by attribute, positioning by intangible factor, positioning by customer benefits,* and *positioning by distributor's service capability.*

The Cognitive Structure Index

The Cognitive Structure Index is constructed from items asking subjects to indicate their level of agreement with brand attribute statements. For example, items for an RCA portable radio might include: "delivers high quality sound," and "is small and lightweight." These perceptions are measured on seven-point scales anchored by "extremely unlikely" (−3) and "extremely likely" (+3).[6]

To judge the effectiveness of a marketing campaign in terms of brand knowledge, the precampaign average score pertaining to each belief item is compared with its corresponding postcampaign score. For example, the precampaign average score pertaining to the belief that the RCA radio brand "delivers high quality sound" is +1.2, whereas the post-campaign score is +2.8. Therefore, the campaign has changed the belief that the brand delivers high quality sound from a +1.2 to a +2.8, or an average change of +1.6 units. This measure, like the image measure of brand knowledge, is particularly suitable to assess the effectiveness of the following positioning strategies: *positioning by attribute, positioning by intangible factor, positioning by customer benefits,* and *positioning by distributor's service capability.*

The Belief Strength Measure

Belief strength is measured by asking subjects, "How likely do you think it is that (the brand) has (attribute *x*)?" Responses are plotted on a seven-point scale labeled from "zero likelihood" to "certain" (coded 1 to 7).[7] The idea here is that the communications campaign is responsible for increasing the certainty or strength of certain beliefs about the brand (the belief that the brand has attribute *x*). The campaign effectiveness is judged by comparing the average belief strength score of each attribute dimension derived before the launch of the campaign with those derived after the launch of the campaign. This measure may be particularly suitable to assess the effectiveness of the following positioning strategies: *positioning by relative price, positioning by low price, positioning by use or application, positioning by competitors, positioning by country of origin, positioning by brand-distributor tie-in,* and *positioning by distributor's location.*

Projective Methods of Brand Associations

In many instances, consumers feel uncomfortable or may be unable to elicit associations stored in their memories, perhaps because these associations are buried in the subconscious memory. Also, many of the self-report tests and measures of brand knowledge may bias respondents toward logical/rational responses, while in actuality the brand associations that may matter the most are those that are not logical or rational. In these instances, projective methods are effective to tap brand associations.

Typical projective methods include free-association tests, picture-interpretation tests, describing-the-brand-as-a-person tests, describing-the-brand-as-an-animal-or-thing tests, in-depth examination of the person's use experience with the brand, dis-section of the decision process, description of the brand user, description of how brands are different from one another, and discovery of personal values driving choice.[8]

A *free-association* test involves word associations. Subjects are presented with a list of objects, including the brand in question, and asked to provide the first set of words that comes to mind.

The *picture-interpretation* test involves presenting subjects with a picture of a scene in which the brand is embedded in the picture. For example, a brand association test involving BMW may show a person standing in front of the car and looking at it. The subject is asked what this person is thinking and feeling.

The *brand-as-a-person* test asks subjects to select from a set of 50 personality-related words to describe the brand in question. For example, in a study conducted at Young and Rubicam (one of the largest ad agencies in the world), Holiday Inn was described as "cheerful, friendly, ordinary, practical, modern, reliable, and honest"; Atari was described as "youthful"; Oil of Olay was described as "gentle, sophisticated, mature, exotic, mysterious, and down-to-earth."

The *brand-as-an-animal-or-thing* test involves asking subjects to think of animals or animal characteristics that come to mind when thinking about a certain brand. For example, in a study conducted at Young and Rubicam ad agency, subjects were given a list of 29 animals and were asked, "If each of these brands were an animal, what one animal would it be?" They asked similar questions for 25 different activities, 17 fabrics, 35 occupations, and 20 nationalities. The results showed that Oil of Olay was associated with mink, France, secretaries, silk, swimming, and *Vogue* magazine. Kentucky Fried Chicken was associated with Puerto Rico, a zebra, a housewife dressed in denim, camping, and reading *TV Guide*.

The *use-experience* test is an in-depth interview with consumers who have a history of using the brand in question. The discussion focuses on past experience with the product. The subject is encouraged to open up, to remember and express feelings and situations in which the brand was used. Ernest Dichter, a psychologist who was once well known for using projective techniques to uncover hidden motives associated with the use of products and brands, reported the following encounter with Ivory Soap. He interviewed more than 100 users of Ivory Soap, allowing them to express themselves about their bathing habits. One finding was that young women would take an unusually thorough bath before going out on a date. This finding resulted in the ad theme: "Be smart, get a fresh start with Ivory soap."

The *decision-process* test involves tracking a consumer's decision process, traditionally done through an in-depth personal interview. The interviewer starts from the decision to purchase and probes backward to understand the dynamics and the reasons why the consumer has made that decision.

The *brand-user* test is a simple procedure in which subjects are asked to describe the typical brand user. More specifically, subjects are asked how a user of one brand is different from the user of another brand and how the needs and motivations of the users of the two brands differ. For example, a classic study showed that people perceive the brand user of Maxwell House drip-grind coffee to be very different from the user of Nescafé instant coffee. The instant-coffee woman was perceived as a lazy, bad homemaker, whereas the woman buying the drip-grind coffee was perceived as industrious, a good homemaker.

The *how-brand-is-different* test asks subjects to distinguish between various brands in a particular product category. Specifically, this test uses a pairwise comparison. Two brands at a time are shown to a subject, and the subject is asked to point to differences between the two brands. Subtle differences among the different brands may be uncovered using this method, and these differences may play a significant role in brand purchase.

In a more sophisticated version of this method, similarity judgments (judgments of the extent to which two brands are similar) are used in a mutidimensional scaling algorithm. The multidimensional scaling procedure produces spatial maps in which the different brands are plotted in two- or three-dimensional space. The distance between any two brands represents the perceptual similarity/differences between them. Thus, the closer two brands are on the map, the more similar they are in the judgment of consumers.

The *personal values* test, sometimes referred to as the "laddering technique," involves using in-depth interviews to uncover the person's motivation to purchase and use a specific brand. Here the subject is asked to describe the brand attributes. For each attribute the interviewer probes the personal significance of the attribute through a series of "why" questions. Probing why a certain concrete attribute is important to the individual may result in an abstract attribute, which may reveal functional consequences, psychosocial consequences, and personal values.

For example, a consumer may describe a certain brand of car as traveling 45 miles per gallon of gasoline (concrete attribute), which is interpreted as "high" miles per gallon (abstract attribute). The reason this product attribute is important to the individual may be that it helps him/her save money (functional consequence). He thinks that his parents would approve of his buying an economy car (psychosocial consequence). Saving money makes the consumer feel good because he sees himself as responsible and disciplined (instrumental value), which in turn enhances his self-esteem (terminal value). See Figure 7.4 for an example of how this technique is used in a test on Nike shoes.

Projective measures and methods can be effectively employed to assess the more "subtle" positioning strategies, such as *positioning by user or customer, positioning by lifestyle or personality,* and *positioning by brand-distributor tie-ins.*

Associative Strength Measures of Brand Awareness

Associative strength is defined as the strength of the association in memory between the product category and the brand.[9] One study identified two direct measures of associative strength. One measure involves assessing how early a brand was named in response to a directive to list all the members of a given product category. The other measure tests the time it takes consumers to identify correctly a brand name belonging to a given product category. Specifically, subjects are presented with a product category name (e.g., toothpaste) on a monitor, followed by a brand name (e.g., Crest) that is either a member or nonmember of that product category. Subjects press either a "yes" or "no" button to indicate as rapidly as possible whether the brand is a mem-

Researcher: "You said that a shoe's lacing pattern is important to you in deciding what brand to buy. Why is that important to you?"

Consumer: "A staggered lacing pattern makes the shoe fit more snugly on my foot." **[physical attribute and functional consequence]**

Researcher: "Why is it important that the 'shoe fit more snugly on your foot'?"

Consumer: "Because it gives me better support." **[functional consequence]**

Researcher: "Why is better support important to you?"

Consumer: "So I can run without worrying about injuring my feet." **[psychological consequence]**

Researcher: "Why is it important for you not to worry while running?"

Consumer: "So I can relax and enjoy the run." **[psychosocial consequence]**

Researcher: "Why is it important that you can relax and enjoy your run?"

Consumer: "Because it gets rid of tension I have built up at work during the day." **[psychosocial consequence]**

Researcher: "Why is it important for you to get rid of tension from work?"

Consumer: "So when I go back to work in the afternoon, I can perform better." **[instrumental value—high performance]**

Researcher: "Why is it important that you perform 'better'?"

Consumer: "I feel better about myself." **[terminal value—self-esteem]**

Researcher: "Why is it important that you feel better about yourself?"

Consumer: "It just is!" **[the end!]**

FIGURE 7.4 An Example of a Laddering Interview

ber of the specified product category. Associative strength is measured in terms of response latency (how long it took the subject to respond).

Associative strength measures are used to assess the effectiveness of a marketing communications campaign in significantly increasing brand awareness. This is done by administering one associative strength test before the launch of the campaign and another after a period of time. The assumption is that if the campaign is successful in significantly increasing brand awareness, then consumers will more readily associate the brand in question with the product category. Note that this method is most suitable to assess the effectiveness of the *positioning-by-product-class* strategy.

MEASURES OF MARKETING COMMUNICATIONS OBJECTIVES

We'll organize the discussion of the marketing communications measures based on the five objective dimensions discussed in chapter 6. These are *brand awareness, brand comprehension* (or *learning association*), *brand attitude* or *liking, brand trial or purchase,* and *brand loyalty* (*repeat purchase*). It should be noted that the brand comprehension dimension is essentially the same as brand knowledge, the objective dimension used to identify and describe the various objective measures pertaining to *marketing* performance. This is because positioning strategies focus on brand associations, brand image, or brand knowledge. Therefore, since these measures have been covered by the preceding section related to measures of marketing objectives, they will not be repeated here. The various constructs of marketing communications objectives and their measures are shown in Table 7.4.

Brand Awareness

Brand awareness is important because without awareness the consumer cannot travel up the hierarchy. That is, the consumer is not likely to learn about the brand features, feel positive about the brand, make a preference decision, or be convinced to purchase the product. In other words, the consumer has to be aware of the brand before feeling any desire or conviction to use it.

Brand awareness is the ability to recall or recognize a certain brand as being a member of a certain product class, and thus this objective fits well with the positioning-by-product-class strategy. Consider the following brands of housewares: Rubbermaid,

---

TABLE 7.4 Measures of Marketing Communications Objectives and Performance

Brand Awareness
  The Recognition Measure of Brand Awareness
  Aided Recall Measure of Brand Awareness
Brand Attitude
  Cognitive-Brand Attitude
    The Multiattribute Index
    The Thought-Elicitation Procedure
    The Mushiness Index
  Affective-Brand Attitude
    The Semantic Differential Measure of Brand Attitude
    Projective Techniques of Brand Attitude
  Brand Acceptance
    The Brand Listing Procedure
    Unaided Self-Report Questions
  Brand Preference
    The Ranking Method
    The Paired Comparison Method
Brand Trial or Purchase
  Attitude Toward Brand Purchase
    The Semantic Differential Measure of Attitude Toward Purchase
    The Favorability Measure of Attitude Toward Purchase
  Purchase Intention
    A Measure of Purchase Intention Given Product Need
    A Planned Purchase Measure
  Brand Purchase
    Tracking Studies
    Purchase Incentive Measures
Repeat Purchase
  Repeat Purchase
    Repurchase Measures
    Percent of Purchase Measures
  Brand Satisfaction
  Brand Loyalty
    A Multivariate Measure of Brand Loyalty
    A Measure of Entrenched Loyalty

General Electric, Corning, Cannon, Corelle, Ecko, Visions, Sunbeam, Black & Decker, and Libbey. Some consumers may be aware of Corning, for example, as a brand of houseware, while others may fail to recognize the connection. Aaker views brand awareness as a hierarchy consisting of five layers. At the bottom of the hierarchy are the consumers who are unaware of the brand. These people simply do not recognize the brand as belonging to a given product class. The next layer includes those who have *brand recognition*, the minimum level of awareness. *Brand recall* is the layer above it, which includes consumers who can retrieve information from memory concerning the various brands belonging to a product class. Finally, at the top of the hierarchy, we have the *top-of-mind awareness*. These consumers recall the brand first and foremost. The brand name is on the "top of their minds." When asked about a certain product, the brand in question is evoked quickly and with relative ease compared to other brands.[10]

It is important to note the difference between recognition measures of brand awareness and brand knowledge. Brand awareness recognition measures deal mostly with the recognition of the brand name, while recognition measures of brand knowledge deal with the recognition of specific aspects (mostly product benefits) of the brand in question.

The purpose of awareness measures is to tap consumers' memory about the product over a specific time. More specifically, brand awareness tests and measures tap whether consumers remember the brand name before and after the implementation of a marketing program. I will describe three popular measures of brand awareness: the recognition method, the unaided recall method, and the associative strength method.

The Recognition Measure of Brand Awareness

Here is an example of a brand recognition measure that was used to gauge the level of brand awareness before and after an ad campaign. I have already discussed an industrial company, Johnson Controls, that introduced a total building automation system that permits all automatic building systems to be monitored, coordinated, and operated by a single computer. The company wanted to make key people *aware* of the new system, specifically people who make major decisions regarding buildings. So the company ran an ad campaign in the *Wall Street Journal*. They measured brand awareness before the campaign and six months after the ad campaign had been launched. A sample of consumers were asked before the launch of the ad campaign whether they recognized the brand or its name. Responses were coded as "yes" or "no," and the percentage of those who said "yes" was determined.

Before the launch of the ad campaign in the *Wall Street Journal,* the brand awareness of the total building automation system was close to zero percent among the decision makers. After six months of the ad campaign, the same recognition measure of brand awareness was administered to another sample of the target population. The results indicated that brand awareness increased to 63% for the same target population. In other words, since all other promotion and marketing elements were held constant, the 63% change in brand awareness may be attributed to the ad campaign.[11]

Aided Recall Measures of Brand Awareness

Aided recall measures usually involve asking a sample of consumers from the target market to list the names of different brands of the product in question. Aided recall measures are used in tracking studies. Tracking studies use the same measure over a period of time to "track" changes or shifts in a behavioral phenomenon. (In this case the behavioral phenomenon is brand awareness measured through an aided recall testing procedure.)

Some researchers argue that the recognition-type measures are more realistic than aided recall measures because, when faced with a buying decision, consumers are exposed to different brands (as in the supermarket). This exposure to the different brands may serve to facilitate the recognition of the brand in question.[12]

Brand Attitude

Brand attitude is another major marketing communications objective. Marketing communications managers not only try to educate target consumers about the brand itself but also try to do so in such a way that the brand image will result in a positive feeling about the brand. Marketing scholars distinguish between two types of brand attitude—cognitively based and affectively based. They also make a distinction between brand attitude and brand acceptance.

Cognitive Brand Attitude

Cognitive brand attitude refers to the overall positive or negative opinion consumers have about the brand based on "rational" beliefs and cognitions. We define "rational" beliefs and cognitions as the kind of beliefs that are generated by conscious thought. To fully understand the concept of cognitive brand attitude, we need to distinguish cognitive brand attitude from "affective brand attitude." *Affective brand attitude* refers to the overall positive or negative opinion consumers may have about the brand based on emotional considerations. In other words, consumers may form an overall judgment of the "goodness" or "badness" of the brand based on some good reasoning, the kind of reasoning that they may be conscious of and that allows them to articulate the "reasons why" they like or dislike the brand. Thus, a brand attitude formed as a result of well-articulated cognitions (e.g., one's belief that Crest toothpaste is reasonably priced, has a nice color, whitens teeth, and has tartar control) is a cognitively-based brand attitude. In contrast, if a consumer forms an overall opinion of the brand based on an association with an attractive celebrity and is not conscious of the underlying reason, the brand attitude is said to be affective. That is, the consumer's attitude is not based on conscious reasoning. If one were to ask the consumer why he or she likes or dislikes the brand, he or she may not be able to respond accurately, since the information processing occurred at a basic, subconscious, emotional level.

Three methods for assessing cognitive-based brand attitude will be described here. These are the multiattribute index, the thought-elicitation procedure, and the mushiness index.

The Multiattribute Index   Many marketing researchers use a multiattribute attitude index to establish brand attitude scores that are firmly embedded in "reasons why" consumers may like or dislike the brand. The typical multiattribute index takes the following form:

$$A = \Sigma B_i I_i$$
where

> A = cognitive-type attitude score toward the brand
> B_i = belief that the brand has attribute i
> I_i = importance of attribute i in relation to the other attributes

For example, suppose the communications campaign is directed to college students. The goal is to convince the local residents who are college students of large universities to stick around in the summer and take summer courses at the community college. That is, the focus of the ad campaign is to persuade the local residents to attend the community college during the summer by educating them about the college's lower tuition costs, proximity to home, academic reputation of the faculty, party atmosphere, and summer athletic program.

Before the launch of the campaign, a sample of local residents who attend large universities outside of their community would respond to a survey questionnaire in which they are asked the extent to which they believe the local community college has lower tuition costs (compared to the large state universities), is indeed conveniently located, has a good academic reputation, is the kind of place where students would have a good time at parties and other social events, and has a good summer athletic program. These questions are in essence the belief strength (B_i) measures. An example of a measure is as follows:

> Indicate your agreement or disagreement with the following statement: Community College X has a good summer athletic program.

(−3)	(−2)	(−1)	(0)	(+1)	(+2)	(+3)
Highly disagree	Moderately disagree	Slightly disagree	Neither agree nor disagree	Slightly agree	Moderately agree	Highly agree

Traditionally, belief strength measures are comparative. That is, the subject responds to the belief strength questions pertaining to the focal brand (Community College X) in relation to competitive brands (State University Y and Z).

The importance weights (I_i) are usually assigned by instructing respondents to rank the attributes (tuition costs, proximity, academic reputation, party atmosphere, summer athletic program) in terms of importance. The greater the importance, the higher the rank. Here is an example. "Rank these decision criteria in order of importance, using the following scale: 5 = first most important criterion, 4 = second most important criterion, 3 = third most important criterion; 2 = fourth most important criterion; and 1 = fifth most important criterion." See Table 7.5.

Each belief-strength-agreement score is then multiplied by its corresponding importance-weight-rank score. The resulting scores pertaining to each attribute are then summed across all attributes. The higher the total score (in the positive direction), the more favorable the attitude based on the designated attributes (the "reasons why").

TABLE 7.5 Example of Ranking Decision Criteria

Decision Criteria	Rank
Tuition costs	4
Proximity	3
Academic reputation	5
Party atmosphere	2
Summer athletics	1

Note: The higher the score the more important the decision criterion.

At a specific time after the launch of the campaign, the same survey is readministered, and the attitude of the local residents who attend the state universities is reassessed. The campaign is deemed effective (based on a cognitive brand attitude objective) if the postcampaign attitude scores are significantly higher than the precampaign scores.

The Thought-Elicitation Procedure The thought-elicitation procedure is another test of brand attitude (the cognitive component). Subjects are presented with the actual brand (or a description of it in words and/or pictures). They are then asked to evaluate the brand strengths and weaknesses (possibly in relation to competitive brands) and to record their thoughts in writing. A variation of this procedure is to request the subject to think out loud and record the verbal expressions on a tape recorder. The thoughts are then analyzed by trained judges. The judges identify favorable and unfavorable thoughts about the brand and record their frequency.

A subject's brand attitude score is computed in terms of a simple arithmetic difference by subtracting the number of negative thoughts from the number of positive thoughts. Of course, the test is administered before the onset of the campaign and after the ad campaign. The effectiveness of the ad campaign is judged in terms of the extent to which it is able to generate more positive than negative thoughts about the brand.

The Mushiness Index Attitude strength can be measured through different methods. One method that is gaining popularity in advertising/public opinion literatures is Yankelovich, Skelly, and White's "Mushiness Index."[13] The mushiness index was specially designed to determine the firmness of an attitude. The measure contains four items. Two sample items are shown in Table 7.6.

It should be noted that the mushiness score is not used exclusively as a measure of the cognitive component of brand attitude. The mushiness score is used with some other measures of brand attitude that capture the valence of the attitude. As with other tests and measures of campaign effectiveness, a survey is done before the launch of the campaign, and the attitude strength and valence scores are computed. Another survey is conducted using the same measures after a specified period of time, and attitude strength and valence scores are computed again. The precampaign score is then compared with the postcampaign score to judge effectiveness.

Affective Brand Attitude

The focus here is on attitude, the kind of attitude that is formed or changed as a direct function of subtle and emotional factors. For example, consider a communica-

TABLE 7.6 Examples of Mushiness Index Items

"On some issues, people feel that they really have all the information that they need in order to form a strong opinion on that issue, while on other issues they would like to get additional information before solidifying their opinion. On a scale of 1 to 5, where 1 means that you feel you definitely need more information, where would you place yourself?"

| Definitely need | 1 | 2 | 3 | 4 | 5 | Do not need |
| more information | | | | | | more information |

"People have told us that on some issues they come to a conclusion and they stick with that position, no matter what. On other issues, however, they make take a position but they know that they could change their minds easily. On a scale of 1 to 5, where 1 means that you could change your mind very easily on this issue, and 5 means that you are likely to stick with your position no matter what, where would you place yourself?"

| Could change your | 1 | 2 | 3 | 4 | 5 | Likely to stick with |
| mind very easily | | | | | | your position no matter what |

tions program involving an ad that employs a very attractive celebrity (one who is considered a sex symbol). It is likely that the target consumers may form a positive attitude toward the advertised brand mostly because of the celebrity. Here the attitude is formed (or changed) not because the consumers thought about the brand, its benefits, its costs, and so on but because of uncontrollable factors operating in the subconscious. In this section, I'll describe two tests or measures of affectively-based brand attitude. These are the semantic differential scale and projective techniques.

The Semantic Differential Measure of Brand Attitude   Measuring the effects of a marketing campaign on brand attitude usually involves testing a given sample of consumers regularly over a period of time with the same test to see if there is any change in their attitudes toward the product.

The test most often used is the semantic differential, which uses adjectives about the product.[14] Examples of adjectives used in the semantic differential measure of brand attitude are shown in Table 7.7.

An average composite is computed from the before-the-campaign survey and pitted against the average composite from the after-the-campaign survey. The ad campaign is expected to significantly raise the average composite score.

TABLE 7.7 An Example of Semantic Differential Scales Used to Measure Brand Attitude

	4	3	2	1	
very appealing	___	___	___	___	very unappealing
very good	___	___	___	___	very bad
high preference	___	___	___	___	low preference
very beautiful	___	___	___	___	very ugly
very special	___	___	___	___	not special
very happy	___	___	___	___	very unhappy
very much like	___	___	___	___	very much dislike
very favorable	___	___	___	___	very unfavorable

Projective Techniques of Brand Attitude   Projective techniques are research tests that avoid the pitfalls of a direct question, such as, "Do you like this brand?" Projective techniques permit subjects to indirectly project their feelings. Examples of indirect questions include: "What thoughts come to your mind when you think of Brand X?" "What do you think of the person who buys Brand X?" "What motives, needs, or desires does this product serve?"

Some projective tests involve sentence completion or drawing pictures. For example, researchers at McCann-Erickson used a projective technique to investigate why women continued to buy a brand of roach killer in canned sprays. Women subjects were asked to draw pictures of roaches and write stories about their sketches. The results indicated that the subjects identified all the roaches in the pictures as male roaches. The interpretation was that these male roaches symbolized men who had abandoned the women subjects and left them feeling poor and powerless. Killing the roaches with a bug spray and watching them squirm and die allowed the women to express their hostility toward the men who abandoned them.[15]

The effectiveness of a marketing program using projective techniques is judged using the before-after campaign method.

Brand Acceptance

Marketing researchers have distinguished between brand attitude and "brand acceptance." *Brand acceptance* refers to the psychological process involving information assimilation about the brand leading to the judgment the advertised brand is an acceptable alternative. Brand acceptance is considered highly important from a marketing point of view because it is a precursor to brand choice and purchase. That is, acceptable brand alternatives are pitted against each other in decision making, leading to brand choice and purchase. Acceptable brands are evoked from memory for further consideration. Therefore, an ad campaign can be developed for the purpose of making a brand acceptable to target consumers. Two tests or measures will be described as research techniques operationalizing brand acceptance. These are the brand listing procedure and unaided self-report questions.

The Brand Listing Procedure   For the brand listing procedure, respondents are asked at the moment of purchase to indicate the brand they chose in a given situation, as in the moment of purchase. The interviewer comes up to the consumer in the supermarket (or some other retail outlet) and asks the consumer to grant an interview about the brand choice he or she has just made. Next, respondents are asked to list the names of any other brands they considered while making their choice. They are usually given 30 seconds for the brand listing task.[16]

The effectiveness of a marketing communications program can be judged by running the brand listing procedure twice, once before the launch of the program and a second time after a specified period of time. An effective program will significantly increase the percentage of respondents listing the brand in question.

Unaided Self-Report Questions   Consideration set content (the set of brand considered for purchase) is measured by a subject's response to unaided self-report questions.[17] Examples of questions include:

1. What brands are you are willing to buy?
2. What brands do you consider acceptable for purchase?
3. What brands would you consider buying?
4. What brands did you find acceptable for purchase the last time you purchased the product?
5. What brands did you consider buying the last time you purchased the product?

A percentage of respondents listing the brand in question is derived from responses to any of these questions. A marketing communications program is deemed effective if it is instrumental in raising the percentage score.

Brand Preference

Brand preference refers to the liking consumers have for one brand over competitor brands in the same product category. Brand preference is different from brand attitude in the sense that a consumer may have a positive attitude toward one brand but may feel the same way about other brands. From the vantage point of the marketing communications manager, brand liking, therefore, is not good enough. The marketing communications manager needs to ensure that the positive feelings consumers have toward the brand are such that the consumer will prefer the brand over alternative brands. Similarly, brand acceptance merely indicates to the marketing communications manager that consumers will consider the brand when they need to purchase an item in the product category. But marketing communications managers need to know whether the brand is preferred over competitors' brands because preference is very likely to lead to brand purchase. Two tests or measures of brand preference will be described here. These are the ranking method and the paired comparison method.

The Ranking Method   For the ranking method, respondents judge their liking of a specific brand by ranking it in relation to other brands. For example, suppose we have five brands. The subjects are asked to express their liking of each brand by ranking each from 1 to 5, 1 being the brand that is most preferred and 5 being the brand that is least preferred. This method is commonly used when the number of brands to be judged is small, usually fewer than six. The viability of this method declines drastically when the subject has to rank more than six brands. When a large pool of brands must be judged, the paired comparison method is used.

The Paired Comparison Method   This method involves instructing the subjects to indicate whether they like or dislike a given brand in relation to another brand. For example, if the marketing communications manager's brand is *A,* and there are seven other alternatives *B, C, D, E, F, G,* and *H,* then subjects indicate their liking of each brand in relation to each of the other brands in turn (see Table 7.8).

Brand Trial or Purchase

Brand trial or purchase refers to the extent to which consumers have psychologically committed themselves to trying the product and therefore buying it. This commitment may be in the form of an intention to purchase the brand given the right circumstances, such as on the next shopping trip or when the current brand is worn out or de-

TABLE 7.8 The Paired Comparison Method

	A	B	C	Referent Brands D	E	F	G	H	Total Score
Brand A		yes	no	yes	yes	no	no	no	3/7
Brand B			yes	yes	yes	yes	yes	yes	7/7
Brand C				no	no	no	no	yes	2/7
Brand D					yes	no	yes	no	4/7
Brand E						yes	yes	yes	4/7
Brand F							no	no	2/7
Brand G								yes	4/7
Brand H									4/7

Note: A "yes" response means that the brand is liked better than the referent brand, e.g., the "yes" response for Brand A in relation to Brand B (referent brand) means that Brand A is preferred over Brand B.

The total score for each brand per subject is derived by summing all the "yes" responses for that brand. For example, Brand A received a total preference score of 3/7. This means that Brand A was preferred in relation to three other brands. Brand F was preferred in relation to two other brands. This score is computed by adding all the "yes" responses going down the Brand F vertical column and across the Brand F horizontal row.

The results of this matrix shows that the particular respondent indicates that he or she prefers Brand B the best, followed by a tie among brands D, E, G, and H, followed by Brand A. Brands C and F are the least preferred.

pleted. There are a number of concepts that marketing communications managers usually refer to that are highly related to brand conviction. These are *attitude toward brand purchase*, *purchase intention*, and *brand purchase*.

Attitude toward Brand Purchase

Attitude toward brand purchase refers to the attitude a consumer may have, not about the brand itself and its attributes, but toward the purchase and use of the brand. Many studies in social and consumer psychology have made the distinction between attitude toward the object versus attitude toward the act since attitude toward the act is a better predictor of behavior than attitude toward the object.[18] For example, if we play the role of scientists trying to predict purchase of Crest toothpaste, we would do better if we know how consumers feel about the purchase of Crest (attitude toward the act) than if we know how consumers feel about Crest (attitude toward the object). In other words, attitude toward brand purchase is the next best thing to brand purchase intention in predicting brand purchase.

Attitude toward purchase is defined as the consumer's disposition to purchase the brand given the need for the product category. This is different from purchase intention in that purchase intention is defined as the extent to which the consumer plans to purchase the brand in the foreseeable future. Two measures of attitude toward brand trial or purchase are briefly described here: the semantic differential measure and the favorability measure.

The Semantic Differential Measure of Attitude toward Purchase   Attitude toward purchase is traditionally measured by asking subjects to indicate their feelings about buying Brand *X* using the bipolar adjectives shown in Table 7.9.

These items have been demonstrated to have high internal consistency and are therefore very reliable.[19] An average composite is computed. This average composite is derived twice, once before the marketing campaign and again after a specified period of time. A successful campaign should be responsible for a significant shift in the attitude composite score.

The Favorability Measure of Attitude toward Purchase   Another rather simple measure of attitude toward purchase is as follows: Subjects are asked to evaluate the act of purchasing the brand in question on a six-point scale anchored by "very favorable" and "very unfavorable."[20] This measure is administered in the context of a survey, which is taken before the launch of the communications campaign and again after a specified period of time. An effective campaign should produce a higher average score for attitude toward purchase after the designated time.

Purchase Intention

Purchase intention refers to the decision to purchase the brand given the need for the product category. That is, consumers decide that when they go shopping next time to purchase the product in question, they intend to buy the designated brand.

Two measures of purchase intention are described here, one in which consumers consider the hypothetical situation of needing the product or shopping for the product category, and another in which consumers indicate the likelihood of purchase within an upcoming period of time.

A Measure of Purchase Intention Given Product Need   Purchase intention is usually measured by a question such as: "If you were in the market today shopping for product *x*, how likely would you be to buy Brand *A*?"[21] Response scales are of the semantic differential variety. Examples are shown in Table 7.10.

A mean composite score is computed before and after the campaign. Significant positive changes in the mean purchase intention composite scores is taken as an indication that the ad campaign was effective in changing consumers' purchase intention toward the brand.

The Planned Purchase Measure   An equally popular measure of purchase intention involves asking respondents to indicate whether they plan to purchase Brand *X* during the next *x* (days, months, or years). Responses are coded on one or more semantic differential scales comparable to the scales used in the measure of purchase in-

TABLE 7.9   The Semantic Differential Measure of Attitude Toward Purchase

good	__ __ __ __ __ __ __ __ __ __	bad
foolish	__ __ __ __ __ __ __ __ __ __	wise
pleasant	__ __ __ __ __ __ __ __ __ __	unpleasant
unsafe	__ __ __ __ __ __ __ __ __ __	safe
punishing	__ __ __ __ __ __ __ __ __ __	rewarding

TABLE 7.10 Response Scales for the Measure of Purchase Intention Given Product Need

very unlikely	—— —— —— —— —— ——	very likely
very improbable	—— —— —— —— —— ——	very probable
very impossible	—— —— —— —— —— ——	very possible
very nonexistent	—— —— —— —— —— ——	very existent

tention given product need. Two average composites are computed, one before the launch of the ad campaign, the other after the launch. The campaign effectiveness is judged in terms of the positive shift in the mean planned purchase score.

Brand Purchase

Brand purchase refers to a one-time purchase. It can refer to a brand trial, in which the consumer buys the brand in order to try it out. Two measures of brand purchase are described here, one that uses tracking studies, and another that provides sample consumers with purchase incentives.

Tracking Studies   Tracking studies are conducted to track the behaviors of consumers at the supermarket checkout counter. Consumer panel participants are given a card (similar to a credit card) that identifies their household and the household demographics. The households are split into matched groups, one group receiving the marketing communication and the other not. The purchases of these consumer panelists are recorded from the bar codes of the product bought. Exposure to the marketing communications is also measured using a diary method. Communications exposures are then correlated with brand purchases.

Popular firms in tracking studies include BehaviorScan by Information Resources, AdTel by SAMI-Burke, and ERIM by A.C. Nielsen. Advantages of tracking studies include control and the ability to measure the effects of the ads on sales as directly as possible. Disadvantages include the focus on short-term sales and the high cost of data collection.[22] (See Table 7.11.)

Purchase-Incentive Measures   Subjects are recruited to participate in a marketing study. The subjects are told: "As a participant in this study you may purchase (same brand) for (certain cents or dollars) per package. [The price is heavily discounted.] If you want to buy any, please provide your name and the number of packages below." Purchase is coded as the number of packages requested. The assumption is that the more packages requested, the greater the motivation to purchase the brand in general.[23]

This type of study is conducted before and after the marketing communications campaign. The precampaign score for the average number of packages of the brand requested is compared with the postcampaign score.

Repeat Purchase

Repeat purchase, on the other hand, refers to the situation in which the consumer purchases the same brand over and over again. Every time the need arises for the product, the consumer buys the same brand. Also, the same construct refers to brand satisfaction and brand loyalty. We will discuss the measures of all three constructs in this section.

TABLE 7.11 Ten Rules for Conducting Tracking Studies

1. Objectives must be properly defined.
2. These objectives must be aligned with sales objectives.
3. Sampling must be proper, e.g., random sampling.
4. Consistency must be achieved through replication of the sampling plan.
5. Evaluative measures must be related to behavior.
6. Asking critical evaluative questions early must be done to reduce bias from response to early questions.
7. Competitors' performance must be measured.
8. Use "moving averages" to spot long-term trends and avoid seasonality.
9. Report data in terms of relationships rather than as isolated facts.
10. Relate variables such as advertising expenditures, price changes, introduction of new brands, etc. to brand and product sales.

Types of Repeat Purchase:

Two repeat purchase measures are discussed here, one based on anticipated repeat purchase and the other based on past repeat purchase.

Repurchase Measure   The repurchase measure of brand loyalty involves ascertaining what percent of the owners of the brand go on to purchase the same brand on their next product purchase.[24] The precampaign repurchase average score is compared to the repurchase score after the campaign. The greater the change in the repurchase scores, the more effective the communications campaign.

Percentage-of-Purchase Measure   The percentage-of-purchase measure involves asking users of the product class questions such as, "Of the last [number of] purchases, what percentage went to [Brand X], [Brand Y], and [Brand Z]?"[25] The higher the average percentage that went to the brand in question, the higher the repeat purchase of that brand. Of course, the effectiveness of the communications campaign in terms of repeat purchase is judged by the difference between the percentage-of-purchase score before and after the campaign.

Brand Satisfaction

Brand satisfaction refers to the positive (or negative) feelings consumers may have about the brand after using it. In other words, after brand purchase, consumers evaluate the brand against their expectations. If they perceive that the brand did better than expected, they may have high brand satisfaction. If the brand is perceived to do as expected, then they are likely to have moderate levels of brand satisfaction. Similarly, if consumers perceive the product to do worse than expected, they may have low levels of satisfaction. Hence, brand satisfaction refers to the psychological process leading to brand evaluation after purchase and usage. Brand satisfaction is traditionally measured through a variety of rating scales.[26] Examples are shown in Table 7.12.

Professors Peterson and Wilson have shown that self-reports of consumer satisfaction invariably have frequency distributions that are skewed toward the high satisfaction

TABLE 7.12 Examples of Satisfaction Scales

Completely satisfied   1 2 3 4 5 6 7   Completely dissatisfied

Satisfaction percentage: 91–100
81–90
71–80
61–70
51–60
41–50
31–40
21–30
11–20
1–10

Very satisfied	Somewhat satisfied	Somewhat dissatisfied	Very dissatisfied	Uncertain
Very satisfied	Somewhat satisfied	Unsatisfied	Very unsatisfied	
Completely satisfied	Very satisfied	Fairly satisfied	Somewhat dissatisfied	Very dissatisfied
Very satisfied	Quite satisfied	Not very satisfied	Not at all satisfied	
Very satisfied	Somewhat satisfied	Completely unsatisfied		

end of the scale, reflecting a "positivity bias." In other words, most people tend to indicate inflated levels of satisfaction, perhaps more than they actually feel. Peterson and Wilson discussed other methodological problems: response-rate bias, data-collection-mode bias, problems with question form, problems with question context, measurement timing, response styles, and mood. Marketing communications managers must take these methodological shortcomings into account when evaluating such self-reports.

The effectiveness of a communications campaign in terms of increasing brand satisfaction is judged by comparing the precampaign satisfaction scores against the postcampaign satisfaction scores.

Brand Loyalty

With respect to *brand loyalty,* Professor Aaker has conceptualized this construct in terms of a five-layer hierarchy varying from the nonloyal buyer (bottom layer) to the committed buyer (top layer).[27] At the bottom layer are the nonloyal consumers who are completely indifferent to the brand. They do not buy out of loyalty for the brand. Perhaps factors such as price and convenience are important motivators. The second layer of the brand loyalty hierarchy includes the satisfied consumers. These are the habitual buyers. They buy the brand not necessarily out of a sense of loyalty and commitment but merely because of habit. They do not have a reason to change the brand. The third layer includes a different type of satisfied consumers. What distinguishes these consumers from the layer below them is the fact that these people cannot think of switching brands because of the high cost of switching. These people are "financially stuck" with the brand; they simply cannot afford to switch to another brand. The fourth layer involves those who like the brand. They consider the brand a friend. There is an emotional/feeling attachment to the brand. Finally, on top of the hierarchy, are the committed consumers. They are proud of being users of the brand. The brand is important to them either functionally and/or in the way the brand expresses their identity. I will discuss two measures of brand loyalty here, one referred to as the multivariate measure of brand loyalty, and the other referred to as the measurement of entrenched loyalty.

A Multivariate Measure of Brand Loyalty   One of the more popular measures of brand loyalty is the multivariate measure.[28] The multivariate measure is composed of the following questions:

1. Did you repurchase the old brand?   Yes   No
2. If you answered "Yes" to Question 1, how many brands did you think of at the outset of your decision process?   Many   Few   One
3. If you answered "One" to Question 2, did you think mainly of the old brand?   Yes   No
4. If you answered "Yes" to Question 3, did you seek any brand-related information?   Yes   No

Brand loyalty is estimated as the percentage of consumers who respond affirmatively to all of these four questions. As with other tests and measures of the effectiveness of a communications campaign, these measures are used before and after the campaign.

A Measure of Entrenched Loyalty   Another measure of brand loyalty involves asking target consumers, "Which other brands (or options) would you consider if your favorite were not available?" Entrenched loyalty is revealed when the answer is something like, "None—I'll shop no further. I'll wait until the brand becomes available."[29]

Summary

This chapter introduced the reader to tests and measures of campaign effectiveness. Campaign effectiveness tests and measures were grouped in terms of the hierarchy-of-effects components—brand awareness, brand knowledge, brand attitude, brand trial and purchase, and repeat purchase. We further examined the same hierarchy-of-effects components in greater detail and discussed common tests and measures used to operationalize these constructs. These tests and measures are used to assess effectiveness of any marketing communications campaign.

In assessing the effectiveness of a marketing communications campaign, marketing researchers traditionally employ a pre-post experimental design. That is, before the launch of the communications campaign (considered here as the experimental treatment), measures of selected components of the hierarchy of effects (e.g., brand awareness, purchase intention) are taken. These measures are administered on a sample of target consumers. These are referred to as "pre-measures." After the launch of the campaign, the same measures are administered to either the same sample or a comparable sample. The measures administered to assess the effectiveness of the ad campaign are referred to as "post-measures." Campaign effectiveness is judged by examining the magnitude of change between the pre-measure scores (let's say on brand awareness) and the post-measure scores. The greater the change (e.g., reflecting greater brand awareness) the more likely the campaign will be judged as effective.

Questions for Discussion

1. Assume that you are working for a major pharmaceutical company. The company develops a nicotine patch that cigarette smokers stick on their shoulder to transmit nicotine directly through the skin into the bloodstream. The nicotine patch helps cigarette smokers stop smoking by preventing or reducing the nicotine craving. The product has been branded as "Nicofit." You, the VP for marketing communications, are planning a major ad campaign. The objectives of the ad campaign involve (1) getting cigarette smokers who are trying to quit to know the benefits of the nicotine patch, (2) getting cigarette smokers to become aware of the brand name, Nicofit, (3) getting cigarette smokers to believe that the use of Nicofit can significantly help only if accompanied by other therapeutic techniques dealing with the psychological addiction, and (4) getting cigarette smokers to develop a positive attitude toward Nicofit as a direct function of its primary benefit of being able to reduce the craving for nicotine. Now is the time to plan how you will assess the effectiveness of the ad campaign. To do this, you need to get together with the research people and select suitable tests and measures. Review the different tests and measures associated with the objectives of the ad campaign, and select one test/measure for each objective. Defend your selection.

2. Suppose you are the VP for marketing communications in a multinational cosmetics company. The R&D department has just developed a new cologne for men. The cologne has the kind of fragrance which is said to "drive women crazy." The company is now counting on you and your people to launch a major ad campaign for this new cologne, branded as "Crazy." The market research people at your company are convinced that men in their twenties who are fashion-conscious are likely to find this cologne very appealing and purchase it. Therefore, the ad campaign is directed at young men in their twenties who are fashion-conscious. The objective of the ad campaign is to have these men develop a positive attitude toward (and preference for) Crazy. You have a meeting with the research people tomorrow to talk about possible effectiveness measures for this ad campaign. You need to prepare some ideas about the suitability of certain tests and measures to assess the effectiveness of the ad campaign against the campaign objective. Generate some ideas in preparation for this meeting.

3. Suppose you are working for one of the fastest-growing fast-food restaurant chains in the country, and you just have been promoted to the position of advertising manager within the marketing department. This position became available after the current advertising manager was lured by another company to become VP for marketing. He gave you a big file on the current ad campaign and, right before he said his good-byes, dropped a hint that the ad campaign might be in trouble. He pointed to the brand acceptance figures, and the figures showed a constant decrease in acceptance over the last three years. After staring at the figures for a while, it dawns on you that the objective of the ad campaign should be repeat purchase, not brand acceptance. You start thinking about coming up with a marketing communications strategy to enhance repeat purchase. You come up with some ideas that you will bounce off the creative

people in the next few days. Now you start to think about effectiveness measures. How are you going to show by the next quarter that your strategy worked? Think about the various options of tests and measures for repeat purchase. Which test and/or measure would you suggest for the research people? How do you think they will react to your suggestions?

4. Consider the pro-life ad campaign sponsored by the Moss Foundation. The ad campaign shows how parents are happy with their children whose births were neither planned nor wanted by the parents and how the children relish their own lives. The message is that life is a gift and that we should not consider abortion as a viable option just because the pregnancy is unplanned or ill-timed. What do you think is the objective of this ad campaign? Explain.

5. Suppose you are the marketing communications manager of Adidas athletic shoes. The market research people tell you that there is a niche for Adidas shoes among mature consumers (ages 40 to 60) who are health-conscious and tend to wear athletic shoes for casual occasions. These people purchase and use athletic shoes but are not involved with Adidas. You are now preparing a plan for the forthcoming ad campaign. What campaign objectives would you set for the campaign? Explain.

6. You are an advertising manager for Procter & Gamble. The research and development department has just developed a new laundry detergent that has the power of removing extremely tough stains. The ad campaign is to be directed to housewives of blue-collar families. What kind of ad campaign would you come up with? What kind of campaign objectives would be advisable for this type of ad campaign?

7. Suppose you are the advertising manager of RCA. RCA is competing against many others in the TV market. The TV market is in the mature stage of the product life cycle. The competition is fierce, and RCA's TVs have lost their differentiation advantage. In other words, the RCA brand does not seem to be significantly differentiated from most of the competitor brands of TV. RCA has just changed advertising agencies, providing you with an opportunity to strongly influence the creative people of the new agency. What would be the major thrust of the new ad campaign? In other words, what would you say to the creative people of the new agency about the goals of the RCA ad campaign?

8. Have you seen DuPont ads showing college students who are highly motivated to make a difference in improving the quality of life on this planet? This ad campaign is classified as a corporate-image campaign or institutional advertising. What do you think DuPont is trying to accomplish with this ad campaign? Explain.

9. "If target consumers are highly involved and knowledgeable about the product, the ad campaign should be designed to. . . ." Complete this sentence. Provide an example of a product that the target consumers are highly involved with and are knowledgeable about. Develop an ad campaign for this product, and explain how the ad campaign is designed to meet the advertising objectives.

Notes

1. Kevin Lane Keller, "Brand Equity and Integrated Communication," in *Integrated Communication: Synergy of Persuasive Voices,* edited by Esther Thorson and Jeri Moore (Mahwah, N.J.: Erlbaum, 1996), p. 114.

2. Benjamin Lipstein and James P. Neelankavil, "Television Advertising and Copy Research: A Critical Review of the State of the Art," *Journal of Advertising Research* 24 (April/May 1984), pp. 18–25.

3. Gary L. Lilien and Philip Kotler, *Marketing Decision Making* (New York: Harper & Row, 1983).

4. Philip Kotler, *Marketing Management: Analysis, Planning, Implementation, and Control,* 8th ed., (Upper Saddle River, N.J.: Prentice Hall, 1994), pp. 112–3.

5. E. H. Krugman, "What Makes Advertising Effective," *Harvard Business Review* 53, (March/April 1975), pp. 96–103.

6. Scott B. MacKenzie and Richard J. Lutz, "An Empirical Examination of the Structural Antecedents of Attitude Toward the Ad in an Advertising Pretesting Context," *Journal of Marketing* 53 (April 1989), pp. 48–65; Darrel D. Muehling, Russell N. Laczniak, and Jeffery J. Stoltman, "The Moderating Effects of Ad Message Involvement: A Reassessment," *Journal of Advertising* 20 (June 1991), pp. 29–38.

7. Robert E. Smith and William P. Swinyard, "Cognitive Response to Advertising and Trial: Belief Strength, Belief Confidence and Product Curiosity," *Journal of Advertising* 17, no. 3 (1988), pp. 3–14.

8. David A. Aaker, *Managing Brand Equity: Capitalizing on the Value of a Brand Name* (New York: The Free Press, 1991), pp. 136–46.

9. Russell H. Fazio, Paul M. Herr, and Martha C. Powell, "On the Development and Strength of Category-Based Associations in Memory: The Case of the Mystery Ads," *Journal of Consumer Psychology* 1, no. 1 (1992), pp. 1–14.

10. David A. Aaker, *Managing Brand Equity: Capitalizing on the Value of a Brand Name* (New York: The Free Press, 1991).

11. J. Thomas Russell, Glenn Verrill, and Ronald Lane, *Kleppner's Advertising Procedure,* 10th ed. (Upper Saddle River, N.J.: Prentice Hall, 1988), p. 134.

12. E. H. Krugman, "What Makes Advertising Effective," *Harvard Business Review* 53 (March/April 1975), pp. 96–103.

13. Karyln H. Keene and Victoria A. Sackett, "An Editor's Report on the Yankelovich, Skelly, and White's Mushiness Index," *Public Opinion* (April/May 1981), pp. 50–1.

14. Kathleen Debevec and Jean B. Romeo, "Self-Referent Processing in Perceptions of Verbal and Visual Information," *Journal of Consumer Psychology* 1, no. 1 (1992), pp. 83–102.

15. Ronald Alsop, "Advertisers Put Consumers on the Couch," *The Wall Street Journal* (May 13, 1988), sec. 2, p. 21.

16. Prakash Nedungadi, "Recall and Consumer Consideration Sets: Influencing Choice without Altering Brand Evaluations," *Journal of Consumer Research* 17 (December 1990), pp. 263–76.

17. Juanita J. Brown and Albert R. Wildt, "Consideration Set Measurement," *Journal of the Academy of Marketing Science* 20 (Summer 1992), pp. 235–43.

18. Icek Ajzen and Martin Fishbein, *Understanding Attitudes and Predicting Social Behavior* (Upper Saddle River, N.J.: Prentice Hall, 1980).

19. Chris T. Allen, Karen A. Machleit, and Susan Schultz Kleine, "A Comparison of Attitudes and Emotions as Predictors of Behavior at Diverse Levels of Behavioral Experience," *Journal of Consumer Research* 18 (March 1992), pp. 493–504; Richard P. Bagozzi, "Attitudes, Intentions, and Behavior: A Test of Some Key Hypotheses," *Journal of Personality and Social Psychology* 41 (October 1981), pp. 606–27.

20. Chris T. Allen, Karen A. Machleit, and Susan Schultz Kleine, "A Comparison of Attitudes and Emotions as Predictors of Behavior at Diverse Levels of Behavioral Experience," *Journal of Consumer Research* 18 (March 1992), pp. 493–504.

21. Kathleen Debevec and Jean B. Romeo, "Self-Referent Processing in Perceptions of Verbal and Visual Commercial Information," *Journal of Consumer Psychology* 1, no. 1 (1992), pp. 83–102.

22. Dave Kruegel, "Television Advertising Effectiveness and Research Innovation," *Journal of Consumer Marketing* 5, no. 3 (Summer 1988), pp. 40–50.

23. Robert E. Smith and William P. Swinyard, "Cognitive Response to Advertising and Trial: Belief Strength, Belief Confidence and Product Curiosity," *Journal of Advertising* 17, no. 3 (1988), pp. 3–14.

24. David A. Aaker, *Managing Brand Equity: Capitalizing on the Value of a Brand Name* (New York: The Free Press, 1991).

25. Ibid.

26. Robert A. Peterson and William R. Wilson, "Measuring Customer Satisfaction: Fact or Artifact," *Journal of the Academy of Marketing Science* 20 (Winter 1992), pp. 61–72.

27. David A. Aaker, *Managing Brand Equity: Capitalizing on the Value of a Brand Name* (New York: The Free Press, 1991).

28. Joseph W. Newman and Richard A. Worbel, "Multivariate Analysis of Brand Loyalty for Major Household Appliances," *Journal of Marketing Research* 10 (November 1973), pp. 404–8.

29. James F. Engel, Roger D. Blackwell, and Paul W. Miniard, *Consumer Behavior,* 6th ed. (Chicago: Dryden Press, 1990), p. 33.

Suggested Reading

Aaker, David A. *Managing Brand Equity: Capitalizing on the Value of a Brand Name.* New York: The Free Press, 1991.

Ajzen, Icek, and Martin Fishbein. *Understanding Attitudes and Predicting Social Behavior.* Upper Saddle River, N.J.: Prentice Hall, 1980.

Axelrod, Joel N., and Hans Wybenga. "Perceptions that Motivate Purchase." *Journal of Advertising Research* (June/July 1985): pp. 19–22.

Bagozzi, Richard P. "Attitudes, Intentions, and Behavior: A Test of Some Key Hypotheses." *Journal of Personality and Social Psychology* 41 (October 1981): pp. 606–27.

Barry, Thomas E. "The Development of the Hierarchy of Effects: An Historical Perspective." *Current Issues and Research in Advertising* 10, no. 2 (1987): pp. 251–95.

Bartos, Rena. "Ernest Dichter: Motive Interpreter." *Journal of Advertising Research* (February–March 1986): pp. 15–20.

Britt, S. H. "Are So-Called Successful Advertising Campaigns Really Successful?" *Journal of Advertising Research* 9 (June 1969): pp. 3–9.

Broadbent, Simon, ed. *The Leo Burnett Book of Advertising.* London: Business Books, 1984: pp. 86–98.

Brown, Juanita J., and Albert R. Wildt. "Consideration Set Measurement." *Journal of the Academy of Marketing Science* 20 (Summer 1992): pp. 235–43.

Colley, R. H. *Defining Advertising Goals for Measured Advertising Results.* New York: Association of National Advertisers, 1961.

Colley, R. H. *Defining Advertising Goals in Modern Marketing Management.* Edited by R. J. Lawrence and M. J. Thomas. Penguin Books, 1971: pp. 282–92.

Colman, Stephen, and Gordon Brown. "Advertising Tracking Studies and Sales Effects." *Journal of the Market Research Society* 25, no. 2 (1983): pp. 165–83.

Corkingdale, David. "Setting Objectives for Advertising." *European Journal of Marketing* 10, no. 3 (1976): pp. 109–26.

Haire, Mason. "Projective Techniques in Marketing Research." *Journal of Marketing* (April 1950): pp. 649–56.

Kruegel, Dave. "Television Advertising Effectiveness and Research Innovation." *Journal of Consumer Marketing* 5, no. 3 (Summer 1988): pp. 40–50.

Krugman, E. H. "What Makes Advertising Effective." *Harvard Business Review* 53 (March–April 1975): pp. 96–103.

Lang, Annie, ed. *Measuring Psychological Responses to Media Messages*. Hillsdale, N.J.: Erlbaum, 1994.

Lavidge, Robert J., and Gary A. Steiner. "A Model for Predictive Measurements of Advertising Effectiveness." *Journal of Marketing* (October 1961): pp. 59–62.

Lipstein, Benjamin, and James P. Neelankavil. "Television Advertising Copy Research: A Critical Review of the State of the Art." *Journal of Advertising Research* 24 (April/May 1984): pp. 18–25.

Lucas, D. B., and S. H. Britt. *Measuring Advertising Effectiveness*. New York: McGraw-Hill, 1963.

Majaro, S. "Advertising by Objectives." *Management Today* (January 1970): pp. 71–3.

Moriarity, Sandra Ernest. "Beyond the Hierarchy of Effects: A Conceptual Framework." *Current Issues and Research in Advertising* 6, no. 1 (1983): pp. 45–55.

Nedungadi, Prakash. "Recall and Consumer Consideration Sets: Influencing Choice without Altering Brand Evaluations." *Journal of Consumer Research* 17 (December 1990): pp. 263–76.

Palda, Kristian S. "The Hypothesis of a Hierarchy of Effects: A Partial Evaluation." *Journal of Marketing Research* 3 (Februray 1966): pp. 13–24.

Peterson, Robert A., and William R. Wilson. "Measuring Customer Satisfaction: Fact and Artifact." *Journal of the Academy of Marketing Science* 20 (Winter 1992): pp. 61–72.

Ray, Michael L., Alan G. Sawyer, Michael L. Rothschild, Roger M. Heeler, Edward C. Strong, and Jerome B. Reed. "Marketing Communications and the Hierarchy of Effects." In *New Models for Mass Communications Research*. Edited by Peter Clarke. Beverly Hills, Calif.: Sage, 1973.

Reynolds, Thomas J., and Jonathan Gutman. "Advertising is Image Management." *Journal of Advertising Research* 25 (February-March 1984): pp. 29–37.

Schwartz, D. A. "Measuring the Effectiveness of Your Company's Advertising." *Journal of Advertising* 33 (April 1969): pp. 20–5.

Smith, Robert E., and William P. Swinyard. "Cognitive Response to Advertising and Trial: Belief Strength, Belief Confidence, and Product Curiosity." *Journal of Advertising* 17, no. 3 (1988): pp. 3–14.

CHAPTER 8

Budget

Recently it has been announced that Colgate (a packaged-goods giant) has consolidated all worldwide advertising at one agency, Young and Rubicam's, giving them 85% of its $650 million advertising budget. This means that Colgate's annual advertising budget alone is approximately $765 million. Have you ever wondered how these giant companies allocate resources? How does a company like Colgate determine an annual advertising budget of $765 million? But this budget is small potatoes compared to the budgets of other giants such as Procter & Gamble, which spends approximately $2 billion in marketing communications on an annual basis.[1]

Allocating resources to the elements of the strategic mix is, in essence, a budgeting decision. The marketing communications manager must decide what resources are needed to implement the selected strategy and its respective strategic mix. For example, given the decision to advertise the product through TV, the manager determines the amount of money needed to launch a TV advertising campaign to achieve a certain level of brand awareness.

Many methods are used to make budgeting decisions. An example of a budgeting method is the "build-up approach" commonly used in advertising. (Sometimes this budgeting method is also referred to as the "objective-task method.") Using the build-up method, resource allocation is determined by a two-stage process: First, the manager identifies the subordinate tasks needed to implement the superordinate task and accomplish its goals (e.g., the TV programs and number of insertions needed to meet a stated objective of brand awareness). Then, he or she sums up the total costs related to the implementation of the subordinate tasks.

Many other methods are commonly used by managers to allocate resources at the corporate, marketing, and marketing communications levels. However, since the focus of this book is on marketing communications, it would serve little purpose to thoroughly review and address budgeting methods at either the corporate or marketing levels. Nevertheless, it is important to show how corporate and marketing strategies and tactics influence the budget at the marketing communications level. We will refer to the process by which corporate and marketing strategies and tactics influence the marketing communications budget as a top-down ("build-down") process. Before discussing the build-down process of resource allocation, first let us discuss some of the traditional methods of budgeting. (See Figure 8.1.)

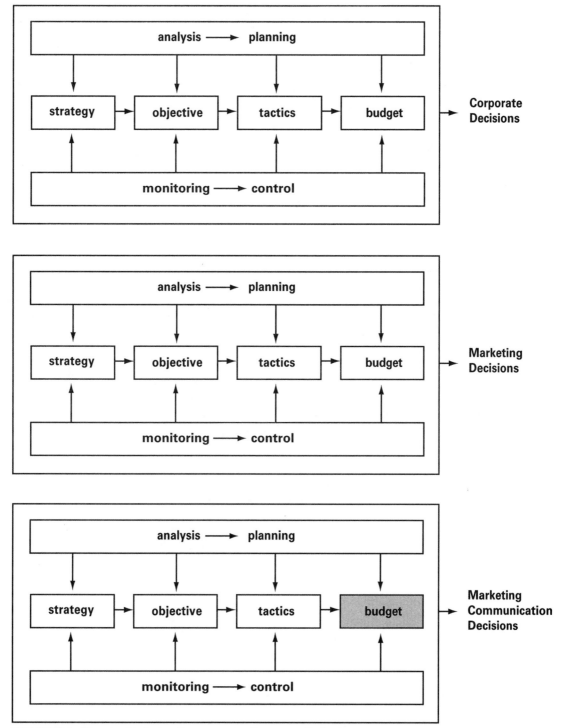

FIGURE 8.1 Allocating Marketing Communication Resources (Budget)

TRADITIONAL BUDGETING METHODS OF MARKETING COMMUNICATIONS

Many methods are traditionally used in allocating communications expenditures. Among the popular methods are ratio-to-sales methods, competitive parity methods, quantitative methods, the return-on-investment (ROI) method, the objective-task method, the all-you-can-afford method, and the previous budget method.[2] We'll discuss these in some detail (see Table 8.1).

Ratio-to-Sales Methods

Ratio-to-sales methods calculate a budget based on *percentage anticipated sales, unit anticipated sales, percentage past sales,* and *unit past sales.* The marketing communications budget thus becomes a percentage of past sales or projected sales, or a percentage of past unit sales or projected unit sales. These methods rely heavily on industry norms and customs. Many communications scholars have argued that relying too much on past sales or forecasted sales is not an effective method of budgeting because if sales were down last year, the marketing communications budget for next year is likely to be smaller. This smaller budget may weaken the effectiveness of marketing communications, which, in turn, will likely cause further decreases in sales. The various ratio-to-sales methods are described below.

Percentage of Anticipated Sales

This method states that a marketing communications budget can be determined as a percentage of forecasted sales. For example, suppose a marketing communications manager of a software such as Microsoft Office has traditionally allocated 3% of sales to marketing communications. Sales are expected to increase by 10% in the next

---

TABLE 8.1   Traditional Budgeting Methods of Marketing Communications

Ratio-to-Sales Methods
   Percentage of Anticipated Sales
   Percentage of Unit Anticipated Sales
   Percentage of Past Sales
   Percentage of Unit Past Sales
Competitive Parity Methods
   Match Industry Norms
   The Share-of-Voice/Market Method
   Match or Outspend Competitors
Quantitative Methods
   The Experimental Method
   The Historical-Statistical Method
The Return-on-Investment (ROI) Method
The Objective-Task Method
The All-You-Can-Afford Method
The Previous Budget Method

12 months. Sales of Microsoft Office for 1994 was $75 million. The sales forecast for 1995, therefore, is $82.5 million. The marketing communications manager allocates 3% of the $82.5 million (sales forecast), not the $75 million (past sales). Therefore, the marketing communications budget for Microsoft Office for 1995, based on the percentage of anticipated sales, is $2.48 million.

Percentage of Unit Anticipated Sales

This method states that a marketing communications budget can be determined as a percentage of unit cost. In the Microsoft example, suppose each Microsoft Office unit is expected to be sold next year at $550. Suppose Microsoft expects to sell 10 million units next year. The tradition has been to allocate 2% of the unit sales to marketing communications. Therefore, the marketing communications budget is determined as $110 million ($550/unit × 10 million units to be sold × 0.02).

Percentage of Past Sales

This method states that a marketing communications budget can be determined as a percentage of last year's sales. The only difference between this method and the percentage of anticipated sales method is the source of the sales figure. The sales figure in the percentage of anticipated sales method is based on a sales forecast, while this method relies on past sales, perhaps last year's sales.

Percentage of Unit Past Sales

This method states that a marketing communications budget can be determined as a percentage of the unit price for last year's sales. Again, the only difference between this method and the unit-anticipated-sales method is the source of the sales figure. The sales figure in the unit-anticipated-sales method is based on a sales forecast assuming a certain price level, while this method relies on past sales based on a fixed price.

Competitive Parity Methods

At least four budgeting methods are known as competitive parity methods. These are: *match industry norms, match competitors, outspend competitors,* and *share of voice/ market.* All these methods are based on a basic assumption—namely, that the competition's level of expenditure is effective and is based on well-articulated logic. The problem with this method is that marketing communications managers cannot rely on a major competitor to determine their own budget. It is hard to justify that a major competitor "knows best" and should be an industry guide for followers. Too many factors are unique to different firms within a product/market, each factor requiring special considerations in budget formulation.

Match Industry Norms

This budgeting method states that an effective marketing communications budget is equivalent to the industry average, or "norm." Marketing communications managers who rely on this method seek and fund studies to gather data establishing the industry norms. For example, a five-year study examined how industrial marketing communications managers set their advertising budgets. The study involved 66 industrial products from 12 firms. The study objective was to establish marketing expenditure norms for industrial marketing communications managers. The study found that most industrial marketing communications managers spend 6.9% of the previous year's budget on marketing tasks, with a range from 3% to 14%. With respect to advertising expenditures, the norm was that industrial marketing communications managers spend 9.9% (range 5 to 19%) of their marketing budgets on advertising, or 0.6% of total sales (range 0.1 to 1.8%). The same study also found that most industrial marketing communications managers allocate their advertising budget in the following manner:

41% on print medium advertising (trade, technical press, and house journals),

24% on direct mail (leaflets, brochures, catalogs, and other direct mail pieces),

11% on shows (trade shows and industrial films), and

24% on promotion (sales promotion).[3]

A more recent study conducted for the American Marketing Association in business-to-business (biz-to-biz) marketing showed that biz-to-biz firms devoted an average of 3.49% of their sales to marketing. The marketing budget is broken down as follows: 2.14% of sales have gone to direct selling (this includes sales staff salaries, bonuses, commissions, travel, and entertainment); 0.88% of sales went to marketing communications (defined as print ads, direct mail, trade shows and exhibits, radio, TV, out-of-home media, public relations, catalogs/directories, literature, coupons, point-of-purchase materials, and dealer and distributor materials); 0.37% of sales went to marketing support (marketing/advertising planning, advertising salaries, and presentations); 0.07% of sales went to market research; and 0.03% of sales went to telemarketing.[4]

The Share-of-Voice/Market Method

This budgeting method entails the examination of one's market share in relation to the major competitors in the product/market. What do the major competitors spend on marketing communications? The rule of thumb is that the marketing communications manager's budget for marketing communications should be in direct proportion to past and desired market share.

For example, suppose we are in the motel business. We are marketing a motel chain; let's call it Hampton Inn. Let's say, hypothetically speaking, that Hampton Inn's market share last year was 20%. The major competitor that Hampton Inn is directly competing against is Holiday Inn, which reported a market share of 30% last year. We know that Holiday Inn spent $20 million on marketing communications last year. Suppose that Hampton Inn's market share objective is to increase market share by 5% (from 20% to 25%). How much money should Hampton Inn allocate for marketing communications? The answer is $16.67 million ($20 million multiplied by 25%, the product of which is divided by 30%).

Match or Outspend Competitors

For most industries, published figures showing marketing communications expenditures as a percentage of sales are used as a guide by many marketing communications managers. For example, a marketing communications manager may read that a major competitor has allocated 20% of the dollar sales from this year to cover marketing communications costs for next year. The manager may then decide to outspend the competition by allocating 23%. Or the manager may simply match the competition by allocating 20%. Typically, firms such as automobile manufacturers and oil companies rely on published data to figure out what certain competitors are doing and then make the decision either to match or outspend them.

Quantitative Methods

Two common types of empirical methods are used to determine the optimal level of communications expenditures—the experimental method and the historical-statistical method.

The Experimental Method

This empirical method states that an effective way to determine an optimal amount of expenditures is to experiment with different amounts and observe the effects. For example, a firm may set its rate for communications based on its most current information about the sales-response function. In market A it may have spent X amount on communications; in market B it may have spent Y amount; and in market C, Z amount. Which level of expenditure produced the highest sales response? Thus, an optimal level of expenditure is chosen.[5] An example of the use of this method involves a DuPont study. DuPont Paint Division divided 56 sales territories into high-, average-, and low-market-share territories. Across these territories, Dupont spent a "normal" amount of advertising in one-third of the territories, two and one-half times as much in another third of its territories, and four times as much in another third of the territories. At the end of the designated period, sales were estimated. The question was: How much were extra sales created by higher levels of advertising expenditures? The study revealed that higher advertising expenditure increased sales at a diminishing rate, and that the sales increase was weakest in the high-market-share territories.[6]

Another common experimental method is an industry study in which communications expenditures and sales data is collected from as many firms as possible within the industry in relation to a particular time period (e.g., the previous two years). From this data, an attempt is made to estimate the elasticity coefficients of various communications tools. The tool that is found to have the greatest elasticity warrants the highest level of expenditure. For example, one study estimated the sales effectiveness of three communications tools used in the pharmaceutical industry.[7] The study showed that journal advertising had the highest long-run advertising elasticity at 0.365; samples and literature had an elasticity of 0.108; and direct mail had an elasticity of only 0.018. Thus, firms in that industry should allocate expenditures to the various communications tools as a direct function of the elasticity coefficients.

The Historical-Statistical Method

Here statistical data from the company's archives are manipulated. The goal is to build a regression model in which sales are predicted by past sales, communications expenditure levels, plus other factors. The hope is that the variable pertaining to communications expenditure levels turns out to be a significant predictor of sales and that the entire regression equation (involving all the predictors) accounts for a large percentage of the variance in the criterion variable (i.e., the sales variable). Given a statistically valid regression model, the marketing communications manager experiments with different expenditure levels to identify the level of expenditure increment that accounts for the highest level of sales increase.[8]

For example, one study focused on the effect of advertising expenditures on the sales of Lydia Pinkham's Vegetable Compound between 1908 and 1960.[9] The study found that the marginal advertising dollars increased sales by only $.50 in the short term. However, the long-term marginal sales effect was three times as large. The marginal rate of return on company advertising was estimated to be 37% over the whole period.

The Return-on-Investment (ROI) Method

This method assumes that money spent today is an investment that is likely to pay off in sales tomorrow. Implementing this budgeting method requires payout planning. For example, launching a new product is likely to result in higher levels of expenditures on communications the first year or two. In the first year, sales are not likely to be high, and profits are likely to be in the red. This picture may begin to change in the second year. Sales are likely to pick up, and profit is likely to be still in the red or close to breakeven. The third year may be quite different, and the payoff (i.e., the return on investment) starts to become evident. Sales may be high, and profits are likely to grow.

Although this is a very reasonable budgeting model, the problem lies with implementation. The marketing communications manager still does not know exactly how much to spend on communications tools the first year, the second year, and so on. Because this method lacks specificity, many marketing communications managers work with the method more implicitly than explicitly.

The Objective-Task Method

This method of allocating expenditures for marketing communications is considered to be the ideal method, but it is also the most tedious. It is tedious because it is based on a precise account of how much money is needed to build a marketing communications campaign that will meet certain communication, marketing, and/or corporate objectives. That is, the method calls for marketing communications managers to develop their marketing communications budgets by defining their objectives clearly, determining the marketing communications programs (tasks) to achieve these objectives, and estimating the costs of these programs.[10] Here is an example involving a direct-response campaign.

> . . . for a lead generation program, we might set a campaign objective of 1,000 sales, determine the average close ratio (leads to sales) to be 30%, and determine the number of qualified leads needed to generate 1,000 sales (4,000 responses). Then determine how much it will cost to bring in 4,000 qualified leads. That equals your budget. If past response is 1%, then 400,000 pieces need to be mailed out to yield 4,000 qualified leads. For print, if past response is 0.2%, then a reach of two million is needed to yield 4,000 qualified leads. You then price a 400,000-piece direct mail campaign or a print campaign that reaches two million readers. If you can't run a campaign that mails this many pieces or reaches this many readers due to budget constraints, then your objectives need to be modified.[11]

The All-You-Can-Afford Method

This method is quite arbitrary and states that a good marketing communications budget is as much as the firm can afford to spend. Small businesses usually use this method because of resource scarcity. They usually cannot or will not borrow money to finance a marketing communications campaign. They feel the risk is high. In contrast, some medium and large businesses use this method, thinking that marketing communications are a form of investment. The more one spends, the bigger the investment. Since marketing communications pay off in the long run, the firm will spend whatever it can afford. Of course, this method of budgeting for marketing communications is ineffective because it ignores the role of marketing communications as an investment and the impact of marketing communications on corporate and marketing objectives.

The Previous Budget Method

This is not really an analytical method to determine communications expenditures. It is very simple. It states that an effective budget is the previous budget, possibly with some adjustments. Many marketing communications managers in large companies that have rich and long histories tend to rely on tradition. They don't want to "rock the boat." They think the company had good reasons for spending certain amounts of money for marketing communications in the way it did in the past. The company has survived and prospered. Therefore, previous efforts at budgeting should be considered successful, and previous budgets can be used to set new ones.

Of course, the logic of this method is not very defensible. One can argue that the company could have done even better with a different budget. Or perhaps the company has survived and prospered despite a "faulty" budget.

RECOMMENDED BUDGETING METHOD

We recommend that a marketing communications budget should be determined using the following procedure (see Table 8.2).

TABLE 8.2 Recommended Budgeting Method

1. Determine the corporate objective.
2. Determine the corporate mix to achieve the stated objective.
3. Determine the marketing strategy to achieve the corporate objective.
4. Determine the marketing objective that operationalizes the marketing strategy.
5. Determine the marketing communications strategy to achieve the marketing objective.
6. Determine the marketing communications objectives that operationalize the marketing communications strategy.
7. Determine the marketing communications mix to achieve the marketing communications objectives.
8. Determine the cost of implementing the selected marketing communications programs.
9. Adjust the marketing communications budget as a function of monitoring/control and analysis/planning.

Determine the Corporate Objectives

The first step is to determine the corporate objectives in terms of sales, market share, profit, and/or cash flow. As a refresher, look back at chapter 6, "Objectives and Measures." Consider the following example throughout this discussion. A software company is now ready to launch a new product. The software is a music encyclopedia. The next quarterly goal is to increase sales of this software by 50%.

Determine the Corporate Mix to Achieve the Stated Objective

The second step is to develop a corporate mix that is capable of achieving the stated objective (e.g., the sales objective). As a refresher, look back at chapter 5, "Corporate Strategies and Tactics." We can implement the *growth* strategy through an aggressive marketing effort. Therefore we need to allocate more resources to marketing to match the increased effort. In other words, the marketing function is viewed as playing a key role in achieving the goals of the growth strategy. All eyes are now focused on marketing. The marketing communications manager is now charged with developing a marketing plan that can achieve the sales objective of a 50% increase in the quarter. Now, let's say a 50% increase in sales translates to the sale of an additional 50,000 units.

Determine the Marketing Strategy to Achieve the Corporate Objective

The third step is to develop a marketing strategy that is capable of achieving the stated corporate objective (e.g., the 50% increase in sales of the music encyclopedia software). Refer to chapter 6, "Marketing Strategies and Tactics." The marketing manager determines that a *focus* strategy is likely to be most effective. This software can be easily used in high school and college music courses. Therefore, the strategy is to focus on music teachers and professors and convince them that this software can be highly useful in their teaching of music to their students. Market analysis indicates that there are at least 250,000 high school teachers and college professors who teach music in the United States. Thus, a *positioning by user or customer* is likely to be most effective here.

Determine the Marketing Objective That Operationalizes the Marketing Strategy

The idea here is to figure out an exact marketing objective that captures the essence of the marketing strategy and ties it back to the corporate objective. In other words, the marketing communications manager has to come up with a marketing objective that is most likely to result in the attainment of the corporate objective too. The marketing objective is to establish an *association between this software brand and the typical music teacher or professor*. A possible goal is to successfully position the product in the minds of at least 20% of this population. The likely result would be sales of 50,000 units, thus achieving the objective of 50% increase in sales.

Determine the Marketing Communications Strategy to Achieve the Marketing Objective

The focus here is to figure out the best marketing communications strategy to convince 20% of high school teachers and college professors who teach music to adopt this software for classroom use by the end of next quarter. The decision is to use an *informative (thinker)* communications strategy. This strategy is likely to be more effective than other communications strategies such as the affective (feeler), habit formation (doer), and self-satisfaction (reactor) strategies.

Determine the Marketing Communications Objective That Operationalizes the Marketing Communications Strategy

The goal here is to figure out those exact marketing communications objectives that reflect the selected marketing communications strategy and to link these objectives with the superordinate marketing objectives. In the context of the software company, the question becomes, What communications objectives reflect an effective implementation of the informative (thinker) communications strategy? These objectives may be stated in the form of specific sequence of objectives related to awareness→attitude→purchase. Perhaps the total marketing communications campaign can be broken into three phases, the first phase reflecting the awareness component, the second phase reflecting the attitude component, and the third phase reflecting the purchase component. Specifically, the most effective implementation of the informative (thinker) strategy that is likely to achieve marketing objective of 20% brand association may be a 60% brand awareness/learning. That is, if the company can get 60% of all high school music teachers and college professors to become aware of the music software and learn something about it in the next quarter, 20% are likely to realize that this software is most used by people like them. This should be the focus of the first phase of the marketing communications campaign (the awareness phase). The objective of the second phase of the campaign should focus on the attitude component. A possible objective would be to ensure that at least 40% of the teachers and professors who have been exposed to the software by now will form a positive attitude toward the software. The objective of the third phase of the campaign should focus on the purchase component. A possible objective would be to ensure that at least 25% of the teachers and professors who now have formed a positive attitude toward the software will purchase the software at least on a trial basis (see Table 8.3).

TABLE 8.3 Setting Marketing Communications Objectives as a Direct Function of the Informative (Thinker) Strategy

	Learning about the Software	Liking the Software	Purchasing the Software
First phase of the campaign	**60%**	20%	5%
Second phase of the campaign	70%	**40%**	10%
Third phase of the campaign	80%	50%	**25%**

Note: The consumer population are high school teachers and college professors who teach music.

Determine the Marketing Communications Mix to Achieve the Marketing Communications Objectives

This step involves selecting the best marketing communications tools or programs that are capable of achieving the stated marketing communications objective. As a refresher, look back at chapter 5, "Marketing Communications Strategies and Tactics." For the music encyclopedia software, the best communications tool is advertising in trade and academic journals that music teachers and professors commonly read. The first phase of the campaign should involve informative direct-response ads placed in the trade and academic journals. The second phase of the campaign should involve variations of the first informative direct-response ads but with less information and more emotional cues (vivid pictures of emotional events or characters). The third phase of the campaign may involve a variation of the ads of the second phase, but now an economic incentive is offered to induce purchase.

Determine the Cost of Programs

The next step is to determine the cost of the selected marketing communications programs. Suppose that advertising in three magazines/journals (in combination with a direct mail campaign) may be most effective in attaining the stated marketing communications objectives. Also, the manager determines that 12 insertions in these weekly magazines/journals would be sufficient to generate the desired levels of awareness/learning, attitude, and purchase. Suppose that advertising this software in these three magazines/journals, with three ad insertions each in the next three issues, will cost $100,000. Also, suppose that the cost for creative production of the ads is $5,000.

Adjust the Budget as a Function of Monitoring/Control and Analysis/Planning

This marketing communications budget is then adjusted as a direct function of monitoring/control and analysis/planning. As Figure 8.1 shows, budgeting at the marketing communications level is determined by considering three factors: (1) marketing communications tactics, (2) marketing communications monitoring and control, and (3) marketing communications analysis and planning. The previous discussion shows how the marketing communications manager can set the marketing communications budget by assessing the cost of the tactics (programs) needed to implement the marketing communications strategy. Chapter 9 will describe how the marketing communications budget can be adjusted by trial-and-error—that is, monitoring and control. The manager adjusts the budget based on past marketing communications expenditures and the goals achieved with these expenditures. For example, past experience dealing with the music teachers' and professors' market may suggest that two ad insertions in three issues can achieve a high level of awareness/learning. Hence, three ad insertions in the next three issues may be too much. Here the marketing communications manager may adjust the budget as a direct function of past experience. Analysis and planning work the same way. The manager adjusts the budget after considering factors likely to affect marketing communications performance. Suppose that by conducting a competitive analysis, the manager realizes that a key competitor is likely to target music teachers and professors using the same trade and academic journals. Because of this, the manager decides that more ad insertions are needed to offset the competition. This should increase the budget by another $15,000 to $20,000. The marketing communications manager then requests a budget of approximately $110,000 from the marketing manager or VP for marketing. Chapter 11, "Analysis and Planning: Resource Allocation," describes in some detail how many factors are considered in adjusting the marketing communications budget and how many of the traditional budgeting methods can be incorporated into the analysis.

Summary

This chapter introduced the reader to traditional budgeting methods of marketing communications. They were discussed in terms of ratio-to-sales methods, competitive parity methods, quantitative methods, the objective-task method, the return-on-investment method, the all-you-can-afford method, and the previous budget method. The shortcomings of these methods were discussed. Then a budgeting method was recommended based on the traditional objective-task method. Many of the other traditional methods can be subsumed in the recommended method.

Questions for Discussion

Assume the following scenario. You are a corporate executive in the Ritz Carlton Resort of Naples, Florida. Recently, upper management decided to aggressively pursue the business conference market—that is, corporate businesses that have educational seminars and workshops throughout the United States. Determine a marketing communications budget for next year using ratio-to-sales methods. The following figures are available. Assume that Ritz Carlton spent $350,000 on marketing communications last year. Their sales from last year were $150 million, of which only $30 million came from the business conference market. A recent study projected a 25% industry increase in sales due to increasing demand for business conferences. Assume the major competitor of Ritz Carlton is the Hyatt in Naples. The Hyatt has 70% of the business conference market, compared to 25% for Ritz Carlton. Hyatt spent approximately $700,000 on marketing communications costs last year. It was determined that an aggressive marketing communications campaign could increase the use of business conference facilities at the hotel by at least 20%, which could generate a 25% increase in revenues. This goal can be accomplished by hiring three additional sales reps with good experience in recruiting corporate business to hotels. The cost of these three reps is expected to be $70,000 a person, with approximately $10,000 needed for additional sales materials and miscellaneous expenses (phone, mailing, etc.).

1. Describe ratio-to-sales methods and discuss their disadvantages. Examine the Ritz-Carlton scenario above and determine a marketing communications budget for next year using the ratio-to-sales methods.
2. Describe the competitive parity methods and discuss their disadvantages. Examine the Ritz-Carlton scenario above and determine a marketing communications budget for the next year using a competitive parity method.

3. Describe the objective-task method. Examine the Ritz-Carlton scenario above and determine a marketing communications budget for the next year using the objective-task method.

Notes

1. Mark Gleason and Pat Sloan, "$500M in Colgate Eggs in 1 Y&R Basket," *Advertising Age* (December 4, 1995), pp. 1, 35.

2. George E. Belch and Michael A. Belch, *Introduction to Advertising and Promotion: An Integrated Marketing Communications Perspective,* 3rd ed. (Chicago: Irwin, 1995), p. 252.

3. Gary L. Lilien and John D. C. Little, "The ADVISOR Project: A Study of Industrial Marketing Budgets," *Sloan Management Review* (Spring 1976), pp. 17–31; Gary L. Lilien, "ADVISOR 2: Modeling the Marketing Mix Decision for Industrial Products," *Management Science* (February 1979), pp. 191–204.

4. Cyndee Miller, "Marketing Industry Report: Who's Spending What on Biz-to-Biz Marketing," *Marketing News* (January 1, 1996), pp. 1, 7.

5. John D. C. Little, "A Model of Adaptive Control of Promotional Spending," *Operations Research* (November 1966), pp. 1075–97.

6. Robert D. Buzzell, *Mathematical Models and Marketing Management* (Boston: Division of Research, Harvard Business School, 1964), p. 166.

7. David B. Montgomery and Alvin J. Silk, "Estimating Dynamic Effects of Market Communications Expenditures," *Management Science* (June 1972), pp. 485–501.

8. Gary L. Lilien, Philip Kotler, and K. Sridhar Moorthy, *Marketing Models* (Upper Saddle River, N.J.: Prentice Hall, 1992), ch. 6.

9. Kristian S. Palda, *The Measurement of Cumulative Advertising Effect* (Upper Saddle River, N.J.: Prentice Hall, 1964), p. 87.

10. G. Maxwell Ule, "A Media Plan for 'Sputnik' Cigarettes," *How to Plan Media Strategy* (American Association of Advertising Agencies, 1957 Regional Convention), pp. 41–52.

11. Karen J. Marchetti, "Direct-Response Skills for the 21st Century," *Marketing News* (July 29, 1996), p. 5.

Suggested Reading

Aaker, David A., and James M. Carman. "Are You Overadvertising?" *Journal of Advertising Research* 22, no. 4 (August-September 1982): pp. 57–70.

Eastlack, Joseph O., Jr., and Ambar G. Rao. "Modeling Response to Advertising and Pricing Changes for V-8 Cocktail Vegetable Juice." *Marketing Science* 5, no. 3 (Summer 1986): pp. 245–59.

Gilligan, Colin. "How British Advertisers Set Budgets." *Journal of Advertising Research* 17 (February 1977): pp. 47–9.

Jones, John P. "Ad Spending: Maintaining Market Share." *Harvard Business Review* (January-February 1990): pp. 38–42.

Lancaster, Kent M., and J. A. Stern. "Computer-Based Advertising Budgeting Practices of Leading U.S. Consumer Advertisers." *Journal of Advertising* 12, no. 4 (1983): pp. 4–9.

Little, John D. C. "A Model of Adaptive Control of Promotional Spending." *Operations Research* 14 (November-December 1966): pp. 175–97.

Patti, Charles, and Vincent Blasko. "Budgeting Practices of Big Advertisers." *Journal of Advertising Research* 21 (December 1981): pp. 23–9.

Piercy, Nigel. "Advertising Budgeting: Process and Structure as Explanatory Variables." *Journal of Advertising* 16, no. 2 (1987): pp. 34–40.

Schroer, James C. "Ad Spending: Growing Market Share." *Harvard Business Review* (January-February 1990): pp. 44–8.

CHAPTER 9

Monitoring and Control

A recent *Fortune* magazine article on Kmart documented its business ills. Kmart's market share dropped from approximately 5.2% in 1990 to 4.7% in 1995, while Wal-Mart's market share increased from approximately 5.2% in 1990 to 10% in 1995. Kmart stock price plummeted from $15 per share in 1990 to $6 per share in 1995. In an interview, Floyd Hall, CEO of Kmart, showed that he does not have a thorough understanding of either Kmart customers or its competitors and that he does not have a corporate strategy. The challenge of saving Kmart is indeed formidable. In 1990 Kmart was the world's biggest discount retailer. Now it is about one-third the size of Wal-Mart. It has problems everywhere—in merchandise selection, service, and value. Often there are stockouts of items on sale. Employees' morale is down in the dumps. The previous CEO, Joseph Antonini, employed a diversification strategy, getting involved in other ventures, such as OfficeMax, the Sports Authority, and Builders Square. Wal-Mart, Kmart's key competitor, focused on its core discount store and used a growth strategy to achieve ambitious sales, market share, and profit goals. Hall says that Kmart's typical shopper is a 55-year-old consumer who has no kids at home and has less than $20,000 in income. Independent marketing researchers consulted by *Fortune* magazine indicate that Kmart's typical shopper is very much like Wal-Mart's. To better serve Kmart's shoppers, Hall is planning to install large sections upfront carrying cheap consumables like laundry soap, snacks, cereals, and dog food. These items are likely to be appealing to the low-income shoppers. Also, he is planning to build more supercenters, which combine the general discount store with a supermarket. However, Wal-Mart is well ahead of Kmart in this area.[1]

Here we have a company that desperately needs a good job of what we call "monitoring and control." Kmart needs to assess its performance not only at the corporate level, but also at the marketing and communications levels. It needs to determine how discrepant its performance (at the corporate, marketing, and communications levels) is from what is considered acceptable goals. It needs to exert control by reassessing its strategies, its tactics, the way resources are allocated, and so on. In this chapter, we will start to grasp the complex issues involved in monitoring and control.

At any given level of the process hierarchy, the decision maker is faced with a set of organizational tasks.[2] These are: (1) deciding on a strategy and assembling the strategic mix, (2) allocating resources to the elements of the strategic mix, (3) setting objectives, and (4) monitoring performance and exerting control. This chapter concentrates on the last system component—monitoring and control (see Figure 9.1). Also, since this

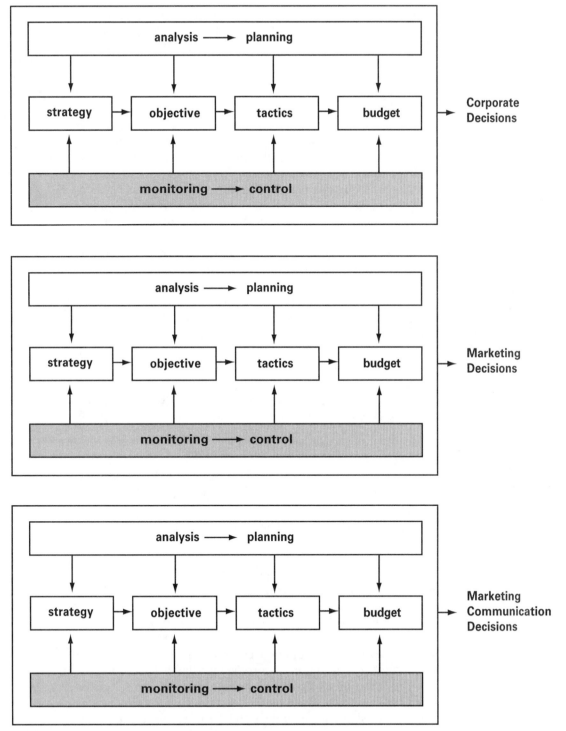

FIGURE 9.1 Corporate, Marketing, and Marketing Communication Control

book is about marketing communications, we will address monitoring and control issues strictly from the viewpoint of the marketing communications manager.

The control function involves the use of a feedback mechanism. A feedback mechanism generates a warning signal when a specific measured outcome is significantly below the stated objective. For example, a marketing communications objective may be a 50% increase in brand awareness as measured by a brand recognition method six months after the launch of the communications campaign. After six months, the marketing communications manager assesses the outcome using the designated method and finds out that brand awareness inched up only 10%. That is, a negative deviation of 40% from the goal is detected. A significant negative deviation "raises a red flag" and motivates the manager to make adjustments. These adjustments may involve one or more of the following: (1) change the strategy and/or tactics, (2) change the budget, and/or (3) change the objective. We'll illustrate how the monitoring and control system works at the three different levels—corporate, marketing, and marketing communications.

The control aspect of marketing communications comes into play when the marketing communications manager conducts marketing research to ascertain the extent to which the explicitly stated objectives at the marketing communications level, as well as the marketing and corporate levels, have been met. Let's use the MapLinx software package as an example to illustrate the control dynamics related to marketing communications. MapLinx is a software program that keeps track of sales data using geographic plots, as was shown in Figure 5.4.

Suppose the *corporate objective* of MapLinx has been stated as follows:

> Increase sales and market share of MapLinx software by 25% in relation to the U.S. market. The current sales are 5,500 units, and the market share was 58% all of last year. Specifically, the goal is to raise unit sales to 6,875 and to achieve a market share of 72.5% by the end of next year.

The corporate strategy is to *gain market share* (or *grow*). The president is taking an aggressive posture because of the perceived quality and superiority of the software over several key competitor brands.

Suppose the *marketing objective* has been stated as follows:

> Increase the association between MapLinx and visual mapping clarity by 40% in the next 12 months. Currently, 50% of sales managers in the United States describe MapLinx by referring to its visual mapping clarity. The goal is to have 70% of sales managers describe MapLinx by making reference to its visual mapping clarity. This should be accomplished by the end of the next 12-month period.

The marketing strategy is differentiation by positioning MapLinx as having "visual mapping clarity," that is, *positioning by product attribute*. This product attribute was chosen because it is the most distinctive feature that differentiates MapLinx from other sales-tracking softwares on the market and because the same attribute is found to be an important decision criteria in the purchase of sales-tracking software.

Suppose the marketing communications objective pertaining to MapLinx software has been stated as follows:

Increase brand trial by 30%. Last year we had approximately 4,000 units that were sent out on a trial basis, and 97% of them were ultimately purchased. Next year we want to increase brand trial to 5,200.

Here the marketing communications strategy involves a habit formation (doer) strategy. That is, sales managers (potential customers) are to be encouraged to try the software package and either pay the invoice or return the software. Personally trying the software would allow sales managers to readily learn about the software and its key benefit, the clarity of visual mapping. With a high rate of satisfaction, the majority of brand trials are likely to translate into brand purchase and sales.

At the end of the designated period, the marketing communications manager conducts research to ascertain the extent to which the marketing communications programs have been successful in increasing brand trial by 30%, brand association by 40%, and sales and market share by 25%. The performance assessment may show that the objectives at the three levels (corporate, marketing, and marketing communication) have been met. This state of affairs signifies that the selected strategies and tactics have been successful. However, what happens when corporate, marketing, or marketing communications performance fail to meet their stated objective? We'll address this situation next (see Table 9.1).

FAILING TO MEET MARKETING COMMUNICATIONS OBJECTIVES

What happens if the research results show that marketing communications objectives were not met? What should the company do in a situation like this? For example, what if the research findings signal a significant shortfall from the stated marketing communications objectives such that brand trial increased from 4,000 to only 4,200, the stated goal being 5,200. In this situation the marketing communications manager can exert control by taking one or more of the following corrective actions.

Reassess the Marketing Communications Strategy

The selected communications strategy for MapLinx was a habit formation (doer) one. Is it possible that this strategy was not effective? Is it likely that a different communications strategy would have produced better results? Perhaps so much emphasis was placed on the habit formation (doer) strategy because the company assumed that most sales managers were aware of MapLinx. Perhaps a strategy that emphasized learning (i.e., the informative [thinker] strategy) should have been employed.

Reassess the Strategic Mix

Perhaps the marketing communications mix of elements used to implement the marketing communications strategy was not the most effective to meet the marketing communications objectives. The marketing communications mix may have to be reconfigured. Suppose the MapLinx software had been advertised in airline magazines and general business magazines. Perhaps these two elements of the marketing communications mix were not effective. Perhaps a direct mail campaign to sales managers

TABLE 9.1 Possible Corrective Actions When Failing to Meet Corporate, Marketing, and Marketing Communications Objectives

- Failing to meet marketing communications objectives
  - Reassess the marketing communications strategy
  - Reassess the marketing communications mix
  - Reassess the implementation of each element of the marketing communications
  - Reassess the extent of coordination among the elements of the marketing communications mix
  - Reassess the realism of the marketing communications objectives
  - Reassess the amount of resources that have been allocated toward the elements of the marketing communications mix and their implementation
- Failing to meet marketing objectives
  - Reassess the marketing strategy
  - Reassess the marketing mix
  - Reassess the implementation of each element of the marketing mix
  - Reassess the extent of coordination between the marketing strategy and the strategies pertaining to the other elements of the marketing mix
  - Reassess the realism of the marketing objectives
  - Reassess the amount of resources that have been allocated toward the elements of the marketing mix and their implementation
- Failing to meet corporate objectives
  - Reassess the corporate strategy
  - Reassess the corporate mix
  - Reassess the implementation of each element of the corporate mix
  - Reassess the realism of the corporate objectives
  - Reassess the amount of resources that have been allocated toward the elements of the corporate mix and their implementation

accompanied by advertising in several key sales management magazines would be more effective.

Reassess the Implementation of the Mix Elements

Was each element of the marketing communications mix implemented effectively? Were there problems in their implementation? Can these implementation problems be corrected? For example, although the designated number of insertions were bought in the airline magazines, only half of them were actually printed in the magazines. Perhaps the creative people at the advertising agency failed to meet the magazines' publication deadlines.

Reassess the Coordination of the Mix Elements

Perhaps there was a coordination problem. The elements of the marketing communications mix may have been successful on an individual basis, but perhaps the problem was with the coordination among the elements. Suppose that the logos, slogans, colors, copy styles, and illustrations in the airline magazines were different from those in the general business magazines. The lack of consistency may have blocked reinforcement opportunities.

Reassess the Realism of the Communications Objectives

Perhaps an expected increase of 30% in brand trial is unrealistic given the short period of time allotted to achieve the objective. Perhaps a more realistic objective would have been an increase of 15% instead of 30%.

Reassess the Amount of Resources Allocated

Examples of questions that the marketing communications manager asks here include: Was the budget for creating the magazine ad sufficient? Could the agency have developed a better ad, given more resources? Was the person responsible for placing the print ad in the airline magazine competent? Could media placement be improved by hiring a more experienced person for more pay?

FAILING TO MEET MARKETING OBJECTIVES

What happens if the research results show that marketing objectives were not met? For example, what if the research findings signal a significant shortfall from the stated marketing objectives such that the brand association with visual clarity increased from 50% to only 55%, the stated goal being 70%. In this situation, the marketing communications manager can exert control by taking any one or more of the following corrective actions.

Reassess the Strategy

Perhaps the differentiation strategy involving positioning by the *product attribute of visual mapping clarity* was not the best marketing strategy to meet the marketing objectives. Perhaps another marketing strategy would have been more effective. Perhaps sales managers are more sensitive to the price of the software rather than visual mapping clarity. Perhaps other sales-tracking software packages were selling for a significantly lower price than MapLinx. If so, a *cost leadership* strategy might have been more effective. The price should have been reduced.

Reassess the Strategic Mix

Perhaps the marketing mix of elements used to implement the marketing strategy was not the most effective to meet the marketing objectives. The marketing mix may have to be reconfigured. Suppose too much emphasis was placed on the communications element without much regard to the pricing of MapLinx. A better pricing program should have been conceptualized and implemented, such as one in which sales managers could purchase or lease the product. Perhaps the company could have offered a lease arrangement that leads to purchase after a number of lease payments. Credit financing could have been arranged.

Reassess the Implementation of the Mix Elements

Was each element of the marketing mix implemented effectively? Were there problems in the implementation? Can these implementation problems be corrected? Perhaps there were disk-related problems. Several customers called and complained that some of the installation disks were damaged. Perhaps there was a problem with a virus infection. How were these problems handled and were they handled effectively? How can the marketing communications manager work closely with the other managers to prevent a recurrence of these problems?

Reassess Coordination between the Marketing Strategy and Related Strategies

Perhaps there was a coordination problem. The marketing strategy may have been successful, but perhaps the shipping department failed to handle the surplus of orders on time, a failure that caused the shortfall in the expected brand trial.

Reassess the Realism of the Marketing Objectives

Perhaps the marketing objective of increasing the association of MapLinx with visual clarity by 40% is unrealistic. Brand association edged up from 50% to only 55%, an increase of only 5%, while the objective was a 20% increase (the goal being to increase brand association with visual mapping clarity from 50% to 70%). Perhaps the best that can be achieved is 10%.

Reassess the Amount of Resources Allocated

Examples of questions that the marketing communications manager may ask here include: Was the budget allocated for marketing communications at large sufficient? Could the agency have developed a better marketing communications plan, given more resources? Was the person responsible for developing the strategic communications plan competent? Could a better plan have been developed by hiring a more experienced person for more pay?

FAILING TO MEET CORPORATE OBJECTIVES

What happens if the research results show that corporate objectives were not met? For example, the research findings signal a significant shortfall from corporate objectives—sales dipped from 5,500 units to 5,100 units, and market share changed from 58% to 53%. The objective was to increase sales and market share by 25%. Specifically, the goal was to raise unit sales to 6,875 and market share to 72.5% by the end of the year. Here, the marketing communications manager can exert control by taking any one or more of the following corrective actions.

Reassess the Corporate Strategy

Perhaps the growth strategy was not well chosen. Perhaps certain key competitors were able to produce and market comparable software with the same quality of visual mapping clarity at a lower price. Perhaps when the growth strategy was selected as *the* corporate strategy, the firm did not know much about the competition and its capabilities. In this situation, the marketing communications manager should attempt to convince corporate executives to change the corporate strategy, perhaps to a *maintain share* strategy.

Reassess the Corporate Mix

Perhaps the corporate mix used to implement the corporate strategy of growth was not the most effective to meet the corporate growth objectives of sales and market share. The corporate mix may have to be reconfigured. Suppose too much emphasis was placed on the R&D and engineering elements without much regard to the marketing aspects. The R&D and engineering people were calling the shots. The software was developed and given to marketing, which in turn was charged with selling it. The marketing communications manager may believe that the R&D and engineering people have to be led and guided by the marketing people to develop the product that meets customers' specifications. And who is better equipped to know customers' specifications than the marketing people within the firm?

Reassess the Implementation of the Mix Elements

Was each element of the corporate mix implemented effectively? Were there problems in their implementation? Can these implementation problems be corrected? For example, the accounting department had significant problems with its staff. Numerous invoices were not sent out on time; some were not sent out at all. Correctable returns (software packages that were sent back because of disk damage) were not followed up. Periodic sales reports were not generated. In this situation, an element of the corporate mix that is not marketing related may have caused the dip in sales and market share. The dip may have very little to do with marketing, although the marketing communications manager may be blamed for failing to achieve the stated sales and market share objective. By investigating the problem, the marketing communications manager may be able to point to the source and exert pressure to have the problem corrected.

Reassess the Realism of the Corporate Objectives

Perhaps the corporate objectives of increasing sales and market share by 25% are not realistic. Perhaps maintaining the same level of sales and market share is more realistic since the competition was not part of the equation when the corporate objectives were set. Note that the data show that sales dipped from 5,500 units to 5,100 units and market share changed from 58% to 53%. In this situation, the marketing communications manager may be able to account for the performance shortfall by showing the gains made by the competition. The manager may then work closely with corporate executives to set more realistic sales and market share goals for the near future.

Reassess the Amount of Resources Allocated

Examples of questions that the marketing communications manager may ask here include: Was the budget allocated for marketing at large sufficient? How about the other departments? Were they able to function effectively, given the resources made available? Could the marketing department have developed a better marketing plan, given more resources? Was the person responsible for developing the strategic marketing plan competent? Which department can use more resources, and how will the department use the resources to increase sales and market share?

Summary

In this chapter the reader was exposed to the concepts of monitoring and control. Monitoring and control was discussed from the viewpoint of the marketing communications manager. The manager assesses marketing communications performance in relation to communications objectives (e.g., brand awareness, brand liking, brand trial/purchase, repeat purchase) and also in relation to marketing objectives (e.g., brand association with a product attribute) and corporate objectives (e.g., sales, market share, and profit). Negative deviations between performance and the objective prompts the marketing communications manager to take corrective action at three different levels—communications, marketing, and corporate. Corrective action can be in the form of:

- reassessment of the selected strategy,
- reassessment of the strategic mix (or tactics),
- reassessment of the extent of coordination among the elements of the strategic mix,
- reassessment of the implementation of each element of the strategic mix,
- reassessment of the realism of the stated objectives, and
- reassessment of the amount of resources allocated for implementing the elements of the strategic mix.

Questions for Discussion

Consider the case of Kmart that was discussed at the beginning of this chapter. Kmart's market share dropped from approximately 5.2% in 1990 to 4.7% in 1995, while Wal-Mart's market share increased from approximately 5.2% in 1990 to 10% in 1995. At Kmart, products are often not available; the employees often provide poor service; many prices seem too high to consumers. You probably have been exposed to Kmart's advertising and other forms of marketing communications. You probably have also visited Kmart on a number of occasions. You probably have visited its key competitor, Wal-Mart. Respond to the following questions by relying on your own knowledge of Kmart and Wal-Mart.

1. Describe the typical Kmart advertising message. Compare it with Wal-Mart's.
2. What communications objectives do you think Kmart is trying to achieve with its advertising? How about Wal-Mart?
3. Do you think Kmart's advertising campaign is effective? Comment on the effectiveness of Kmart's advertising campaign in relation to what you think may be Kmart's advertising objectives.
4. Do you think Wal-Mart's advertising campaign is effective? Comment on the effectiveness of Wal-Mart's advertising campaign in relation to what you think may be Wal-Mart's advertising objectives.

5. If you think Kmart's advertising campaign is not effective, would you recommend that Kmart change its marketing communications strategy? From what to what?

6. Would you recommend changes in the marketing communications mix? Explain.

7. Would you recommend changes in marketing strategy? What is Kmart's current positioning strategy? Do you think it is an effective strategy? If not, what other positioning strategy is likely to be more effective?

8. Would you recommend changes in the marketing mix? Explain.

9. What is Kmart's current corporate strategy? Do you think it is an effective strategy? If not, what other corporate strategy is likely to be more effective for Kmart? Would you recommend changes in the corporate mix? Explain.

Notes

1. Patricia Seller, "Kmart is Down for the Count," *Fortune Magazine* (January 15, 1996), pp. 102–3.

2. J. Baumler, "Defined Criteria of Performance in Organizational Control," *Administrative Science Quarterly* (September 1971), p. 340; C. W. Churchman, *The Systems Approach* (New York: Dell, 1968); E. Flamholz, "Organizational Control Systems as a Managerial Tool," *California Management Review* 22, no. 2 (1979), pp. 50–9; D. Katz and R. Kahn, *The Social Psychology of Organizations* (New York: John Wiley, 1966); A. Y. Lerner, *Fundamentals of Cybernetics* (London: Chapman and Hall, 1972); W. T. Powers, *Behavior: The Control of Perception* (Chicago, Ill.: Aldine, 1973); G. Richardson, *Feedback Thought in Social Science and Systems Theory* (Philadelphia: University of Pennsylvania Press, 1991); F. F. Robb, "Cybernetics in Management Thinking," *Systems Research* 1, no. 1 (1985), pp. 5–23; M. Joseph Sirgy, "Toward a Theory of Social Organization: A Systems Approach," *Behavioral Science* 34 (1989), pp. 272–85.

Suggested Reading

Baumler, J. "Defined Criteria of Performance in Organizational Control." *Administrative Science Quarterly* (September 1971), p. 340.

Churchman, C. W. *The Systems Approach*. New York: Dell, 1968.

Flamholz, E. "Organizational Control Systems as a Managerial Tool." *California Management Review* 22, no. 2 (1979): pp. 50–9.

Katz, D., and R. Kahn. *The Social Psychology of Organizations*. New York: John Wiley, 1966.

Lerner, A. Y. *Fundamentals of Cybernetics*. London: Chapman and Hall, 1972.

Powers, W. T. *Behavior: The Control of Perception*. Chicago, Ill.: Aldine, 1973.

Richardson, G. *Feedback Thought in Social Science and Systems Theory*. Philadelphia, Pa.: University of Pennsylvania Press, 1991.

Robb, F. F. "Cybernetics in Management Thinking." *Systems Research* 1, no. 1 (1985): pp. 5–23.

Sirgy, M. Joseph. "Toward a Theory of Social Organization: A Systems Approach." *Behavioral Science* 34 (1989): pp. 272–85.

PART FOUR

Analysis and Planning

Do you know what strategic planners are? Many medium- and large-sized ad agencies have been hiring strategic planners for years. These people specialize in gathering intelligence and filtering relevant information to key decision makers. New types of planning positions are opening up too, such as positions for people who have expertise gathering intelligence through cyberspace or on-line information services. Strategic planners may work on either the client side or the agency side. At client companies, many strategic planners work in marketing departments. On the agency side, many people who become strategic planners previously held account management positions. These people tend to think strategically and focus on information that can assist managers in strategic planning. They are also leaders in the sense that they not only provide information to decision makers but also inspire managers. They inspire them to think creatively; they challenge them to think strategically; they motivate them to focus on what's important. Planners help identify a brand's strategy and then communicate it to all those who work with different facets of marketing communications. Recently, many agencies have created new departments for strategic planning. These departments work closely with upper management. The success

FIGURE IV.I Analysis and Planning

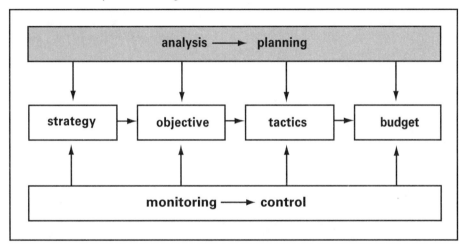

of marketing communications campaigns such as those of Burger King and MasterCard have been attributed to good, solid strategic planning.*

This part of the book (Part IV) discusses analysis and planning. Here we concentrate on how the marketing communications manager can conduct meaningful situation analysis. Situation analysis helps the marketing communications manager select the best strategies at the corporate, marketing, and marketing communications levels (chapter 10). Chapter 11 describes the kind of situation analysis that can assist the marketing communications manager in setting objectives at the three hierarchical levels. And similarly, chapter 12 describes situation analysis for the purpose of determining an effective marketing communications budget (see Figure IV.1)

---

*Mark Gleason, "Strategic Planners Hold the Cards," *Advertising Age* (December 11, 1995) pp. 30–1.

CHAPTER 10

Analysis and Planning: Selecting a Strategy

onsider the following case. Compaq Computer Corporation and preschool toy giant Fisher-Price have created a joint venture to develop a new product line. This product line allows consumers to turn home PCs into toys for preschoolers. There are 18 million U.S. families with children under the age of seven. The idea is to get these families to buy computer attachments, such as an oversized keyboard and car-like controls, to make a PC appealing to preschoolers. With this hardware comes a variety of software programs that involve both learning and adventure—exciting stuff for kids. The electronic learning toy market has been growing at about 28% per year and is estimated to reach $290 million per year in 1995. Compaq and Fisher-Price are clearly using an innovation strategy to tap this market. Wonder how Compaq and Fisher-Price arrived at that strategy? What analysis did these companies perform to make this decision? Did they examine the market potential and recognize a tremendous opportunity? Did they study competitors such as Packard Bell, IBM, and Microsoft, all of which are pursuing the kiddie market? Game makers, such as Sega Enterprises, are already in this market. Sega's Pico computer is a device that attaches to a regular TV and does what Compaq and Fisher-Price have in mind. What about consumer analysis? Have Compaq and Fisher-Price done their homework—that is, analysis and planning—to figure out whether families with young children are willing to fork over an additional $150 for the computer attachment and an additional $40 for each game? Managers engage in *analysis and planning* to assist them in selecting effective strategies and tactics.

This chapter is about analysis and planning, the process by which the marketing communications manager conducts an analysis of the situation, allowing him or her to make effective decisions. Managers traditionally refer to analysis and planning as *situation analysis*, sometimes as *strategic analysis*. Marketing communications managers often study a variety of factors, both internal and external to the firm, for the purposes of gathering information that would assist them in decision making. Traditionally, *external situation analysis* refers to the following:

- *market analysis* (gathering information about the size and geographic distribution of the market),
- *customer analysis* (dividing the market into customer segments and establishing a demographic, psychographic, and media habits profile of each segment),

- *competitive analysis* (discovering the marketing profile of each major competitor—that is, the products that each competitor provides to consumers, the price of each product, the channel of distribution used by each competitor, and the elements of the communications mix used by each competitor and the amount of resources allocated to the entire communications budget and its various elements), and

- *environmental analysis* (information about changes in technology, culture, consumption habits, political structures, laws and regulations, and/or the economy that are likely to affect the market).

Internal situation analysis focuses on factors internal to the organization, such as plotting sales trends from accounting data to determine those factors that have affected changes in sales over time or developing a sales forecasting model from data on past sales and communications expenditure levels.

The information obtained from situation analysis is used to make a host of decisions. Specifically, situation analysis may help marketing communications managers select corporate, marketing, and marketing communications strategies. How do marketing communications managers assist in the selection of a corporate strategy (grow, maintain position, harvest, innovate, or divest)? What factors should the manager consider in selecting the most effective corporate strategy? How do marketing communications managers select (or assist in the selection of) a marketing strategy? What analysis is needed to help them select the most effective marketing strategy (differentiation, cost leadership, or focus)? How about marketing communications? What analysis is needed to help the marketing communications manager select the most effective marketing communications strategy? Should it be an informative (thinker) strategy? An affective (feeler) strategy? A habit formation (doer) strategy? Or should it be a self-satisfaction (reactor) strategy? What information does the marketing communications manager need to make an effective strategy selection? (See Figure 10.1.)

FIGURE 10.1 Analysis and Planning in Relation to Strategy and Tactics

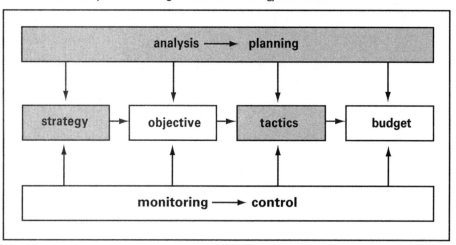

SITUATION ANALYSIS IN SELECTING A CORPORATE STRATEGY

As previously stated, situation analysis can be conducted to help the manager make three decisions. One is which corporate strategy to select. The second major decision is which corporate objectives to set. And the third decision is how to allocate resources. In this chapter we concentrate only on strategy selection.

At the corporate level, many corporate strategists employ *portfolio models* as a prerequisite to strategy selection. Two popular portfolio models are well accepted in the corporate strategy literature and can provide the reader with a good understanding of how to select a corporate strategy. These are: (1) the Boston Consulting Group matrix and (2) the multifactor portfolio matrix.

The Boston Consulting Group (BCG) Matrix

This model is commonly used to select the best mix of businesses or SBUs (strategic business units) to maximize the long-term earnings growth of the firm.[1] It helps determine the potential value of a particular SBU for the firm. This assessment is based on how a particular product/market stands in relation to market share and market growth (see Figure 10.2).

As shown in the figure, a product/market in a high-growth market but with low market share is called a "problem child." Successful competition transforms a "problem child" into a "star." Thus, a "star" is a business unit that is in a high-growth market and has high market share. The corporate strategy used to transform a "problem child" into a "star" is called the "gain share strategy."

FIGURE 10.2 The Boston Consulting Group Matrix

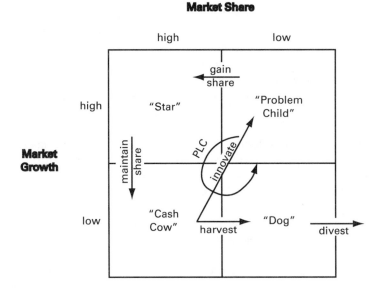

Implicit in the logic of the BCG matrix is the notion of the *product life cycle*. SBUs starting out in a high-growth market are the "problem children." They compete against others in a high-growth industry. The result of this competition produces winners and losers. The winners in a high-growth market are "stars"—the SBUs that attain high levels of market share. Then, market growth levels off and decreases over time. During this period, a "star" attempts to maintain its high market share in a mature market. With full market maturation, the "star" turns into a "cash cow." In this situation, the rate of return is high for the product, but the market is at low levels of growth. When a "star" starts to make good profit, it becomes a "cash cow." A "cash cow" makes a high level of profit because of *experience effects*—that is, the business unit cuts costs by learning to become highly efficient. After lowering costs, the profit margin increases, and the business unit generates the highest level of profit.

Further movement of the product comes from loss of sales and market share. Thus, a "cash cow" eventually turns into a "dog." A business unit classified as a "dog" has a poor competitive position and is in a declining market. Most firms select one of two strategies when they realize that a "cash cow" is moving toward a "dog" position. One strategy is to *innovate*—to focus on turning the product around by making a new and improved version. Thus, through innovation the product is resuscitated into a "problem child" and starts a new product life cycle of its own. The other strategy is to *harvest*. For the harvest strategy, the manager stops expending resources to nourish and sustain the product acknowledging that the end for the product is near. Thus, the firm tries to make the best of a bad situation. It does not spend money to save the product; instead, the firm makes as much profit as possible from the product and then lets it fade into extinction. When the product starts losing money, a *divest* strategy is selected. The divestment strategy entails selling off the business unit. The company divests it from its product portfolio.

The Multifactor Portfolio Matrix

The BCG matrix is a very popular and well-accepted model in the corporate strategy field. However, it has been criticized for being too narrow in its focus because it employs only two factors (market share and market growth) as a guide to strategy selection. In the real world, many businesses do not even know what their market share is. Market growth is also not easy to assess. Some managers consider return on investment as a more appropriate consideration for investment purposes than market share and cash flow. These difficulties have led companies such as GE and the Shell Group to adopt a portfolio model that allows a multifactor approach to assess market share and market growth.[2]

Figure 10.3 illustrates the multifactor portfolio matrix. The matrix has two dimensions: (1) company position (or business strength) and (2) market position (or industry or market attractiveness). *Company position* can be viewed as an equivalent construct to that of market share but broader in scope. Similarly, *market position* can be viewed as equivalent to market growth but broader in scope.

The multifactor portfolio matrix shown in Figure 10.3 recommends that the organization should invest in products assessed as high-to-medium in strength of company or market position. These products have good growth potential. The organization should harvest or divest products assessed as medium-to-low in strength of

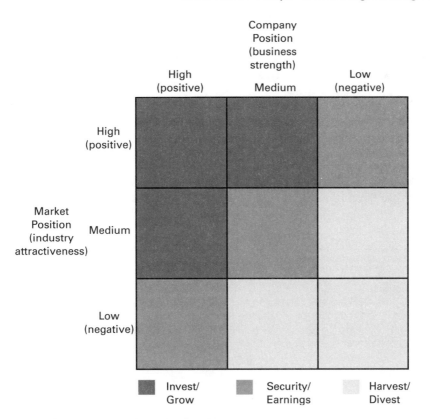

FIGURE 10.3 The Multifactor Portfolio Matrix

company or market position. Products assessed as medium should be managed very "selectively" to enhance earnings.

But how does the marketing communications manager assess company position (or business strength) and market position (or industry attractiveness)? GE has developed the multifactor portfolio matrix. GE used the following factors to assess and operationalize company position: (1) market position operationalized by indicators such as three-year average market share (total dollars) and three-year average international market share; (2) competitive position operationalized by indicators of product quality, technological leadership, manufacturing/cost leadership, and distribution/marketing leadership; and (3) relative profitability operationalized by a three-year average SBU return on sales (ROS) less the average ROS pertaining to the largest three competitors.

The factors used by GE to assess market position are (1) market size operationalized by a three-year average of industry market dollars; (2) market growth operationalized as the market growth rate of a ten-year constant dollar average; (3) industry profitability operationalized by indicators such as the three-year average return on sales of the three largest competitors; (4) cyclicality operationalized by the average annual percent variation of sales from a trend; (5) inflation recovery operationalized by the five-year average ratio of combined selling price and productivity change to change in cost due to inflation; and (6) importance of non-U.S. markets operationalized by the ten-year average ratio of international to total market.[3]

However, marketing scholars have expanded the list of factors that can be considered in the assessment of both business strength and industry attractiveness.[4] Table 10.1 shows the list of factors that can be used to assess company position strength, and Table 10.2 shows the factor list in relation to market position.

Assessing Company Position

Table 10.1 shows that company position can be assessed using four major factors: (1) market factors, (2) profit factors, (3) competitive factors, and (4) marketing factors.

TABLE 10.1 Assessing Company Position

Factors	$Ei \times Ii = Ej$			
		$Ej \times Ij = Ek$		
Market Factors				
• Sales	$5 \times$	$.50 =$	2.50	
• Customer satisfaction	$3 \times$	$.10 =$	.30	
• Brand loyalty	$4 \times$	$.20 =$	.80	
• Corporate image	$4 \times$	$.20 =$	.80	
		100%	$4.40 \times .20 =$	.88
Profit Factors				
• Gross profit/margin	$5 \times$	$.40 =$	2.00	
• Net profit/margin	$3 \times$	$.60 =$	1.80	
		100%	$3.80 \times .20 =$	.76
Competitive Factors				
• Market share	$4 \times$	$.40 =$	1.60	
• Value added	$4 \times$	$.20 =$	.80	
• Brand preference	$3 \times$	$.20 =$	.60	
• Experience curve effects	$2 \times$	$.20 =$	.40	
		100%	$3.40 \times .20 =$	.68
Marketing Factors				
• Product effectiveness	$4 \times$	$.10 =$	.40	
• Price competitiveness	$5 \times$	$.20 =$	1.00	
• Distribution effectiveness	$3 \times$	$.10 =$	.30	
• Mktg. comm. effectiveness	$5 \times$	$.20 =$	1.00	
• Sales effectiveness	$2 \times$	$.00 =$	.00	
• Marketing organization	$5 \times$	$.40 =$	2.00	
		100%	$4.70 \times .40 =$	1.88
			100%	4.20

Notes: The company position is evaluated in relation to each of the subfactors (i) on a scale varying from 1 ("poor") to 5 ("excellent"). These are shown in the table as Ei. These evaluations are derived through subjective judgments made by the marketing communications manager. The Ei scores are weighted by importance weights (Ii), which are also subjective judgments made by the marketing communications manager. The sum of the Ei × Ii scores of a given factor makes up the Ej score of that factor, which in turn is weighted by importance weights for that factor (Ij), producing the factor evaluation (Ek) scores. The sum of the Ek produce an overall evaluation score varying from 1 and 5, 1 being "poor" and 5 being "excellent." The hypothetical example here shows that the company position is good-to-excellent (4.20 rating out of 5).

TABLE 10.2 Assessing Market Position

Factors	$Ei \times$	$Ii =$	Ej / $Ej \times$	$Ij =$	Ek
Financial Factors					
• Market sales	5 ×	.40 =	2.00		
• Rate of growth (sales)	4 ×	.30 =	1.20		
• Profit margin	4 ×	.30 =	1.20		
		100%	4.40 ×	.30 =	1.32
Competitive Factors					
• Number of competitors	2 ×	.40 =	.80		
• Competitive structure	3 ×	.20 =	.60		
• Capital intensity	3 ×	.20 =	.60		
• Barrier of entry	4 ×	.20 =	.80		
		100%	2.80 ×	.20 =	.56
Customers Factors					
• Market size	4 ×	.30 =	1.60		
• Rate of growth (market size)	4 ×	.20 =	.80		
• Demand cyclically	3 ×	.10 =	.30		
• Availability of substitutes	2 ×	.20 =	.40		
• Concentration of customers	3 ×	.20 =	.60		
		100%	3.70 ×	.25 =	.93
Supply Factors					
• Availability of supplies	4 ×	.30 =	1.20		
• Availability of suppliers	5 ×	.40 =	2.00		
• Concentration of suppliers	3 ×	.30 =	.90		
		100%	4.10 ×	.25 =	1.03
Environmental Factors					
• Economy	4 ×	.25 =	1.00		
• Government regulations	5 ×	.25 =	1.25		
• Changes in technology	3 ×	.25 =	.75		
• Labor market	5 ×	.25 =	1.25		
		100%	4.25 ×	.10 =	.43
				100%	4.27

Notes: The market position is evaluated in relation to each of the subfactors (i) on a scale varying from 1 ("poor") to 5 ("excellent"). These are shown in the table as Ei. These evaluations are derived through subjective judgments made by the marketing communications manager. The Ei scores are weighted by importance weights (Ii), which are also subjective judgments made by the marketing communications manager. The sum of the Ei × Ii scores of a given factor makes up the Ej score of that factor, which in turn is weighted by importance weights for that factor (Ij). The sum of the Ej × Ij scores produce an overall evaluation score varying from 1 and 5, 1 being "poor" and 5 being "excellent." The hypothetical example here shows that the market position or its relative attractiveness is good-to-excellent (4.27 rating out of 5).

Market Factors   A company is in good position when the company's sales are high and *the rate of growth* (in sales) is high too. Furthermore, a company is strong if the customers are *loyal* to the company product. Another indicator of company position is *corporate image*. Does the organization have a good image among customers? The rule is: The more positive the corporate image, the better the company position.

Profit Factors   The company position is positive if the product generates a high level of *gross and net profit* and a high level of *profit margin*. That is, the higher the company's level of profitability, the more positive is its position in the market.

Competitive Factors   The company is said to be in good position if the product has a high *market share*. Also, if the product has *value-added* relative to the competition, then the company is in good position. If market research shows that customers *prefer* the company brand more than competitor brands, then the company is in good position. Finally, the company is said to be in good position if it achieved high levels of cost efficiencies as a direct function of *experience effects*.

Marketing Factors   Marketing factors are also used as indicators of business strength. Specifically, the higher the effectiveness of product, price, distribution, and promotion, the better the company's position. Also, the company may be judged as in good position if it has a marketing organization (the corporate culture that reflects customer service throughout the entire organization) and if it has a high level of organizational synergy.

Product effectiveness can be measured through indicators such as product quality, the breadth of the product line, number of products manufactured, timeliness of product development, capacity and productivity, R&D advantage, and cost efficiency in product manufacturing.

Price competitiveness can be measured in terms of consumer perceived value. The higher the perceived value, the greater the price competitiveness. Also, price competitiveness may be suggested by the extent to which consumers perceive the price to fall within the acceptable price range (within the upper and lower price limits). Furthermore, the company is in good position when consumers perceive the product as significantly different and better than the leading competitor product.

Distribution effectiveness can be measured in terms of consumers' access to the product in question. The greater the access, the better the company position. Just-in-time delivery is another distribution goal. The company is in good position if it delivers the product to the consumer when it is needed and where it is needed.

Promotion effectiveness can be measured in terms of the following indicators: the extent to which the target consumers are aware of the product, are familiar with the product benefits, have a positive attitude toward the product, make a decision to buy the product, and, after purchase and trial, would feel committed to the product.

Marketing organization, as a factor to assess company position, refers to the extent to which the organization is structured to reflect marketing dominance. Table 10.3 contrasts different types of organizations, organizations dominated by marketing versus organizations dominated by manufacturing, sales, and technology.

General managers who are marketing oriented tend to be unconstrained by functional boundaries (departments such as marketing, manufacturing, engineering,

TABLE 10.3 Organizations Dominated by Different Functional Units

	Orientation			
	Manufacturing	*Sales*	*Technology*	*Marketing*
Typical strategy	Lower cost	Increase	Push research	Build share profit-ability
Normal structure	Functional	Functional or profit centers	Profit centers	Market or product or brand; decentralized profit responsibility
Key systems	Plant P&L's Budgets	Sales forecasts Results vs. plan	Performance tests R&D plans	Marketing plans
Traditional skills	Engineering	Sales	Science and engineering	Analysis
Normal focus	Internal efficiencies	Distribution channels; short-term sales results	Product performance	Consumers Market share
Typical response to competitive pressure	Cut costs	Cut price Sell harder	Improve product	Consumer research, planning, refining
Overall mental set	"What we need to do in this company is get our costs down and our quality up."	"Where can I sell what we make?"	"The best product wins the day."	"What will the consumer buy that we profitably make?"

R&D, accounting, finance, personnel, etc.). Thus, a marketing organization typically does the following:

- The company identifies specific markets for each of its products—that is, it identifies several product/markets.
- It monitors profitability for each product/market.
- It conducts research to determine the needs, wants, and preferences of the consumers in each product/market.
- It assesses the strengths and weaknesses of the major competitors in relation to each product/market.
- It assesses the impact of environmental trends on each product/market.
- The company prepares and uses an annual marketing plan.
- "Marketing investment" (money spent on marketing is considered as an investment that pays off sooner or later) is understood and practiced.
- Everyone in the company assumes the responsibility of making the business successful and profitable.
- Everyone in the company "talks" marketing.
- Top executives of the company are marketing people.[5]

Assessing Market Position

Like assessing company position, assessing market position is multifaceted. There are financial, competitive, customer, and environmental factors to consider.

Financial Factors   Several financial factors that managers consider in assessing the attractiveness of a specific market are market sales, sales growth rate, and profit margin. Here the marketing communications manager should identify *current sales* (in dollars and in units) of the entire market and project these sales into the future. The higher the current and forecasted sales, the more attractive the market. The marketing communications manager also should compute *sales growth* (percentage of change from one year to the next) and project the rate of growth into the future. The higher the rate of past, current, and forecasted sales growth, the more attractive that market becomes. Similarly, the manager identifies the average *profit margins* as reported by all the companies in that market. Also, given the means, the manager extrapolates future profit margins. The higher the industry past, current, and forecasted profit margin, the more attractive the market.

Competitive Factors   The manager considers a variety of competitive factors, such as the *number of competitors*, the industry *competitive structure*, *capital intensity*, and *barriers of entry*. The more competitors, the less attractive the market. However, in many situations the market is not attractive even with zero competitors. This situation is common with new product introductions, especially the kind of products that require consumers to change existing habits. In this situation, it is very difficult to build primary demand through the efforts of only one firm. The efforts of several firms help build primary demand for the product. Therefore, one can describe the relationship between attractiveness and number of competitors as follows: Market attractiveness is very low when there are no competitors; the market is highly attractive when there are a few competitors; the market becomes decreasingly attractive as more competitors enter the market (see Figure 10.4).

In assessing market position, the competitive structure of the industry is another significant factor. The *competitive structure* of any industry can be described in terms of a dimension varying from complete monopoly to pure competition. The gradients are: a monopolistic industry in which one large firm has complete control of the market, followed by monopolistic competition in which there is one leader and many small and insignificant competitors, followed by an oligopoly in which there are several large firms competing head-to-head and many smaller firms, all the way to pure competition, in which the industry has many small-to-medium-sized firms. Market attractiveness is highest in situations resembling pure competition and least attractive in monopolies. This is because it is very difficult to compete against giant monopolies, and less so against oligopolies, and, by the same token, it is easiest to compete in markets approaching pure competition.

Capital intensity refers to the situation in which the firms in that market have invested a great deal of capital in land, equipment, and machinery. The higher the capital intensity in the industry, the lower its attractiveness. This is because higher levels of capital intensity usually lead firms to be ineffective in countering changes in the environment. Also, when the going gets tough, the firms become fierce and ugly competitors. On the other hand, an industry having very low levels of capital intensity is also considered unattractive. This is because the low *barrier of entry* encourages many new competitors to enter the market. A moderate barrier is often deemed desirable.

FIGURE 10.4 The Relationship between Number of Competitors and Market Attractiveness

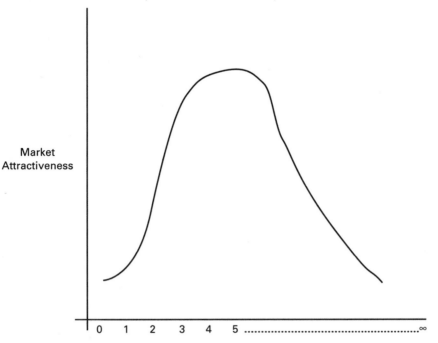

Number of Competitors

Customer Factors   In assessing the attractiveness of a market, managers consider factors such as market size, market growth size, demand cyclicality, availability of substitutes, and concentration of customers. Here, the marketing communications manager should estimate the number of people that can be characterized as "customers" in the designated market. Past and current figures are identified and future projections estimated. The bigger the *size of the market* is and is likely to be in the future, the more attractive the market.

With respect to the *rate of market growth*, managers compute changes in the size of the market from year to year and make future projections too. Managers look for stability in the rate of growth. If many change coefficients are negative, this may signal market instability.

Related to rate of growth is *demand cyclicality*. Many markets are besieged by cyclical demand. That is, demand tends to fluctuate significantly, perhaps as a direct function of seasonal demand or the business cycle. The greater the demand cyclicality, the less attractive the market.

Availability of substitutes is a factor that, if relevant to a market, makes the market unattractive. For example, cable technology is rapidly evolving to the extent that consumers of video rentals are increasingly ordering the pay movies offered by cable networks. Pay movies are a substitute for video rentals. The increasing availability of and demand for this substitute makes the video rental market unattractive.

Concentration of customers doesn't have anything to do with how dispersed the customers are in a certain geographic region. Concentration of customers is a power construct. It refers to the extent to which customers have bargaining power over the seller firms. For example, in the military aviation market, the entire industry is subject to the whims of the defense departments of the United States and its allied countries. There are a few customers, and these customers wield enormous power over the sellers. Such a situation is not attractive because losing key customers may likely mean the demise of key players in the industry and perhaps even the demise of the industry as a whole. The converse situation, however, is attractive. This is a situation in which there are many customers, and these customers are not organized to transact with industry players with one voice.

Supply Factors   Managers usually consider at least three supply factors in assessing market attractiveness: availability of supplies, availability of suppliers, and concentration of suppliers. *Availability of supplies* refers to the situation in which adequate raw materials are available for the industry to manufacture, distribute, and promote the product. Consider a foreign market, such as Albania (next to former Yugoslavia). A company may consider entering the coffee maker manufacturing business. The plant needs a continuous water supply and uninterrupted electric power to run the equipment. But Albania's infrastructure is in shambles. Water and power are scarce commodities. Therefore, the Albanian market is considered unattractive.

The same can be said about *availability of suppliers*. Even if the parts and raw materials are available, are there suppliers to sell and deliver the supplies? The more suppliers, the more attractive the market because more suppliers generate greater competition among suppliers, which in turn serves to reduce the price of supply and/or enhance its quality.

However, if the suppliers are organized and attempt to sell their products through price collusion, the buyers of this supply are not likely to benefit significantly. This is because *concentration of suppliers* enhances the bargaining power of suppliers to the detriment of the organizations needing that supply. This situation makes the market unattractive. For example, in the early 1970s, many manufacturing industries relying heavily on oil were hurt by the OPEC oil cartel. OPEC decided to restrict the flow of oil to the United States because of the U.S. support of Israel in the 1973 Arab-Israeli war.

Environmental Factors   Managers consider many environmental factors in assessing the relative attractiveness of a given market or industry. Among the important factors are the economy, government regulations, changes in technology, and the labor market. For example, if the *economy* is anticipated to take a downturn, it may adversely affect the market. Thus, marketing communications managers should consider the effects of the economy on the market. Consider doing business in a country like Mexico. Could the fall of the peso have been forecasted? Many markets in Mexico look very unattractive because the devaluation of the peso has adversely affected consumer demand for many products.

Government regulation is an important factor in assessing the attractiveness of a market. A market that is besieged by all kinds of government regulations is considered unattractive, while markets that have little or no regulation are attractive. Consider the tobacco industry. That industry is subject to all kinds of government regulations. For example, tobacco managers cannot advertise on television or radio. In print ads, they cannot show a person in the act of smoking. All kinds of warning labels have to be included in an ad. Also, government regulations are expected to be exacerbated in the future, making managers in that industry feeling that the tobacco market has increasingly lost its luster.

The extent to which *changes in technology* are likely to affect any aspect of the industry have an impact on its attractiveness. For example, an advertising agency assesses the market and examines the changing role of computer technology. Many advertisers have been establishing in-house advertising departments with the capability of producing sophisticated graphics and designing software packages. These firms do not need advertising agencies as much as they did in the past. Also, many media firms have adopted computer technology, allowing an advertiser to produce an ad directly through the media firm, thereby bypassing the ad agency. Here is an example in which change in computer technology has adversely affected the attractiveness of the market for ad agencies.

The *labor market* is another important environmental factor managers pay close attention to. Is there a shortage or a surplus of qualified personnel to man the manufacturing plants? What is management's relationship with unions within the industry at large? Is there an amicable relationship? Is it likely to turn sour? How is the relationship likely to affect developing the product in time? Will the labor market be adequate to manufacture the desired number of units, to deliver the promised product quality, to maintain a certain price for the product? These considerations are important since they affect directly and indirectly the level of attractiveness of the market.

Having illustrated how business strength (company position) and industry attractiveness (market position) can be determined (as illustrated in Table 10.1 and Table 10.2), we are ready to plug these numbers back into the multifactor portfolio matrix and ascertain the exact position of the hypothetical product/market in question. Figure 10.5 shows the result. The figure shows that both the company and market position of the hypothetical product/market falls in the high/high quadrant, which signals that the product/market should be nurtured to growth and that the firm ought to invest in this product/market to allow it to realize its full growth potential.

Also, it should be noted that there are many situations in which the application of the multifactor portfolio matrix may show that the product category is significantly discrepant from the ideal position (see Figure 10.6). In these situations, the marketing communications manager may attempt to articulate a strategy projecting a trajectory from the current position in the direction of the ideal position. This trajectory may take a variety of forms as a direct function of the current position.

SITUATION ANALYSIS IN SELECTING A MARKETING STRATEGY

Like corporate analysis and planning, marketing analysis and planning have to be discussed in relation to marketing strategy selection. Remember the various positioning strategies discussed in chapter 5, "Marketing Strategies and Tactics." Fifteen positioning strategies were identified and discussed. These were classified under three key

FIGURE 10.5 An Illustration of the Use of the Multifactor Portfolio Matrix

Note: Location of product/market as derived from the assessments shown in Table 10.1 and 10.2, which means that this product/market is assessed as being strong in business strength and is in a very attractive market or industry. The recommendation is to invest in this product/market and nurture its growth.

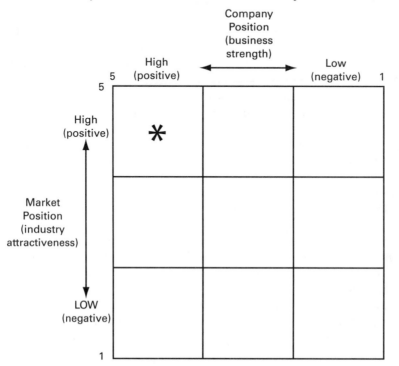

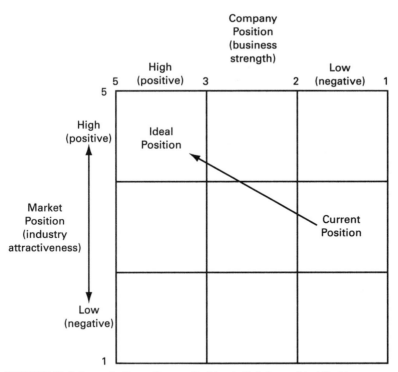

FIGURE 10.6 Strategic Gap—Current Position in Relation to Ideal Position

strategies (differentiation, cost leadership, and focus). Under differentiation we identified several positioning strategies. These include positioning by: product attribute, intangible factor, relative price, product class, competitors, country-of-origin, brand-distributor tie-in, distributor location, distributor's service capability, celebrity or person, and lifestyle or personality. The focus strategy was discussed in terms of market segmentation and was examined especially in relation to three key positioning strategies. These are positioning by customer benefits, positioning by user or customer, and positioning by use or application. The cost leadership strategy was described in terms of positioning by low price.

Situation analysis is conducted to help the marketing communications manager determine the best marketing strategy for the situation at hand. In this section, we will discuss conditions under which each marketing strategy is thought to be most effective. Situation analysis is therefore required to ascertain these conditions and select the most effective strategy. It should be noted that instead of discussing those factors affecting strategy selection one at a time as we have done in the preceding section, we'll discuss situation analysis *per* positioning strategy. This is because the factors or conditions that we have to address *interact*.

Situation Analysis Pertaining to the Differentiation Strategy

Remember the 11 positioning strategies that were discussed as alternative means to implement the differentiation strategy. We described them in some detail in chapter 5.

These are positioning by product attribute, positioning by intangible factor, positioning by product class, positioning by competitors, positioning by country-of-origin, positioning by relative price, positioning by brand-distributor tie-in, positioning by distributor location, positioning by distributor's service capability, positioning by celebrity or person, and positioning by lifestyle or personality. We'll discuss the conditions under which each of these strategies is considered best.

When to Use the Positioning-by-Product-Attribute Strategy

This strategy should be used under the following conditions:

1. When consumers make buying decisions using product attributes. For example, the purchase of mineral water may be based on certain decision criteria. Examples of decision criteria are whether an alternative brand has attributes such as "in-between color," "nonalcoholic," and "not too sweet, less sugar." In other words, consumer analysis has to be conducted to identify the product attributes that consumers regard as important and consider these attributes in making their purchase decisions.

2. When product attributes can be clearly connected with functional and psychosocial consequences. Returning to the mineral water example, the product attributes that were referred to ("in-between color," "nonalcoholic," and "not too sweet, less sugar") may be connected with functional and psychosocial consequences such as "dry, clean taste," "light taste," "doesn't mask taste of food," "doesn't inhibit ability to concentrate," among others. Thus, the marketing communications manager should conduct consumer analysis to identify and measure the strength of the connections between the concrete attributes and functional/psychosocial consequences. For a model and measurement techniques to carry this out, the reader should refer to the means-end chain model discussed in Appendix 5.1 at the end of chapter 5.

3. When the product is functional in nature—that is, when the product serves a functional or practical purpose. For example, mineral water is a practical type of product. People consume it for practical reasons. In contrast, jewelry doesn't have a strong utilitarian purpose; it mostly serves to express the consumer's values. Thus, consumer analysis has to be conducted to measure the extent to which the product is functional or value-expressive. Of course, this can be done through a scientific consumer study or judged subjectively by the marketing communications manager.[6]

4. When the product attributes are clearly attributed to the brand in question and not the competition. Consider an example such as fluoride in Crest. For years and years Crest had positioned its toothpaste brand in terms of fluoride (a product attribute). But almost all toothpaste brands now have fluoride. It wouldn't be very smart for Crest or any toothpaste brand to position itself in terms of fluoride anymore because all or most brands now have this attribute.

When to Use the Positioning-by-Intangible-Factor Strategy

This strategy should be used when the marketing communications manager is aware of a specific intangible factor that marks his or her product's superiority over the competitors'. For example, if the marketing communications manager knows that the product is marked by technological distinction, he or she may be able to use this intangible factor as the focus of a marketing communications campaign. For a method to identify important intangible factors, see the means-end chain model described in Appendix 5.1 at the end of chapter 5.

When to Use the Positioning-by-Product-Class Strategy

This strategy should be used under one condition: when the product is in the early stages of its life cycle. The Nivea shower and bath moisturizing gel is an example of a product in the early stages of the product life cycle (PLC). Thus, the focus of any marketing communications campaign pertaining to products in the introduction stage of the PLC is *primary demand*, not selective demand. For example, primary demand advertising of personal computers focuses on educating consumers about personal computers and how they can be used in a variety of settings. In contrast, *selective demand* advertising of personal computers focuses on differentiating a brand of PC from other competitor brands. This is done by showing how a given brand of PC is better in terms of product attributes or customer benefits such as portability, compatibility with certain computer environments and applications, multimedia compatibility, speed, storage capacity, and so on. Note that in the early stages of the PC market, probably about 10 or 15 years ago, most of the PC advertising focused on primary demand. Now, much of the PC advertising can be characterized as selective demand advertising.[7]

When to Use the Positioning-by-Competitors Strategy

This strategy should be used under two conditions:

1. When the brand is competing against another that is well established in the marketplace. Relating the strength of one's brand by comparing it to the leading brand is very advantageous to the brand because it allows consumers to bring the brand into their evoked set. The *evoked set* refers to those alternative brands that consumers consider when they contemplate purchase of a given product. A situation analysis involving market share of the various brands can reveal which other brands are well established.

2. When the marketing communications manager's brand has a significant strength beyond that of the leading brand(s). This information can be obtained from product engineers and technical reports from independent agencies that have reviewed the product's strengths and weaknesses from a technical standpoint.

When to Use the Positioning-by-Country-of-Origin Strategy

This strategy should be used under the following conditions:

1. When the majority of the consumers in the target market use quality as an important criterion in evaluating product alternatives. For example, when consumers evaluate alternative car models, they tend to ascertain the quality of each, and that quality is indeed an important evaluative criterion in their purchase decision. The method described in Appendix 5.7 at the end of chapter 5 can be helpful in identifying important customer benefits.

2. When the country or geographic area where the product is manufactured has a clear image of quality in direct relation to the marketing communications manager's product. For example, watches manufactured in Switzerland have a clear image of quality; however, cars manufactured in Switzerland may not. A consumer analysis can be conducted to measure the image of the country in question.[8]

3. When the marketing communications manager has little concrete evidence to claim high quality for his or her product. For example, if the marketing communications manager has more substantial evidence of quality, such as quality ratings by *Consumer Reports*, he

or she should use that evidence. Only in the absence of such evidence should the country-of-origin cue be used as a symbol for quality.

When to Use The Positioning-by-Relative-Price Strategy

Marketing communications managers should use the positioning-by-relative-price strategy under the following conditions:

1. When most of consumers in the target market are confident that there is a direct correspondence between price and quality and that a higher-priced product has better quality. For example, most consumers feel that the more they pay for an automobile, the better its quality. A consumer price-quality study is recommended to make this determination.[9]

2. When there are significant quality variations among the brands in the product category. For example, the automobile market has a wide range of quality variations. These can be assessed through technical reports of quality rankings of all or most of the brands in the product category.

3. When actual quality is difficult to judge without having experienced the product first-hand. Again, the example is a car. It is difficult to judge the quality of a car without having driven it for some time.[10]

When to Use the Positioning-by-Brand-Distributor-Tie-in Strategy

This strategy should be used under the following conditions:

1. When the manufacturer (distributor) does not have much of a reputation, while the distributor (manufacturer) has a good and solid reputation in the minds of target consumers. For example, a new brand of washing machine (called "Washer") may be manufactured by a medium-sized company. This company does not have an established reputation in the washing machine industry and market. This firm contracts with a reputable retailer, such as Sears, to distribute its line of washing machines.[11]

2. When the distributor (manufacturer) is impressed by the innovativeness of the manufacturer's product and its appeal to the distributor's customers. That is, the distributor believes that the manufacturer's product can be easily sold to its customers. Using the Washer/Sears example, Sears may be convinced that the Washer line is highly innovative and better than its current line and that Sears customers are very likely to buy the Washer brand.

When to Use the Positioning-by-Distributor-Location Strategy

This strategy should be used when consumers feel that the convenience of the distribution outlet and product access are very important criteria in purchase decisions. For example, a consumer survey indicates that the decision to patronize a fast-food restaurant such as Subway is determined not only by the restaurant's "good food" but also by their convenient access. Based on this finding, many of the Subway franchises are located inside convenience stores.[12]

When to Use the Positioning-by-Distributor's-Service-Capability Strategy

Like the preceding strategy, this positioning strategy should also be used when getting good customer service from the retailer is a very important decision criteria for consumers.

When to Use the Positioning-by-Celebrity/Person Strategy

Marketing communications managers typically use this strategy in the following circumstances:

1. When the competition is fierce and the mass media are cluttered with ads. For example, the market for teenagers' sneakers can be characterized as fiercely competitive. Celebrity endorsement is very common here.[13]

2. When most consumers in the target market are not heavily involved (emotionally speaking) with the product category. Thus, a celebrity serves to heighten consumers' involvement with the product and the advertised brand.[14]

When to Use the Positioning-by-Lifestyle/Personality Strategy

This strategy should be used under one condition; when the product has been associated with certain symbols that carry certain meanings and images over an extended period. Examples include the use of a magazine "cover girl" as a symbol to identify Cover Girl cosmetics; the use of Pillsbury dough boy as symbol for Pillsbury baked goods, among others. Marketing communications managers can capitalize on this opportunity to clearly and forcefully reinforce this position in the minds of target consumers.

Situation Analysis Pertaining to the Focus Strategy

Remember the three positioning strategies that were discussed as alternative means to implement the focus strategy. We described them in some detail in chapter 5. These are positioning by customer benefits, positioning by user or customer, and positioning by use or application. We'll discuss the conditions under which each of these strategies is considered best.

When to Use the Positioning-by-Customer-Benefits Strategy

Marketing communications managers should use this strategy under the following conditions:

1. When the selected customer benefits are perceived as very important by target consumers. In chapter 5, we described a method in Appendix 5.7 to ascertain the importance of various customer benefits. Please refer to that method for a measurement method that can be used in the situation analysis here.

2. When most of the consumers are at least moderately familiar with the product and may have different feelings about its various benefits. For example, people who like to eat pickles are likely to have tried a variety of brands of pickles. Similarly, a radio station in a given locality may be another example. Most residents in a locality, at some point in time, have probably tuned into most radio stations in the area.

3. When the cost of getting the product is small or negligible to the consumer. For example, the cost of tuning one's radio to a specific radio station is indeed minimal. Similarly, the cost of a jar of pickles is also very small.

When to Use the Positioning-by-Use/Application Strategy

This strategy can be used under the following conditions:

1. When the product can be used in a variety of applications. For example, a PC can be used for a variety of purposes at home, at school, and at work.

2. Early in a product's life cycle. At this stage, many consumers have not yet used the product and may not be very familiar with how and why to use it. PCs are a good example.

When to Use the Positioning-by-User/Customer Strategy

This marketing strategy can be used under the following conditions:

1. When the product has to be value expressive. Examples of value-expressive products include computer notebooks, watches, clothes, cars, and magazines. Each of these reflect a user image. In other words, in order for this strategy to work, the product has to have a clear user image already established, or the marketing communications manager must be willing to establish that image.[15]

2. When the market is likely to be in its mature stage, when the market is dominated by an oligopoly, and when competitive brands and product differentiation are minimal. An example may be the economy/sports market. The market is dominated by a handful of well-established brands with little differentiation among them.

Situation Analysis Pertaining to the Cost Leadership Strategy

Recall the one and only positioning strategy that was discussed as a means to implement the cost leadership strategy. We described it in some detail in chapter 5. It is positioning by low price. We'll discuss the conditions under which this strategy is considered best.

When to Use The Positioning-by-Low-Price Strategy

This strategy can be employed under one or more of the following conditions:

1. When a significant segment of the target market consists of consumers who are brand switchers. For example, many consumers using cosmetic products such as lipstick, eye shadow, and makeup tend to switch from one brand to another. Switching behavior can be easily induced by price reductions and discounts. A consumer study can be conducted to determine the level of switching behavior in the product category. A measure of brand commitment or loyalty can be used to measure the extent of brand switching. Various measures of brand loyalty are discussed in chapter 7, "Objectives and Performance Measures."

2. When a significant segment of the target market consists of nonproduct users—that is, people who haven't had a chance to try the product yet. For example, personal computers may fall under this category. PCs are expensive, and there many nonusers. But many nonusers can be persuaded to buy a PC if they find a good bargain. This possibility can be ascertained through a market potential study.[16]

3. When a significant segment of the target market is price or deal conscious. That is, the positioning-by-low-price strategy can be very effective when directed to consumers who frequently shop around and are seeking good bargains. An example of a consumer segment with this profile is traditional homemakers who are bargain seekers. These consumers tend to shop around for savings. A consumer study can be conducted here to identify the extent to which target consumers are price or deal conscious.[17]

4. When the product/market is considered price elastic. A positioning strategy based on price may work best when consumers are responsive to price differences. If price is not an important consideration for the average consumer in the target market, then this strategy

should not be used. For example, marketing communications managers should not use this strategy if the product is women's jewelry directed to upscale clientele. These consumers are not likely to be price sensitive.[18]

SITUATION ANALYSIS IN SELECTING A MARKETING COMMUNICATIONS STRATEGY

As we've done in relation to both the corporate and marketing levels, we'll address analysis and planning with respect to the selection of a marketing communications strategy. How do marketing communications managers select among these four different communications strategies (informative, affective, habit formation, and self-satisfaction)? What are the decision criteria, or factors, guiding their strategy selection? In the following section we'll discuss several factors that can help the marketing communications manager conduct a situation analysis that can be highly instrumental in selecting an effective communications strategy.

Organizational Factors

Organizational factors are perhaps the most important factors in the selection of a marketing communications strategy because they force the marketing communications manager to consider those decisions made at both the corporate and marketing levels. The superordinate decisions are supposed to guide marketing communications decisions. Examples of important organizational factors follow.

Corporate Strategy and Objective

When the corporate goal is a large volume of *sales* (or *market share*), an informative (thinker) or an affective (feeler) strategy is recommended. This is because a goal of a large volume of sales (or an ambitious market-share goal) entails reaching out to new consumers in new markets. New customers, by definition, need to become aware of the brand, need to be educated about the brand's benefits (or costs), and need to feel good about the possibility of purchasing it. Also, advertising, which is the communications mix element commonly deployed as a means to generate the highest level of brand awareness possible, may not be cost efficient if the corporate goal does not involve a large volume of sales.[19] When the corporate goal is small-to-moderate sales volume, other personal forms of communications that induce an immediate response (e.g., personal selling, certain forms of direct marketing, and reseller support) are used.[20] It should be noted too that the corporate strategies of *growth* and *innovation* are consistent with the objective of maximizing sales and, therefore, point to the need for informative (thinker) or affective (feeler) communications strategies. The reason is that a growth strategy may entail marketing to new consumers in new markets, which in turn entails the use of marketing communications to reach out to these new consumers, educate them about the product, and help them develop a preference for it. These goals are consistent with informative (thinker) and affective (feeler) communications strategies.

With respect to *profit*, if the goal is immediate or short-term profit, then the emphasis is placed on the bottom line—sales, sales, sales, and NOW, NOW, and NOW. Much pressure is placed on the marketing communications manager to get consumers to buy, buy, and buy, a goal that entails either a habit formation (doer) or self-satisfaction (reactor) strategy. Usually, two forms of marketing communications are used to get people to buy and buy *now*. The first is direct marketing. This form of communications has more impact than other communications tools in generating immediate customer response. For example, many financial brokerage firms use telemarketing (a direct marketing technique) to generate immediate business. Second, sales promotion promote immediate purchase. Both of these communications devices can be highly effective in generating an immediate response from the consumer, and both are highly consistent with the habit formation (doer) and self-satisfaction (reactor) strategies. Also, it should be noted that a *harvest* corporate strategy, where the ultimate goal is to maximize profit, may entail getting consumers to repeat purchase. This goal is consistent with either the habit formation (doer) or the self-satisfaction (reactor) communications strategies because the firm may not want to lose its customers to competition. Therefore, the focus is on using marketing communications tools and techniques to encourage repeat purchase, thus increasing profit.

These factors pertaining to corporate strategy and objective call for an "internal" situation analysis; that is, the marketing communications manager has to gather and analyze information about the current corporate strategy and objectives.

Marketing Strategy and Objective

Certain kinds of positioning strategies (and their corresponding objectives) can be carried out most effectively through certain strategies of marketing communications. For example, examine the following positioning techniques: *positioning by user or customer*, *positioning by celebrity or person*, and *positioning by lifestyle or personality*. These marketing strategies can be best implemented through affective (feeler) or self-satisfaction (reactor) communications strategies. Either strategy can generate feelings that can spill over to the brand. Specifically, both strategies can generate feelings of brand liking through positive affect felt for a celebrity, a lifestyle, or a personality. The idea here is to use a lifestyle or a personality that consumers feel an affinity for, which in turn will generate positive feelings toward the brand through association. Thus, different positioning strategies may entail different marketing communications strategies.

Accounting for the marketing strategy and objective calls for conducting an internal situation analysis. The marketing manager needs to be acutely aware of the current marketing strategy and objectives.

Marketing Communications Past Performance

New marketing communications strategies are determined as a direct function of what has been already accomplished in relation to the brand awareness, brand learning, brand attitude, brand trial and purchase, and repeat purchase communications goals. If past marketing communications efforts have achieved sufficient levels of brand awareness, brand knowledge, and brand preference but have achieved little in relation to brand purchase and repeat purchase, then perhaps the manager should now change strategies and adopt one that gets consumers to purchase the product (e.g., habit formation or self-satisfaction). These strategies are selected as a direct function of what has already been accomplished and what still needs to be accomplished. Marketing communications campaigns are usually planned to accomplish the communications goals in a sequential fashion. After achieving one goal (or one set of goals), the marketing communications manager should change communications strategies to attain a new set of goals.

This factor calls for "customer analysis." This kind of situation analysis focuses on target consumers and measures the extent to which they are aware of the brand, how much they know about the brand, their attitude toward the brand, and their purchase history in relation to the brand and its competitors. This information can be very helpful in selecting a suitable communications strategy. The various measures that can be used to gather this information are described in some detail in chapter 7, "Objectives and Performance Measures".

Product Factors

Product factors are considerations related to product characteristics. For example, whether the product is a "thinking" type product or a "feeling" type may make a difference in selecting an appropriate communications strategy. The level of product involvement may also make a difference.

Thinking-Type versus Feeling-Type Products

Products can be classified as the "thinking type" or "feeling type." The distinction between thinking and feeling products is based on the distinction between right- and left-brain information processing. The left brain processes semantic information through "rational," or cognitive, thinking. The right brain, in contrast, processes information that is more spatial and visual in nature. The right brain engages in the affective, or "feeling," functions. Consumers tend to process information about cars, houses, furnishings, new products, and household items more with the left brain than the right one. Information processing for these products is more cognitive or rational than emotional. These products are characterized as "thinking products." For thinking products, either the informative (thinker) or habit formation (doer) strategy is suitable. In contrast, either the affective (feeler) or the self-satisfaction (reactor) strategy is better suited for "feeling products." Examples of feeling products include jewelry, cosmetics, fashion apparel, motorcycles, cigarettes, liquor, and candy.[21]

Product Involvement

Nondurable products of low value and frequently purchased products requiring routine decision making are low-risk products and therefore are not highly involving for consumers. Marketing communications managers working with low-involvement products commonly use either a habit formation (doer) or self-satisfaction (reactor) strategy. Examples include toothpaste, mouthwash, soap, razor blades, and shaving cream. The goal is to get consumers to experience the product directly. After using the product, consumers form preferences and habits that influence repeat purchase.

However, when the perceived risk of product purchase is high, consumers become highly involved. They tend to be highly receptive to information, and therefore an informative (thinker) or affective (feeler) strategy is likely to be best here. For example, durable products of high value, such as a refrigerator, a color TV, a VCR, a car, or a camcorder, tend to be perceived as risky purchases. In buying durable products, consumers gather much information in an attempt to reduce their perception of risk. Much of this information may come from credible sources, such as consumer reports, consumer buyer guides, certain magazines that specialize in the product category (some magazines conduct their own surveys and endorse certain products as a direct result of their research), and the advice of friends, neighbors, relatives, and opinion leaders.[22] Products that generate such high involvement call for an informative (thinker) strategy.[23] Of course, for durable products that are equally risky but whose attributes tend to be processed through the right brain (feeling-type products, such as jewelry and cosmetics), the best strategy is the affective (feeler) one.[24]

Summary

How is corporate strategy selected? Optional corporate strategies are: grow or gain market share, maintain market share, harvest, innovate, and divest. We introduced to the reader two models of corporate strategy selection, the Boston Consulting Group matrix and the multifactor portfolio matrix. Both are used to help corporate executives select suitable strategies as a function of a variety of industry/market factors and factors related to their own business. Situation analysis is used to assess these factors and apply the models, the result of which is a selection of an effective corporate strategy. We recommended the multifactor portfolio matrix because of its conceptual strength.

The marketing communications manager has to select an effective positioning strategy from a pool of at least 15 positioning strategies that are viewed as alternative means of operationalizing three key strategies (differentiation, cost leadership, and focus). We discussed the kind of situation analysis needed for each one of the 15 positioning strategies.

Finally, the marketing communications manager is faced with the task of choosing an effective marketing communications strategy. The choices are informative (thinker), affective (feeler), habit formation (doer), and self-satisfaction (reactor). We discussed the kind of situation analysis that can assist the marketing communications manager in selecting an effective strategy. Situation analysis calls for internal analysis, focusing on understanding current corporate and marketing strategies and objectives. Also, we recommended that managers should conduct customer analysis to assess the extent of current brand awareness, brand learning, brand attitude, brand purchase, and repeat purchase. Furthermore, we urged managers to assess product factors such as whether the product is of the thinking or feeling type and whether it has a high degree of consumer involvement.

Questions for Discussion

Consider the following situation. A software company called Lintronics has been recently established and manned by three people. The company developed their first software, called Apple Pie Music. The product is a CD-multimedia software that contains an encyclopedia of music and a history of music in the United States. The three partners are very excited about the launch of this software and have high hopes for it. They decide to focus on the school library market and launch a marketing communications campaign directed to that market. Use this case to select appropriate strategies. Specifically, respond to the following questions, making as many assumptions as needed to conduct the desired situation analysis:

1. Apply the Boston Consulting Group matrix to Apple Pie Music. Recommend a corporate strategy as a direct function of this application.
2. Apply the multifactor portfolio matrix to Apple Pie Music. Recommend a corporate strategy as a direct function of this application.
3. Select an effective positioning strategy for Apple Pie Music. Use sound analysis and planning to justify your selection.
4. Select an effective marketing communications strategy for Apple Pie Music. Use sound analysis and planning to justify your selection.

Notes

1. Bruce D. Henderson, "The Product Portfolio," Boston: The Boston Consulting Group, Inc., *Perspectives* no. 66 (1970); Philippe Haspeslagh, "Portfolio Planning: Uses and Limits," *Harvard Business Review*, (January-February 1982), pp. 60, 73.
2. Francis J. Aguilar and Richard Hamermesh, "General Electric: Strategic Position: 1981," 25, Harvard Business School Case 9-381-174; Subash C. Jain, *Marketing Planning and Strategy* (Cincinnati, Ohio: South-Western, 1994), pp. 271–86.
3. *Organizing and Managing the Planning Function* (Fairfield, Conn.: GE Company, n.d.); Francis J. Aguilar and Richard Hamermesh, "General Electric: Strategic Position: 1981," 25 (Harvard Business School Case 9-381-174).
4. William E. Rothschild, *Putting It Together* (New York: AMACOM, 1976).
5. Subash C. Jain, *Marketing Planning and Strategy*, 4th ed. (Cincinnati, Ohio: South-Western, 1993), p. 183; Benson P. Shapiro, "What the Hell Is 'Market Oriented'?" *Harvard Business Review* (November-December 1988), pp. 119–25; Gordon Canning, Jr., "Is Your Company Marketing Oriented?" *Journal of Business Strategy* (May-June 1988), pp. 34–6.
6. For those who want to conduct a consumer study and measure the level of functionalism (utilitarianism) and value-expressiveness of the product in question, please see the following article: J. S. Johar and M. Joseph Sirgy, "Value-Expressive versus Utilitarian Advertising Appeals: When and Why to Use Which Appeal," *Journal of Advertising* 20 (September 1991), pp. 23–34.
7. Readers who want to know more about the product life cycle (PLC) and know of methods and ways to measure the stage of their product in its PLC may consult the following sources: Chester R. Wasson, *Dynamic Competitive Strategy and Product Life Cycles*, Austin, Tex.: Austin Press, 1978; John A. Weber, "Planning Corporate Growth with Inverted Product Life Cycles," *Long Range Planning* (October 1976), pp. 12–29; and Peter Doyle, "The Realities of the Product Life Cycle," *Quarterly Review of Marketing* (Summer 1976), pp. 1–6.
8. For measures of country image, the reader may consult the following sources: Richard Ettenson, Janet Wagner, and Gary Gaeth, "Evaluating the Effect of Country of Origin and the 'Made in the U.S.A.' Campaign: A Conjoint Approach," *Journal of Retailing* 64 (Spring 1988), 85–100; and Sung-Tai Hong and Robert S. Wyer, Jr., "Effects of Country-of-Origin and Product-Attribute Information on Product Evaluation: An Information Processing Perspective," *Journal of Consumer Research* 16 (September 1989), pp. 175–87.
9. For methods of measuring the price-quality relationship, the reader should consult the following sources: Gary M. Ericksen and John K. Johansson, "The Role of Price in Multi-Attribute Product Evaluations," *Journal of Consumer Research* (September 1985), pp. 195–9; and George J. Szybillo and Jacob Jacoby, "Intrinsic versus Extrinsic Cues As Deter-

minants of Perceived Product Quality," *Journal of Applied Psychology* (Februrary 1974), pp. 74–8.

10. Valerie Zeithaml and Merrie Brucks, "Price as an Indicator of Quality Dimensions," paper presented at the 1987 Association for Consumer Research Annual Conference, October 9–11, Cambridge, Mass.; Kent B. Monroe and Akshay R. Roa, "Testing the Relationship between Price, Perceived Quality, and Perceived Value," paper presented at the 1987 Association for Consumer Research Annual Conference, October 9–11, Cambridge, Mass.

11. For those who want to conduct a consumer study to ascertain the strength of the company image, the following measure is recommended: David W. Cravens, Gerald E. Hills, and Robert B. Woodruff, *Marketing Decision Making: Concepts and Strategy*, Homewood, IL: Richard D. Irwin, 1976, p. 234; the same measure appears in Philip Kotler, *Marketing Management*, 8th ed. Upper Saddle River, N.J.: Prentice Hall, p. 568.

12. To determine the relative importance of location as a purchase decision criterion, the reader may consult the model described in Appendix 5.1 in chapter 5.

13. John C. Mowen and Stephen W. Brown, "On explaining and Predicting the Effectiveness of Celebrity Endorsers," in *Advances in Consumer Research* 8 (Ann Arbor: Association for Consumer Research, 1981), pp. 437–41; Charles Atkin and M. Block, "Effectiveness of Celebrity Endorsers," *Journal of Advertising Research* 23, no. 1 (February-March 1983), pp. 57–61.

14. For a measure of consumer involvement, the reader should consult: Gilles Laurent and Jean-Noel Kapferer, "Measuring Consumer Involvement Profiles," *Journal of Marketing Research* 22 (February 1985), pp. 41–53.

15. For a measure of value expressiveness, the reader may consult: M. Joseph Sirgy, J. S. Johar, and Michael Wood, "Determinants of Product Value-Expressiveness: Another Look at Conspicuousness, Differentiation, and Common Usage," in *Developments in Marketing Science* 9, edited by Naresh Malhotra (Atlanta, Ga.: Academy of Marketing Science, 1986), pp. 35–9.

16. For a method to determine market potential, the reader should consult Philip Kotler, *Marketing Management: Analysis, Planning, Implementation, and Control*, 8th ed. (Upper Saddle River, N.J.: Prentice Hall), pp. 245–54.

17. For a good measure of price or deal consciousness, the reader may consult the following source: Donald R. Lichtenstein, Richard G. Netemeyer, and Scott Burton, "Distinguishing Coupon Proneness from Value Consciousness: An Acquisition, Transaction Utility Theory Perspective," *Journal of Marketing* 54 (July 1990), pp. 54–67.

18. Marketing researchers traditionally measure price sensitivity through price elasticity of demand. This is a mathematical measure of percentage change in quantity demanded divided by percentage change in price.

19. Subash C. Jain, *Marketing Planning and Strategy*, 4th ed. (Cincinatti, Ohio: South-Western, 1993), pp. 509–16.

20. Ibid.

21. Richard Vaughn, "How Advertising Works: A Planning Model," *Journal of Advertising Research* 20, no. 5 (October 1980), pp. 27–33; Richard Vaughn, "How Advertising Works: A Planning Model Revisited," *Journal of Advertising Research* 26, no. 1 (February-March 1986), pp. 57–66.

22. Michael A. Houston, "Consumer Evaluations and Product Information Sources," in James H. Leigh and Claude R. Martin, Jr., eds., *Current Issues and Research in Advertising* (Ann Arbor, Mich.: University of Michigan Graduate School of Business, 1979), pp. 135–44.

23. Ibid.

24. For a better appreciation of the concept of product involvement and its measures, the reader may consult the following sources: Anthony G. Greenwald and Clark Leavitt, "Audience Involvement in Advertising: Four Levels," *Journal of Consumer Research*, 11, no. 1 (June 1984), pp. 581–92; Judith L. Zaichkowsky, "Conceptualizing Involvement," *Journal of Advertising*, 15, no. 2 (1986), pp. 4–14.

Suggested Reading

Day, George. "Diagnosing the Product Portfolio." *Journal of Marketing* (April 1977): pp. 29–38.

Ferrell, O. C., George H. Lucas Jr., and David Luck. *Strategic Marketing Management*. Cincinnati, Ohio: South-Western, 1994.

Hambrick, Donald C., and Ian C. MacMillan. "The Product Portfolio and Man's Best Friend." *California Management Review* (fall 1982): pp. 84–95.

Haspeslagh, Philippe. "Portfolio Planning: Uses and Limits." *Harvard Business Review* (January-February 1982): pp. 60, 73.

Hawkins, Scott A., and Stephen J. Hoch. "Low Involvement Learning: Memory without Evaluation." *Journal of Consumer Research* 19, no. 2 (September 1992): pp. 212–5.

Krugman, Herbert E. "The Impact of Television Advertising: Learning without Involvement." *Public Opinion Quarterly* 29 (Fall 1965): pp. 349–56.

Lavidge, Robert J., and Gary A. Steiner. "A Model for Predictive Measurements of Advertising Effectiveness." *Journal of Marketing* 24 (October 1961): pp. 59–62.

Schnaars, Steven P. *Marketing Strategy: A Customer-Driven Approach*. New York: The Free Press, 1991.

Smith, Robert E., and William R. Swinyard. "Information Response Models: An Integrated Approach." *Journal of Marketing* 46, no. 2 (Winter 1982): pp. 81–93.

Smith, Robert E. "Integrating Information from Advertising and Trial: Processes and Effects on Consumer Response to Product Information." *Journal of Marketing Research* 30 (May 1993): pp. 204–19.

Vaughn, Richard. "How Advertising Works: A Planning Model." *Journal of Advertising Research* 20, no. 5 (October 1980): pp. 27–33.

Vaughn, Richard. "How Advertising Works: A Planning Model Revisited." *Journal of Advertising Research* 26, no. 1 (February-March 1986): pp. 57–66.

Wind, Yoram, and Vijay Mahajan. "Designing Product and Business Portfolios." *Harvard Business Review* (January-February 1980), pp. 155–65.

Wind, Yoram, Vijay Mahajan, and Donald J. Swire. "An Empirical Comparison of Standardized Portfolio Models." *Journal of Marketing* (spring 1983): pp. 89–99.

CHAPTER 11

Analysis and Planning: Setting Objectives

Consider the following case. The company is R. R. Donnelley & Sons, the world's largest commercial printing company. The company prints *Time*, *Newsweek*, and *Business Week* magazines. Its 1995 sales were $6.4 billion, and its earnings (net income) were $301 million. In 1995, the company managed to boost sales by 31% and earnings by 12%. The forecast is that sales will increase another 18% and earnings (net income) another 17% over 1 year's time. Early in 1996, the company began a series of new contracts, ranging from the printing of phone books in China to a 10-year deal to print 15 million copies a month of *Reader's Digest* in the United States. The company's business mission is to transform itself from an old-line printer to a marketing-and-services company providing customers with editorial products such as directory information in magazines, software disks, on-line material, and other media forms. However, Donnelley has strong competitors. Rivals such as Quebecor, Banta, and Quad Graphics—all old-line printers—are also going electronic. The inside story is that John R. Walter, Donnelley's current chairman and CEO since 1995, has changed the company from a rigid, bureaucratic company besieged by internal rivalries to a fast-moving company with a participatory management style. Walter has decentralized the organization by allowing business-unit managers to negotiate contracts and decide on pricing independently of headquarters executives.[1]

Now imagine yourself in the CEO's shoes. Armed with the above information, could you set sales objectives for next year? Would you set a 31% increase, as forecasted? Would you go higher? Lower? Why? What information would you use to set your sales objectives? Why? This chapter is designed to sensitize the reader to the kind of analysis and planning that can be done to help managers, especially marketing communications managers, set objectives.

Note that the situation analysis discussed in the previous chapter pertains to strategy selection at the corporate, marketing, and marketing communications levels. Situation analysis can also be conducted to assist marketers in setting objectives and allocating resources. We will start out by discussing situation analysis that focuses on setting objectives at the corporate level and then proceed to discuss situation analysis at the marketing and marketing communications levels (see Figure 11.1).

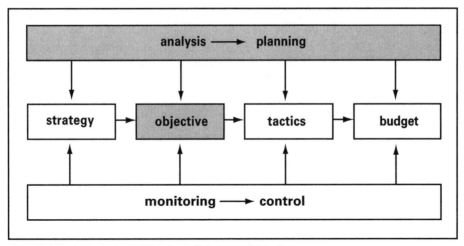

FIGURE 11.1 Analysis and Planning in Relation to Objectives

USING SITUATION ANALYSIS TO SET CORPORATE OBJECTIVES

As previously stated, situation analysis can be conducted to help the manager make three decisions. One is how to select corporate strategy. The second major decision is what corporate objectives to set. And the third decision is budgeting.

Remember what corporate objectives are? They are objectives typically set in relation to four performance dimensions: (1) sales, (2) market share, (3) profit, and (4) cash flow (see chapter 7, "Objectives and Performance Measures" for a refresher). Remember that all corporate objectives, like corporate strategy and tactics, are constrained to a very specific strategic business unit (SBU). We previously recommended that objectives be set using a three-stage process: (1) identification of one or more objective dimensions, (2) identification of the measures used to gauge outcomes related to each objective, and (3) identification of the desired level and time frame associated with each objective dimension. We will now focus on how situation analysis can assist in the third stage of this three-stage decision model.

In chapter 7, we argued that the objective dimensions have to be selected as a direct function of the selected strategy. In other words, knowing what the strategy is helps the manager determine (at least partly) possible objective dimensions. For example, sales and market share are usually most consistent with a growth strategy. On the other hand, a harvest strategy may lead the manager to select a profit objective. An innovation strategy entails a sales objective. A divestment strategy focuses on cash flow.

In order to set objectives quantitatively and concretely, the manager has to work with valid measures of sales, market share, profit, and cash flow. Managers must use objective measures that are based on sound accounting principles. The accounting calculus used to measure sales, market share, profit, and cash flow must be well established and accepted by the accounting profession because the manager has to gather data pertaining to the norms of the measure, especially in relation to past performance and the performance of other firms in the industry. The norms of these measures are very important in determining the desired level and time frame associated with each objective. Now, we will talk about this in more detail.

After determining the norms of the objective measure (e.g., average yearly sales of comparable competitor brands), the manager sets the desired level (and the time frame) in relation to past profit, sales, and/or market share. For example, suppose a company is in the retail telephone business. The average yearly retail telephone sales for the company in question has been determined to be $1.5 million per store. The store manager then sets a sales objective for next year in direct relation to the $1.5 million. Should it be $1.5 million? Should it be greater or less than $1.5 million? At least six factors should be considered in setting corporate-level objectives. These are shown in Table 11.1 and will be discussed in some detail in the following sections.

Industry Average in Relation to Objective Level

The industry average of sales, market share, profit, and/or cash flow figures can help the manager determine whether the desired level of the selected objective should be at, above, or below the firm's own norm (past profit, sales, and/or market share). For example, if the industry at large has an average gross profit margin of 35%, whereas the firm has averaged 30% gross margin for the past five years, then next year's gross margin objective should be set at a higher level than 30%, perhaps somewhere between 30% and 35%.

Forecasted Sales, Market Share, Profit, and/or Cash Flow

Similarly, forecast figures can help the manager figure out whether the desired level of the objective(s) should be set at, above, or below the firm's norm. For example, if the firm's sales forecast is very positive (e.g., a forecast of 5 million units to be sold next year, a jump from 3.9 million sold this year), then the sales objective should be set at a level between 3.9 and 5 million.

Past Sales, Market Share, and Profit of Key Competitors

Many managers select key competitors and gather as much data as possible about these companies. Usually the key competitors are "comparable" competitors. These competitors may be looked at as "role models" to be emulated in most respects. If the manager knows the past sales data of a key competitor, then the manager's sales objective for next year may be somewhat influenced by the competitor's past sales. For example, if a key competitor had a market share of 25%, whereas the manager's firm

TABLE 11.1 Factors Considered in Setting Corporate Objectives

1. Industry average in relation to profit, sales, and/or market share
2. Forecasted profit, sales, and/or market share
3. Past profit, sales, and/or market share of key competitors
4. Anticipated profit, sales, and/or market share of key competitors
5. Anticipated market changes that may affect future profit, sales, and/or market share
6. Anticipated changes within the firm that may affect future profit, sales, and/or market share

had a market share of 20%, then next year's market share objective is likely to be set somewhere between 20% and 25%.

Anticipated Profit, Sales, and/or Market Share of Key Competitors

Similarly, knowing the anticipated profits, sales, and/or market share of key competitors can be quite valuable. For example, if the manager finds out that the anticipated market share of a key competitor is 30%, whereas the manager's firm had a last-year market share of 20%, then next year's market share objective is likely to be set somewhere between 20% and 30%.

Anticipated Market Changes That May Affect Objectives

The focus here is on market changes. Suppose the firm acquires information about an industry study that indicates that the market is likely to increase by 5%. This new information should help the manager set sales objectives for next year.

Anticipated Changes within the Firm That May Affect Objectives

Changes within the firm can certainly affect corporate level performance and, therefore, future objectives. Imagine the following scenario. A corporate level executive of a Fortune 500 firm is told that a new VP for marketing has agreed to join the company. The new VP comes from another Fortune 500 company and has had much experience in the industry of the recruiting firm. Knowing this, the corporate executive is likely to feel quite optimistic in setting the sales and market share objectives of next year.

Table 11.2 shows how setting corporate level objectives can be done in a quantitative and mathematical way. Note that we first need to start out with a baseline. The best baseline is the firm's past performance on the objective dimension. The example shown in Table 11.2 involves an average of unit sales over the past five years (5,000 unit sales). If the product is new, the manager may examine comparable products and their past performance in the first year of product launch. The six factors discussed above (industry norms, forecasted performance, past performance of key competitors, anticipated performance of key competitors, anticipated market changes that may affect the firm's performance, and anticipated changes within the firm that may affect the firm's performance) are used to estimate other performance referents. Note that each of these referents is assigned an importance weight. In other words, the manager may have higher confidence in certain referents than others and therefore is likely to weigh these referents more heavily. An average referent is then computed (7,100 unit sales). Then an average is computed between the firm's past performance (5,000) and the weighted average referent (7,100). The unit sales objective is therefore determined to be 6,050. Of course, if one wishes to obtain a weighted average rather than a simple average, then both the firm's past performance and the average referent can be similarly weighted by importance scores, and a weighted average can be similarly derived.

TABLE 11.2   An Example of Setting a Unit Sales Objective

The firm's past unit sales (average of past 5 years)						**5,000**

Factor	Estimated Unit Sales		Importance Weight			Weighted Score
Average unit sales of industry at large	4,000	×	10%	=		400
Sales forecast	6,000	×	25%	=		1,500
Past sales of key competitor	8,000	×	20%	=		1,600
Anticipated sales of key competitor	9,000	×	10%	=		900
Anticipated market changes that may affect sales	7,000	×	10%	=		700
Anticipated changes within the firm that may affect sales	8,000	×	25%	=		2,000
The firm's unit sales based on analysis					100%	**7,100**
Final objective unit sales for next year						**6,050**
(average of past unit sales and unit sales based on analysis)						

USING SITUATION ANALYSIS TO SET MARKETING OBJECTIVES

Like corporate analysis and planning, marketing analysis and planning have to be discussed in relation to strategy selection, objective setting, and resource allocation. Here we will concentrate on the use of situation analysis to set effective marketing objectives.

Remember what marketing objectives are? They are objectives typically set in relation to specific brand associations and are directly related to the type of positioning strategy selected. For example, a positioning-by-product-attribute strategy automatically leads the marketing manager to focus on the association between the marketer's brand and a significant product attribute, an important product feature that is unique to the marketer's brand. Similarly, the positioning-by-intangible-factor strategy guides the marketer to focus on establishing, maintaining, or reinforcing an association between the brand and an intangible factor. That intangible factor is supposed to be a significant criterion in consumer purchase decision. We should note that identification of the objective dimension is predicated on the selected positioning strategy. Knowing the positioning strategy automatically allows the marketing manager to identify the objective dimension.

However, as stated in the section on setting corporate objectives in this chapter, the manager must work with objective measures of brand association that studies have shown to be reliable and valid. This is important because the manager has to gather data pertaining to the norms of the measure, especially in relation to past performance and the performance of other firms in the same industry. The norms of these measures are very important in determining the desired level and time frame associated with each objective.

Once the norms of the objective measure used are determined (e.g., recognition of brand X as part of product class Y using measure Z), then the manager sets the desired level and the time frame in relation to past data on brand association. For example, suppose the firm that markets a toothpaste to teenagers—let's call it "Sexy Smile"—wants to reinforce a brand association with the benefit of "sexy smile." That is, the firm wants to imply, "If you brush your teeth with Sexy Smile toothpaste, you'll have a sexy smile." Suppose that through a consumer survey it has been determined that only 30% of the teenagers in the United States recognize the brand name and its key benefit of "making one's smile more sexy." The brand manager then sets the following objective for next year: Increase recognition of the brand name and its key benefit of sexy smile by 200% by the end of next year. In other words, the goal is to have 90% of all teenagers in the United States recognize the brand and its key benefit of sexy smile by the end of next year. But then how did the manager come up with 90%—an increase of 200%? Actually, once the referent is determined, how much to increase (or decrease) from the referent can be determined by taking into account several factors shown in Table 11.3. These will be discussed in some detail in the sections that follow.

Industry Average in Relation to a Particular Measure of Brand Association

Marketing communications managers should gather information about the norms of brand association measures, especially the norms of the measure that they use to gauge brand association performance. The industry average of brand association performance can help marketers determine whether the desired level of the selected objective should be stated at, above, or below the brand's past performance. For example, if the industry at large has an average brand association of 50% using brand association X, whereas the brand in question has averaged 30% over the past year, then next year's brand association objective should be set at a higher level than 30%, perhaps somewhere between 30% and 50%.

Forecasted Changes in the Brand Association

Similarly, forecast figures can help marketing communications managers figure out whether the desired level of the objective(s) should be set at, above, or below the firm's norm. For example, one study indicated that at least 60% of all teenagers in the United States will come to believe that all brands of toothpaste can make their smiles more sexy. This may be due to the collective industry advertising that implies that all brands of toothpaste can produce sexy smiles. This collective industry effort is likely to cause more teenagers to believe that Sexy Smile brand of toothpaste, as well as others, enhances smiles by making them look sexy. If the consumer survey conducted last year revealed that 30% of all teenagers believed that Sexy Smile toothpaste enhanced their sexy smile and that approximately 60% of the same population are expected to believe in the same benefit next year, then what should the objective be? Perhaps somewhere between 30% and 60%.

TABLE 11.3 Factors Considered in Setting Marketing Objectives

1. The industry average in relation to the use of this particular measure of brand association
2. Forecasted changes in the brand association in question
3. Past brand associations of key competitors
4. Anticipated brand associations of key competitors
5. Anticipated market changes that may affect the brand association in question
6. Anticipated changes within the firm that may affect the brand association in question

Past Brand Association of Key Competitors

Many marketers select key competitors and gather as much data as possible about them. Usually the key competitors are "comparable" competitors. If marketers have data about past brand associations of a key competitor, then the marketers' brand association objectives for the next year may be somewhat influenced by the competitor's past experience. For example, if the association with sexy smile of a key competitor—let's call it X— was 25% among all teenagers, then next year's brand association objective is likely to be set somewhere between 25% and 30%.

Anticipated Brand Association of Key Competitors

Similarly, information about the anticipated brand association of key competitors can be quite valuable. For example, if the marketing communications manager of Sexy Smile finds out that the anticipated association with sexy smile of a key competitor X is likely to be 40% next year, whereas the manager's firm had a last-year association of 30%, then next year's brand association objective is likely to be set somewhere between 30% and 40%.

Anticipated Market Changes That May Affect Brand Association

The focus here is on market changes. Suppose the Sexy Smile manager acquires information about an industry study that indicates that there is a market trend among teenagers toward adopting products that make them look and feel sexy. Shouldn't this new information help the marketer of Sexy Smile toothpaste set the brand association objective for next year? Yes, of course. If past brand association with sexy smile was 30%, then next year's objective should be set at a level definitely higher than 30%, perhaps 40%.

Anticipated Changes within the Firm That May Affect Brand Association

Changes within the firm can certainly affect brand association performance and, therefore, the setting of future objectives. Imagine the following scenario. The marketing communications manager of Sexy Smile toothpaste has successfully recruited a new advertising specialist. This person has much experience with developing advertising for products directed at teenagers. Knowing this, the marketing manager is likely to feel quite optimistic in setting next year's brand association objective.

USING SITUATION ANALYSIS TO SET MARKETING COMMUNICATIONS OBJECTIVES

Just as we have discussed analysis and planning at both the corporate and marketing levels, we will now address analysis and planning with respect to marketing communications objectives. Remember what the five marketing communications objectives are? They are brand awareness, association, attitude, trial, and repeat purchase. However, since we argued that brand association goal comes under marketing objectives, we'll concentrate on the other four.

As stated in the section on setting corporate and marketing objectives in this chapter, the manager has to work with reliable and valid measures of brand awareness, brand attitude, brand purchase, and repeat purchase. It is important for managers to use objective measures that studies have demonstrated are reliable and valid (refer to chapter 7, "Objectives and Performance Measures" for a refresher). This is important because the manager has to gather data pertaining to the norms of the measure, especially in relation to past performance and the performance of other firms in one's industry. The norms are crucial in determining the desired level and time frame associated with each objective.

Once the norms of the objective measure used are determined (e.g., brand name recognition using measure X), then the manager sets the desired level and the time frame. Let's go back to the example of the firm that markets the Sexy Smile toothpaste to teenagers. Suppose the marketing communications goal is to reinforce a positive brand attitude. Suppose that through a consumer survey it has been determined that only 50% of the teenagers in the United States like this brand. The marketing communications manager then sets the following objective for next year: Increase positive brand attitude by 50% by the end of next year. In other words, the goal is to have at least 75% of all teenagers in the United States feel good about Sexy Smile toothpaste by the end of next year. But then how did the manager come up with 75%—an increase of 50%? Actually, once the referent is determined, knowing how much to increase (or decrease) from the referent can be determined by taking into account several factors shown in Table 11.4. These will be discussed in some depth in the following sections.

The Industry Average in Relation to the Selected Measure

Marketing communications managers should gather information about the norms of brand awareness (and/or brand attitude, brand purchase, and repeat purchase) measures, especially the norms of the measure that they use to gauge communications performance. Knowing the industry average of communications performance can help the manager determine whether the desired level of the selected objective should be at, above, or below the brand's past performance. For example, if the industry at large usually attains an average brand attitude of 40% using a certain measure, whereas the brand in question has averaged 50% as indicated by a consumer survey conducted last

TABLE 11.4 Factors Considered in Setting Marketing Communications Objectives

1. The industry average for the selected measure of the communications objective
2. Forecasted changes in the selected communications measure
3. Past performance of key competitors along the selected communications measure
4. Anticipated performance of key competitors along the selected communications measure
5. Anticipated market changes that may affect the selected communications objective
6. Anticipated changes within the firm that may affect the selected communications objective

year, then next year's brand attitude objective should be set at a lower level than 50%, perhaps somewhere between 40% and 50%.

Forecasted Changes in the Selected Measure

Similarly, forecast figures can help marketing communications managers figure out whether the desired level of the communications objective should be set at, above, or below the firm's norm. For example, one study may indicate that at least next year's brand attitude toward Sexy Smile toothpaste may increase by 25%, perhaps due to a social contagion effect. That is, the more teenagers use the product, the more they talk about it, and the better they feel about it. If the consumer survey conducted last year revealed that 50% of all teenagers had a positive attitude toward Sexy Smile toothpaste, then what should the objective be? Perhaps somewhere between 50% and 67.5%.

Past Performance of Key Competitors along the Selected Measure

Many marketing communications managers select key competitors and gather as much data as possible about them. Usually the key competitors are "comparable" competitors. Suppose in the same survey conducted last year, consumers were asked to indicate their brand preference and the marketer's brand was included among a list of key competitor brands. Thus, the marketing communications manager would have an idea how the brand in question stands in relation to key competitors along a communications performance dimension such as brand awareness, brand attitude, brand purchase, and repeat purchase. This information may be very helpful to the marketing manager in setting communications objectives for next year. For example, if a comparable competitor brand called Close-Up toothpaste was preferred by 60% among all teenagers, then next year's attitude objective for Sexy Smile toothpaste is likely to be set somewhere between 50% and 60%.

Anticipated Performance of Key Competitors along the Selected Measure

Similarly, discovering the anticipated communications performance of key competitors can be quite valuable. For example, the marketing communications manager of Sexy Smile may find out that teenagers' attitude toward Close-Up is likely to increase by 10% because the marketing communications manager of Close-Up toothpaste fired the firm's ad agency and gave the account to another agency that has a reputation for great creative advertising. The Sexy Smile manager thus surmises that because of the new advertising campaign that is currently being developed, brand attitude toward Close-Up is likely to increase by at least 10% next year, bringing it to a level of 66% brand preference. Based on this information, the marketing communications manager of Sexy Smile toothpaste decides to set the brand attitude objective for next year somewhere between 50% and 66%.

Anticipated Market Changes That May Affect Communications Objectives

Suppose the Sexy Smile communications manager becomes informed of an industry study that reveals a market trend toward sexiness and sensuality among the teen population. Shouldn't this new information help the marketer of Sexy Smile toothpaste set the brand attitude objective for next year? Perhaps. If past brand attitude toward Sexy Smile was 50% last year, then next year's objective may be set at a level higher than 50% as a direct function of this market trend.

Anticipated Changes within the Firm That May Affect Communications Objectives

Changes within the firm can certainly affect the performance of any communications objective, and consequently the setting of future communications objectives. Imagine the following scenario. The marketing communications manager of Sexy Smile toothpaste finds out that several outstanding, key creative people at the ad agency that services the Sexy Smile account have left the agency and joined the agency that services the Close-Up account. This is bad news that may dampen any high expectations in relation to next year's communications performance. Knowing the situation, the manager is likely to feel pessimistic in setting next year's brand attitude objective.

Summary

How are objectives set? Corporate objectives? Marketing objectives? Marketing communications objectives? The reader was introduced in this chapter to situation analyses that can be performed to help managers set objectives at the corporate, marketing, and marketing communications levels. The basic situation analysis model calls for gathering information about past performance in relation to the selected objectives to establish a baseline. Once a baseline is established using past performance data, then new data should be gathered in relation to several referents. These referents include industry norms, forecasted changes, past performance in relation to key competitors, anticipated performance in relation to key competitors, anticipated market changes, and anticipated changes within the firm. These referents are compared against the baseline parameter (established based on past performance), and the baseline parameter is adjusted in the direction of these referents.

Questions for Discussion

Study the following case. The marketing plan of a certain bank—let's call it United States Bank—calls for it to increase operations in the mid-Atlantic states. The bank offers the traditional banking services plus consumer and business loans, home mortgage loans, and its own credit card. The bank wants to make greater inroads in the mid-Atlantic states. The marketing plans call for a growth strategy. Its present market share in the mid-Atlantic states is only 2%. There is a plethora of banks in the mid-Atlantic states, and the average market share seems to hover around 6%. The United States Bank regards First States Bank as a key competitor. First States Bank has a market share of 12% in the designated states. An article about banking in the mid-Atlantic states reveals that First States is planning to launch an aggressive marketing campaign to significantly increase its market share to 15% in the next year or two. A situation analysis revealed that a major strength of the United States Bank is consumer and business loan divisions. These divisions have aggressively marketed themselves as providing fast, low-interest loans with top-notch service. A recent consumer survey reveals that 68% of the bank customers rated the bank as excellent in terms of fast loans, low-interest loans, and top-quality service in relation to loans. The same survey also revealed that 85% of the bank's customers have positive feelings toward the bank and 60% intend to use the bank to obtain loans when the need arises. An industry study has shown that most banks achieve an average of 45% of their customers indicating excellent on the dimensions of fast-speed loans, low-interest loans, and high-quality service in relation to loans. The same study also indicated there is a trend away from traditional banking. Many consumers are increasingly using specialized financial services, and a significant segment is also beginning to bank using on-line computer services. Now respond to the following questions:

1. What would be a reasonable corporate objective for the United States Bank for the next two or three years? Explain the logic you used to set the objective.
2. What would be a reasonable marketing objective for the United States Bank for the next two or three years? Explain the logic you used to set the objective.
3. What would be a reasonable marketing communications objective for the United States Bank for the next two or three years? Explain the logic you used to set the objective.

Notes

1. Richard A. Melcher, "The Press of New Business," *Business Week* (January 15, 1996), pp. 64–65.

Suggested Reading

Day, George. "Diagnosing the Product Portfolio." *Journal of Marketing* (April 1977): pp. 29–38.

Ferrell, O. C., George H. Lucas Jr., and David Luck. *Strategic Marketing Management.* Cincinnati, Ohio: South-Western, 1994.

Hambrick, Donald C., and Ian C. MacMillan. "The Product Portfolio and Man's Best Friend." *California Management Review* (Fall 1982): pp. 84–95.

Haspeslagh, Philippe. "Portfolio Planning: Uses and Limits." *Harvard Business Review* (January–February 1982): pp. 60, 73.

Schnaars, Steven P. *Marketing Strategy: A Customer-Driven Approach.* New York: The Free Press, 1991.

Wind, Yoram, and Vijay Mahajan. "Designing Product and Business Portfolios." *Harvard Business Review* (January–February 1980): pp. 155–65.

Wind, Yoram, Vijay Mahajan, and Donald J. Swire. "An Empirical Comparison of Standardized Portfolio Models." *Journal of Marketing* (Spring 1983): pp. 89–99.

CHAPTER 12

Analysis and Planning: Budgeting for Marketing Communications

Consider the following case. The focus is on the photo industry. The product is an advanced photo system. This is the hottest new photo technology in years. The system does not allow any errors: no more pictures that are poorly exposed; no more pictures that are poorly colored; and no more pictures that are printed badly. The product has been jointly developed by a consortium of industry leaders that include Fuji Photofilm and Eastman Kodak. The product is expected to raise industry sales by at least 10% in 1996. These industry leaders are expected to spend at least $150 million on marketing support in 1996. The marketing communications campaign will focus on consumer education. Fuji, which spent $6.5 million on measured media in 1994, is expected to spend twice this amount in 1996. Kodak spent $65.4 million in the United States on its brand last year; Canon spent $10.3 million on media in 1994; Nikon spent $9 million; and Minolta spent $5.1 million. Film sales hit 864 million units in 1994.[1]

Now imagine you are a marketing communications executive at Kodak. Your goal is to determine an effective marketing communications budget for 1996 and 1997. How would you use this information? Or would you use this information at all? Would you want to gather additional information? What kind and why? This chapter explains how marketing communications managers can use analytic techniques in making budgeting decisions.

In the previous two chapters situation analysis was discussed in relation to strategy selection and objective setting at the corporate, marketing, and marketing communications levels. Situation analysis is also conducted to assist marketing communications managers with budgeting decisions. We will start out by discussing situation analysis that focuses on corporate resource allocation, then proceed to discuss situation analysis for resource allocation at the marketing and marketing communications levels (see Figure 12.1).

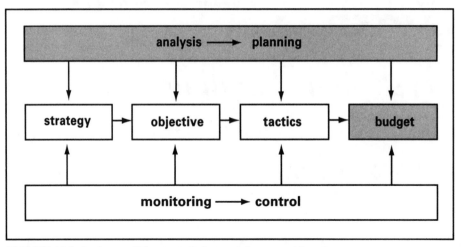

FIGURE 12.1 Analysis and Planning in Relation to Resource Allocation

USING SITUATION ANALYSIS IN BUDGETING FOR MARKETING COMMUNICATIONS

It should be noted that we are not interested in how to allocate resources for all functions at the corporate level. We are interested only in how to allocate the portion of marketing resources that will ultimately go toward marketing communications and its elements. Chapter 8 described a method for IMC budgeting. This section will describe those factors that the marketing communications manager should consider in making budgeting decisions. The manager needs to gather information about organizational, market, product, and customer factors and then analyze the information to guide decision making. These factors are shown in Table 12.1 and discussed in some depth in the following sections.

ORGANIZATIONAL FACTORS

Three major organizational factors are likely to influence the marketing communications budget as determined at the corporate level. These are objectives, strategy and tactics, and control at the three levels (corporate, marketing, and marketing communications).

Objectives

At the corporate level, the rule is, the higher the market share objective, the greater the marketing budget and, possibly, the larger the marketing communications budget.[2] Research has shown that firms with large market share have an advantage over smaller firms. Although they spend more money on marketing and communications, they get better returns for the money. This may be due to economies of scale.[3] In contrast, an objective to significantly increase profit may not necessarily mean a

TABLE 12.1 Factors Affecting Resource Allocation for Marketing Communications

Organizational factors
    Objectives
    Strategy and tactics
    Control
Industry factors
    Industry norm
    Competition
    Product life cycle
    Market growth
    Market size
    Market potential
Product factors
    Product involvement
    Brand differentiation
    Product newness
Customer factors
    Purchase frequency
    Consumer involvement
    Consumer familiarity
    Customer demand for the product
    Growth in customer base

significantly larger marketing or marketing communications budget. This is because increasing profits tends to be a goal consistent with a harvest strategy, which specifically prohibits increases in expenditures in whatever form.

Therefore, increases or decreases in the marketing budget should closely match changes in corporate objectives. If sales and market share objectives increase, then proportional increases in the marketing budget may be justified. For example, marketing expenditures as a percentage of past sales or profit can be easily computed. Suppose the corporate objective is to increase sales by 50% in the next year. This would call for a corresponding 50% increase in the marketing budget. Therefore, the marketing communications manager needs to keep track of changes in corporate objectives to see if increases or decreases in the marketing budget are consistent with those changes.

At the marketing level the same rule applies. That is, the higher the brand association objective, the larger the marketing communications budget. Consider these two scenarios. The first scenario involves a new product, let's say a new dental device with which consumers can remove plaque from their teeth without having to go to the dentist. The marketing objective is to create an association between the brand, called The Plaque Remover, and the major product class, namely, dental products designed to remove plaque. The marketing objective is to establish a brand association with the benefit of removing plaque. In one year, 50% of the U.S. consumers between the ages of 40 and 60 should learn about this new product. Now compare this scenario to the scenario involving Interplak, an electric toothbrush that is also designed to remove plaque but that is less effective than the new device. Interplak has been around for a number of years. Currently, 60% of U.S. consumers between the ages of 40 and 60 are aware of Interplak and its major benefit. The Interplak marketing objective is to increase this brand association to 80% next year. Which marketing program is likely to require a higher level of marketing communications expenditure? Obviously, the program for The Plaque Remover would cost more because the marketing objective is much more ambitious than the objective for Interplak, which has been around for a few years.

The same rule also applies at the marketing communications level. Increases in certain marketing communications objectives may warrant proportional increases in resources for certain elements of the marketing communications mix. For example, if the goal is to increase brand trial and purchase by 50% in the next six months, and we know that telemarketing is a suitable communications tool to achieve this objective, then a 50% increase in resources allocated to telemarketing may be warranted too.

A caveat: It should be noted that an increase (or decrease) in an objective at a superordinate level may not necessarily mean a proportional increase (or decrease) at a subordinate level. For example, if the sales objective at the corporate level is increased by 40%, should every element of the marketing communications mix (e.g., coupons) be proportionately increased? The answer is a resounding NO. Perhaps the use of coupons as a marketing communications tool is deemed to be ineffective in this situation. Perhaps a combination of other tools should be selected.

Strategy and Tactics

Different strategies call for different approaches to resource allocation. For example, market share objectives tend to go along with a growth strategy, which in turn places much emphasis on the marketing function. Resources are shifted so that the marketing department is provided with more resources to carry out the growth strategy and achieve the higher market share objectives. However, a maintain share strategy may not entail an increase in the marketing and marketing communications budgets. Actually, resource allocation may depend on the fierceness of the competition. A harvest strategy dictates decreasing marketing communications expenditures for the exact purpose of increasing profit. An innovation strategy may entail assigning more resources to help launch the new product. A divestment strategy, on the other hand, requires that the marketing communications budget be significantly reduced or even cut off.

The marketing communications manager should know the corporate strategy in place and the role of the marketing department in achieving the goal of the corporate strategy. If the marketing budget is inadequate for the goal, the marketing communications manager should point this out to top management and ask for a budget increase.

At the marketing and the marketing communications levels, the same logic holds. Specific brand association objectives tend to go along with specific positioning strategies, which in turn may place increased or decreased emphasis on the marketing communications function. Resources may need to be shifted so that the marketing communications department will be provided with more resources to carry out the positioning strategy. For example, a positioning strategy such as positioning by celebrity is likely to require more marketing communications than, let's say, positioning by product class. Therefore, resources are allocated to marketing communications as a direct function of the nature of the positioning strategy and its communications requirements.

Control

Control can be viewed as learning from experience. Some managers are very good at learning from experience. This experience may be personal (data stored qualitatively in their memories) or quantitative (data stored in the firm's accounting archives). Budgeting decisions can be partly guided by the lessons of experience. Here is an example of how budgeting decisions can be made based on past experience. Suppose by examining the company archive, a manager is able to develop a regression equation. The regression equation has a criterion variable of sales and a predictor variable of marketing expenditures. Sales data are dated from 1945 to 1995, comprising 50 observations. The regression coefficient turns out to be statistically significant and accounts for 75% of the variance in sales scores. This regression equation is extremely useful because it allows the manager to manipulate potential increases or decreases in the marketing budget and observe the effect of these increases or decreases on sales. Thus, an optimal marketing budget is selected based on a regression simulation. The regression equation indicates that a 5% increase in the marketing budget is likely to increase sales by 8%, but further increases in the marketing budget above 5% are not likely to generate significant increases in sales. Thus, the manager chooses to increase the marketing budget by 5%.

This quantitative method described here is also described in chapter 8, "Budget," as the "historical/statistical method," a traditional method commonly used in budgeting. Here, too, it is one of the many tools that the marketing communications manager should consider using in making budgeting decisions.

Please note that expenditures and performance dimensions at different levels should not be mixed. That is, expenditures on an element of the marketing communications mix (e.g., trade shows) should not be used as a predictor of sales. Sales is a performance dimension at the corporate level, whereas a trade show is a tactical program belonging to the marketing communications level. This is an important caveat.

A more qualitative version of the use of control to allocate expenditures is the percentage of past sales, or the profit method (or the previous budget method). Again, this method has been described in chapter 8, "Budget." Managers commonly set a marketing (or a marketing communications) budget as a percentage of sales, perhaps 5%. When asked why they chose 5%, they might say something to the effect that 5% of sales has worked well in the past. Why change?

INDUSTRY FACTORS

At least six industry factors are likely to influence communications budgeting decisions at the corporate level. These are industry norm, competition, product life cycle, market growth, market size, and market potential.

Industry Norm

Most industries publish expenditure norms. Many trade journals of specific industries conduct industry studies and publish norms such as average marketing (and marketing communications) expenditures as a percentage of sales. For example, *Advertising Age* usually publishes ad dollars as percentages of sales of industry categories. For example, automobiles is 4.4%, bottled and canned soft drinks is 6.5%, personal computers is 12.4%, dairy products is 5.7%, movies is 9.5%, while perfumes, cosmetics, and toiletries is 9.4%.[4]

Many managers seek out these data and rely on industry norms to increase or decrease the marketing budget in the direction of industry norms. For example, if a firm has spent 5% of its sales on marketing, while the industry average is 3%, top management may be motivated to decrease next year's marketing budget to make it more consistent with the industry norm. Studies are also conducted to find out average expenditures in relation to the various elements of the marketing communications mix. These data are used as a guide to determine future expenditure level.

Competition

In discussing the effect of corporate strategy on allocating resources to marketing and marketing communications, we noted that a maintain share strategy may or may not entail an increase in the marketing budget. It depends on the competition. If the competition is fierce, the corporate executives may recognize the need for a larger marketing communications budget to prevent the competition from "stealing" market share. Competitors may take away customers by using effective marketing communications methods in the form of sales promotion. In order to combat the competition, the firm has to counteract the sales promotion by matching, and possibly outmatching, its monetary incentives. This may call for a bigger marketing budget (and also a proportional increase in the marketing communications budget). In general, the greater the competition, the greater the need for greater marketing (and marketing communications) resources to fight it.

Consider the recent case of Revlon, the cosmetics giant that is No. 1 in market share. Revlon's competitors have been developing new cosmetic products and spending more and more on marketing communications in an attempt to derail Revlon. Specifically, Maybelline, the second largest cosmetics manufacturer (ranking No. 2 in market share at 18.4%), was planning to spend $30 million, or 60% of its media budget, to introduce The Greats, a product line involving a collection of makeup products. The Greats is a defense against Revlon's ColorStay eye makeup and foundation and ColorStay Lash Color mascara. Proctor & Gamble was planning to spend $20 million on U.S. media advertising Max Factor, which had a market share of 7.3% in December 1995, up from 6.1% at the start of 1995. Cover Girl, which had a market share of 23.5% in 1995, was planning to spend $15 million of 1996's $40 million-plus media budget on Continuous Wear foundation. Also, Simply Powder, a lightweight powder that acts like a foundation, was to be launched supported by $15 million in media advertising.[5] How should Revlon have reacted to this kind of competition? Should it have raised its media budget to counteract the competition?

Remember reading about the competitive parity methods as traditional budgeting methods in chapter 8, ("Budget"). We described the share-of-voice/market method and the match/outspend-the-competition method. These methods underscore the importance of competition, and top management should consider this factor in determining the marketing budget. To use these methods, the marketing communications manager has to gather information about key competitors and their marketing and marketing communications expenditures. This can provide them with ammunition to make a case for increases or decreases in the marketing and marketing communications budget.

Product Life Cycle

As a product ages through its PLC, marketing budgets decline proportionately.[6] Specifically, in the introduction stage of the product life cycle, extra resources are allocated to the marketing function (and therefore to marketing communications too). The marketing budget decreases as the product enters into its growth stage and decreases significantly during the late maturity and decline stages. Why? Because in the early stages of the PLC, resources are allocated to create brand awareness and educate consumers. In the later stages of the PLC, the objective is to get consumers to switch from competitor brands or to maintain their loyalty and encourage repeat purchase. The resources needed for marketing communications tasks to create awareness and educate consumers are likely to be significantly higher than the resources needed to, let's say, encourage repeat purchase.

Hence, the marketing communications manager should have a good understanding of the product and the stage of the product in its overall life cycle. Such understanding may help the marketing communications manager make a case for increases (or decreases) in the marketing budget to top management.

Market Growth

The higher the customer growth rate, the greater the marketing need to exploit the market growth opportunity. This, of course, necessitates higher levels of marketing and marketing communications expenditures.[7] For example, the growth of the telecommunications market is phenomenal. More opportunities are available today than ever before. One telecommunications product is the cellular phone. Cellular phone marketers are recognizing the growth in this market and are increasing their marketing communications expenditures to exploit this emerging opportunity. Again, by having information about market growth, the marketing communications manager can make a justifiable case to top management for increases in the marketing budget.

Some managers use quantitative models to forecast sales by taking into account changes in the trends related to technology, law, society, culture, environment, economics, and so on. They develop these sales models to forecast market growth and brand sales. They then allocate a certain percentage of the forecasted sales to marketing or marketing communications. That percentage of sales may be based on the industry norm. This method has been described in chapter 8 ("Budget") as the percentage of anticipated sales. We recommend the use of this method to provide the marketing communications manager with additional information based on another potentially significant factor. The idea is not to rely on one factor alone, but to take into account as many factors as possible.

Market Size

The size of the market is an important factor. Small and concentrated markets are easier to communicate to, while larger and more disperse markets are more difficult. Larger and more disperse markets warrant higher levels of marketing communications expenditures.[8] Consider the case of the computer software company Microsoft and its marketing of Windows 95. Microsoft has developed a marketing program and a marketing communications campaign that covers the world. Such a campaign requires enormous amounts of resources.

Market Potential

The focus here is on potential. If the difference between actual and potential sales is large, much of the market remains unserved. This situation warrants a significant increase in communications expenditures. Let's revisit Microsoft's Windows 95. After a year or two, Microsoft will compare its sales to market potential. If a significant discrepancy still remains between market penetration versus market potential, another aggressive marketing communications effort should be launched. This new effort would require significantly more resources.

PRODUCT FACTORS

At least three product factors are likely to influence the proportion of the total marketing budget assigned to marketing communications. These are product involvement, brand differentiation, and product newness.

Product Involvement

The higher the product involvement, the less need for marketing communications, and, therefore, the lower the marketing communications budget. This is because products that create involvement are likely to motivate consumers to seek information about the product. When they are exposed to any information about the product, they will process it. Marketers do not need to launch an extensive marketing communications campaign with many repeated exposures to achieve the goals of a positioning strategy. For example, compare the marketing of two products that vary significantly in their capacity to elicit involvement in message processing. One is an automobile, the other is candy. Consumers who are shopping around for a sports car are likely to actively seek and process most messages related to sports cars. In contrast, consumers who want to purchase candy are not likely to feel highly involved in processing most messages related to candy. This is because automobiles are more involving than candy. Marketing communications messages about products that elicit more consumer involvement are more likely to be attended to and processed than messages about products that elicit less involvement.

Brand Differentiation

If the marketer's brand is highly differentiated from competitor brands, the opportunity is present to communicate the differential uniqueness of the brand to consumers. On the other hand, if the marketer's brand is not at all differentiated, then perhaps marketing communications is not likely to be effective, and a large budget may not be warranted. Similarly, if the basis for differentiating a brand is hidden and cannot be readily judged at the time of the purchase, then more money should be spent on marketing communications to make consumers aware of the hidden benefit.[9]

Product Newness

It takes substantially more money to communicate about a new product than to communicate about an established brand.[10] This is because consumers need to be educated about new products. Communication about new products involves many message repetitions and the placement of the message in a variety of media. This effort requires money, lots of money, compared to communicating about an established brand.

CUSTOMER FACTORS

Four customer factors can be used to help the marketing manager allocate a marketing communications budget. These are purchase frequency, consumer involvement, consumer familiarity, and customer demand of the product.

Purchase Frequency

The higher the purchase frequency of a given product, the greater the need for marketing communications. For example, conducting a marketing communications campaign for staple products, such as food items commonly found in supermarkets and convenience stores, may require more resources than a marketing communications campaign for a durable good, such as a kitchen appliance.[11]

Consumer Involvement

What is the difference between product involvement and consumer involvement? When marketing scholars talk about product involvement, they refer to the fact that consumers become involved in one product more than another, mostly because of the characteristics of certain products. For example, more people get involved in the purchase of an automobile than a staple good such as toothpaste. Automobiles tend to be perceived by most consumers as a risky purchase, whereas toothpaste is not. There, the involvement comes from the product, not from the consumer per se. In contrast, consumer involvement refers to the kind of involvement that comes mostly from the consumer, not the product per se. For example, design engineers, by virtue of their occupation, tend to be more involved with computers than are homemakers.

The higher the consumer involvement, the less need for marketing communications and, therefore, the lower the marketing communications budget, because consumers who care greatly about a product will probably seek more information about it themselves. They will naturally pay close attention to any information about the product. Marketers can achieve the goals of a positioning strategy without launching an extensive marketing communications campaign with many repeated exposures. Imagine launching a marketing communications campaign to sell a sophisticated software design package to design engineers. Most of these people are highly involved with design software because it is a vital tool in their profession. Any message directed to them would be readily processed. Now compare design engineers to other consumers. Perhaps the firm decides to target parents of teenagers who have a proclivity for design. Many more resources are needed to conduct this marketing campaign because, compared to design engineers, the parents, as consumers, are not likely to be highly involved with design software.

Consumer Familiarity

If the marketer's product and brand are well known to consumers, then the need for marketing communications is less pressing, and therefore, fewer marketing communications resources are required. Going back to the example of design engineers, we can easily surmise that design engineers are likely to be more familiar with design software and various software brands than the parents of teenagers who are interested in design. A substantially more costly marketing communications campaign is needed to communicate with the parents' market than the design engineers' market. Since the parents are not familiar with the product and the various design software brands, a campaign must involve a more compelling message with a high level of message repetition.

Customer Demand for the Product

If the product class in general is in high demand, it is easier to stimulate brand preference through advertising and other means of marketing communications.[12] That is, when there is primary demand for the product, there is also the opportunity to use marketing communications to attain higher levels of sales, profit, market share, and cash flow. Consider the case of many small and medium-sized businesses in industrializing countries. These entrepreneurial enterprises are motivated to become economically efficient as they realize that the use of computers would help achieve efficiency in the operation of their business. The demand for PCs is high. In this situation, PC marketers can take advantage of this situation and launch a marketing communications campaign targeting these potential customers.

Growth in Customer Base

As the customer base grows, the marketing communications budget should grow proportionately. Increases in resources allocations are needed to continue reaching a larger number of customers.[13] This typically occurs with technological innovations. In time, a technological innovation becomes increasingly accepted by the general population, thereby increasing the customer base for the firm's product. For example, the customer base of the home computer market has been increasing in the last decade or so. Computer companies targeting the home market spend more than ever to communicate to that market.

Summary

What kind of situation analysis can the marketing communications manager perform to assist in making budgeting decisions at the corporate, marketing, and marketing communications level? Several organizational, industry, product, and customer factors are closely related to marketing and marketing communications expenditures. Organizational factors include objectives, strategy and tactics, and control. Industry factors include industry norms, competition, the product life cycle, market growth, market size, and market potential. Product factors include product involvement, brand differentiation, and product newness. Customer factors include purchase frequency, consumer involvement, consumer familiarity, and growth in customer base.

Information about these factors should assist the manager in determining a suitable budget for marketing, marketing communications, and the various elements of the marketing communications mix.

Questions for Discussion

Study the following case about the advanced photo system that we discussed at the beginning of the chapter. The product is expected to raise industry sales by at least 10% in 1996. Kodak and Fuji are expected to spend at least $150 million on marketing support in 1996. Fuji spent $6.5 million on measured media in 1994 and is expected to spend twice this amount in 1996. Kodak spent $65.4 million in the United States on its brand last year; Canon spent $10.3 million on media in 1994; Nikon spent $9 million; and Minolta spent $5.1 million. The strategic alliance between Fuji and Kodak expects to capture a large chunk of the market share in this new product market in 1996. The goal is to rapidly capture this market. Suppose that Kodak executives recall that they spent approximately $10 million on marketing communications when they marketed a comparable but less sophisticated product several years ago with outstanding results. Kodak was able to achieve a 70% brand awareness. Let's say that in relation to this new photo system, both Kodak and Fuji feel that they need to achieve a 70% brand awareness in the next six months. Both Kodak and Fuji may expect sales revenues to exceed $100 million the first year of operation. From projected sales, Kodak has traditionally allocated 3% of sales to marketing support, whereas Fuji's marketing support traditionally amounts to 5%. Suppose you are the marketing communications manager for this advanced photo system. Make the following decisions.

1. Describe those organizational factors that you need to take into account in determining an optimal marketing communications budget for the advanced photo system. How would these factors affect the budget?
2. Describe those industry factors that you need to consider in determining an optimal marketing communication budget for the advanced photo system. How would these factors affect the budget?
3. Describe those product factors that are relevant to determining an optimal marketing communications budget for the advanced photo system. How would these factors affect the budget?
4. Describe those customer factors that may affect the planning of an optimal marketing communication budget for the advanced photo system. How would these factors affect the budget?

Notes

1. Michael Wilkie, "New Photo Tech Ready for '96 Flash," *Advertising Age* (December 4, 1995), p. 36.
2. Gary L. Lilien and John D. C. Little, "The ADVISOR Project: A Study of Industrial Marketing Budgets," *Sloan Management Review* (Spring 1976), pp. 17–31; Gary L. Lilien, "ADVISOR 2: Modeling the Marketing Mix Decision for Industrial Products," *Management Science* (February 1979), pp. 191–204.
3. Randall S. Brown, "Estimating Advantages to Large-Scale Advertising," *Review of Economics and Statistics* 60 (August 1978), pp. 428–37; Kent M. Lancaster, "Are There Scale

Economies in Advertising?" *Journal of Business* 59, no. 3 (1986), pp. 509–26; Johan Arndt and Julian Simon, "Advertising and Economies of Scale: Critical Comments on the Evidence*," Journal of Industrial Economics* 32, no. 2 (December 1983), pp. 229–41.

4. *Advertising Age* (October 24, 1988), p. 51.

5. Pat Sloan, "Cosmetics Competitors Try to Slap Down Revlon," *Advertising Age* (December 4, 1995), p. 38.

6. Gary L. Lilien and John D. C. Little, "The ADVISOR Project: A Study of Industrial Marketing Budgets," *Sloan Management Review* (Spring 1976), pp. 17–31; Gary L. Lilien, "ADVISOR 2: Modeling the Marketing Mix Decision for Industrial Products," *Management Science* (February 1979), pp. 191–204.

7. Ibid.

8. Michael L. Ray, *Advertising and Communication Management* (Upper Saddle River, N.J.: Prentice Hall, 1982), pp. 161–2.

9. Ibid.

10. Ibid.

11. Ibid.

12. Ibid.

13. Ibid.

Suggested Reading

Aaker, David A., and John G. Myers. *Advertising Management*, 3rd ed. Upper Saddle River, N.J.: Prentice Hall, 1987: ch. 3.

Blasko, Vincent J., and Charles H. Patti. "The Advertising Budgeting Practices of Industrial Marketers." *Journal of Marketing* 21 (Fall 1984): pp. 104–10.

Broadbent, Simon. *The Advertiser's Handbook for Budget Determination.* Lexington, Mass.: Lexington Books, 1988.

Jones, John Philip. *How Much Is Enough: Getting the Most from Your Advertising Dollar.* New York: Lexington Books, 1992.

Patti, Charles H., and Vincent J. Blasko. "Budgeting Practices of Big Advertisers*." Journal of Advertising Research* 21 (November 1981): pp. 23–9.

Ray, Michael L. *Advertising and Communication Management.* Upper Saddle River, N.J.: Prentice Hall, 1982.

PART FIVE

The Marketing Communications System at Large

Professor Schultz writes a column in the *Marketing News* on integrated marketing. In one of his recent columns, he discussed IMC as practiced in Australia and New Zealand. Based on Schultz's view of IMC, firms integrate their marketing communications programs by adopting the customers' views and bringing "the entire value chain into line."* An example of total integration Professor Schultz uses is a large entertainment organization that licenses its products, characters, and properties around the world. This organization is challenged to align its marketing communications efforts with the efforts of the licensees, the wholesalers, and the retailers. This can be done through being customer focused, knowing the channels, training the sales force, and sharing database.

By being *customer focused* Professor Schultz means that the organization should focus on the end user. In other words, the entertainment firm has to start at the far end, beginning with the customers, and work backward toward the organization relating customers' values to specific products, services, and programs. Professor Schultz also talked about *knowing the channels*. He alluded to the notion that IMC requires aligning marketing communication efforts with those of the channel members; that is, the firm should align all internal marketing and communications activities (customer service, technical support, management information systems, etc.) with external marketing and communications activities (advertising, personal selling, event marketing, public relations, etc.). Next, the firm should *train the sales force* in integration. Instead of simply selling or merely taking orders, they should build alliances. Finally, Professor Schultz recommends that customer *database be shared* with all channel members; that is, all members of the channel have to cooperate to share customer information and align their efforts to serve the end users.

So the reader can appreciate what Professor Schultz is saying, we will review the principles of integration as deduced from the application of the IMC systems model, specifically discussing principles of integration in chapter 13 and advising the marketing communications manager on how to best use these principles.

*Don E. Schultz, "At Least in Melbourne They Understand IMC," *Marketing News* (May 6, 1996), p. 8.

CHAPTER 13

Lessons in Integration

At one point in time, I helped a small publishing company that specializes in Appalachian history. This company published an extensive line of books dealing with the history of the region, its geography, and its culture. The company had been established for 20 years or so and was essentially a two-person operation (the owner/publisher and a copyeditor). The owner expressed to me her frustration over her failure to do a good job promoting the book line. I gathered the following information from meeting with the owner. She was convinced that a sizable population in and around the Appalachian Mountains is highly interested in books related to the history, geography, and culture of the region. This interest was indicated by the many college courses and community noncredit courses on the subject offered in the Appalachian region. For the previous five years, the publisher had sold approximately 3,000 books a year. Most of the books used in the college courses and noncredit community seminars were published by major publishers, but none of those publishers had a book line on Appalachian studies. She thought that she had an advantage over the competition. She also thought that she could sell a whole lot more than 3,000 books a year, perhaps at least double that number.

My first impression was that her marketing communications efforts were "all over the place." That is, they lacked cohesion. Things were done rather haphazardly without any plan or systematic effort on her part. The corporate strategy seemed to be growth, as indicated by her statement of her objective. However, the more we talked, I learned that she had become frustrated and had even contemplated selling the business several times in the past. I thought then that this corporate strategy did not mesh with her objective of doubling sales. I asked her what she had done in terms of marketing. From what she told me, I got the impression that she was selling her books very cheaply. In other words, she thought she was competing by positioning the book line as a bargain—a cost-leadership strategy. But then she acknowledged that many of her customers would have bought her books at higher prices. She was very reluctant to change her pricing strategy for fear that a change would make matters worse. I then realized that this cost-leadership strategy was not the best marketing strategy to meet her sales objective. I asked her about her marketing objective. She didn't understand! I asked her about her promotion strategy and goals. She didn't understand! She responded that she had tried a variety of communications tools, such as direct mail using a mailing list of households in several selected towns in the Appalachian Mountains; once in a while she had advertised in the regional newspapers, usually in the classified section of the newspaper. She showed me several newspaper articles that had been written about her company and book line, and she seemed very proud of this exposure. She also indicated that she has small ads in the yellow pages of the phone books of a number of Appalachian towns and renews them year after year. She admitted that she didn't know which communication method was best. She didn't keep track of the effectiveness of any of them. Moreover, each year she spent whatever she could afford on promotion, and this amount varied from year to year.

This is a classic example of lack of system integration and is typical of most businesses, especially those run by businesspeople who are not well trained in the managerial sciences. Each component in the overall marketing communications system did not seem to be linked, even slightly, with other components as our systems model shows they should be. There was no systematic method for making marketing communications decisions, and no decision seemed to be guided or influenced by other decisions. *The system lacked integration.* In this chapter, the reader will be sensitized to issues of integration. The message of this chapter is very simple. Integration comes about by establishing strong links among the system components. We have already seen how this can be done. This chapter emphasizes the importance of the system's connections.

INTEGRATING THE MARKETING COMMUNICATIONS SYSTEM

Having gotten a sense of the working dynamics of the marketing communications system, the reader is now in a position to appreciate some lessons in *system integration.* As briefly discussed in the "Systems Concepts" chapter (chapter 2), system integration can be effectively managed by ensuring strong links between the system components. Specifically, the system can be effectively integrated by ensuring strong links among the following system components. These links are shown in Table 13.1 and will be discussed in some detail in the following sections (also see Figure 13.1).

Linking Strategy, Objective, and Tactics

Systems tend to break down and become ineffective when there is no logical connection among a given strategy, the way this strategy becomes a goal guiding tactics, and the way tactics are formulated to achieve the objective. For a system to be effectively integrated, strategy has to be translated into a quantifiable objective, and tactics have

---

TABLE 13.1 Strengthening System Links to Ensure Integration

- Links between strategy, objective, and tactics
- Links between strategy/objective/tactics and resource allocation
- Links between monitoring and control
- Links between monitoring/control and strategy/objective/tactics
- Links between monitoring/control and objectives
- Links between monitoring/control and resource allocation
- Links between analysis and planning
- Links between analysis/planning and strategy/objective/tactics
- Links between analysis/planning and objectives
- Links between analysis/planning and resource allocation

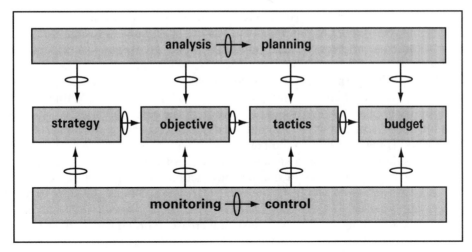

FIGURE 13.1 Reinforcing System Links = System Integration

to be developed to achieve the stated objective. Each tactic, in turn, becomes a strategy or a goal to guide subordinate-level tactics, and so on. This is a necessary but not sufficient principle of system integration.

At the corporate level, a corporate strategy has to be operationalized in terms of a quantifiable goal. If the corporate strategy is growth and expansion into new markets, then this strategy has to be articulated concretely as a goal to guide corporate tactics. Should the goal be an increase in sales and market share? If so, what percentages could be expected? What is the logic supporting these expectations? How will the corporate objectives of a specified level of increase in sales and market share help guide corporate tactics? Corporate tactics, in this instance, would be implemented by the various functional departments of the organization—marketing, finance, personnel, operations, engineering, R&D, and so on. How does a certain percentage of increase in sales and market share (corporate objective) guide the strategies of the various departments? Will the VP for marketing, for instance, have to come up with a new marketing strategy to meet the new challenge? What changes in the marketing plan must be effected to achieve the desired level of sales and market share? Perhaps the marketing manager decides that a focus strategy could be highly instrumental in accomplishing the corporate objectives of increased sales and market share. How should this marketing strategy be operationalized and quantified in terms of a goal (i.e., marketing objective)? Perhaps the marketing manager figures that targeting specific consumers with a highly select psychographic profile should do the trick. Thus, the marketing objective can be stated in terms of establishing or reinforcing brand association in the minds of the target consumers. In other words, the objective is to get a certain percentage of the target consumers to identify with the firm's brand.

What marketing tools (elements of the marketing mix) should be deployed to achieve this new marketing objective? Does the product need to be redesigned to appeal to the target consumers (using product tactics)? If so, how? Does the price have to be changed to increase target consumer's willingness to buy (using price tactics)? If so, how much? Should the product be distributed to the target consumers using a unique channel or distributor (using place tactics)? If so, what channel or distributor? How should the product be communicated to target consumers (using promotion tactics)? What marketing communications strategy is likely to be most effective for target consumers?

Perhaps the marketing communications manager decides that a self-satisfaction (reactor) strategy is likely to be most effective in achieving the marketing objective of establishing a certain level of brand association in the minds of target consumers. The marketing communications manager thinks that getting target consumers to buy the product first is the best way to familiarize them with the product. Once familiar with it, they are likely to develop a strong preference for it and to buy it again. Now the question becomes, How should the self-satisfaction (reactor) strategy be translated into concrete and quantifiable goals (i.e., marketing communications objectives)? How should the marketing communications objectives be stated? Here, the objectives have to be stated in terms of percentages of increase in brand trial and preference because the self-satisfaction (reactor) strategy dictates the use of these objective dimensions. Once concrete marketing communications objectives are set, the marketing communications manager has to assemble the most effective communications mix to achieve the stated marketing communications objectives. What would be the most effective communications mix? What forms of advertising? Perhaps interactive forms of advertising are likely to be most effective. Perhaps premiums and a contest can get target consumers to buy and experience the product.

Note that this exercise is extremely important as a first step of system integration. The corporate strategy has to be strongly linked with corporate objectives. Corporate objectives have to be strongly linked with marketing strategy. Marketing strategy has to be strongly linked with marketing objectives. Marketing objectives have to be strongly linked with marketing communications strategy. Marketing communications strategy has to be strongly linked with marketing communications objectives. And finally, marketing communications objectives have to be strongly linked with the selection and implementation of certain elements of the marketing communications mix (see Figure 13.2).

FIGURE 13.2 Reinforcing the Strategy-Objective-Tactics Link

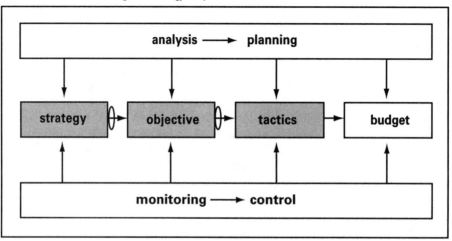

Linking Strategy/Objective/Tactics to Budget

The marketing communications system lacks integration when marketing communications resources are allocated in a manner that has little to do with the resource requirements of the selected marketing communications programs. In many instances, top management allocates resources using methods (e.g., 5% of last year's sales) that do not take into account the resource requirements to accomplish the goals of certain strategies. Such misallocation of funds can put the marketing communications system in jeopardy (see Figure 13.3).

For example, examine the case of a relatively new business magazine called *Management Theorems* that has been developed and marketed by, let's say, McGraw-Hill, one of the giant publishers in the United States. The CEO decides that the corporate strategy for *Theorems* is to grow in new markets. This strategy is translated in terms of a 15% increase in sales and market for next year. It has been determined that a differentiation strategy could effectively achieve the 15% increase in sales and market share. Specifically, the marketing manager decides to position the product by creating a psychological tie-in with a computer on-line service such as America Online. The goal is articulated as establishing brand association with the selected distributor so that 80% of readers of management-related magazines would associate *Theorems* with America Online by the end of next year. The marketing communications manager decides to use a habit formation (doer) strategy. She feels that this strategy is likely to be highly instrumental in achieving the goal of getting target consumers to adopt the magazine on a trial basis. The corresponding objective is to increase product trial by 30% in the next year. She knows that such an objective will require at least two mass direct mailing campaigns to America Online users and would cost approximately $100,000. However, top management has traditionally allocated a marketing communications budget based on 2% of forecasted sales. The sales forecast is $4 million, and 2% of $4 million allocates only $80,000. The marketing communications

FIGURE 13.3 Reinforcing the Link between Strategy-Objective-Tactics and Resource Allocation

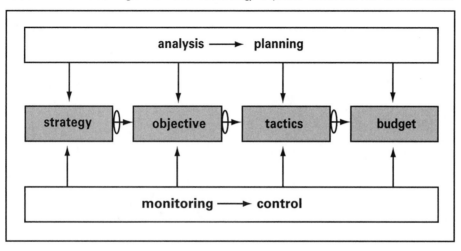

manager needs at least $100,000 to accomplish the goals of the communications strategy and its stated objective. There is a problem here! The resources allocated do not mesh with the required strategies and the cost of the program required to achieve the goal of the strategy.

Linking Monitoring and Control

A lack of system integration in marketing communications may also occur when performance monitoring at any level (corporate, marketing, or marketing communications) is not followed by control. In other words, a manager at any hierarchical level may monitor system performance based on certain well-thought-out objective dimensions, but no control is exerted. The manager may fail to observe deviations from desired states or may fail to respond to observed deviations by taking corrective action. Corrective action may be completely dissociated from monitoring (see Figure 13.4).

For example, suppose the marketing communications manager observes that the direct mail campaign designed to increase product trial by 30% in six months has failed. He does nothing! There is no corrective action! There is no learning from mistakes! Failure is imminent! Effective organizations learn from trial and error. Effective organizations take corrective action to improve future performance. If the link between monitoring and control is weak, then the organization does not learn. Here, the marketing communications manager should take some corrective action. An example of corrective action might be to investigate the cause of the failure by focusing on the marketing communications tactics (or programs) that were put in place to achieve the 30% product trial. In this case, the marketing communications program is the direct mail campaign. Perhaps a direct mail campaign is less effective than direct response advertising in a magazine that targets the right consumers. Perhaps the direct mail campaign was not implemented effectively. Have you heard stories about certain mail workers dumping bags and bags of what they consider junk mail? Yes, it

FIGURE 13.4 Reinforcing the Link between Monitoring and Control

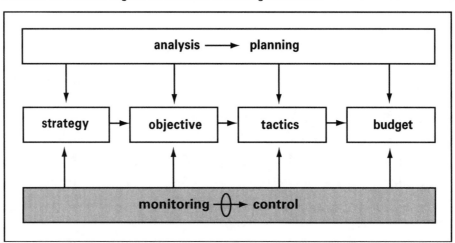

can happen. Perhaps the mailing list used was outdated. A significant percentage of the mailings went to wrong addresses. This happens too. As a matter of fact, it happens quite frequently. What can the manager learn from this so that the same mistake will not recur in future direct mail campaigns?

Linking Monitoring/Control to Strategy/Objective/Tactics

The focus here is on how monitoring and control is exerted to change strategy-objective-tactics links. This is part of the monitoring and control function. If the marketing communications system fails to meet certain performance objectives, corrective action can be instituted by changing the strategy, its objective, and the corresponding tactics (supporting programs) at any of the three levels (corporate, marketing, and marketing communications). The system lacks integration if the monitoring and control function fails to reassess the strategy-objective-tactics link in the face of negative feedback (see Figure 13.5).

Let's focus on the direct mail example used in the preceding section. The marketing communications objective was set as a 30% increase in brand trial in six months. Let's assume that after six months we find that only 10% ordered the product on a trial basis. This is a negative deviation of 20%, which is highly significant. What should we do? In the previous section, we talked about examining the link between the marketing communications objective and the use of the direct mail campaign and about possible problems with the implementation of the direct mail campaign. The focus was on the link between marketing communications objective and marketing communications tactics. The same examination and evaluation is needed for superordinate links; the link between the marketing communications strategy and objective, the link between the marketing objective and marketing communications strategy, the link between the marketing strategy and the corporate objective, and the link between the corporate objective and the corporate strategy. In other words, any of the strategy-objective-tactics links can be faulty and should be reassessed.

FIGURE 13.5 Reinforcing the Link between Monitoring/Control and Strategy/Objective/Tactics

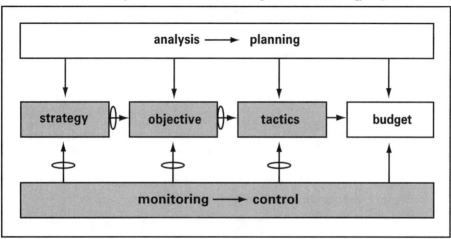

Linking Monitoring/Control to Objectives

The focus here is on how the monitoring and control function serves to make changes to the stated objectives. The desired level of an objective is reassessed in light of failure. The manager asks whether the objective was set unrealistically high and whether it should be adjusted to reflect the system's true capabilities. The system lacks integration if the manager fails to reassess the objectives in light of performance outcomes reflecting significant deviations from those objectives (see Figure 13.6).

For example, suppose an advertiser, such as Nike, runs an ad campaign to create awareness of a new model of athletic shoes. The objective is to create 90% awareness of the new shoes in the minds of those who are athletically inclined after six months of the campaign. After six months, Nike finds out that only 60% of the target consumers have become aware of the new model of shoes. That is, a negative deviation of 30% points is detected. Why did the ad campaign not reach its objective of 90% awareness? Perhaps because the 90% awareness objective was too inflated and unrealistic to begin with. A 60% awareness objective should have been set from the beginning.

Linking Monitoring/Control to Budget

The monitoring and control function serves to motivate the marketing communications manager to reassess the appropriateness of the resources allocated. Given failure, the manager asks whether the failure might be attributed to the lack or misallocation of resources. If so, changes in resource allocations are the recommended corrective action. Failure to reassess the method and outcomes of resource allocation when a program does not succeed is a signal of system breakdown or lack of system integration (see Figure 13.7).

Let's go back to our Nike example. Nike is running the ad campaign to create 90% awareness of a new model of athletic shoes. The goal is to accomplish this in six months. About $20 million were allotted to run this ad campaign in athletic magazines nationwide. After six months, Nike finds out that only 60% of the target consumers

FIGURE 13.6 Reinforcing the Link between Monitoring/Control and Objectives

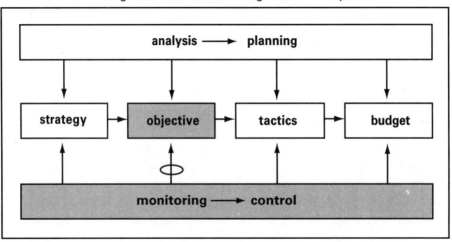

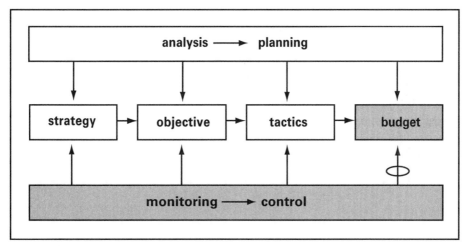

FIGURE 13.7 Reinforcing the Link between Monitoring/Control and Budget

have become aware of the new model of shoes. That is, a negative deviation of 30% points is detected. Why did the ad campaign not reach its objective of 90% awareness? Was it because the $20 million budget did not go a long way? More money was needed to achieve the 90% awareness objective. Perhaps more insertions in these magazines were needed. Perhaps the reach of these magazines was more limited than originally thought. Therefore, ads in more magazines were needed to extend the reach to the targeted population. This would require additional resources.

Linking Analysis and Planning

Lack of integration in the marketing communications system may be due to a lack of a strong link between analysis and planning. Many managers engage in research; they set up elaborate intelligence apparatus; they hire consultants and gather enormous amount of data. But the same managers may fail to use this information in their decision making. Most business, marketing, and marketing communications textbooks show managers how to conduct all kinds of analyses—analyses about the competition, about the market, about the environment. Managers commission studies of consumer behavior to establish demographic and psychographic profiles of consumers. Markets are segmented into groups, and elaborate profiles are established. Sales data are analyzed, and fancy regression models are developed. Much sophistication in information gathering? Yes! The failure is in how little this information is used. Textbooks usually provide very little guidance in this area. A breakdown between analysis and planning is a strong sign of a lack of system integration (see Figure 13.8).

Let's use Nike again as an example to illustrate the breakdown between analysis and planning. Suppose Nike has conducted a consumer survey of those who are athletically inclined. The survey was rather extensive. Questions were asked about demographics and lifestyle. That is, respondents were asked about their activities, interests, and opinions regarding all kinds of sports activities. Terrific information, right? Not really. The marketing communications manager needs appropriate information to

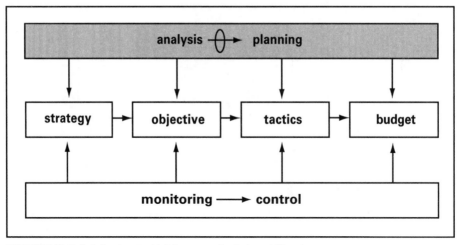

FIGURE 13.8 Reinforcing the Link between Analysis and Planning

make a host of decisions. Let's focus on strategy selection. The manager has a choice among four strategies: informative (thinker), affective (feeler), habit formation (doer), and self-satisfaction (reactor). He or she needs information that would assist in making this decision. What kind of information? According to the FCB planning model (chapter 6), two key factors may help the manager decide on the best strategy. Specifically, these factors relate to product involvement and to thinking versus feeling. That is, the manager needs to find out whether Nike shoes are a high- or low-involvement item for the athletically inclined. Are these consumers likely to be highly involved in processing messages about the new Nike shoes? What is their extent of involvement? The consumer survey should have included questions, items, and measures concerning consumer involvement with the product so that the manager would be in a better situation to make a strategic selection than if he or she were to make a decision based on sheer guessing. The same can be said in relation to the thinking-versus-feeling factor. The manager needs to find out whether Nike shoes are a thinking or feeling product. The same consumer survey may have included a measure for this factor. Are messages about this Nike shoe likely to be processed mostly through the right brain (indicating that the product is a feeling-type product) or left brain (indicating a thinking-type product)? Again, hard information is better than guessing. All the information about demographics and lifestyle is not really helpful. Remember that analysis is supposed to empower the marketing communications manager to plan. If the link between analysis and planning is not strong, the system cannot be effectively integrated.

Linking Analysis/Planning to Strategy-Objective-Tactics Links

Analysis and planning are used to help marketing communications managers plot strategy, articulate objectives from strategy, and formulate tactics guided by objectives. Analysis and planning are imperative. Strategy selection (at the corporate, marketing, and marketing communications levels) that is not guided by a thorough analysis of the situation can lead to ineffective decisions. If the wrong strategy is selected, the wrong objectives are articulated and the wrong tactics are deduced. Analysis and planning are aids to the marketing communications manager—aids assisting in strategy selection, setting of objectives, and developing tactics. The literature on marketing strategy, marketing management, and marketing communications is rich with models that allow managers to determine what strategies are effective under what conditions. Failure to use these analytic models may lead the manager to make misguided decisions, leading to disintegration of the marketing communications system (see Figure 13.9).

Let's go back to the Nike example used in the previous section. The marketing communications manager needs to select one of the four strategies (informative, affective, habit formation, and self-satisfaction). The manager gathers information about the extent to which the product in question induces consumer involvement and the extent to which the product is a thinking or feeling type. Situation analysis reveals that the Nike shoes in question are a high-involvement product and more of a thinking-type than a feeling-type product. Therefore, an informative (thinker) strategy is selected based on this analysis. Now the question is how to set an objective that directly reflects the goal of the informative (thinker) strategy. We know that the objective dimension should be brand awareness and learning. But then the manager needs to determine those marketing communications tools that are most effective in maximizing the stated objectives. Should he or she decide to work with advertising? What form of advertising? How about public relations? What form? How about sales promotion? What form? Which marketing communications tools or programs are likely to be most effective in achieving the objective of 90% awareness? Here the marketing communications manager needs information to help him or her make tactical decisions. What does he or she know about the relative effectiveness of each tool under various conditions? How do these conditions translate in the context of the situation at hand? This kind of analysis and planning is very helpful in making effective decisions. Lack of a strong link between analysis/planning and strategy/objective/tactics is indicative of a lack of system integration, a situation that must be corrected.

FIGURE 13.9 Reinforcing the Link between Analysis/Planning and Strategy/Objective/Tactics

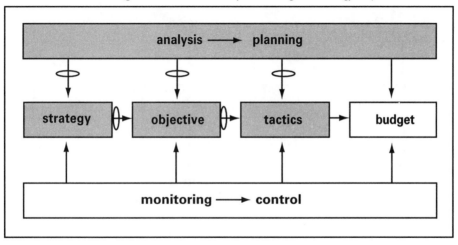

Linking Analysis/Planning to Objectives

In the previous section, we addressed analysis and planning in relation to the links connecting strategy, objective, and tactics. Part of the discussion included objectives. Here, we want to exclusively focus on objectives and how analysis and planning is used to help managers set realistic ones. Objective setting that is not guided by situation analysis may lead managers to set unrealistic and unreasonable objectives. This is again symptomatic of a lack of system integration (see Figure 13.10).

We have talked about how analysis and planning assist the Nike manager in selecting a marketing communications strategy and how this strategy leads to the specification of objective dimensions, which in turn guide the formation of marketing communications tactics. But the million-dollar question is what level of brand awareness and learning should be set. The manager has to conduct additional analyses to be able to determine a desired level of brand awareness and learning. The manager might gather information from past marketing communications campaigns to see what has been achieved in the past. He or she might gather information about the norms of brand awareness and learning measures to be used. What level of performance did most "comparable" products register on the brand awareness/learning measures? This information can help a manager to form reasonable expectations.

Linking Analysis/Planning to Budget

Analysis and planning also assist managers to allocate resources effectively. Remember how the marketing communications budget is determined—through the objective-task method. In other words, the manager examines the marketing communications tasks (elements) needed to achieve the stated marketing communications objectives and determines the costs of the tasks. The sum of these costs makes up the marketing communications budget. However, we also discussed the importance of monitoring and control as well as analysis and planning in making adjustments to the budget. Failing to make

FIGURE 13.10 Reinforcing the Link between Analysis/Planning and Objectives

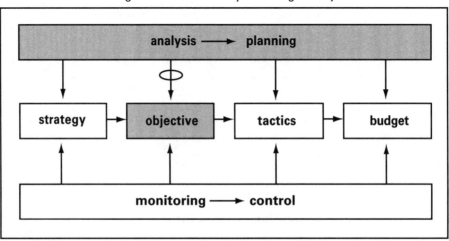

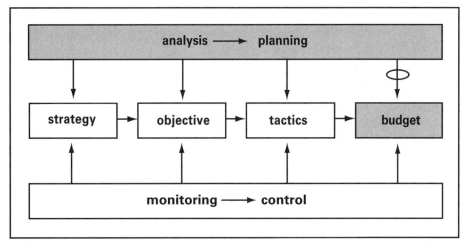

FIGURE 13.11 Reinforcing the Link between Analysis/Planning and Resource Allocation (Budget)

these adjustments, which may be at least partly due to failure to conduct adequate analysis and planning, may contribute to system disintegration (see Figure 13.11).

The Nike example helps illustrate the importance of analysis and planning in resource allocation. The marketing communications objective is to create 90% awareness of the new shoes in the minds of those who are athletically inclined after six months of the campaign. About $20 million was allotted to run this ad campaign in athletic magazines nationwide. In other words, it was determined that $20 million was needed to place a certain number of ads in so many magazines over a 12-month period. The reach and the number of insertions in these magazines were expected to be sufficient to achieve the 90% awareness objective. But then, through situation analysis, the marketing communications manager began to understand that the cost of placing the specified number of ad insertions in the selected magazines was expected to increase by at least 8%. Knowing this, the manager has to adjust the marketing communications budget by 8% to reflect the increased media costs. If the manager has failed to do a thorough analysis of the situation, the manager will not be able to take this factor into account and develop an effective marketing budget, a budget capable of achieving the designated objectives.

Summary

This chapter highlights the importance of strengthening links between the systems components as a means to enhance system integration. Specifically, system integration can be effectively managed by ensuring that the links remain strong among the following system components: (1) the link connecting strategy, objective, and tactics, (2) the link between strategy/objective/tactics and resource allocation, (3) the link between monitoring and control, (4) the link between monitoring/control and strategy/objective/tactics, (5) the link between monitoring/control and objectives, (6) the link between monitoring/control and resource allocation, (7) the link between analysis and planning, (8) the link between analysis/planning and strategy/objective/tactics, (9) the link between analysis/planning and objectives, and (10) the link between analysis/planning and resource allocation.

Questions for Discussion

Let's revisit the small publishing company that we first talked about at the beginning of this chapter. Remember that the company specializes in Appalachian history. This publisher has an extensive line of books dealing with the history of the region, its geography, and its culture. The company has been around for the last 20 years or so and is a two-person operation (the owner/publisher and a copyeditor). Now, attempt to answer the following questions.

1. Develop an overall marketing communications plan that spells out the corporate strategy. Make sure that the corporate objectives are strongly linked with the corporate strategy. What do you think is an effective marketing strategy? Connect the marketing strategy with the corporate objective. Now translate the marketing strategy into a marketing objective. Explain the logic of the link. What is an effective marketing communications strategy? Why did you select that strategy, and how is it linked with the marketing objective? Explain. What is a reasonable marketing communications objective? How is this tied to the marketing communications strategy? What communications tools and programs are best here? Why? Explain how these communications programs can achieve the stated marketing communications objective.

2. How much do you think this company should spend on marketing communications annually? How can you go about figuring out the best way to develop a marketing communications budget? Is the budget linked to strategy, objectives, and tactics? Explain.

3. Is there a problem with monitoring and control? Explain. What would you advise the publisher to do?

4. If you were to focus on the link between strategy/objective/tactics and monitoring/control, what would you say about this publisher? Come up with a script that would educate the publisher about the importance of this system link. Happy scripting!

5. Now focus on the link between monitoring/control and objective setting. Use what you've learned from this chapter and previous ones to educate the publisher about how she should set her corporate, marketing, and marketing communications objectives.

6. Do the same thing in relation to the monitoring/control–resource allocation link. That is, come up with a script to educate the publisher about the importance of feedback and trial-and-error to figure out an effective budget over the long haul.

7. Now focus on analysis and planning. What advice would you give this publisher about analysis and planning? What kind of analysis should she do, and how can she use this analysis in planning marketing communications campaigns?

8. What kind of information should the publisher gather to help her with determining the best strategies at the corporate, marketing, and marketing communications levels? Explain.

9. What kind of information should the publisher gather over time to help her set reasonable objectives? Explain.

10. What kind of information should the publisher gather over time to help her figure out the best marketing communications budget possible? Explain.

Suggested Reading

Baumler, J. "Defined Criteria of Performance in Organizational Control." *Administrative Science Quarterly* (September 1971): p. 340.

Cavaleri, Steven, and Krzysztof Obloj. *Management Systems: A Global Perspective.* Belmont, Calif.: Wadsworth Publishing, 1993.

Churchman, C. W. *The Systems Approach.* New York: Dell, 1968.

Flamholtz, E. "Organizational Control Systems as a Managerial Tool." *California Management Review* 22, no. 2 (1979): pp. 50–9.

Katz, D., and R. Kahn. *The Social Psychology of Organizations.* New York: John Wiley, 1966.

Lerner, A. Y. *Fundamentals of Cybernetics.* London: Chapman and Hall, 1972.

Miller, James G. *Living Systems.* New York: McGraw-Hill, 1978.

Morell, R. W. *Management: Ends and Means.* San Francisco: Chandler, 1969.

Powers, W. T. *Behavior: The Control of Perception.* Chicago: Aldine, 1973.

Powers, W. T. "Control Theory: A Model of Organisms." *Systems Dynamics Review* 6, no. 1 (1990): pp. 1–20.

Rahmation, S. "The Hierarchy of Objectives: Toward an Integrating Construct in Systems Science." *Systems Research* 2, no. 3 (1985): pp. 237–45.

Richardson, G. *Feedback Thought in Social Science and Systems Theory.* Philadelphia, Pa.: University of Pennsylvania Press, 1991.

Robb, F. F. "Cybernetics in Management Thinking." *Systems Research* 1, no. 1 (1985): pp. 5–23.

Simon, Herbert A. *Administrative Behavior.* New York: The Free Press, 1965.

Sirgy, M. Joseph. *Marketing as Social Behavior: A General Systems Theory.* New York: Praeger Publishers, 1984.

Sirgy, M. Joseph. "Strategies for Developing General System Theories." *Behavioral Science* 33, no. 1 (1988): pp. 25–37.

Sirgy, M. Joseph. "Toward a Theory of Social Organization: A Systems Approach." *Behavioral Science* 34 (1989): pp. 272–85.

Sirgy, M. Joseph. "Toward a Theory of Social Relations: The Regression Analog." *Behavioral Science* 35, no. 4 (1990): pp. 195–206.

Sirgy, M. Joseph. "Self-Cybernetics: Toward an Integrated Model of Self-Concept Processes." *Systems Research* 7, no. 1 (1990): pp. 19–32.

Glossary

A

absolute cost The total amount of money needed to purchase advertising in certain media. The term "absolute cost" is used in contrast to "relative cost" in media planning. Media costs can be compared in relation to one another, and therefore media are selected in relation to their relative costs. However, certain media are selected or eliminated from consideration based on the total dollar cost needed for advertising. For example, many media planners do not consider national television advertising because the total costs are too high and prohibitive, in an absolute sense.

advertising One of the elements or tools of marketing communications for use in mass media, such as television, radio, newspaper, magazine, outdoor, transit, aerial, mobile billboards, specialty, directory, interactive, in-store, in-flight, movie theater, and videotape advertising.

affective brand attitude A marketing communications goal. It describes a desirable situation in which target consumers establish a favorable attitude toward a firm's brand. The attitude is based on an emotional response.

affective (feeler) strategy A marketing communications strategy that guides the marketing communications manager to elicit an affective response, a feeling that helps build a positive attitude toward the firm's brand. The focus here is on feelings, much more so than learning or inducing purchase.

analysis The process of identifying factors that may assist the decision maker in selecting an effective strategy, setting objectives, determining tactics, and/or allocating resources. Once these factors are identified and specific information about the case in question is gathered (guided by the identified factors), then the decision maker is ready for planning. In other words, analysis assists the decision maker in planning.

attitude toward brand purchase A marketing communications goal. It describes a desirable situation in which target consumers have established a positive attitude toward the act of purchasing the firm's brand.

attribute sensory modality The sensory component associated with information processing of a particular message. For example, an ad shown in a magazine is processed through the visual sense, and a radio commercial is processed through the auditory sense.

aware objective A marketing communications goal to establish, increase, or maintain a certain level of brand awareness in the minds of target consumers.

B

barriers of entry Hurdles or obstacles for a firm to penetrate a given industry. Some industries have high barriers (e.g., aviation industry) while others have low barriers (e.g., local janitorial business).

brand acceptance A marketing communications goal. It describes a desirable situation in which target consumers recognize the firm's brand as an acceptable choice for the product category.

brand association A marketing goal. The term is used interchangeably with terms such as *brand equity*, *brand image*, and *brand knowledge*. It describes a desirable situation in which target consumers associate the brand with desirable features, events, and/or people.

brand attitude A marketing communications goal. It describes a desirable situation in which target consumers establish a favorable attitude toward the firm's brand.

brand awareness A marketing communications goal. It describes a desirable situation in which target consumers recognize or recall the brand name as related to a product category.

brand differentiation A situation in which a given brand is perceived to be different from competitor brands in the same product category.

brand equity A marketing goal. The term is used interchangeably with terms such as *brand association, brand image,* and *brand knowledge.* It describes a desirable situation in which target consumers associate the brand with desirable features, events, and/or people.

brand image A marketing goal. The term is used interchangeably with terms such as *brand association, brand equity,* and *brand knowledge.* It describes a desirable situation in which target consumers associate the brand with desirable features, events, and/or people.

brand knowledge A marketing goal. The term is used interchangeably with terms such as *brand association, brand equity,* and *brand image.* It describes a desirable situation in which target consumers associate the brand with desirable features, events, and/or people.

brand loyalty A marketing communications goal. It describes a desirable situation in which target consumers feel psychologically committed to the firm's brand after purchase and use.

brand preference A marketing communications goal. It describes a desirable situation in which target consumers recognize the firm's brand as preferable to competitor brands.

brand purchase A marketing communications goal. It describes a desirable situation in which target consumers have actually purchased the firm's brand.

brand sales A corporate performance standard traditionally measured in terms of total amount of monetary sales of a given brand during a certain time period.

brand satisfaction A marketing communications goal. It describes a desirable situation in which target consumers feel satisfied with the firm's brand after purchase and use.

brand trial or purchase A marketing communications goal. It describes a desirable situation in which target consumers have psychologically committed themselves to trying the firm's brand and then buying it.

budget The amount of monetary resources allocated to implement certain tactics (or a course of action).

C

campaign continuity The situation in which all messages communicated in different media through different marketing communications tools are interrelated.

capital intensity The situation in which firms in a given industry have invested a great deal of capital in land, equipment, and machinery. For example, the aviation industry or the space industry are characterized as highly capital-intensive industries.

cash cow A common term used by corporate strategists for a product considered to have high market share in a low-growth market.

cash flow A corporate performance standard traditionally measured in terms of cash availability after a given time.

cognitive brand attitude A marketing communications goal. It describes a desirable situation in which target consumers establish a favorable attitude toward the firm's brand. The attitude is formed based on "rational" beliefs and cognitions.

competitive analysis The process in which competitors are identified and selected competitors are profiled in terms of their product offerings, the prices of their products, the channels of distribution of their products, promotional messages, and the media carrying these messages.

competitive structure The nature of competition among firms within a given industry. Competition can be characterized as monopolistic (the market is controlled mostly by one large firm), oligopolistic (the market is controlled by several large firms), and purely competitive (the market is composed of many small firms who are "equally" competing for resources).

consumer-based integration A goal of marketing communications in which marketing communications decisions are guided by marketing strategy.

consumer involvement The situation in which a given consumer feels a certain amount of excitement or anxiety in relation to a particular product before, during, and/or after purchase. Product involvement is different from consumer involvement in that in product involvement the source of excitement or anxiety comes from the product; that is, the product has the ability to arouse "involvement." In contrast, the source of excitement or anxiety in consumer involvement is the consumer himself or herself.

control The process by which a warning signal is generated to trigger corrective action. The strength of the signal is determined by the degree of the negative deviation between an objective and a performance outcome—the greater the negative deviation, the greater the warning signal.

coordinated integration A goal of marketing communications in which the personal selling function is directly integrated with other elements of marketing communications (advertising, public relations, sales promotion, and direct marketing).

corporate image The evaluation of a firm's goodwill in the minds of certain stakeholders, such as customers, employees, distributors, suppliers, government, and so on.

corporate objective A formal statement that represents a concrete and precise desired state of affairs articulated at the corporate level. Corporate objectives are usually stated in terms of sales, market share, profit, and cash flow in relation to a given strategic business unit (SBU).

corporate strategic mix A firm's functional elements, such as marketing, R&D, engineering, manufacturing, personnel, finance, and accounting. Any corporate strategy is implemented through corporate tactics—through selected changes in the corporate strategic mix. For example, a growth strategy at the corporate level is likely to be implemented through significant changes in marketing, R&D, and/or engineering—selected elements of the corporate strategic mix or corporate tactics.

corporate strategy A course of action taken at the most superordinate level of the organizational hierarchy. There are at least five alternative corporate-level strategies: grow, maintain position, harvest, innovate, and divest.

corporate tactics Elements of the corporate strategic mix selected to be implement a corporate strategy. The typical elements of the corporate strategic mix are marketing, R&D, engineering, manufacturing, personnel, finance, and accounting. For example, a growth strategy at the corporate level is likely to be implemented through significant changes in marketing, R&D, and/or engineering—selected elements of the corporate strategic mix or corporate tactics.

cost leadership strategy A marketing strategy that guides the marketing communications manager to communicate low price as a key benefit. The aim here is to generate a brand association that can significantly and positively differentiate the firm's brand from competitor brands through its lower price.

cost per thousand (CPM) A media cost-efficiency index commonly used by media planners to help them select cost-efficient media vehicles. The formula is as follows:

CPM = [($ cost of an ad) × 1,000] / [number of people in target audience]

customer analysis The process in which the market is divided into customer segments, and selected segments are profiled in terms of demographics, psychographics, and media habits.

D

database marketing Marketing communications that is directly facilitated by a large database containing relevant information about customers and prospects.

demand cyclicality   Demand cyclicality refers to seasonal fluctuations in product demand. Some products, such as sun-block lotion, are seasonal and, therefore, are said to have high demand cyclicality.

differentiation strategy   A marketing strategy that guides the marketing communications manager to identify a distinguishing feature that helps the firm gain a competitive advantage over competitor brands. This distinguishing feature may be product related (positioning by product class, product attribute, intangible factor, competitor, or country of origin), price related (positioning by relative price), distribution related (positioning by brand-distributor tie-ins, distributor location, and distributor service), or promotion related (positioning by celebrity/spokesperson or lifestyle/personality). The focus here is to generate a brand association that can significantly and positively differentiate the firm's brand from competitor brands.

direct marketing   An element or tool of marketing communications. It involves various forms of marketing communications couched in direct channels of distribution, such as direct mail, catalogs, telemarketing, direct response advertising, the new electronic media (e.g., teleshopping and videotext), and direct selling.

divestment strategy   A corporate strategy that guides the corporate executive to set corporate objectives in terms of cash flow. The focus here is to generate needed cash flow by selling off the firm's least prosperous organizational entities.

do objective   A marketing communications goal to establish, increase, or maintain a certain level of brand trial/purchase (or intention to purchase) among consumers in a target market.

dog   A common term used by corporate strategists for a product considered to have low market share in a low-growth market.

E

environmental analysis   Environmental analysis refers to the process in which certain factors are identified that may have an impact on the size and geographic distribution of the market. Such factors may involve technology, economy, culture, media, politics, and so on.

experience curve effects   The cost saving gained as a direct result of learning, business experience, and the use of economies of scale.

external situation analysis   The process in which certain factors external to the organization are analyzed to help marketers with strategic planning. These external factors include the competition, the market, customers, and the environment.

F

feel objective   A marketing communications goal to establish, increase, or maintain a certain level of brand liking (or preference or positive attitude) in the minds of target consumers.

focus strategy A marketing strategy that guides the marketing communications manager to target a highly select audience and to communicate with this audience by making references to a specific customer benefit/problem, a user/customer image, or use/application. The goal here is to generate a brand association that the target audience can identify with and relate to in the context of their daily lives.

functional integration A goal of marketing communications in which decisions are made as a direct function of marketing goals, such as sales and market share.

G

geographic selectivity The targeting of select geographic areas, commonly used in media planning to help select media.

gross audience A measure commonly used by media planners to assess the effectiveness of a media schedule in terms of its maximum reach of a target market. It is computed by adding the audience of all media vehicles without taking into account the duplication among the vehicles. For example, a 5 million gross audience is the ability of a combination of media vehicles to reach 5 million of the target market, assuming that there is no audience duplication among the media vehicles. Net audience is computed by subtracting audience duplication from gross audience and is considered to be a more accurate index of media schedule effectiveness than gross audience.

gross reach A measure commonly used by media planners to assess the effectiveness of a media schedule in terms of its maximum reach of a target market. It is computed by adding the percentages of reach of all media vehicles without taking into account the duplication among the vehicles. For example, a 90% gross reach is the ability of a combination of media vehicles to reach 90% of the target market, assuming that there is no audience duplication among the media vehicles. Net reach is computed by subtracting audience duplication from gross reach and therefore is considered to be a more accurate index of media schedule effectiveness than gross reach.

growth strategy A corporate strategy that guides the corporate executive to set corporate objectives in terms of increases in sales and market share. The aim here is to expand the market by going after new prospects and/or encouraging customers to purchase more.

H

habit formation (doer) strategy A marketing communications strategy that guides the marketing communications manager to induce purchase or an overt behavioral response. The focus here is on inducing action. Action, in turn, is likely to prompt consumers to learn about the brand's costs and benefits, and this learning is likely to facilitate the development of a positive attitude toward the brand. The positive attitude is likely to motivate consumers to purchase the brand when the need for the product arises in the future.

harvest strategy A corporate strategy that guides the corporate executive to set corporate objectives in terms of maximizing profit. The intent here is to stop investing and making improvements and thus reduce costs of doing business. Therefore, profit maximization can be achieved through cost reduction.

I

image integration   A goal of marketing communications in which decisions are made to ensure message/media consistency.

informative (thinker) strategy   A marketing communications strategy that guides the marketing communications manager to provide target consumers with information about the firm's brand—that is, to educate consumers about the product costs and/or benefits. The focus here is on learning, much more so than eliciting an affective response or inducing purchase. The goal is that learning about the brand's costs and benefits is likely to help consumers develop a positive attitude toward the brand. In turn, these positive feelings for the brand are likely to motivate consumers to purchase the brand.

innovation strategy   A corporate strategy that guides the corporate executive to set corporate objectives in terms of increases in sales. The aim here is to develop a new product to increase sales.

integrated marketing communications (IMC)   A concept that recognizes the added value in a program that integrates a variety of strategic disciplines—such as general advertising, direct response, sales promotion, and public relations—and combines these disciplines to provide clarity, consistency, and maximum communication impact.

intermedia selection   The decision to select among media categories such as television, radio, magazines, newspapers, billboards, transit advertising, interactive advertising, and so on.

internal situation analysis   The process in which certain factors internal to the organization are analyzed to help marketers with strategic planning. These internal factors include the firm's past sales, past profit, past media expenditures, past promotional messages, and so on.

intramedia selection   The decision to select among media vehicles within a particular media category. For example, given that magazines are chosen as a viable media category for advertising, the media planner ponders what specific magazines should be selected.

L

learn objective   A marketing communications goal to establish, increase, or maintain a certain level of brand association (or knowledge) in the minds of a target market.

M

maintain position strategy   A corporate strategy that guides the corporate executive to set corporate objectives in terms of maintaining current levels of sales and market share. The intent here is to defend the firm's position against offending competitors.

market analysis   The process of estimating the size and geographic distribution of the market for a particular product.

market growth   The expansion of a particular product market. That is, consumers' demand for the product is increasing.

market potential   An estimate of the size of the market that is unrealized. It is that portion of the market composed of individuals or groups that are likely to consume the product but have not yet done so.

market share   A corporate performance standard traditionally measured in terms of the percentage of the total amount of monetary sales of a given product category that went to a given brand during a certain time period.

marketing communications objective   A formal statement that represents a concrete and precise desired state of affairs articulated at the marketing communications level. Marketing communications objectives are usually stated in terms of increases in brand awareness, learning about the benefits and costs of the brand, establishing positive attitude or liking toward the brand, and inducing trial purchase.

marketing communications strategic mix   The typical elements of the marketing communications strategic mix are advertising (print, broadcast, outdoor specialty, and interactive), reseller support (training, trade shows, cooperative advertising, trade allowances, contests and incentives, in-store advertising, POP displays, and personal selling), public relations (press release, publicity, press conference, corporate advertising, event sponsorship, and product placement in movies and TV), direct marketing (direct mail, newsletter, direct response advertising, catalogs, telemarketing, and direct selling), sales promotion (coupons, sampling, refunds and rebates, bonus packs, price-off deals, premiums and contests, and sweepstakes), and word-of-mouth (WOM) communications (stimulating WOM through advertising and sampling, simulating WOM through advertising, and referral system). Any marketing communications strategy is implemented through marketing communications tactics, i.e., through selected changes in the marketing communications strategic mix. For example, an informative (thinker) strategy at the marketing communications level is likely to be implemented through significant changes in the advertising (mostly print), reseller support (mostly through training and trade shows), public relations (mostly through press releases and publicity), and WOM communications (mostly through stimulating WOM communications through advertising and sampling, and using a referral system)—selected elements of the marketing communications strategic mix or marketing communications tactics.

marketing communications strategy   A course of action taken at the marketing communications level of the organizational hierarchy. There are at least four alternative strategies at this level: informative (thinker), affective (feeler), habit formation (doer), and self-satisfaction (reactor).

marketing communications tactics   Elements of the marketing communications strategic mix selected to implement a marketing communications strategy. The typical elements of the marketing communications strategic mix are advertising (print, broadcast, outdoor specialty, and interactive), reseller support (training, trade shows, cooperative advertising, trade allowances, contests and incentives, in-store advertising, POP displays, and personal selling), public relations (press release, publicity, press conference, corporate advertising, event sponsorship, and product placement in movies and TV), direct marketing (direct mail, newsletter, direct response advertising, catalogs, telemarketing, and direct selling), sales promotion (coupons, sampling, refunds and rebates, bonus packs, price-off deals, premiums and contests, and sweepstakes), and word-of-mouth (WOM) communications (stimulating WOM through advertising and sampling, simulating WOM through advertising, and referral system). For example, an informative (thinker) strategy at the marketing communications level is likely to be implemented through significant changes in the advertising (mostly print), reseller support (mostly through training and trade shows), public relations (mostly through press releases and publicity), and WOM communications (mostly through stimulating WOM communications through advertising and sampling, and using a referral system)—selected elements of the marketing communications strategic mix or marketing communications tactics.

marketing objective   A formal statement that represents a concrete and precise desired state of affairs articulated at the marketing level. Marketing objectives are usually stated in terms of brand equity or brand associations. An example of a marketing objective is "Establish an image of quality for Brand X."

marketing strategic mix   The typical elements of the marketing strategic mix are product, price, distribution, marketing communications, and customers/ prospects. Any marketing strategy is implemented through marketing tactics, that is, through selected changes in the marketing strategic mix. For example, a differentiation strategy at the marketing level is likely to be implemented through significant changes in the product and possibly price—selected elements of the marketing strategic mix or marketing tactics.

marketing strategy   A course of action taken at the marketing level of the organizational hierarchy. There are at least three key strategies at the marketing level: differentiation, cost leadership, and focus. From the vantage point of marketing communications, these marketing strategies are further operationalized in terms of positioning strategies. Each marketing strategy necessitates certain positioning strategies. Specifically, the differentiation strategy can be operationalized through a variety of positioning strategies, such as positioning by product class, product attribute, intangible factor, competitor, country of origin, relative price, brand-distributor tie-ins, distributor location, distributor service, celebrity or spokesperson, and lifestyle or personality. The cost leadership strategy entails only one positioning strategy, namely positioning by low price. The focus strategy entails three positioning strategies. These are positioning by customer benefit/problem, user/customer image, and use/application.

marketing tactics   Elements of the marketing strategic mix selected to implement a marketing strategy. The typical elements of the marketing strategic mix are product, price, distribution, marketing communications, and customers/prospects. For example, a differentiation strategy at the marketing level is likely to be implemented through significant changes in the product and possibly price—selected elements of the marketing strategic mix or marketing tactics.

mass-media communications Traditional forms of marketing communications that employ impersonal media, such as television, radio, billboards, transit advertising, magazines, and newspapers.

media habits Consumers' frequent use of certain media classes and vehicles. Market researchers typically develop profiles of the media habits of target consumers.

media selectivity Reaching a consumer group through highly select media. For example, avid cyclists can best be reached through cyclists' magazines. Cyclists' magazines are considered highly select media.

monitoring The process by which performance outcomes are measured.

N

net audience A measure commonly used by media planners to assess the effectiveness of a media schedule in terms of its maximum reach of a target market. It is computed by adding the audience of all media vehicles and then taking into account the duplication among the vehicles. For example, a 3 million net audience is the ability of a combination of media vehicles to reach 3 million consumers of the target market. Net audience is computed by subtracting audience duplication from gross audience and is therefore considered to be a more accurate index of media schedule effectiveness than gross audience.

net reach A measure commonly used by media planners to assess the effectiveness of a media schedule in terms of its maximum reach of a target market. It is computed by adding the percentages of reach of all media vehicles minus duplication among the vehicles. For example, a 90% net reach is the ability of a combination of media vehicles to reach 90% of the target market.

O

objectives Formal statements of a strategy that serve as goals. These formal statements are precise, quantifiable, and guide the formulation of tactics or action. For example, a corporate strategy of "Maintain position" can be quantified and treated as a goal to guide action as follows: "Maintain current market share for the next quarter."

P

planning Making decisions related to strategy, objectives, tactics, and resource allocation that are based on information obtained through analysis.

portfolio models Strategy models designed to help managers select among alternative corporate strategies. Examples of alternative strategies at the corporate level include growth, maintain position, harvest, innovation, and divestment.

positioning by brand-distributor tie-in A message strategy that focuses on creating a mental association between the firm's brand and a credible and reputable distributor, or vice versa. For example, Sears advertises heavily the fact that it carries Kenmore appliances. Both Sears and Kenmore appliances benefit from this tie-in.

positioning by celebrity or spokesperson   A message strategy that focuses on creating a mental association between the firm's brand and a specific celebrity or spokesperson. For example, Wendy's fast-food restaurant is positioned through Wendy's father, the president of Wendy's. People associate Wendy's with this spokesperson.

positioning by competitor   A message strategy that focuses on creating a mental association between the firm's brand and a specific attribute that the brand possesses that makes it appear superior to competitor brands. For example, Aleve, the nonprescription pain reliever, is positioned as having a longer lasting effect than Tylenol, Advil, and Bayer.

positioning by country of origin   A message strategy that focuses on creating a mental association between the firm's brand and a specific country that has a good reputation for making the product. For example, Walker cookies is positioned as being made in Scotland, where this cookie recipe originated.

positioning by customer benefit or problem   A message strategy that focuses on creating a mental association between the firm's brand and a specific customer benefit or problem. For example, Claussen pickles is positioned as being crunchy. Consumers perceive crunchiness as a significant benefit.

positioning by distributor location   A message strategy that focuses on creating a mental association between the firm's brand and easy access to the product through specific channels and retail outlets. For example, many companies are advertising their homepage to allow target consumers to access their products and services directly and more conveniently.

positioning by distributor's service capability   A message strategy that focuses on creating a mental association between the firm's brand and how well it can be delivered through specific channels and retail outlets. For example, many banks have positioned themselves on customer service.

positioning by intangible factor   A message strategy that focuses on creating a mental association between the firm's brand and a general attribute that captures a host of important attributes. For example, Ford positions itself in terms of "quality." "Quality" is an intangible factor that relies on a host of tangible factors, such as materials, construction, design, and so on.

positioning by lifestyle or personality   A message strategy that focuses on creating a mental association between the firm's brand and a certain personality or lifestyle. For example, Cover Girl makeup is associated with the personality of a young, free-spirited, wholesome, and very attractive woman.

positioning by low price   A message strategy that focuses on creating a mental association between the firm's brand and a lower price than products of most, or certain, other competitors. For example, Wal-Mart is positioned as a low-price, discount store.

positioning by product attribute   A message strategy that focuses on creating a mental association between the firm's brand and an important product attribute. For example, Crest toothpaste positioned itself as containing fluoride because consumer research indicates that fluoride is perceived to be an important attribute in toothpaste.

positioning by product class   A message strategy that focuses on creating a mental association between the firm's brand and the product class. For example, 7-Up soft drink positioned itself as the logical alternative to the "uncolas." The "uncola" soft drink is essentially a product class that subsumes a variety of non-cola soft drinks.

positioning by relative price   A message strategy that focuses on creating a mental association between the firm's brand and quality based on price. For example, the Mercedes automobile is positioned as a luxury car and therefore highly priced. The high price communicates luxury and quality.

positioning by use or application   A message strategy that focuses on creating a mental association between the firm's brand and a specific use of the product. For example, a brand of coffee can be positioned as highly suitable for a social get-together. Another brand may be positioned as most suitable to help people wake up and get going in the morning. Another brand may be positioned as most suitable for after meals, especially dinners.

positioning by user or customer   A message strategy that focuses on creating a mental association between the firm's brand and a type of product user or customer. For example, Nike shoes are positioned for the serious athlete. The message is that if you are a serious athlete, then Nike shoes are made for you.

positioning strategy   The same as a *message strategy*. That is, the marketing communications manager translates corporate and marketing strategies in terms of specific message to be communicated to target consumers. For example, a growth strategy at the corporate level may translate into a differentiation strategy at the marketing level, which further translates into positioning by intangible factor such as quality. That is, the marketing communications manager may believe that a message about product quality may be most effective in differentiating the firm's product from competitor products, which in turn may be an effective way to grow.

problem child   A common term used by corporate strategists for a product considered to have low market share in a high-growth market.

process hierarchy   A decision tree—a hierarchy of decisions reflecting a hierarchical link between strategy, objective, and tactic. For example, the following can be described as a process hierarchy: A corporate strategy of "Gain market share" leads the decision maker to set a corporate objective of "Increase market share by 20% by next quarter." Certain corporate tactics are then selected to meet this objective, such as to hold the marketing department responsible to develop a marketing program that can achieve the corporate objective.

product involvement   The situation in which a given product creates a certain amount of excitement or anxiety among consumers before, during, and/or after purchase. Product involvement is different from consumer involvement in that in product involvement the source of excitement or anxiety comes from the product; that is, the product has the ability to arouse "involvement." In contrast, the source of excitement or anxiety in consumer involvement is the consumer himself or herself.

product life cycle (PLC)   The stages that a product (product category, not a single product brand) goes through, from the early stages of inception and commercialization to eventual decline and extinction. The stages are usually referred to more specifically as introduction, development, early maturity, late maturity, and decline.

production flexibility   The ability of certain media to accommodate the scheduling demands of advertisers. For example, radio advertising is highly flexible; radio script can be easily modified, and changes can be easily made to within the last few days of the airing of the radio commercial.

profit   A corporate performance standard, traditionally measured in terms of product's revenues minus costs for a given time period.

public relations   An element, or tool, of marketing communications. It involves promotional activities that focus on enhancing or protecting the overall image of the firm at large. It consists of communication activities such as press releases, press conferences, exclusives, interviews, publicity, cooperative advertising, event sponsorship, and product placements in movies and television.

purchase intention   A marketing communications goal. It describes a desirable situation in which target consumers have formed a behavioral intention to purchase the firm's brand.

R

relationship management integration   A marketing communications goal in which messages are not guided only by marketing strategy but by corporate strategy as well. That is, decisions related to manufacturing, engineering, research and development, finance, accounting, human resources, accounting, and legal are all considered.

repeat objective   A marketing communications goal to establish, increase, or maintain a certain level of brand repeat purchase (or brand commitment and loyalty) among consumers in a target market.

repeat purchase   A marketing communications goal. It describes a desirable situation in which target consumers have purchased the firm's brand repeatedly over time.

reseller support   An element, or tool, of marketing communications that involves promotional activities by distributors, such as contests and incentives, trade allowances, in-store displays, point-of-purchase materials, training programs, trade shows, cooperative advertising, and personal selling. It is often called *trade promotion*.

S

sales promotion   An element, or tool, of marketing communications. Sometimes it is referred to as *consumer promotions* because it involves promotional activities directed to consumers. It involves communication activities, such as coupons, sampling, premiums, contests and sweepstakes, refunds and rebates, bonus packs, and price-off deals.

seasonal usage in media   This refers to seasonal variation in the use of certain media. For example, radio is listened to more frequently in the summer months than during other times. Primetime television is typically watched more frequently during mid-fall and winter than during other times of the year.

self-satisfaction (reactor) strategy   A marketing communications strategy that guides the marketing communications manager to induce purchase. That is, the focus here is on inducing action, which in turn sparks certain positive feelings for the brand. This emotional response, in turn, is likely to motivate consumers to learn about the brand's costs and benefits. This learning is expected to help establish a positive attitude toward the brand, thereby inducing future purchase.

share of voice   The marketer's share of mass-media expenditures. The more money the marketer spends in mass-media advertising, the greater the share of voice.

situation analysis   Another term for *strategic analysis*. Situation analysis refers to the process in which certain factors internal and external to the organization are analyzed to help marketers with strategic planning. Examples of internal factors include the firm's past sales, past profit, past media expenditures, past promotional messages, and so on. Examples of external factors include the competition, the market, customers, and the environment.

stakeholder-based integration   The goal of marketing communications in which messages directed to target consumers, employees, suppliers, distributors, stockholders, the community, and certain government agencies are coordinated.

star   A common term used by corporate strategists to signify a product considered to have high market share in a high-growth market.

strategic analysis   Another term for *situation analysis*. It refers to the process in which certain factors internal and external to the organization are analyzed to help marketers with strategic planning. Examples of internal factors include the firm's past sales, past profit, past media expenditures, past promotional messages, and so on. Examples of external factors include the competition, the market, customers, and the environment.

strategic business unit (SBU)   A product/market unit—a specific product related to a specific customer group. For example, a mercury-based thermometer needed in cooking and directed to restaurants is an SBU. A mercury-based thermometer designed to measure atmospheric temperature and directed to households is another SBU.

strategic mix   Those managerial components or elements at a given organizational level that must be manipulated to produce certain outcomes. For example, the strategic mix at the corporate level involves engineering, R&D, manufacturing, marketing, human resources, legal, finance, and accounting. At the marketing level, the strategic mix involves the four Ps—product, price, place, and promotion. At the marketing communications level, the strategic mix involves advertising, publicity, reseller support, sales promotion, personal selling, direct marketing, and word-of-mouth communications.

strategy   A course of action that emphasizes certain elements of the strategic mix. For example, at the corporate level, a "Gain market share" strategy would manipulate the marketing element of the corporate mix in such a way as to generate a different outcome—a higher share of the market. At the marketing level, an example of a marketing strategy is "cost leadership," which is essentially a marketing strategy that manipulates the price element of the marketing mix to gain a competitive advantage. At the marketing communications level, an "informative" strategy involves manipulating certain elements of advertising (mostly print), reseller support (mostly training and trade shows), and public relations (mostly press release and publicity).

system integration   The extent to which the system components (strategy, objective, tactics, budget, analysis, planning, monitoring, and control) are strongly or weakly linked. A system is said to lack integration if any one link between the system components is weak. In contrast, a system is said to be fully integrated when all the system components are strongly linked.

T

tactics   Selected courses of action guided by objectives of the superordinate level of the organization's hierarchy. For example, at the corporate level an objective such as "Increase market share by 10% by next quarter" has to be implemented within the confines of each corporate department—engineering, R&D, manufacturing, marketing, accounting, finance, legal, and so on. The implementation of specific programs in relation to each corporate element reflects corporate tactics. At the marketing level, an objective of, let's say, "Establish reputation of quality that by the end of next quarter at least 50% of target consumers would recognize the brand as high quality" guides tactical action. The marketing manager has to configure a marketing program involving the four Ps in a manner to meet this objective. Similarly, a marketing communications objective such as "Increase positive affect toward the brand by 10% the end of next quarter" would motivate the marketing communications manager to put together a marketing communications program that can meet this objective. The elements of this program would involve selected communication tools (selected elements of advertising, public relations, sales promotion, reseller support, and direct marketing). These, in turn, become the marketing communications tactics.

V

value added   A common term used by marketer to refer to the consumers' perception of a significant advantage of one or more product features added to the firm's brand.

W

word-of-mouth (WOM) communications   An element, or tool, of marketing communications that focuses on consumers communicating among themselves about the firm's product. WOM communications involve both controllable and uncontrollable forms of communications. Controllable forms of WOM communications include stimulating WOM through advertising and sampling, simulating WOM communications through advertising, and using a referral system.

Credits

CHAPTER 1

Figure 1.1 Reprinted from *Integrated Marketing Communication* by Don E. Schultz, Stanley I. Tannenbaum and Robert F. Lauterborn. © 1993. Used with permission of NTC/Contemporary Publishing Company.

Figure 1.2 Reprinted from *Integrated Marketing Communication* by Don E. Schultz, Stanley I. Tannenbaum and Robert F. Lauterborn. © 1993. Used with permission of NTC/Contemporary Publishing Company.

CHAPTER 5

Figure 5.1 Reprinted with Permission by the California Milk Processor Board.

Figure 5.2 Reprinted with Permission by Norwegian Cruise Lines.

Figure 5.4 Reprinted with Permission from Nivea Products.

Figure 5.5 Reprinted with Permission by MapLinx Corp.

Figure 5.6 Reprinted with Permission of Seimens Corp.

Figure 5.7 Reprinted with Permission by Bayer Corp.

Figure 5.8 Created by Landey & Partners Grounds Morris.

Figure 5.9 © 1995 GM Corp. All Rights Reserved.

Figure 5.10 Reprinted with Permission by IBM Inc.

Figure 5.11 © 1997 Federal Express Corporation. All Rights Reserved.

Figure 5.12 Reprinted with Permission by Wendy's International, Inc.

App. 5.1.1 J. Paul Peter and Jerry C. Olson, *Consumer Behavior: Marketing Strategy Perspectives,* Richard D. Irwin Inc. © 1987, p. 119. Used with permission of the Mc-Graw-Hill Companies.

App. 5.1.2 Reprinted with permission from Jerry C. Olson and Thomas J. Reynolds, "Understanding Consumers' Cognitive Structures: Implication for Advertising Strategy," in *Advertising and Consumer Psychology,* edited by L. Percy and A.G. Woodside (eds.), fig. 4.1. Copyright © 1983 Jossey-Bass Publishers. First published by Lexington Books.

App. 5.4 Adapted from David W. Cravens, Gerald E. Hills, and Robert B. Woodruff, *Marketing Decision Making: Concepts and Strategy,* Richard D. Irwin, Inc., 1976, p. 234. Used with permission of the McGraw-Hill Companies.

CHAPTER 6

Table 6–4 Reprinted from *Strategic Media Planning* by Kent M. Lancaster and Helen E. Katz © 1989. Used with permission of NTC/Contemporary Publishing Company.

CHAPTER 7

Figure 7.3 From William A. Mindak, "Fitting the Semantic Differential to the Marketing Problem," *Journal of Marketing,* 25, April 1961. Used with the permission of the American Marketing Assoc., Chicago.

Figure 7.4 Peter K. Olson, *Consumer Behavior,* © 1987, Richard D. Irwin Inc. Used with permission of the McGraw-Hill Companies.

Table 7.11 Adapted from Cuba, Fred, "Fourteen Things That Make or Break Tracking Studies," by *Journal of Advertising Research,* 15, no. 1, February/March, 1985, p. 21–23. Used with permission.

CHAPTER 10

Table 10.3 Reprinted from Edward G. Michaels, "Marketing Muscle: Who Needs It?", *Business Horizons,* May/June 1982 p. 72. Copyright © 1982 by the Foundation for the School of Business at Indiana University. Used with permission.

Index

A

Aaker, David A., 179–180
absolute cost, 123, 124
abstract attributes, 104
acceptance stage, 12. *See also* purchase cycle
actual self-congruity, 112–113
Acuvue, 3, 4
ad hoc approach, 12
advertising
  aerial, 128
  affective (feeler) strategy, 131–132
  agencies, 4
  cooperative, 132
  corporate, 133
  creativity in affective strategy, 132
  creativity in informative strategy, 128–129
  direct response, 136, 140
  habit formation strategy, 134–135
  informative strategy, 121–129
  in-store, 142
  interactive, 135
  intermedia selection, 121–125, 131–132
  intramedia selection, 125–126, 132
  legal issues, 124
  media categories list, 121–122
  package deals in, 11–12
  radio, 128
  reminder, 139
  self-satisfaction strategy, 139
  stimulating word-of-mouth with, 130
aerial advertising, 128
affective brand attitude, 171–173
  definition of, 169
  projective techniques for, 173
  semantic differential measure of, 172
affective (feeler) strategy, 19
  advertising for, 131–132
  definition of, 281

feel/learn/do sequence in, 46–48
  marketing strategies/tactics, 131–134
  public relations, 132–133
  reseller support, 132
  typical application of, 44
  word-of-mouth communications, 133–134
aided recall measures
  brand awareness, 168–169
  brand knowledge, 161
Aleve ad, 81, 82
all-you-can-afford method, 193
American Marketing Association, 190
analysis/planning, 32–34
  competitive, 214
  in corporate objective setting, 241–244
  in corporate strategy selection, 215–216
  customer, 213
  environmental, 214
  external situation, 213–214
  internal situation, 214
  linking, 36, 273–274
  linking with budget, 37, 276–277
  linking with objectives, 37, 276
  linking with strategy/objective/tactics, 37, 274–275
  market, 213
  in marketing communications objective setting, 246–249
  in marketing communications strategy selection, 233–236
  in marketing objective setting, 244–246
  in marketing strategy selection, 226–233
  and objective setting, 33, 50–51, 240–250
  resource allocation and, 33–34, 51, 251–262
  strategies/tactics in, 32–33
  and strategy selection, 49–50, 213–239
  in systems model, 49–51
  uses of, 214
associative strength measures, 165–166

299

group selling, 141
growth
    customer base, 260
    rate of, 220
growth strategy
    objectives in, 46
    tactics for, 61–63

H

habit formation (doer) strategy, 19, 139
    advertising for, 134–135
    direct marketing for, 135–136
    do/learn/feel sequence in, 46–48
    objectives of, 134
    product involvement and, 153
    public relations, 139
    reseller support, 138–139
    sales promotions, 136–138
    typical application of, 44
habits, media, 124
Hall, Floyd, 200
harvest strategy, 216
    objectives in, 46
    tactics for, 64–65
HealthMax Treadmill, 93
Hewlett-Packard, budgeting/control in, 147
hierarchy of effects, 18
historical-statistical method of budgeting,
    191–192
HMO referral systems, 131
Home Shopping Network, 140
horizontal cooperative advertising, 132
how-brand-is-different tests, 165

I

IBM Corp.
    image consistency, 117
    Lotus takeover, 59
    positioning, 87, 88
ideal point construct, 107
ideal point model, 106–107
ideal social self-congruity, 114
image
    brand, 159–160
    brand-user, 112–115
    corporate, 220
    integration, ensuring, 6–7
    measure of brand knowledge, 162–163

media, 126
    positioning through user/customer, 99,
        112–115
importance construct, 106–107
incentives, 93, 142
Indiana Middle Grades Reading program case,
    55–57
industry factors, in resource allocation, 255–258
infomercials, 136
    as direct response advertising, 140
information technology, shift of, 10
informative (thinker) strategy, 19
    advertising creativity and, 128–129
    advertising for, 121–129
    intermedia selection, 121–125
    intramedia selection, 125–126
    learn/feel/do sequence in, 46–48
    marketing communications elements for, 120
    net reach computation for, 126–128
    public relations and, 129–130
    reseller support and, 129
    tactics, 118, 120–131
    typical application of, 44
    word-of-mouth communications and,
        130–131
ingredient-sponsored cooperative advertising,
    132
innovation strategy
    objectives in, 46
    tactics for, 65
instant coupons, 137
in-store advertising, 142
instrumental values, 104
intangible factor positioning, 79, 80, 81, 228
*Integrated Marketing Communications: Pulling
    It Together and Making It Work*
    (Schultz, Tannenbaum, Lauterborn),
    13
integrated marketing communications (IMC),
    3–23
    awareness of need for, 6
    campaign characteristics, 5–6
    case study, 265–266
    definitions of, 3–5, 6–7
    developmental view of, 6–8
    effectiveness of, 5
    lessons in, 266–277
    planning approaches for, 10–21
    systems model for, 40–57
    trends/conditions that lead to, 8–10
interactive advertising, 135
intermedia selection

terminal values, 104
tests, 163–166
themelines approach, 11
thinker strategy. *See* informative (thinker)
    strategy
thinking-type products, 235
thought-elicitation procedure, 171
time frames, identifying appropriate, 29,
    154
tone, consistency in, 5–6
top-of-mind awareness, 168
tracking studies, 168–169
trade allowances, 138–139
trade promotion. *See* reseller support
trade shows, 129
training
    informative strategy and, 129
    sales force, 263

U

unaided self-report questions, 173–174
usage stage, 13. *See also* purchase cycle
use-experience tests, 164
use or application positioning, 70, 71, 98,
    231–232
user/customer association, 98–99
user/customer image, 99
    active strategy for, 115
    actual self-congruity, 112–113
    ideal self-congruity, 113–114
    ideal social self-congruity, 114

passive strategy for, 114–115
selecting important, 112–115
social self-congruity, 114
user/customer image positioning, 114–115
user or customer positioning, 98–99

V

valence
    message, 132
    properties, 159
value-added products, 220
vehicles
    identifying in Moore/Thorson model, 13
    images of, 126
vertical cooperative advertising, 132
Virginia Slims, 5
voice
    consumer perception of, 5–6
    share of, 10
    share of resource allocation method, 190

W

Walkers cookies ad, 83, 84
Wal-Mart, 200
Wendy's ad, 89, 91, 92
Wilson, William R., 178–179
word-of-mouth (WOM) communications
    affective strategy, 133–134
    informative strategy, 130–131
    simulating, 133–134
    unethical, 133–134
World Wide Web, advertising on, 135